W9-BXP-591

Woody Guthrie,
American Radical

MUSIC IN AMERICAN LIFE

A list of books in the series appears
at the end of this book.

Woody Guthrie, American Radical

WILL KAUFMAN

University of Illinois Press

URBANA, CHICAGO, AND SPRINGFIELD

A list of prose and lyric writings,
copyright Woody Guthrie Publications, Inc.,
appears at the back of this book.

A portion of the royalties from the sales
of this book will be donated to the
Woody Guthrie Foundation.

Will Kaufman is supported by

 Arts & Humanities
Research Council

Library of Congress Cataloging-in-Publication Data
Kaufman, Will.
Woody Guthrie, American radical / Will Kaufman.
p.   cm. — (Music in American life)
Includes bibliographical references and index.
ISBN-13: 978-0-252-03602-6 (hardcover : alk. paper)
ISBN-10: 0-252-03602-6 (hardcover : alk. paper)
ISBN-13: 978-0-252-07798-2 (pbk. : alk. paper)
ISBN-10: 0-252-07798-9 (pbk. : alk. paper)
1. Guthrie, Woody, 1912–1967.
2. Folk singers—United States—Biography. I. Title.
ML410.G978K38   2011
782.42162'130092—dc22   2010040240
[B]

For Ry Cooder and Martin Carthy,
the two pillars of my musical conscience;
and for Ralph McTell,
the angel of Woody Guthrie on his shoulder

SOCIALISMO

My name is called Socialism
And I was born in you a good
    long time ago.
But I do grow slow.
And I grew up fighting. But
    always was your best working
    child, and your happiest one.
If I do happen to tear a part
    of your house down on my
    way growing up towards your
    sky, don't you be afraid.
I'll fix it back a whole lot
    better than I found it.
I want to raise my own kids
    in a better house.

                Woody Guthrie
                January 21, 1948

Contents

Acknowledgments

At the top of my list are Nora Guthrie of the Woody Guthrie Foundation and Archives and Ralph Jackson of the Broadcast Music Industry Foundation, to whom I owe thanks for the award of a 2008 BMI–Woody Guthrie Fellowship, without which this book could not have been written. I am also grateful to Anna Canoni, Jorge Arévalo Mateus, Bucky Halker, and the judges of my application for this invaluable award.

I am indebted to the members of three households whose hospitality went far beyond the facilitation of my research. Ron and Nancy Cohen opened their doors to me so that I could spend a number of days mining Ron's extensive archive of American folk resources. In addition to this kindness, Ron read through and painstakingly critiqued my manuscript drafts. No one could ask for a more encouraging and inspiring mentor. Ron is not only the most scrupulous of historians and the dean of American folk scholarship (David Hajdu rightly calls him "the guardian angel of folk studies"), he also reminded me of the lesson I had long ago learned from Mark Twain but too often forgot: "Use the right word, not its second cousin."

Barry and Judy Ollman generously hosted me and introduced me to their ever-growing collection of Guthrie Ur-sources—letters, manuscripts, song lyrics, drawings, and the vital ephemera without which a full picture of the life and times can never be attained. The Ollman Collection is an indispensable repository that future Guthrie scholars will ignore only at their peril.

Cathy Fink and Marcy Marxer gave me a home and the warmth of their friendship during my entire period of research in Washington, D.C. It was a memorable time that enabled me to perceive new connections between musical and social activism—and a humbling experience for any musician.

I've never *seen* so large an arsenal of banjos and guitars—of all shapes, sizes, and tunings—put to such expert use on the side of the angels.

During my month at the Woody Guthrie Archives in New York, Tiffany Colannino and Lisa Sparks earned my gratitude for their assistance and, it must be said, all their patience with my minute-by-minute requests. I am also grateful for the knowledge and guidance of Jeff Place and Stephanie Smith at the Smithsonian Institution's Center for Folklife and Cultural Heritage and Todd Harvey and his colleagues at the American Folklife Center of the Library of Congress.

I thank Laurie Matheson and the editorial board at the University of Illinois Press for their trust in this project, and the press's anonymous referees, who were appropriately tough and fair in their responses to the manuscript. This is as good a place as any, too, to acknowledge my debt to Hank Reineke, biographer of Ramblin' Jack Elliott, for keeping me on the straight and narrow in my discussion of Elliott in Britain, and to Dave Arthur and Mike Paris for illuminating crucial aspects of Guthrie's British reception.

For providing me with textual and photographic sources, granting permission when needed, and helping me in myriad other ways to get this book off the ground, I am grateful to Jackie Bishop at the EMI Archives, Bob Brough, Colette Brough, Angela Burton, Martin Butler, Anna Casetta, Prima Casetta, Cope Cumpston, Don Fleming at the Alan Lomax Archives, Caroline Ford at Peekskill's Field Library, Erika Gottfried and Sarah De Mott at the Tamiment Library, everyone at Woody Guthrie Publications, Angela Wesley Hardin, Martin Johnston, Mack A. Ladd, Nancy Ladd, Ramona Love Lampell, Bob McLean, Alison Chapman McLean, Sean Casey O'Brien and Henry Slucki at KPFK radio, Yoko Ono and the Estate of John Lennon, Hank Reineke (again), Aaron Rennert, Pete Seeger, Malcolm Taylor at the Vaughan Williams Memorial Library, and Sarah Woodman at the Kern County Museum.

My comrades at the university chalkface, Janice Wardle, Theresa Saxon, and Alan Rice, have shouldered more burdens on my behalf than I can count. I owe them thanks for their goodwill and for their continued moral and practical support of my teaching and scholarship. I am equally grateful to the UK's Arts and Humanities Research Council and my university's School of Journalism, Media, and Communications for the generous funding that allowed this project's completion.

This book grows out of a series of performance programs on Woody Guthrie that I have been taking to European universities, festivals, folk clubs, and other public venues since 2006 (www.myspace.com/willkaufman). I am grateful to many people for encouraging and facilitating these projects, above all my two brothers, Steve Kaufman (the world's best damn flatpicker) and Mike

Kaufman (the world's best damn music teacher), both of whom have kept the music front and center in our family. I must also thank those singing champions of Woody's—on both sides of the Atlantic—who have backed my musical evangelism with warm words of support: Pete Seeger, Ralph McTell, Tom Paxton, Ry Cooder, Christy Moore, Steve Tilston, and our much esteemed Honorary Fellow of the University of Central Lancashire, Martin Carthy.

For enabling me to introduce these programs to American audiences I am especially grateful to David Ferrard, Jon Andersen (fine radical poet), Cathy Fink, Ashley Kahn, James Grady, Mike and Suzanne Kaufman, Marty Summerour and Mary Cliff at the Folklore Society of Greater Washington, Judy Blazer (Hey, Sis!) and all her colleagues at the Artist's Crossing, David Brouillard at the Bowery Poetry Club, the terrific Sonny Ochs, Evelyn Hershey at the American Labor Museum, Barbara Manners at Acoustic Celebration, Gene Shay, Ray Naylor, Kenny Judge, Phil Cerny and Angus Gillespie at Rutgers University, William Van Vugt at Calvin College, and Mary Anne Trasciatti and Lisa Merrill at Hofstra University.

Finally, I thank my wife, Sarah, and our sons, Reuben and Theo, for their sorely tested forbearance throughout the research and writing of this book. Anything else is not for public eyes—but they know what I owe them.

A quarter of this book's royalties are being donated to the Woody Guthrie Foundation (www.woodyguthrie.org), whose mission is "to promote, perpetuate, and preserve the social, political, and cultural values that Woody Guthrie contributed to the world through his life, his music, and his work." Without the foundation there would be no Woody Guthrie Archives; and without the archives—well, I shudder to think. Please give generously.

Introduction

"I don't agree with you. I don't agree with you at all. Your country was built by people who went there and had something to give, to contribute. It's only now, with all the, you know, migrants coming in, that your country is in danger." This was the stern lecture I received from Britain's Prince Andrew in the State Gallery of his family's rather large, publicly funded house. It was March 2007. The queen and the Duke of Edinburgh were hosting a Buckingham Palace reception for UK-based Americans to commemorate the 400th anniversary of the Jamestown settlement—England's first great migrant colony in North America. The prince had misunderstood me, and now he was visibly upset. I'd simply said that, in some ways, it was a miracle that the United States had held together for so long—not because the society was always on the verge of blowing sky high (as he thought I had implied), but because of the centuries-old tensions between federal and state power, political factions, checks and balances, sectionalism, the Civil War, Articles of Confederation, and so on . . . a commonplace, objective, and, I thought, innocuous observation. But, genuine admirer of America that he is, the prince bristled at the implication of social breakdown. American society was fundamentally sound. If there was a problem, *cherchez le migrant.*

What was his thing about migrants? Wasn't his own father, there by the window, a Greek migrant? Wasn't his mother, just now coming through the gallery, descended from a whole line of German migrants going back to George I? Hell, he was *talking* to a migrant, sprung from migrant grand-parents who had themselves sprung from a line of migrants going back to the diaspora. At one time or another, we'd all had to put on our traveling shoes. I felt uncomfortable arguing with the guy in his own house ... well, somebody's house, anyway.

I was rescued when a palace aide revolved me into an audience with the next royal host, the Duchess of Gloucester, married to the queen's cousin. She herself, I found, hailed from Denmark. *Hello, fellow migrant!* I told her that I had just returned from Copenhagen, where I'd been introducing American Studies undergraduates to the songs and story of Woody Guthrie.

She had never heard of him. I explained that he was an American songwriter who had chronicled the epic trials of the, you know, migrants who had fled the Dust Bowl in the 1930s. Ah, yes, she *had* heard of the Dust Bowl—"a difficult time for America," she said. She expressed amazement that I went around Europe teaching history by singing to people. With a mischievous half smile, she asked me to sing one of this Guthrie chap's songs for her. Not for a minute, I'm sure, did she imagine that I would actually (be drunk enough to) do it. But I took a deep breath, looked around at the chandeliers, oil paintings, and gilded mirrors, and sang, sotto voce, a verse of Guthrie's great ode to America's migrant workers, "Pastures of Plenty":

> California, Arizona, I've worked on your crops;
> Then north up to Oregon to gather your hops;
> Dig beets from your ground, I cut grapes from your vines,
> To set on your table that light, sparklin' wine.

A few heads turned. The duchess looked at me blankly. I tried again:

> This land is your land, this land is my land ...

She brightened and nodded: "Ah, yes! I know that one."

As I recalled it later in the educational press:

> This was good to hear. And for the rest of the evening it was just me and one big sloppy grin. Goddamn, I've sung Woody's songs in Buck House! I have brought Woody Guthrie to the world's greatest seat of hereditary privilege. Maybe something of the man's great heart, his empathy with the hard hit and the hard traveling, is seeping into the foundations of this palace *right now*. Maybe a few notes of his music are still floating up there around the chandeliers, like Tinkerbell—a faint echo in the ears of the powerful. Who knows, maybe Prince Andrew will wake up tomorrow morning humming "Pastures of Plenty" and wondering how the hell *that* tune got into his head. Sheesh, maybe I've had too much champagne.[1]

It was sometime during the dark days of the second Bush administration that I began putting together a series of performance programs on Guthrie.

It was a difficult time to be an American abroad. The belligerent voices of those who claimed to speak and act on the country's behalf—Rumsfeld, Perle, Cheney, Bush himself—invited nothing but hatred for America on a global scale. Woody's voice—the voice of another América—sounded pretty good just then, even as the white phosphorous rained down on Fallujah: "What makes your boats haul death to my people? / Nitro block busters, big cannons and guns?" His songs, it seemed, could have been sung anywhere from Camp Delta to Abu Ghraib to the death-row cells of the Polunsky Unit in Texas: "You keep me in jail and you lock me in prison; / Your hospital's jammed and your crazyhouse full . . ."[2]

Instinctively, I'd seized on Guthrie as a link to an almost forgotten America—perhaps an America that never existed, an America that could contain *as its own,* without denial or neurotic reaction, Gene Debs and Upton Sinclair; Mother Jones and Mother Bloor; the Wobblies and the John Reed Clubs; the International Workers Order and the Southern Tenant Farmers Union; the Communist Party of the USA and the Socialist Workers Party; the defenders of Sacco and Vanzetti; the Highlander Folk School; the Commonwealth and Brookwood labor colleges; the Jefferson School of Social Science; Charles H. Kerr's socialist publishing house; the *Liberator, Masses,* and *New Masses;* the Share Croppers Union; "Red Diaper" babies; Paul Robeson, his passport revoked, singing down the telephone to a British audience; the thousands who held the line at Peekskill; the millions who saw (and see) no conflict between American values and an economic system that takes according to one's ability and gives according to one's needs. Generations of Cold Warriors, conservatives, and neocons (both inside and outside of the labor movement) had so effectively done their job in establishing left-wing radicalism as "un-American" that many people—my students among them—had grown up unaware that there had ever been such a thing as an American radical tradition. To them, the words *socialism* and *American*—let alone *communism* and *American*—were natural contradictions. It had come to such a pass that, were some visionary American to propose even a pale shadow of the National Health Service that my family and I had been enjoying in the UK (and which had been preserved even by Margaret Thatcher and the Tories), he or she would be grossly caricatured as a rabid socialist and pilloried as "un-American."

Woody Guthrie's radical activism was once common knowledge, particularly among those who had their ears tuned to the energetic progressive culture that predated McCarthyism, that poisonous watershed of political erasure. A watered-down version of the radical Guthrie had survived into the 1960s, thanks in part to the generation of young musical activists—"Woody's Children," they were called—who continued to circulate his more popular songs and otherwise champion his legacy. At various times, Bob Dylan, Joan Baez, Phil Ochs, Tom Paxton, and Peter, Paul, and Mary (among others) were honored with this familial designation. Some of Guthrie's younger contemporaries still carried his radical torch around the margins of American society, none more than Pete Seeger, who did not fully reemerge from the shadows of the McCarthyite blacklist until 1967, the year of Guthrie's death. By then, Guthrie himself had become, for the most part, the icon of a vague unconformity among college students, the little guy who had flipped the bird to "the system" and had taken off down the road with a guitar strapped to his back.

At the same time, ironically, Guthrie had achieved a degree of public recognition and a series of official honors that had all but wiped out his radical profile. He was truly America's balladeer. The year before his death, a citation from Secretary of the Interior Stuart Udall marked him out as an officially sanctioned national treasure: "You sang that 'this land belongs to you and me,' and you sang from the heart of America that feels this about its land. You have articulated, in your songs, the sense of identification that each citizen of our country feels toward this land and the wonders which it holds."³ (The morose conclusion of the radical editor Irwin Silber could not have been more accurate: "They're taking a revolutionary and turning him into a conservationist.")⁴ An accompanying honor—having a Bonneville Power Authority substation named after him—did succeed, it is true, in flushing out at least one disgruntled constituent, who wrote to Oregon senator Mark Hatfield: "As a result of Secretary Udall's naming a Bonneville Power substation after Woody Guthrie, a folk singer who has written for The Daily Worker and The People's World, and who is or was alleged to be or to have been a member of the Communist Party, a local controversy has arisen. . . . If he was [a communist], can you take some action to get the name "Woody Guthrie" eliminated as a name for a Federally owned power station[?]"⁵

Such expressions of patriotic umbrage notwithstanding, it was now possible for a former aide to Senator Joe McCarthy—Senator Robert F. Kennedy—to write to Guthrie on his deathbed: "I have long been an admirer of your work and I fully share the opinion of the many people who regard you as one of the finest and most authentic artists our nation has ever produced."⁶ And it was thus possible, thirty years later, for Guthrie to adorn a United States postage stamp, prompting this quip from Arlo Guthrie: "For a man who fought all his life against being respectable, this comes as a stunning defeat."⁷

Occasionally a collection of Guthrie's writings would appear posthumously—say, *Woody Sez* (1975), which charmed one notable radical activist into writing to the Guthrie family:

Dear Whoever,
Woody lives,
and I'm glad!
love,
John Lennon
75[8]

As that collection's descriptive note explained: "The articles collected here first appeared in a column in *People's World,* published in San Francisco, under the title 'Woody Sez,' from May 12, 1939 to January 3, 1940."[9] For whatever the reason, the editors of *Woody Sez* declined to point out for a general readership that the *People's World* was the West Coast's communist daily. Perhaps it didn't matter. Perhaps it mattered much. But it signaled a certain nervousness, a deliberate soft-pedaling of Guthrie's radical history. Not that such timidity was unique to the arenas of popular music or publishing in the mid-1970s and, arguably, afterward. In the late 1980s, the television historian David Marc described the troubles he was still facing in attempting to examine the political agendas of the mildly antiwar television series *M.A.S.H.* (1972–83): "Despite the obviousness of the show's politically-loaded obsessions, it is difficult to get most of the people involved in *M.A.S.H.* to discuss the show's political content—or even the possibility that it had any. The hesitation of television producers to speak frankly on such issues points to a legacy of McCarthyism that continues to cast a shadow over American popular culture."[10]

Unsurprisingly, then, when Hal Ashby's film *Bound for Glory* (1976) introduced David Carradine as Saint Woody (a little too holy, in spite of his philandering; a little too wooden, and certainly too tall), in no manner was Hollywood's version of Guthrie associated with the American communist movement in which the historical figure had been immersed. (And the political nervousness continues: one of Guthrie's publishers, TRO, has denied me permission to quote from "Dear Mrs. Roosevelt" unless I agree to delete this troublesome verse—a verse that the Woody Guthrie Archives has been honest enough to include on its own website:

He said he didn't like DeGaulle, nor no Chiang Kai Shek;
Shook hands with Joseph Stalin, says: "There's a man I like!"
This world was lucky to see him born.[11]

How ironic that in the year 2010, a petty exercise in airbrushing—one of Stalin's own pet practices—should be demanded in order to prevent engagement with some of Guthrie's more inconvenient opinions.)

During my school years, Guthrie was more than anything else the father of "This Land Is Your Land," which I sang, hand on heart, in the daily segue from the Pledge of Allegiance. Not until my midthirties did I learn that Guthrie had written three verses that had never made it into the school songbooks. These were angry verses. One depicted the "hungry" people lined up "in the shadow of the steeple / By the Relief Office," forced to beg for what was rightfully theirs.[12] One condemned the "big high wall" with its forbidding sign, "Private Property."[13] A third vowed that no American shall be stopped or turned back on "that freedom highway"[14]—"Homeland Security" and the Patriot Act notwithstanding. These verses had been scattered between separate written sources and one unreleased recording; I certainly never sang them at school. The version of "This Land Is Your Land" that had emerged into the public consciousness could too easily be misconstrued as a series of empty populist slogans suitable for a Republican Party convention or inauguration ("This Land" as it was sung by Richard Nixon in 1960 and Ronald Reagan in 1980).

Reading Joe Klein's biography *Woody Guthrie: A Life* (1980), I was particularly moved by Arlo Guthrie's recollection of his father's own awareness of the song's political evisceration and his helplessness in the face of it, wracked as he was by the Huntington's disease that had killed his mother and would soon kill him:

> I remember him coming home from the hospital and taking me out to the backyard, just him and me, and teaching me the last three verses to "This Land Is Your Land" because he thinks that if I don't learn them, no one will remember. He can barely strum the guitar at this point, and—can you imagine—his friends think he's a drunk, crazy, and they stick him in a puke green room in a mental hospital. . . .
>
> And then . . . when he can't write or talk or do anything at all anymore, he hits it big. All of a sudden everyone is singing his songs. Kids are singing "This Land Is Your Land" in school and people are talking about making it the national anthem. Bob Dylan and all the others are copying him. And he can't react to it . . . . The disease doesn't affect his mind. He's sitting there in a mental hospital, *and he knows what's going on,* and he can't say anything or tell anyone how he feels.[15]

Beginning in the 1950s, it is true, a scattered handful of academic essays and longer studies had sought to focus on Guthrie's political radicalism. For the most part, these were broad explorations of American protest music or left-wing American culture. In these studies, Guthrie, while prominent or even foundational, was only one among a huge cast of characters.[16] The two major biographies—with Ed Cray's *Ramblin' Man* (2004) following on from Klein's—certainly do not ignore Guthrie's political journey; but it is a thread often disappearing into the epic tales of rambling and womanizing and the Greek tragedy of the voice, body, and life gradually lost to the grim reaper of Huntington's disease. An entire book devoted to the radical Guthrie had yet to be written: a book about a political awakening and its aftermath; a book that would uncover and reclaim the obsessive thinker and fitful strategist practically buried in the romantic celebrations of the Dust Bowl Troubadour.

In 2008 a BMI–Woody Guthrie Fellowship took me to the Woody Guthrie Archives in New York to begin my research. I'd already learned by then that Guthrie was far to the left of the majority of Americans with whom he had been identified, not least the great mass of Dust Bowl migrants whose spokesman he became, almost by accident. As the historian James Gregory had discovered, the "Okies," by and large, were quite a conservative bunch: "When Okies talked of social equality, they usually meant equality for whites and often only native-stock whites. When they sorted out their pantheon of enemies, they frequently figured Communists to be more dangerous than bankers. And when faced with organizational opportunities that might yield collective benefits, they typically fell back instead on habits of individualism and family self-sufficiency."[17]

By contrast, Guthrie, the "Okie bard," had firmly nailed his colors to the mast of the American communist movement, if not the Communist Party itself. Whether or not he ever actually signed a CP membership card—and it remains the subject of tiresome debate[18]—I soon learned that I, for one, had taken far too smug a pleasure in imagining how many right-wing hawks might have licked his backside on a U.S. postage stamp.

As it turned out, Woody could be a bloodthirsty warmonger when he wanted to be:

> I'll bomb their towns and bomb their cities,
> Sink their ships beneath the tides.
> I'll win this war, but till I do, babe,
> I could not be satisfied.[19]

He could be selfish, petulant, bitchy, and snide—and insufferably self-righteous. He climbed on the backs of women, using them and deserting them, pregnant or otherwise; he climbed on the backs of friends. He borrowed guitars and never gave them back. He was a racist into his young adulthood; he neglected his first wife and their children; he could be violent; he never retracted his fondness for Stalin. Some of these things came as a mild surprise; some came as a revelation.

None of this would come as even a mild surprise to Nora Guthrie. When I first arrived at the archives, she urged me to pay attention to her father's contradictions—his "nuances," as she phrased it. She had just finished producing the album of Guthrie's lyrics put to music by Jonatha Brooke—happily for me, Jonatha's *The Works* was the soundtrack to my period of research at the Archives, continually played by the staff in the run-up to the album's official release. Jonatha had chosen the title of her album from an entry in Guthrie's notebooks reproduced in the collection *Woody Guthrie Artworks:*

> Your own people will sing loud yells about Woody Guthrie being two sex maniacs. But if I took the other road these same several yellers would scream that I'm a queer. I fully aim at this time, dear lay man and lay woman, to walk up and to run bare back down both of these trails and to get my soul known again as the two, both, the sexual maniac, the saint, the sinner, the drinker, the thinker, the queer. The works.
>
> The whole
WORKS
>
> It's not till you have called me all of these names that I feel satisfied.[20]

In a radio interview following the album's release, Jonatha responded to the suggestion that many of Guthrie's lyrics "sound like a woman wrote them": "That was another thing that surprised me. There were songs like 'My Flowers Grow Green' which he wrote absolutely from a woman's perspective. I couldn't believe it. How did he know that I would feel something like that, that I could sing that honestly, you know—in my heartbroken tone, that that would be the way I would speak it or the way I would have wished to say it?"[21]

Woody the great seed planter, the "cocksman" (as one unimpressed acquaintance called him),[22] the lovin' and leavin' misogynist—we all know him; the Woody who callously abandoned his domestic responsibilities to ride the boxcars and forge his celebrated reputation as America's favorite hobo. His is truly the classic American male escape narrative "characterized by physical movement" and "primarily associated with an explicit rejection of the female," as Heidi Slettedahl Macpherson describes it in *Women's Movement,* her pioneering study of women's escape narratives.[23] It is unsurprising that Guthrie's most faithful disciple, Ramblin' Jack Elliott, should have recalled: "My wives always mentioned Woody Guthrie in the papers as a reason why they would divorce me."[24] Ellen Steckert, while decrying Guthrie's "sexism," is generous enough to approach it at least in part as "a reflection of [his] times (even within the political left)."[25] Now Jonatha Brooke's recovery work obliges yet another rethink of Guthrie's fraught relationship with women. His misogyny, while an undeniable part of him, was—like so much else about him—"nuanced." This is not to condone, but to attempt an understanding.

This, too, would be no surprise to Nora Guthrie. One day she made a point of directing me to a particular archival source that seemed to have put a great hold on her—a five-page disquisition of Guthrie's in verse, on the deceptively prosaic subject of tipping. Woody, as we all know, was the worker's champion; it is wholly in keeping with his sympathies and his convictions that he should have taken note of the lowest wage slaves of Ithaca, New York, during a tour:

> And we stopped off at a little tavern;
> And one waitress was all they had there
> To wait on several big tables like us;
> I watched her run herself nearly crazy
> Trying to get our orders to us.
>> Every musician and every dancer
>> Pitied the poor girl so awful much
>> They all took money out and paid their bills
>> And then left tips down on the tables . . . .

And then, it was Guthrie—my Woody Guthrie!—who wrote this:

> All but me;
> I argued with the others;
> Told them I don't believe in tipping.

His conclusion was a brutal slap in the face:

> If you need more money,
> Get it off of your owner,
>> Not off of me.

This was Woody Guthrie?—who himself had legendarily played for tips in every bar from California to the New York Island?

> A long number of years;
> Playing for tips my music, singing;
>> Songs for nickels and for dimes;
>>> Which a worker could not pay to hear,
>>> So he could not have his own songs;
>>>> But had to listen to the rich man songs
>>>> That says, "This world is okie dokie!"

What had happened? How could Woody Guthrie have come to conclude that he should withhold the lifeblood of a poor waitress's tip? How dare he, of all people, say, "I don't believe in tipping"?

Do you tip your Nurse or Doctor?
Do you tip your classroom teacher?
Do you tip your union bringers?
    Union organizers?
    Union workers?
        Do you tip your old professor?
            Do you tip your Worker's paper?

Then it dawned on me: Woody was working through a theory. He was looking at the system that was positively oiled by the normalization of tipping rather than fair wages. Tips were coins tossed to a beggar—as he himself had once been:

When I was a bus boy;
    Waiter,
    Driver,
    Shoe Shiner,
    But then I
        Got tired, and sick
        Of living by begging;
    Living on the
        Whims of idle minds.
    Living on the
        favors of money
            owners.

In the end, tipping was just one more bulwark against the dictatorship of the proletariat, an obstacle to the planned economy of the socialist America that remained Guthrie's ideal to his dying day:

You don't have to go across
Any ocean, nor any waters,
To see folks by the untold thousands
Lost in a hungry world of tipping;
    Watching eats, and clothes and work plans
        Tossed back and forth across the tables
        In the form of tips and take offs
            To the union busters,
            To the labor spies and stooges,
               To the cultural misleaders,
               To the clowns and monkey of planlessness.[26]

Whether or not this was Nora's intention, what I took away from this disquisition was a profound sense of both the idealism and the brutality of the struggle to which her father was committed—an often violent struggle, as he signaled in the poem I chose as this book's epigraph:

> If I do happen to tear a part
>   of your house down on my
>   way growing up towards your
>   sky, don't you be afraid.
> I'll fix it back a whole lot
>   better than I found it.
> I want to raise my own kids
>   in a better house.[27]

Woody Guthrie spent his productive life on the warpath—against poverty, political oppression, censorship, capitalism, fascism, racism, and, ultimately, war itself. His commitment to radical struggle forced him to face head-on—and sometimes celebrate—the violence inevitable to the tearing down and reconstruction of an oppressive system, whether fascism in Europe or capitalism at home. Sometimes the violence was physical; sometimes it was violence done to long-held and often cherished beliefs and assumptions. My research showed me that Guthrie was at his most convincing when he acknowledged and wrestled with the moral compromises of his struggle, as he does in his highwayman's song "The Unwelcome Guest":

> I don't know good horse,
> As we trot in this dark here
> That robbing the rich is for worse or for best
> They take it by stealing and lying and gambling
> And I take it my way, my shiny Black Bess.[28]

Otherwise, he could often be simplistic in his hunger for a solution to the degradation he saw all around him—even willfully blind to the corruption of those, like Stalin, in whom he saw a way forward. It was an affliction he shared with many American communists and noncommunist leftists in the first half of the twentieth century, an affliction most conveniently identified with hindsight.

I cannot deny that in my search for the radical Guthrie I learned some things that I would rather not have learned; but they never obliterated what I still consider to be the core of his being and the reason why I continue to broadcast his voice as the representative voice of my America, here at its interface with the rest of the world: once again, it is "the man's great heart, his empathy with the hard hit and the hard traveling." All the negatives and the contradictions simply make him less of a saint, and more of a committed, flawed human being immersed in political complexity and a harrowing personal struggle.

1. Awakenings

On August 24, 1939, the German foreign minister, Joachim von Ribbentrop, and his Soviet counterpart, Vyacheslav Molotov, shook hands across the table in Moscow after signing their mutual nonaggression pact. Josef Stalin stood behind them, beaming. He and Adolf Hitler were now allies, a situation that immediately sent the antifascist Left around the world into a tailspin. The Soviet Union—the mother of the Revolution—had entered into a pact with the devil. The major repercussions of the Hitler–Stalin Pact over the next few months would include the Nazi–Soviet invasion of Poland, the Soviet annexation of the Baltic states, and the Red Army's attack on Finland. One minor repercussion was that an obscure American folksinger named Woody Guthrie lost his job at the Los Angeles radio station KFVD.

Guthrie had gone a step too far, singing his song "More War News" on his morning radio program:

> I see where Hitler is a-talking peace
> Since Russia met him face to face—
> He just had got his war machine a-rollin',
> Coasting along, and taking Poland.
> Stalin stepped in, took a big strip of Poland and give
>   the farm lands back to the farmers.
>
> A lot of little countries to Russia ran
> To get away from this Hitler man—
> If I'd been living in Poland then
> I'd been glad Stalin stepped in—
> Swap my rifle for a farm . . . Trade my helmet for a sweetheart.[1]

Guthrie's boss at KFVD, J. Frank Burke Sr., was a leftist, but he was no Stalinist. When it came to Stalin—and in particular the invasion of Poland—he had no room for an apologist on his station. Guthrie was sent packing.

He had another job, but not one that his family could live on. His topical column "Woody Sez" was still running gratis in the San Francisco–based communist daily the *People's World*. He'd gotten the column through the paper's Los Angeles bureau chief, Ed Robbin, a fellow broadcaster on KFVD. The paper's editor, Al Richmond, recalled how Robbin had come to his office, dragging in tow a "young hillbilly singer from Oklahoma, who turned out to be socially conscious."[2] Richmond also recalled what is nowadays often forgotten: what the safety of the Soviet Union meant to American communists and socialists as fascism took hold in Europe. The world's "first and only Socialist state" had initially sought alliances with the Western powers against Hitler, only to be rebuffed. The subsequent treaty with Germany, however distasteful, was defended by Communist Party ideologues as a diplomatic necessity. Nonetheless, it hit Richmond like "a megaton shock, stunning, sudden, wrenching." As he later admitted: "Unprepared, knocked off balance by this abrupt turn, our reflex defense of the treaty had elements of the frenetic. Scanning the *People's World* of those days one can find much that is reasonable and stands the test of time, and much folly and confusion. I will speak for myself: I was confused. One argument for the treaty was that it created a zone of peace. From this I deduced that surely Hitler would not strike eastward, and so thoroughly persuaded myself that even when the Nazis threatened Poland I gave my personal assurance to the liberal publisher of a modest Beverly Hills newspaper that they would not attack. . . . Despite my personal assurance Hitler invaded Poland two days later."[3]

So did Stalin, two weeks after that. Nobody knows what opinion, if any, Woody Guthrie held about Stalin's purges of 1936–38, through which thousands of suspected "saboteurs and fascists" were executed; the purges were, even at the time, common knowledge for those American communists and fellow travelers brave enough to face the truth.[4] No one knows what Guthrie thought of the great Ukrainian famine and the deaths of up to 20 million in 1932–33, the result of Stalin's brutal collectivization policy. Again, it was no secret to those in the American Left willing to confront it.[5] It was enough that Guthrie spoke—or sang—his mind about Poland.

He'd once boasted: "My contract with KFVD don't give me enough money to get the bighead, but it gives me enough that I don't care what other people think about me."[6] Those days were now gone. KFVD had been his home on the air for the past two years; Burke had given Guthrie his first big break in Los Angeles. Robbin recalled how Guthrie had arrived at KFVD in the summer of 1937—knocking on Burke's door and announcing: "Mr. Burke, I'd like to sing on this here station of yours, if you'd let me, and I don't need any money for it, I just want to sing my songs." Burke had told him that the station already had a hillbilly singer, to which—according to Robbin— Guthrie replied: "His songs are pretty and nice, I guess. Mine aren't so pretty, but they're songs that I learned or I wrote while I was doing stoop labor up and down the highways and byways of California, travelin' with my people in their broken-down old cars and with their kids with bellies swollen from hunger, their mouths full of the dust of Oklahoma. They were fighting to live somehow or other, in the shanties, and with the whole family workin' out there in the fields. That is the kind of song that I'm singin', and believe me, there's thousands of my people out there who would eventually be listenin' because they want someone to speak out for 'em. Why don't you try me for a while and see what kind of response we get?"[7]

This version was myth, like so much else that was to come. Guthrie had done no "stoop labor up and down the highways and byways of California," although he had done some dishwashing, some sign painting, some busking on LA's street corners, and singing for pennies in the Skid Row bars. He hadn't come knocking on Burke's door to be a spokesman for his "people," but rather to see if he and his cousin, "Oklahoma" Jack Guthrie, might get a radio spot to kick-start what they hoped would be a lucrative cowboy music act (the terms *country music* and *country and western* had yet to be invented). It hadn't even been Woody's idea to hit KFVD; it was Jack's, because, he said, "You can get more jobs at saloons, churches and markets if you've got a radio program every day."[8]

But Burke was willing to give them a hearing, and an air check was arranged. The surviving recording shows that, from the very first, Woody Guthrie could write and sing with a political bite to him:

> My banker put me down on the Skid Row.
> Oh, the banker put me down on the Skid Row.
> If you're a-hittin' it hard on the Hollerwood Boulevard,
> You might sleep tonight on the Skid Row.
>
> My senator sent me down on the Skid Row.
> My senator sent me down on the Skid Row.
> I thought he was tops but he's rotten as the crops
> And as filthy as the flops on the Skid Row.[9]

Already Guthrie had developed a viable mode of political and economic critique based on his observations of a newly urban underclass. He disguised his bite with a veneer of faux naiveté, explaining that another audition song had come to him when he "sorta got to watchin' the ways of a big city":

> Brother John moved into town, he rented a flat and settled down,
> Lord, Lord, he's a gettin' them big city ways.
> Brought his wife and kids along, but fifteen dollars didn't last long,
> Lord, Lord, he's a gettin' them big city ways.
>
> The finance company right next door got his paycheck, then some more,
> Lord, Lord, he's a getting' them big city ways.
> The banker got his furniture and the auto company got his car,
> Lord, Lord, he's a getting' them big city ways.[10]

Guthrie sang another song for his air check—"If You Ain't Got the Do Re Mi"—about an illegal blockade that had been set up by the Los Angeles Police Department, hundreds of miles outside their jurisdiction, to prevent the Dust Bowl migrants from entering the state of California unless they had fifty dollars or more to prove that they weren't "unemployable." The blockade had lasted only for a few months in 1936—it was gone by the time Guthrie arrived in California—but the memory of the insult was fresh enough to provoke a stinging musical critique. It was fairly strong stuff for someone who simply wanted to sing cowboy music and make a few bucks.

The Guthrie cousins got the job, playing for free on the station's 8:00 a.m. slot and happy for the opportunity to promote their live shows. Woody Guthrie kept his politics to himself during "The Oklahoma and Woody Show"— not that the station's management would have minded all that much (barring any overly Stalinist rhetoric). Burke and his son, Frank Jr., were on the far left of the Democratic Party. Frank Sr. had supported the visionary socialism of Upton Sinclair's End Poverty in California campaign (EPIC), and both were staunch New Dealers. They gave airtime to all kinds of opinions, from the right-wing evangelism of Robert "Fighting Bob" Shuler to the Popular Front communism of *The People's World,* but their programming was, in the main, proudly of the non-Stalinist left, providing a bulwark, however minor, against the Roosevelt-hating reaction of William Randolph Hearst's KEHE radio station and the business-first agenda of the Chamber of Commerce's *March of Progress* broadcasts.[11]

Jack Guthrie lasted two months before he concluded that he couldn't make a living out of music. Woody Guthrie joined up with a singer from Missouri, Maxine Crissman, and together they launched the "Woody and Lefty Lou" show on KFVD. Their surviving fan mail indicates that they were immediately popular with "working-class listeners, Dust Bowlers, and women."[12] Their repertoire was dominated by hymns, country standards, and traditional ballads; but with the departure of his more commercially focused cousin, Guthrie was able to play more freely off of Crissman's "personal politics of standing up for the underdog."[13] The duo began to venture deeper into direct social commentary—nothing particularly radical at first, simply aware:

> My mama and my papa
> Have eight children sweet and fine;
> Our house is such a little house,
> And soon there will be nine.
>
> And now today I kneel and pray
> Some million dollar man
> Will let my papa go to work;
> He'll do the best he can.[14]

The pair's introduction of "Do Re Mi" into their airplay marked an early radical shift: they were in effect now taking on the LAPD, Governor Frank Merriam, the *Los Angeles Times,* the Chamber of Commerce, and the rest of the state's powerful anti-migrant bloc, which certainly hadn't been dismantled along with the "bum blockade." Guthrie pointed a finger—quietly and ironically, perhaps, but unquestionably:

> The Police at the Port of Entry say:
> You're number fourteen thousand for today!
>
> If you aint got the do re mi, folks,
> If you aint got the do re mi,
> Better hang on in Beautiful Texas,
> Oklahoma, Kansas, Georgia, Tennessee.
> California is a Garden of Eden,
> A Paradise to live in or see,
> But, believe it or not, you won't find it so hot,
> If you aint got the do re mi.[15]

Guthrie's critique was sly, suggestive. "The California newspapers and magazines," he said, "print purty pictures and purty descriptions of the Land of Sunshine and Paradise that is California. And they are right in what they print. They do this to bring folks out here to tour the country and drop off a few midwestern dollars, and to sell 'em some rale estate, like a lot or a farm, or a house. And this is all right. But they also cause all the fairly happy farm folks to swap their stock and machinery for a 'hoopy' or a 'jalopy' and come rattlin' thru to California with nothing but a run down car and a gallon of sorghum. They take the sorghum at the Boundary line, and the car breaks down at Los Angeles."[16] His critique was comic, almost slapstick, crafted with a cartoonist's skill that managed, in spite of all hilarity, to emphasize the tragic conditions that the migrants faced upon their arrival in the Golden State:

> Got to California so dad gum broke,
> So dad gum hungry I thought I'd choke,
> I bummed up a spud or two,
> Wife fixed up some 'tater stew.
>> Fixed th' kids a bait of it . . .
>> Looked like a tribe of thy-mometers runnin' around.[17]

The radio audience loved it, sending in birthday cakes, clothes parcels, invitations to dinner, the odd dollar to "buy yourself and the lady a drink," and letters begging them: "Please don't go modern." Occasionally a listener would see through Guthrie's quickly developing "Okie" persona: "I don't enjoy that faked hill billy language that you give us, Woodie. The reason I know its faked is because I know that if you were really that ignorant, horses couldn't drag you up before a 'microbephone,' I come from the hills myself but I never heard any talking quite so bad as yours."[18] Such criticisms were in the minority.

In the spring of 1938, Crissman quit singing on the grounds of ill health. Guthrie was now "Woody, the Lone Wolf," as his show was retitled. Before one of the broadcasts, Burke Sr. came to Guthrie with a proposal that would change his life and the course of American music. Burke had started a small newspaper, *The Light,* to promote the gubernatorial campaign of the progressive Democrat Culbert Olson, hoping to unseat Merriam. He asked Guthrie to head out to Bakersfield and farther into the San Joaquin Valley, to report on the conditions in the jungle camps and jails, all variously packed with migrants looking for work and—for those daring to organize into unions—getting their heads broken. Thanks to his radio show and his Oklahoma origins, Guthrie would be welcome where few Californians had been or would care to go. "You might even consider getting yourself arrested," Burke proposed.[19]

Guthrie would ever recall what he saw on his travels—the squalid camps of migrant families squatted beneath a railroad bridge or on the banks of a filthy river, named, wherever they were, in honor of the president who, in spite of a long record of relief work on behalf of Belgium, Russia, and the victims of the great Mississippi flood of 1927, had—unaccountably, it seemed—resisted all calls for federal relief to the victims of the Depression. "The camp is called Hooversville," Guthrie wrote, "and if such a bad place as this was named after my name, I believe I'd commit suicide before morning. People take old rusty buckets, rip them apart, beat them out flat, and nail them onto a frame of rickety boards—and that's a plumb good house in Hooversville. It is garbage to garbage and water to water." He recalled the "4000 people hungry and dirty and bogged down" in the "shacktown called Hooversville . . . There are flies crawling over babies faces. There are little pot bellies by the hundreds swelled up with the gas that is caused by malnutrition. There youll see the torn holes in the flour sack dresses that the kids wear. Red, fevered skin is showing through these clothes like the blistered hide of the several hundred thousand Okies that crawled and walked and marched across a couple of thousand miles of red hot desert to get from Oklahoma's trash pile to California's green pretty places."[20] He turned disgust and outrage into poetry, building his verses on a foundation of neglect and despair that had been spreading across America since the Depression hit:

> Ramblin', gamblin', rickety shacks,
> > That's Hooversvill;
> Rusty tin an' raggedy sacks
> > Makes Hooversvill;
> On the skeeter bit end of th garbage dump,
> 30 million people slump
> Down where the big rats run an' jump
> > In Hooversville

He sought the most heartbreaking image to encapsulate the commodification of humanity, often with a grim honesty that would elude even John Steinbeck, Dorothea Lange, John Ford, or the other poets in word or image whose strategy, for the most part, was to ennoble the Dust Bowl migrants in the midst of their adversity. Guthrie's Okies, beyond desperation, could be far less heroic than Steinbeck's Ma Joad, far less stoic than Lange's Migrant Mother:

> Maybe you just didn't know
> > That's Hooversville;
> Guess you didn't never go
> > To Hooversville;
> Maybe you aint never seen
> The little girls around fifteen
> Sold for the price of a bowl of beans
> > In Hooversville.[21]

Guthrie had little in common with the popular image of the Dust Bowl migrants he met in the camps—those fictionalized into Steinbeck's Joad family, who would appear in *The Grapes of Wrath* in 1939. The Joads' real-life counterparts, as one historian notes, "had not come to California out of a sturdy yeoman farmer tradition, nor out of a pastoral landscape. They had

been victims at home too of an exploitative agricultural system: of tractors, one-crop specialization, tenant insecurity, disease, and soil abuse."[22] If
anything, Guthrie came from the exploiting class and an exploiting family;
his father, Charley, was a socialist-hating, fistfighting small-town politician,
real-estate agent, landlord, and sometime property swindler. Guthrie could
recall the flush times of his early childhood in Okemah, Oklahoma, where
his father "had to outwit, outsmart, and out-run a pretty long string of people
to have everything so nice":

> Papa went to town and made real-estate deals with other people, and he brought
> their money home. Mama could sign a check for any amount, buy every little
> thing that her eyes liked the looks of. Roy and Clara could stop off in any store
> in Okemah and buy new clothes to fit the weather, new things to eat to make
> you healthy, and Papa was proud because we could all have anything we saw.
> Our house was packed full of things Mama liked, Roy liked, Clara liked, and
> that was what Papa liked.

When the oil boom hit Okemah around 1920, Charley Guthrie could add
"land speculator" to his list of professions, outsmarting the "oil slickers, oil
fakers, oil stakers, and oil takers":

> Papa met them. He stood up and swapped and traded, bought and sold, got
> bigger, spread out, and made more money.
> And this was to get us the nice things. And we all liked the prettiest and
> best things in the store windows, and anything in the store was Clara's just for
> signing her name, Roy's just for signing his name, or Mama's just for signing
> her name—and I knew how proud I felt of our name, that just to write it on a
> piece of paper would bring more good things home to us. This wasn't because
> there was oil in the wind, nor gushers thrashing against the sky, no—it was
> because my dad was the man that owned the land—and whatever was under
> that land was ours.[23]

But in 1928 the oil ran out, and Okemah went from boom to bust. The following year, Wall Street crashed. Guthrie wrote of his father: "I heard the song that
is in a man's voice when he builds up all of these things by close trading, then
loses them by some mistake, some crazy something in a ticker tape machine.
My dad told me that he was the only man in the world that lost a farm a day
for thirty days."[24] The Guthrie family were thus brought one step closer to the
reality of the migrants defining "the hungry thirties," the majority of whom
were not agricultural workers but white-collar or blue-collar town workers.[25]
    With the breakup of his family (the death of his older sister, Clara, in a
house fire, the near-fatal burning of his father in another fire, and the incarceration of his mother in the Oklahoma State Mental Asylum through her

undiagnosed and misunderstood Huntington's disease), Guthrie joined his recuperating father in another boom-to-bust oil town on the Texas Panhandle, Pampa in Gray County. He became, successively, a high school dropout, odd-jobber, drug store–cum–speakeasy attendant, fortune teller, husband, and father of two. He took up the profession of sign painting.

There, in Pampa, he lived through the catastrophe that would enable him to identify with many of the migrants he would later meet in the California camps—the historical event with which he himself would become most readily identified. As he told his second wife, Marjorie Mazia, after she'd asked why he began writing songs about the Dust Bowl: "Well, I always sort of liked to write about wherever I happen to be. I just happened to be *in* the Dust Bowl. I mean, it wasn't something that I particularly wanted or craved, but since I was there and the dust was there, I thought, well, I'll write a little song about it. . . . I felt it was the most important thing that I had seen, so I had to write about it."[26]

In the Dust Bowl, five thousand square miles of ravaged farmland wreaked its vengeance on the inhabitants of the southern plains—vengeance for the decades of intensive cotton and wheat farming that had wiped out the indigenous prairie grasses holding down the soil for the previous millennia; vengeance for the army of Henry Ford's tractors let loose upon on the land; vengeance for the arrogant belief that no vengeance would ever come. In November of 1933, the dust buried the Midwest. The following spring it came back to bury Chicago as well as Albany and Buffalo, New York. Three hundred miles out in the Atlantic, sailors reported the settling of a fine patina of red Oklahoma dust on their decks and railings. Guthrie later described the worst dust storm that he, or any of the Dust Bowlers, witnessed, on Black Sunday—Palm Sunday—April 14, 1935. The sky had turned black and red with thousands of tons of roiling dust, as winds of more than seventy miles an hour whipped the topsoil and red clay from as far away as Nebraska and dumped it on the already dying town of Pampa. Animals and people choked to death. Toddlers wandered off into dust drifts and suffocated. The plains around Pampa, Guthrie said, were "thirty-six hundred feet high and just as flat as a floor. A thousand miles wide and ain't a thing in the world to stop that wind but just a barb-wire fence, about a hundred miles north of there, and it ain't got a barb on it." When the dust storm hit the huddled town of Pampa, it "looked like a ocean was chompin' on a snail."[27] It looked "like the Red Sea closin' in on the Israel children."[28]

Out of this experience came Guthrie's first Dust Bowl ballad, "Dusty Old Dust" ("So Long, It's Been Good to Know Yuh"), which, even at that early stage in his songwriting career, carried a critical bite as it swiped at the greed of small-town prairie prelates feeding on the trembling and the credulous. Terrorized by promises of hellfire and damnation, the parishioners flock to the church:

> And that dusty old dust storm blowed so black,
> The preacher could not read a word of his text
> And he folded his specs and he took up a collection.
> Said, "So long, it's been good to know yuh . . . ."[29]

When Guthrie left his wife and children to seek a living for them all out west, he carried a part of Oklahoma with him: the prairie socialist tradition that his father had fought so hard to beat down, and which he himself would work to perpetuate. The radical struggle was inscribed into his very birthdate—July 14, 1912. While much has been made of the revolutionary overtones of the day—Bastille Day[30]—it was the year of his birth that was the most significant. The year 1912 marked the near-zenith of the rising and falling tide of Oklahoma socialism, with the militant farmers giving Eugene Debs and his Socialist Party over 16 percent of the state's vote in the national election (whereas the party could claim only 6 percent nationally).[31] Socialism—the "tempting serpent" with "dangerous fangs," as Charley Guthrie described it[32]—had thrown the state's Democrats "into panic," with the Socialists having increased their vote in every cotton-belt ballot since 1907.[33] Debs had inflamed rural radicalism with his visions of a "cooperative commonwealth"[34] and the damnation of capitalism as "inherently unjust, inhuman, unintelligent."[35] In Oklahoma the Socialist Party had championed the interests of "agricultural workers" above all others, declaring them in official platforms the backbone of the state's "working class"; the Party's "Renter's and Farmer's Program" promised to place control of the land in "the hands of the actual tillers of the soil."[36] The Debsian party was populist in its appeal, the people's St. George taking on the political dragon of "rent, credit, and taxes"[37]—upon which the fortunes of all property entrepreneurs, Charley Guthrie included, were founded. The elder Guthrie could take little pleasure in the knowledge that it was *his* state—not New York—that was the epicenter of political radicalism in America.

There were historical reasons for these whirlwinds of prairie radicalism. In the decades after the Civil War, the autonomous Five Nations inhabiting Oklahoma Territory—the Creek, Choctaw, Chickasaw, Seminole, and Cherokee—had leased vast swaths of their lands to railroad speculators, mine owners, ranchers, and other white, moneyed entrepreneurs. Masses of poor whites had also flooded the "Indian Territory," leasing small holdings from both white and tribal landlords in a bid to escape the hard-scrabble farmlands of the defeated Confederacy. But then the Five Nations themselves had succumbed to the clamor of eastern developers claiming that they were too "lazy" and "idle" for the continued stewardship of the land; their governmental and social structures were dissolved and their lands "allotted" to more aggressive or "enterprising" stewards. By the time of Oklahoma statehood in 1907, a whole cadre of merchants, lawyers, bankers, and landlords had grown to preside over the poor whites—both established settlers and newcomers—who watched helplessly as land values inflated along with agricultural prices. Oil discoveries, railroad building, and other capitalist developments snowballed. By Bastille Day 1912, the majority of Oklahoma's farmers were tenants, many of them paying a bitter rent on farms that they had once owned.[38]

But also by Bastille Day of 1912, the state's renters had begun to fight back. Some had organized into unions modeled on those of the southwestern coal miners and timber workers, such as the Oklahoma Renters' Union, founded in 1909. Rural militants took heed of radical newspapers like the Sulpher *New Century*, which proclaimed that "every tenant farmer in Murray county should take steps to organize. . . . There are less than one hundred landlords in the county and about seven hundred tenants; organization is the only remedy. Just so long as you act independent of your neighbor he is your competitor, but when organized you become each other's protectors."[39] In Charley Guthrie's own Okemah, the *Sledge Hammer* went to press with a mission "to hammer the system, not the individual," trumpeting the Debsian credo that "Socialism will not interfere with the farmer who owns and farms his land. On the contrary it will render his possession of it far more secure than it can possibly be under capitalism, for he cannot lose it by debt, crop failure, or sickness. Co-operative farming will gradually develop under socialism, but the feature of the program that should appeal to the tenant farmers with the greatest force is the fact that the occupancy of the land will be in the hands of the men who work it, and they will have permanent homes without having to pay rent."[40]

Two-hundred-odd miles up the road, the Sentinel *Sword of Truth* damned "the banker, the money shark, the merchant, the petty grafter," and "the court-house ring," along with "their slaves, such as clerks, deputies, stenographers, etc." who were "waiting for the harvest of the farmer": "They are of the class that produces not. They get their living out of the sweat and toil of the farmer, the working class. It is the height of folly to expect them to work in the interest of the farmer."[41]

All these expressions of rural radicalism were not merely founded on the foreign theories of pernicious Marxist "kumrids," as Charley Guthrie sneered at them in a series of published essays,[42] but also upon a distinctly home-grown brand of Christian socialism. The "Kingdom of God" was possible on earth; such was the prevailing tenet of Protestant activism in Oklahoma.[43] It was not for nothing that Steinbeck would make his most radical agitator an ex-preacher in *The Grapes of Wrath;* the prototypes for Reverend Jim Casy were to be found in the churches and revival tents, proclaiming the words of Leviticus 25:23 damning the landlords above all other parasites: "The Land shall not be sold forever: for the land *is* mine; and ye *are* strangers and so-journers with me." In 1912 the *New Century* reported that the Socialist Party was gaining "more recruits from the ranks of the ministry than from any other profession."[44] Socialism was by definition Christianity, and vice versa, as Okemah's fiery preacher E. F. McClanahan argued in the *Sledge Hammer:* "On every hand there is a sweeping demand for a righteous government, the toiling of thousands of earth's homeless burden-bearers are demanding it, and the socialist movement is the concrete expression of this demand. For the first time since Christ, there is an intelligent movement toward the conscious organization of a just society. Then children can enjoy childhood, women can be womanly, and men can be manly. The men can organize and cooperate industrially. Then all true Christians will follow the Great Galilean from conquest to victory."[45]

His depictions of greedy preachers notwithstanding, Woody Guthrie him-self would never escape from the hold of this prairie religiosity, maintaining: "I seldom worship in or around churches, but always had a deep love for peo-ple who go there."[46] His producer at Folkways Records, Moses Asch, would later recall: "You know, when people say, 'Communist, and this and that,' they don't realize how much the Bible influenced Woody."[47] In the last tortured years of his life, wasting away under the ravages of Huntington's disease, Guthrie would desperately cling to Jesus as his only "doctor."[48] But always, even when not in extremis, he would plant his feet on the rock of Christian socialism's heaven on earth, conceived on the plains of Oklahoma:

> No debts and no burdens in Heaven,
> No mortgage or loans to repay,
> No banks on the great streets of glory.
> No homes shall be taken away;
> There will never be landlords in Heaven,
> No rent to take from you each day,
> And we all will be equal in glory,
> And happy forever we'll be.
>
> You will all have a pension in Heaven
> But you'll never be aged nor gray;
> You will work for each other in Heaven,

Not for gold to be buried away.
There's a job for us all up in glory,
There's a job and a wealth you can share;
Let's have it here like you've got it up there,
Then: there's no disappointment down here.[49]

As he emerged from the Dust Bowl early in 1937 and pointed his way west-ward, Guthrie passed and mingled with veterans of the long class struggle fought to bring about this earthly paradise—the older, sometimes violent militants from the defunct Working Class Union, which in 1914 had con-demned J. P. Morgan's "great speculation," the "rich man's war" and the "poor man's fight," and had spread across the Oklahoma state line to wage a different war against the "death-producing practice of rent, interest, and profit-taking" that had been "imposed upon the working class of the world."[50] Some of these veterans had participated in the last great outburst of working-class prairie militancy, the doomed "Green Corn Rebellion" of 1917, in which an-gry tenant farmers from the lands around Okemah had set out to march on Washington—sustaining themselves with corn pilfered from fields along the way—to overthrow Woodrow Wilson and the conscription act. They had expected to gather a farmers' army behind them but in the end gathered nothing but green corn, indigestion, and a series of indictments, convictions, and prison sentences.

Other old soldiers on the road were veterans of the Farm-Labor Union (FLU), which between 1923 and 1925 had chosen to do battle with the most powerful rising force in Oklahoma politics, the Ku Klux Klan—not so much in defense of nonwhites as on behalf of the working class. The FLU accurately nailed the Klan as "the legitimate offspring of the Fascista movement in Italy" but expressed only minor interest in the hooded legions' racism. Rather, they focused on the Klan as a band of "avowed open shoppers" whose mission was "to disrupt organized labor and co-operative enterprises" through "mob violence," "white cap methods," and a "black list against all who are not af-filiated or in sympathy with their organization."[51] The fighting spirit of the FLU had not been blown away with Oklahoma's topsoil; it would be carried westward into the militant labor struggles in the fields of Madera and Kern County in California.

Others sharing the tarmac and the boxcars with Guthrie would have been some of the old Wobblies—the Industrial Workers of the World (IWW)—who had once roused fear and hatred among the employing class in Oklahoma, as elsewhere. The IWW presence had predated statehood, with five chapters set up across the territory by 1906. The Wobblies struck particularly hard at the state's oil industry, laying bare the disparity between high oil profits and low wages that placed decent food and housing out of reach of many oil work-ers. As the 1916 IWW pamphlet *Message to the Oil Workers* characteristically goaded: "While you are inhaling poisonous gases, up to your shoe tips in filthy muck, the bosses are wallowing in luxury, eating the choicest of foods and drinking champagne."[52] The Wobblies' political nonalignment and their endorsement of sabotage as a legitimate weapon of class warfare frightened even the Oklahoma Socialist Party, which in the year of Guthrie's birth called the IWW "a mad mob of desperate men moved by hatred to the commission of all forms of violence and destruction."[53] Guthrie would always hold the Wobblies in high regard, although their example would turn him toward a different level of activism. As he later wrote: "They wanted to get control of all of the farms and factories, mines, mills and railroads. They wanted to get good wages, short hours and better treatment all the way 'round. But they steered clear of politics. . . . There's a good word for them in the pages of history, but you just can't outwit these people that's got the money unless you blast away in their face with politics, votes, petitions, letters, unions, speeches and meeting halls running full blast. The rich folks got your money with politics. You can get it back with politics."[54]

What would impress Guthrie most about the Wobblies would be their use of song as a weapon to "Fan the Flames of Discontent" (as their song-book proclaimed).[55] Their most articulate and winning spokespeople had been their songwriters—Ralph Chaplin, composer of "Solidarity Forever"; T-Bone Slim (Matti Valentine Huhta), who wrote "The Lumberjack's Prayer" and "The Popular Wobbly"; "Haywire Mac" McClintock (Harry Kirby Mc-Clintock), composer of "Hallelujah, I'm a Bum" and, so he claimed, "The Big Rock Candy Mountain"; and above all, Joseph Hillstrom—Joe Hill—the Swedish-born immigrant and martyr to the IWW cause, executed on a dubious murder charge in 1915, four years after turning the fundamentalist hymn "In the Sweet By and By" into the great anthem to international labor "The Preacher and the Slave." A year before his death, Hill had written: "A pamphlet, no matter how good, is never read more than once, but a song is learned by heart and repeated over and over."[56] He had also advised would-be musical activists to "put a few cold, common sense facts into a song, and dress them up in a cloak of humor to take the dryness off of them"[57]—a lesson that Guthrie would take to his heart, carrying the IWW songbook in his breast pocket. He would later eulogize Hill: "I lived like a rebel, like a rebel I die. . . . Goodbye Joe Hillstrom you done a pretty good job."[58]

All these militant sons and daughters of Oklahoma would, to be sure, be in the minority among the overwhelmingly conservative migrant population in California. They would provide the radical edge in the agricultural labor struggles of the late 1930s, in sympathy and partnership with the union agitators—both Communist and non-Communist—going up against the fruit crop bosses and labor exploiters in the San Joaquin Valley. They would be the unsung champions of the great mass of Dust Bowl migrants, particularly the recent class of victims who had fallen for what Guthrie called "one of the stinkin'est things that I've run on to," the promises of the California labor contractors flooding the southern plains with offers of crop work at five dollars a day in exchange for a ten-dollar fee. Guthrie would later reconstruct a conversation with one hopeful migrant:

> I said, "You'll go out to California. He'll give you this card with this name and address on it, and you'll go meet this here feller. You'll go out to his place, and he'll say, 'Damn, I never seen nothin' like it before. The fruit's in awful shape, and it ain't gonna be worth nothin' this year. I doubt if it's worth pickin', the price they're payin'—I think maybe I'll just let it rot. But of course, if you boys *want* to pick it . . . if you haven't got no job and nothin' to do, why, you can pitch in there and pick it if you want to; and when you pick and pack and carry and load one ton of peaches, why, I'll give you a dollar.'" And I says, "You're not gonna see a five dollar bill while you're in California, I don't care how long you stay there, unless you just go visiting somewheres—a bank or somewhere, and just stand there and look."[59]

He would bitterly mock the exploitation of the migrants' hope in the song "California California," so easily misread as a paean to the Golden State's open-armed hospitality:

> If you want to see beauty
> And progress abound
> Just open your sad eyes
> Take a look all around
> Her people are healthy
> All happy and free
> When heaven's on earth
> This is where it will be.[60]

In the spring of 1937, Guthrie crossed the state line into California. As he mythologized his first impressions:

> Sign says: "Fruit, see, but don't pick it." Another one reads: "Fruit—beat it." Another one: "Trespassers prosecuted. Keep Out. Get away from Here."
> Fruit is on the ground, and it looks like the trees have been just too glad to grow it, and give it to you. The tree likes to grow and you like to eat it; and there is a sign between you and the tree saying: "Beware The Mean Dog's Master."

Fruit is rotting on the ground all around me. Just what in the hell has gone wrong here, anyhow? I'm not a very smart man. Maybe it ought to be this way, with the crops laying all around over the ground. Maybe they couldn't get no pickers just when they wanted them, and they just let the fruit go to the bad. There's enough here on the ground to feed every hungry kid from Maine to Florida, and from there to Seattle.[61]

He looked for sign-painting work (no "stoop labor"), as he later described it to Marjorie: "You hit the town from the outside edge and hustle all the neighborhood stores, drugs, dry goods, hardware, theaters, saloons, the churches, the libraries, pool hall, road stands, the open air markets, and the office buildings to do names on plaques and tobacco stairways." There was, he said, "not a main street, and few side streets in Los Angeles and the whole state of California that I did not drive, walk, look down for jobs." He was aware that there was so much more to the great migration than agricultural displacement: "There are traveling salesmen, artists, musicians, show-folks, crop chasers, gang workers, road, dam, bridge, railway, and house builders. There are lots more. And there was me in the run with my guitar in one hand and my brushes in the other."[62] He went to stay with family in Glendale, and there hooked up with his cousin "Oklahoma" Jack. Together they worked up their act and beat their way to Frank Burke's door.

Ed Robbin recalled listening to Guthrie's KFVD broadcast for the first time, the day after telling Guthrie of the release from prison of the labor leader Tom Mooney. Mooney had been convicted on the false charge of carrying out the murderous "Preparedness Day Bombing" that killed ten people in San Francisco in 1916, amid a wave of anti-union hysteria. For two decades his supporters had campaigned for his release and the pardon that he eventually received from Governor Culbert Olson. As Robbin heard the broadcast: "'I got a little song I want to sing for my friend Ed and for all the folks out there. It's about this fella Tom Mooney, who's just got out of jail after spending twenty years for something he never done.' He sang a ballad of Tom Mooney, telling the whole Mooney story and the tale of the long struggle for his release. Then he sang some of his dust bowl ballads with easy, rambling, homey talk between songs."[63]

Robbin proved to be Guthrie's route into the communist movement and the California Popular Front. He brought Guthrie to Al Richmond at the *People's World*, who recalled an impromptu offer from "the hillbilly" to contribute a column to the paper: "Since the man asked for no money I advised Robbin, when informed of the offer, to get some samples. They were good. We had a column: brief text, primitive drawings. Being suspicious of folksiness and words misspelled for comic effect, I wondered at first: is this columnist phony or genuine?"[64]

"Fruit, see, but don't pick it . . ." Sketch by Woody Guthrie, c. 1946. Image courtesy of the Ralph Rinzler Folklife Archives and Collections, Smithsonian Institution, with permission from the Woody Guthrie Archives. © Woody Guthrie Publications, Inc.

Guthrie had been reading and listening to the humorist Will Rogers, whom he admired, after Jesus Christ, as "the second most famous man that ever lived on the face of this earth."[65] He patterned his "Woody Sez" column after Rogers's blend of cornpone philosophy and astute political satire. On May 12, 1939, the readers of the *People's World* were introduced to Woody Guthrie through the myth that he and his image makers would continue to perpetuate: "He is one of the 200,000 people who came from the dustbowl looking for work and a little food—the people who have picked the fruit and the crops of California—lived in shanty camps, been beaten and driven about by the bank-landowners."[66]

From the outset the "Woody Sez" column wove a tapestry of myth and fact, but it always kept Guthrie yoked to the proletarian struggle that he had vaguely begun to theorize upon his arrival at KFVD:

> Gawdamighty. I been interested in a world of stuff since I been born. Sold papers, shined shoes, polished spittoons, sold gas and oil, clerked in a hotel, picked that cotton, drilled waterwells, helped a carpenter, drilled wheat, drove tractors, bootlegged whiskey, peddled home brew, jerked soda, stocked groceries, painted signs, traveled in road shows, read hypnotism, studied human nature, tried to preach, played a guitar, sung in saloons, practiced divine healing, played in movies, rode freight trains, begged back doors, slept in a million jails, slept under bridges, broke my arm on a bronco, wrote junk, been from coast to coast the hard way, believe in everybody, joined everything, and still a goin strong. Above statements are all true.[67]

He experimented with placing the Dust Bowl migration in a broader context, combining meteorology with an economic critique and a dash of Oklahoma spirituality:

> You know when the finance folks and the weather both set in on you at the same time, they ain't nothin' else to do but dessert the farm.
> An, you know, when you cause a person to lose faith in old mammy earth, he has really lost a lot.[68]

He depicted the complexities of Marxist theory as well beyond his comprehension, painting himself the Okie rube against the more sophisticated urban discussants who—in the succeeding two decades—he would contemptuously dismiss whenever he wasn't trying to emulate them:

> Ed Robbin & Byron Dunham was ahaving somewhat of a gentlemenly argument about some high fangled terms—about the various planes or phases of consciousness one goes thru (in becoming plumb conscious) among others of which they talked of class consciousness.
> Now Ed & Byron was plumb out of my territory a using them high falutin words, but I enjoyed the consciousness as much as they did.[69]

Guthrie's calculated self-deprecation was, for the most part, justified. Political theory would ever bedevil him. Over the years he would amass a considerable library, but the annotations in the margins of his books would often peter out halfway through or only after a few pages, betraying his exasperation with their density. (In 1945 he would write on the flyleaf of V. I. Lenin's *Theory of the Agrarian Question:* "I wish I knew what I could do to make all the thoughts of Marx and Engels and Lenin and Stalin and Wilkie and Roosevelt and Earl Browder fly down and roost in my brain."[70] The same year, he would scrawl on the inside cover of Marx's *Capital:* "Will memorize contents in a week or so. . . . I'd like to try to write all of these things down in short words".)[71]

In the end, Guthrie would find his greatest artistic and critical strength in humanizing whatever political theory he managed to absorb—stripping it down, animating it, giving it a human face. This, and the compression of images and "short words," was the key—as he demonstrated in "Woody Sez"—to his most memorable observations:

> I never stopped to think of it before, but you know—a policeman will jest stand there an let a banker rob a farmer, or a finance man rob a workin man.
>
> But if a farmer robs a banker—you would have a hole dern army of cops out a shooting at him.
>
> Robbery is a chapter in ettiquette.[72]

Ed Robbin, for one, immediately sensed the instinctive nature of his new friend's radicalism. He recalled introducing Guthrie to the man who would have the greatest influence on his political awakening in California, the actor and progressive activist Will Geer (later known by millions as the Grandfather in the television series *The Waltons*). Guthrie and Geer, Robbin felt, "were very much alike in many ways. Neither was a political theorist. Neither bothered about what was the correct line to follow"[73]—perhaps too generous an observation with regard to Guthrie and the Hitler–Stalin Pact, but otherwise an accurate one.

It was Geer who, in turn, introduced Guthrie to John Steinbeck during a film shoot, in the process perceiving Guthrie's insatiable hunger for political news:

> I remember walking over to John's with Woody one time. We picked up John and we walked right up to the drugstore just about a block away. John stopped on the corner and picked up a copy of the *People's World* at the newsstand and a copy of Hearst's *Examiner.* Glen Gordon, one of the actors in the picture, had joined us. He said, "How in the hell can you read that paper knowing the things you know?" And Steinbeck said, "Well, a writer has to know all sides of a question. I have to know what that old buzzard Hearst is thinking and writing." And Woody was impressed with that. It really made a great impression on him, about learning everything.[74]

Steinbeck lent his name to the "John Steinbeck Committee to Aid Agricultural Organization," and Geer and Guthrie lent their creative and fund-raising talents. Guthrie recalled: "I went around singing for cotton pickers, cannery workers, lettuce grabbers, and all kinds of picket lines, union meetings, and picnics where union people sung and danced."[75] The two were particularly active on behalf of the United Cannery, Agricultural, Packing, and Allied Workers of America (UCAPAWA), engaged in pitched battles with the gun thugs of the Associated Farmers—"perhaps the most virulent and notorious right-wing American group, with the exception of the Ku Klux Klan"[76]— during the bitter cotton strike of 1938 in Kern County.

At one point in the midst of the strike, a cotton worker phoned Guthrie at KFVD with an appeal for help. As the worker's son recalled, Guthrie arranged "a full car load" of supplies to be sent to the strikers—"three fifty-pound bags of flour, lots of suger, corn meal, cookies for the kids, powdered milk and a lot of canned goods. The car was setting on its springs till the people unloaded it, and Woody sent a message with it, saying if more was needed they were to just call anytime."[77] On another occasion, Guthrie himself went down to join the strikers, only to find them burying a dead infant by the roadside. They were soon menaced by deputies carrying pick-handles and batons: "Woody tried to explain that the people were burying a little girl and a man would come there within a few days to help the migrants move on with thier trucks. But the deputies, acting on the sheriff's orders begun herding the people, about thirty or so, toward the highway." As the deputies

Original caption: "Striking cotton pickers talk it over. The strike is failing. Kern County, California. 'I don't care: Let them throw me in jail. There's somebody will take my place.'" Photograph by Dorothea Lange, 1938. FSA-OWI Photograph Collection, Library of Congress.

laid into the migrants, Guthrie fought back at their side: "My dad said people looking at Woody thought him a weakling as he was kinda short and pretty thin too. But Woody was a great fighter, had two good fists and knew how to use them."[78]

When not singing (or fighting) on picket lines and raising money for the Steinbeck Committee and other progressive causes, Guthrie continued with his KFVD broadcasts. His songbooks from the period clearly demonstrate his increasing militancy. He sang for the superfluous workers strewn aside in the rush to mechanization—not only on the farms, but in the mills and mines, as well, identifying a constituency beyond the agricultural migrant group:

> A hundred men used to dig a ditch,
> You could hear them work and sing.
> Along come a big ditch-digging machine
> And done the work of the whole shebang.
>> Boss man fired us—one man run it,
>> And ninety-nine men went hungry.
>
> I got me a job in a packing plant,
> And was a-paying out a little home;
> And they invented a big machine
> That put a hundred thousand on the bum.
>> Stopped our salary; said, We don't need you;
>> Finance man got the little home.[79]

He sang of "the world's mighty gallery of politics" peopled by unemployed fathers, destitute mothers, economically ravaged marriages, and "souls . . . exchanged for gold."[80] He sang of crafty, unscrupulous Chicago bankers bankrolling Death Valley tourist traps.[81]

And he sang—with growing hostility—about Franklin Roosevelt and the New Deal. He could just about see his way in 1938 to giving Roosevelt honorary mention in a celebration of Culbert Olson's gubernatorial victory, most likely as a gesture of loyalty to Burke:

> Our good ship is sailing through the storm,
> Our good ship is sailing through the storm,
> With Olson at the sail, and Roosevelt at the wheel,
> Our good ship is sailing through the storm.[82]

Yet such musical eulogizing went increasingly against the grain of his "Woody Sez" pronouncements, which had become noticeably anti-Roosevelt by late 1939, as the presidential election approached:

The landlord was over at our house in Texas puttering around trying to fix up some old rotten boards that was as flimsy as a Roosevelt speech.[83]

The fall will fall and winter wilt and spring will come again, and summer smother some of us, and roll on 'round again, and Roosevelt and Willkie and all the Rich Guys Crowd will age and grow, but well, you know they're on their last go 'round![84]

Guthrie was unmoved by Roosevelt's reforms. He sang of the "Capital City Cyclone" that would wipe out even the foundations of the hallowed New Deal as it swept Roosevelt and his rich cronies out of office:

> It blowed away the wages and the pay,
> It stretched out the hours of the day—
> It blowed in the night it was an awful sight,
> It blowed down the WPA.[85]

Braving all predictable charges of blasphemy, he challenged FDR's saintliness as the architect of federal relief:

And here's a Definition for Relief:

Relief (noun): It is 2 people and one of them has accumulated the property of both; and then poses as some sort of a "giver"—when in reality he is only giving back a little at a time, the Life that he took at a single grab or two . . .

Most like a poker game where the cards is marked—and set and shuffled and "dealt," and timed, and framed, and organized and arranged to "relieve" you of what you got—and then turned around and gives you a mess of beans in exchange for your Freedom,—and then make a big speech or two about it and call it "Relief."

They first relieve you of what you got, then "Relief" you for what you get.[86]

To be fair, Guthrie had no problem with relief per se. In 1938 he had come out, along with a substantial cross-section of the Okie population, in favor of California's "Ham and Eggs" initiative aimed at funding increased old-age pensions. As he then sang happily over the airwaves:

> I am glad Ham and Eggs is marching on;
> It's a long, long time that they been gone;
> But I hear the people say they are on the way today,
> And I'm glad Ham and Eggs is marching on.[87]

But in October 1939, upon the birth of his son—named Will Rogers Guthrie—he mocked Roosevelt's first inaugural speech, which had ushered in the New Deal in 1933. His new baby, as he wrote in "Woody Sez," was "a Ham & Egger.

If things dont go as they ott to, he proceeds to make 7 speeches in 6 difrent languages, all at th same time. Deciphered some more: 'Two thirds of me is ill-housed, ill fed, and ill clothed—for goodness sake, TRY SOMETHING!'"[88]

Clearly, one thing that had happened between the generosity of 1938 and the hardening of 1939 was the signing of the Hitler–Stalin Pact. The Communist Party of the USA (CPUSA) and its closest fellow travelers had never warmed to Roosevelt in the first place, in spite of the New Deal reforms. As Richmond wrote: "President Roosevelt, utilizing the considerable economic reserves of United States capitalism, displayed the flexibility and skill to go on ruling in the old way (his reforms did not change the essence of rule). And his massive support among those sectors of the population that presumably should have been most ready for revolution (i.e., the working class, the black people, the unemployed) showed they had not concluded it was impossible to go on living in the old way."[89]

Now, after the Hitler–Stalin Pact, any of Roosevelt's menacing gestures toward Germany must logically extend to the Soviet Union. There were those in the Roosevelt administration who openly proclaimed the pact an example of Soviet duplicity (given that FDR had recognized the Soviet Union in the first place only as a barrier to rising German and Japanese fascism).[90] The CPUSA was of course hypersensitive to any criticism of Stalin or the USSR. In any event, Roosevelt was at base an imperialist and the savior of American capitalism: he was no friend to the Revolution. It was such utterances— however implied or disguised in folksy song or aphorism—that ultimately caused Guthrie's break with Burke and lost him his KFVD program.

But it was more than just the Hitler–Stalin Pact: Guthrie was angry at what he had seen over the past year—too angry to placate Burke for the sake of a job or the man's feelings. It seemed that Robbin, Geer, and others in the communist movement were the only ones actively trying to change conditions on the ground, particularly in the fields and the migrant camps. The CPUSA in California had earned the highest badge of honor in the form of the Associated Farmers' enmity, in payment for their brave efforts at organizing the migrant workers at great risk to life and limb. The most embattled of California's agricultural unions in the 1930s—the Cannery and Agricultural Workers Industrial Union, the Agricultural Workers Industrial League, UCAPAWA itself—were either under Communist leadership or were CPUSA affiliates.[91] The Workers' Alliance, holding out in Arvin, Bakersfield, Madera, and Marysville, was staffed with Communists and fellow travelers.[92] Not for nothing did the Associated Farmers justify their brutal vigilantism on the grounds of resistance to "communist agitators,"[93] for in the midst of

Extreme literary criticism: Members of the Associated Farmers
burn a copy of John Steinbeck's *The Grapes of Wrath,* August 1939.
Photograph by Henry Barge. Image courtesy of the Kern County
Museum.

all their lies equating union organization with un-Americanism, this was the
only grain of truth: regardless of the Hitler–Stalin Pact, it was the Communists
who were in the front line against the fascists in the Californian fields.

It was those same fascists—and the free market behind them—who had
turned Guthrie's "people" into *refugees,* a term, it seemed to Guthrie, equally

applicable in California, Hitler's Germany, and Franco's Spain—and so the term appeared with increasing frequency in "Woody Sez."[94] Initially he had recoiled from it, and it would always be problematic for him. As he later recalled with a sigh: "They called us 'dust bowl refugees.' All the newspaper headlines was full of stuff about dust bowl refugees. Refugees here, refugees yonder, refugees everywhere that you look."[95] But by 1939 there was something apt in the term. California-based eugenicists had been targeting the migrants, arguing seriously for "Okie" sterilization, voluntary or otherwise. Even H. L. Mencken, though not a Californian, had jumped onto that platform, declaring: "They are simply, by God's inscrutable will, inferior men, and inferior they will remain until, by a stupendous miracle, he gives them equality among His angels."[96]

Anti-migrant sentiment reached a new high (or low) with the 1939 "anti-Okie" petition sponsored by the California Citizens Association and backed by the *Los Angeles Times,* the *Los Angeles Examiner,* the *Bakersfield Californian,* the American Legion, the Rotary Club, the Lions, the Kiwanis, and the Soroptimists.[97] Route 66 was "a highway marked with blood where a million feet have trod," Guthrie wrote;[98] and still they dared to treat his people this way—to post signs saying "No Okies Allowed in Store"[99] or, above a dockside urinal, "Okie Drinking Fountain."[100] The police had set up an illegal barricade targeting *his* people—and they'd gleefully called it the "bum blockade." The *Los Angeles Times* both laughed about it and celebrated it, with vile cartoons depicting huge California-shaped policemen turning back filthy derelicts at the state line. Musing on the Baptist hymn "I Can't Feel at Home in the World Anymore"—which, in the vein of Joe Hill, he had transformed into the bitter "I Ain't Got No Home"—Guthrie spat: "Reason why you cant feel at home in this world any more is mostly because you aint got no home to feel at."[101]

He was on the road to a reconception that he would commit to paper within the year—yes, his people *were* refugees: "When my cousin got to California he built him a shack in one of those flood basins out there. His house was a big packing box that he got down at the water front and all over it was painted the name of a family of people that managed to get out of Germany just as the Nazis were taking over. My cousin called it his Hitler Box."[102] He issued a grim, vague warning on behalf of an entire people gathering their anger:

Yes, we ramble, yes, we roam,
Since the tractor took our home.
Little whirlwinds make a cyclone,
That's the dust bowl refugees.[103]

Outline Map of California!

"The Bum Blockade": Anti-migrant cartoon by Bruce Russell,
Los Angeles Times, February 5, 1936. Image provided by Martin
Butler, courtesy of the Bruce Russell Papers, Special Collections
Research Center, Syracuse University.

Beneath another set of lyrics to "I Ain't Got No Home" he wrote:

Wish I knowed what kind of a fight it's a comin' to.

* * *

RIVER'S A RISIN'.
RISIN'. RISIN'.
RIVER IS A RISIN'
GONNA SEE HELL.[104]

When Guthrie read Kenneth Crist's slanderous report in the *Los Angeles
Times* calling the migrants—in an echo of Mencken—"relief chiselers" and
praising the authorities for "cleaning out" (read "burning down") the camps,[105]
he came out swinging, nearly losing his grip on the down-home affability so
indispensable to "Woody Sez." "The Author was trying to make you believe

that these weatherbeaten, browbeaten, homeless people are really robbers at heart," he wrote, amazed that anyone would seriously claim that the migrants had *chosen* to live "like wild hogs in a boggy river bottom for a whole year in order to get some of that easy Relief Gold":

> Personal, I've ben in Calif. 2 years—'cause the dust and the cold, run me out of Texas . . . an' I ain't never applied for relief of any kind yet. An' for the past year I've averaged a makin' less than $1 a day.
>
> But before I'd make my livin' by a writin' articles that make fun of the Hungery Folks, an' the Workin' Folks,
>
> I'd go on Relief . . .[106]

"Relief chiselers"? Original caption: "Texas tenant farmer in Marysville, California, migrant camp during the peach season. 1927 made seven thousand dollars in cotton. 1928 broke even. 1929 went in the hole. 1930 still deeper. 1931 lost everything. 1932 hit the road. 1935, fruit tramp in California." Photograph by Dorothea Lange, 1935. FSA-OWI Photograph Collection, Library of Congress.

For the past seven years, Americans had been listening to Bing Crosby and Rudy Vallee crooning—and pitifully begging—"Brother, Can You Spare a Dime?" Although he would soon befriend "Yip" Harburg, the lyricist of that Depression anthem, such sentiments made Guthrie sick. Begging? The capitalists weren't begging for anything; they were *taking* it. He'd rediscovered a fondness for outlaws, the righteous avengers in the old ballads sung to him by his mother. He thought of Oklahoma's Pretty Boy Floyd, whom he would soon dignify with a militant social conscience ("Some will rob you with a six gun / And some with a fountain pen");[107] of the highwayman Dick Turpin, aiming to "take the money and spread it out equal";[108] of Jesus Christ, murdered by "the landlord and the soldiers that he hired" for daring to proclaim that "the poor would win all this world."[109] He jotted below his lyrics to "Pretty Boy Floyd": "I love a good man outside the law just as much as I hate a bad man inside the law."[110] The Associated Farmers were a bunch of bad men inside the law; it was they who had killed Preacher Casy for calling out, "Unite all you working men."[111] Guthrie vowed that the fight-back would soon start: when the sons and daughters of the Dust Bowl "organize and fight for what's right, they'll surprise the whole world" and "strike at the right place stronger and faster than any of us can imagine at the present time."[112]

Will Geer was going to New York to star in the stage version of Erskine Caldwell's *Tobacco Road*. He suggested that Guthrie follow him out there— after all, he'd lost his KFVD show; the UCAPAWA battles were shifting to the canneries after bitter defeat in the cotton fields; there were other battles to fight, and Los Angeles was getting old. After depositing his family in Texas, Guthrie beat his way north and east in the subzero New Year of 1940. As Pete Seeger later marveled: "Woody was hitchhiking through Pennsylvania in the month of February. It was freezing cold—can you imagine him on the side of the highway with his thumb stuck out and the cars going *zzzoom, zzooom* past him? But if he had a nickel he'd go into a roadside diner and get a cup of coffee, and the juke box was playing Kate Smith singing 'God Bless America.'"[113]

Irving Berlin's patriotic tub-thumper was the hit of the year. Guthrie hated it. It was still gnawing at him when he landed in New York and pitched camp in Geer's living room, and later still, after he'd moved into a flea-bag hotel on 6th Avenue, where he sat down to write his own response to the song whose complacency had infuriated him beyond measure. What "America" had Kate Smith been singing of? Not the "big high wall" and the painted sign saying "Private Property"; not the bread line "in the shadow of the steeple," by "the Relief Office" where Guthrie's "people . . . stood hungry."[114] These are the first critical images in the song that Guthrie initially titled "God Blessed America," his explicit rejoinder to Berlin. The "blessing," pointedly, was in the past tense; if there had been any blessing in the first place, it was over and done with. There could be no unearthly solution to earthly problems: America's struggles were grounded in history, economics, and the rough-and-tumble of politics. If there *were* to be a heaven on earth, it was human labor that would build it.

Even after the catharsis of his first draft, Guthrie found that his ire had not been vented. The sanctimoniousness of Berlin's song continued to rankle, and he soon came back to revisit "God Blessed America," which title had also served as the song's refrain. Then, thinking of the Hoovervilles and the swollen bellies of starving migrant children, the club-wielding vigilantes, the "bum blockade," and the barbed-wire gates of California's Eden, Guthrie scratched out his old refrain and wrote a new one into history:

> Nobody living can ever stop me,
> As I go walking that freedom highway;
> Nobody living can ever make me turn back
> This land was made for you and me.[115]

2. Hard-Hitting Songs for Hard-Hit People

Nearly sixty years after they met, Gordon Friesen recalled his first impression of his fellow Oklahoman Woody Guthrie in New York: "He looked just like a dust bowl refugee from Oklahoma: scrawny, underfed, uncut brambly hair, thin-faced, eyes that had learned to stay out of trouble, or at least not push trouble too far."[1] Besides his appearance as "th' Dustiest of th' Dust Bowlers," as Guthrie grew fond of calling himself,[2] there was something else that drew people's attention that freezing February in 1940. Guthrie carried—or, more likely, wore uncased and strapped to his back—a guitar. This was a time, in Millard Lampell's recollection, when "there weren't but about a dozen country or folk singers who had ever ventured north of the Blue Ridge Mountains. When a dude pushed into a subway lugging a guitar, people gawked as though he was carrying a kayak."[3]

If the CPUSA ever held an American bastion in 1940 it was New York, home to the *Daily Worker* as well as half of the Party's membership. However, New York's political culture was hardly a unified one dominated by the Party; rather, the metropolitan Popular Front was scarred by "a zigzag of temporary alliances and broken coalitions" between Communists and other leftists.[4] It was thus a confusing and fluid political milieu, perhaps ideally suited to an independent radical with "eyes that had learned to stay out of trouble."

By the time Guthrie landed in New York, he already had a wealth of urban experience behind him. He had learned early to make creative capital out of his exaggerated persona, the rural rube in the big city. He was thus able to hit the ground running upon his arrival in New York, where he continued to file his "Woody Sez" columns for the *People's World*. "The one and only New York" became the subject of an extended economic critique in his column, in which Guthrie assigned to the city "the best of the least for the most, and the most of the best for the least, and the biggest bunch of people on earth that work like dogs for a living, and the biggest bunch that live a hole lifetime and never hit a lick of work."[5] Guthrie was quick to depict himself as a bemused outsider—or more precisely, an undersider—looking up at the cockeyed distribution of the city's wealth: "In passin out the money, they come to some doors twice every hour, and other doors once a month. Other doors never. Hell, I ain't even got a door."[6]

Occasionally Guthrie's column was restricted to bouts of affected yokelism as he marveled at the urban density with which, in reality, he was quite famil-iar ("The 5 o'clock trains was so crowded today you couldn't even fall down. I changed stations twice and both times I come out with a different pair of shoes on").[7] Usually, however, he embedded a tough kernel of anticapitalist critique in his observations. Thus he addressed the time-honored New York tradition of picking up the early news editions just before midnight: "There's one thing about New York and that is the way you kin get tomorrow's paper last night, that is tonight. The capitalist papers are so far ahead of the news that they know tonight what happened tomorrow, but they never do go to the trouble of informin' their readers about what they really knew yesterday."[8] He noted a menacing undercurrent of police repression, which he success-fully incorporated into a Chaplinesque scenario: "I wore out a pair of new moccasins last night achasin' around the Times Square newspaper building atryin' to kech up on the news. Run around about forty times afollowin' the electric sign to get the end of the disspach but jest then I seen a poleece car and decided it wood be the better part of valor if not comfort ef I went home and read yesterday's paper."[9]

The subject of New York tourism afforded a far-reaching extrapolation, as Guthrie reflected on the nine-year-old Empire State Building, a monument to mammon thrust into the heavens in the midst of the Great Depression:

> Costs you a dollar to go to the top. Elevators really run you down fast. We dropt 34 floors before I could call out my number. That's fast droppin'. Almost dropt as fast as wages.
>
> After we hit bottom my pants kept on a goin'. It never was this a-way back home.
>
> However there are 7,000,000 people here in New York. I would judge 6,000,000 of 'em has already lost their pants.[10]

An observation about the crowded skyline led to a further anticapitalist connection: "Talking about the sky, here in New York you have got to give the taxi company 35 cents cash to get a cab driver to chase some down for you. That's the Capitalist cistern for you, they build up so much buildins to beat you out of money with, that they finally block out the sky, and charge

you 20 cts. a mile to ride around an look at it."[11] In a decidedly more sober
vignette, Guthrie's reflections on a moment in Union Square managed to
comment both upon the dire economic crisis and the knee-jerk equation
of the American radical with the "Russian Red": "Union Square. 20 men
sprawled around asleep at the foot of a statue that says they are blessed with
a bunch of things. One bunch of folks talking a language I didn't under stand.
However they looked just as broke as me. Another bunch talking about the
banking system. What they got to bank? Another bunch yelling their heads
off about Soviet Russia. I never was there. They said they had something to
eat over there. Well, it's a long swim."[12]Beyond the pages of his newspaper
column, the contrasts of New York quickly worked their way into Guthrie's
other writings. Songs spilled into his notebooks as he searched for the human
faces, hands, and voices practically obliterated by the capitalist headquarters
towering so arrogantly around him:

> I'm the town called New York,
> I was struck by the winds;
> I been froze and been blistered
> And then struck again;
>> I was struck by my rich folks,
>> And struck by my bums,
>> Struck by my mansions,
>> And struck by my slums.[13]

Guthrie practiced, and perhaps failed, at capturing the voice of working-
class New York, however much he succeeded on paper in restoring the worker
to a just ownership of his labor's output: "You couldn't build no kinda building
unless I wuz dere ta push my wheelbar on it. So when I help ta gitta town all
built from da bottom to da top, den haddent alla us guys down on da bottom oughtta hit da top once inna while?"[14] Guthrie's "Wheelbarrow Pusher"
allied the urban laborer with the migrants and hoboes he had encountered
farther west, adapting the imagery of the transcontinental wanderer to the
circular, claustrophobic setting of Manhattan's twenty-three square miles:

> I push my wheelbarrow
> Full of rocks and hot tar.
> Rocks and hot tar.
> Yes rocks and hot tar.
> I push my wheelbarrow
> Full of rocks and hot tar.
>> Ten thousand miles I rolled her.
>> Ten thousand miles to roll.[15]

Guthrie was both intellectually and politically energized by New York. With an initial optimism that would be increasingly challenged over the next two decades, he quickly settled on New York as "the main fort and vanguard of the working class movement"[16] and—in the political if not the aesthetic sense—"about the revoltingist place in the country." As he saw it: "You can always go out and take a look at the rest of the country, fist fights, gun fights, strikes, police and legion raids, and everything, and then when you go back to New York, you'll see it just a little bit plainer, or the same thing in just a little cleaner looking glass; you'll see the working folks marching up and down the streets, having meetings, talking, preaching, and always going the rest of the country just one better."[17]

Yet in spite of his applause for the political energy that seemed to electrify his newly adopted city, Guthrie was clearly "revolted" by the sight of one more Skid Row—New York's Bowery—to add to his grim collection of mental postcards, as he would later catalog them: "Lower Pike in Seattle, California Ave. in Oklahoma City, Congress St. in Dallas, Fifth and Main in Los Angeles, Ave. J. in Sacramento, South St. in Philadelphia, the Ski streets of Chicago and several others just as crummy in Duluth, Milwaukee, Akron, Cleveland, Toronto, Phoenix, Baltimore and several dozen ratty roads of New York City."[18] On a few square feet of concrete he found a microcosm of New York's—and the nation's—economic brutality, as he reflected in his sprawling, handwritten "Manifesto on Wage Slaves, Sleep Walking, and Jesus":

> There is one place down there called the Bowery savings bank and the other night I was down there with my old guitar and I was looking for a flop joint to flop in and I passed right by the door of the bank and there was a man piled up on the steps asleep. He was barefooted. His old run over shoes was on the step below his head and he was snoring away. It was the first days of early spring and too cold to sleep very good on a set of cement steps but I honestly believe that man whether he knew it or not was manning the right door. It was a dreary picture. Dark and cold to see him all dirty and ragged in his old greasy overhalls and black dirty feet laying there in the little dim glow of a street lamp a half a block away that struck and reflected against the big brass plate that said Bowery Savings Bank.[19]

Certainly at the forefront of Guthrie's mind during his first weeks in New York was his awareness of his own proximity to the fate of the Skid Row outcasts he described. Thus he defiantly—and perhaps a little fearfully—conjured up a vague impression of the unnamed "you" who capriciously withheld or conferred financial wherewithal upon the masses. His poem "I'll Not Beg" is a cri de coeur from the bowels of Skid Row:

I won't beg nobody
I won't go a begging
I just ain't that lost.
I'm still a man
I can stand up and walk
I can walk and talk
And you can't stop me
You're crazy if you try it
You might want me to
Bow down here to you
But I won't beg you
I won't go a begging nobody.
A feller might give me some help
And I'd be much obliged
But I'll not beg you
I'll take it easy
But I'll dang shore take it.[20]

Guthrie's later annotation to these lines indicates his extremity during his first weeks in New York, where he "froze [his] ballix . . . four times": "I wrote this up one night looking for a home along the stem. It was in New York City during a right big snowy blizzerd in February of Nineteen and Forty. I read it over in my old book here every few nights and it still sounds like I still feel about begging or asking for milk in my saucer like a cat."[21] Here again was the defiance of "Pretty Boy Floyd" pitted against the pathos of "Brother, Can You Spare a Dime?"—but fortunately for Guthrie, history stepped in to ensure that he would not have to choose between starving or begging, at least in the short term.

Just as Guthrie arrived in New York, Will Geer was busy putting together a "Grapes of Wrath" benefit concert for the Steinbeck Committee, to be held on March 3. This concert would prove to be one of the Popular Front's two most important musical events in the immediate wake of the Hitler–Stalin Pact (the other being Paul Robeson's 1939 radio broadcast of Earl Robinson's "Ballad for Americans").[22] Geer had secured a roster of the important New York folk-music figures, the most influential of whom was Alan Lomax, the collector, musicologist, impresario, and power wielder at the Library of Congress Archive of American Folk Song. Along with Lomax and his sister, Bess, there would be a number of established performers—Josh White, the Golden Gate Quartet, the American Square Dance Group, Aunt Molly Jackson, and the up-and-coming Burl Ives—as well as some virtual unknowns: the Harvard dropout Pete Seeger; the radical union activist, teacher, and singer Lee Hays;

the paroled convict and self-proclaimed "King of the Twelve-String Guitar" Huddie Ledbetter (aka Lead Belly),[23] and Geer's old friend Woody Guthrie.

The critical response to the first meeting of these particular unknowns has—perhaps with good reason—tipped into hyperbole. Lomax himself ventured: "Go back to that night when Pete first met Woody Guthrie. You can date the renaissance of American folk song from that night."[24] For Seeger, who considered his own performance that night a "real bust," Guthrie's appearance was the evening's true landmark, both historically and for him personally: "Woody Guthrie just ambled out, offhand and casual . . . a short fellow complete with a western hat, boots, blue jeans, and needing a shave, spinning out stories and singing songs he'd made up. . . . Well, I just naturally wanted to know more about him. He was a big piece of my education."[25]

All hyperbole notwithstanding, the significance of the "Grapes of Wrath" benefit is especially apparent when viewed in light of the history of radical American music at the close of the 1930s. The songs of the Wobblies, familiar and joyous to so many American workers (who had themselves written the bulk of them), were all but forgotten. Instead, the custodians of radical music were to be found in or allied to the CPUSA, with their unshaken conviction that "a new musical form had to be *handed down* to the workers as their own."[26] Folk music, it appeared, would not fit the bill, as one of America's leading musicologists, Charles Seeger, father of Pete, declared in the *Daily Worker* in 1934 (he would dramatically revise his opinion before too long). Writing as "Carl Sands"—a pseudonym chosen to prevent his more conservative fellow musicologists from thinking him "a damn fool"[27]—Seeger argued that folk songs were not "suitable to the revolutionary movement. Many of them are complacent, melancholy, defeatist—originally intended to make slaves endure their lot—pretty, but not the stuff for a militant proletariat to feed upon."[28] Seeger's colleague Henry Cowell agreed: "One of the great faults in the field of workers music has been that of combining revolutionary lyrics with traditional music—music which can by no means be termed revolutionary."[29]

Consequently, a decidedly top-down musical agenda was apparent, among other places, in the Party-sponsored *Red Song Book* published in 1932 and dominated by the inflated rhetoric and musical complexity of semiclassical Russian, German, French, and English compositions (although it did include Joe Hill's "The Preacher and the Slave," Aunt Molly Jackson's "Poor Miner's Farewell," and Ella Mae Wiggins's "I.L.D. Song"). The *Red Song Book* was only one product of the Party's mission to arrive at a scientific approach to workers' music. They also established the Workers Music League (WML), described in the *Red Song Book* as "the central organization of all music forces connected with the American revolutionary working class movement. Its aim is to coordinate, strengthen, and give both ideological and musical guidance to these forces."[30] The WML in turn established the Workers Musicians Club, based in New York and rechristened the Pierre Degeyter Club, after the composer of "The Internationale." The Degeyter Club brought together a radical fellowship of performers, composers, and publishers, while the WML declared itself "ready with advice to help all workers and their organizations," issuing songbooks and articles that—among other patronizing suggestions—advised would-be organizers to form workers' choruses "around a number of 'simplistic' instruments such as (1) harmonica, (2) accordion, (3) bugle and drum, or (4) fife and drum."[31]

The fondness for workers' choruses was a reflection of the strong Party membership among European immigrant groups with an established tradition of choral singing. A host of American choruses sprang from this tradition, the most notable being the Freiheit Chorus, the Daily Worker Chorus, the American Workers' Chorus, and the ILD (International Labor Defense) Song Group. The standard output from these groups was a hortatory barrage of "doctrinaire, European-sounding songs in foreign languages," generally anathema to the mass of American workers outside of particular, relatively localized immigrant-language groups.[32]

Compounding the linguistic isolation of the Party-sponsored music projects was their fixation upon technically complex, classically based musical structures. An experimental modernism, meant to reflect the revolutionary quality of the music, dominated the work of the most significant radical composers who formed the "Composers' Collective" within the Degeyter Club—Harvard, Columbia, Juilliard, and Eastman School graduates such as Elie Siegmeister (the pseudonymous "L. E. Swift"), Jacob Schaefer, Lan Adomian, Charles Seeger, Herbert Haufrecht, Aaron Copland, Earl Robinson, Marc Blitzstein, and Henry Cowell—with many of them acknowledging their debt to the folk-hostile German immigrant composer Hanns Eisler. Charles Seeger recalled one of the collective's "more difficult" efforts: "There's one on Chiang Kai-shek in the five tone scale in five-four time with five-measure phrases, in which I call Chiang Kai-shek a tyrant and a murderer and everything else. We really did sing away, but it didn't catch on very much."[33]

Unsurprisingly, the choral and orchestral works by these composers met with increasingly hostile criticism throughout the 1930s, even from fellow radicals such as the critic and novelist Mike Gold. "Why don't American workers sing?" Gold asked. "The Wobblies knew how, but we have still to develop a Communist Joe Hill."[34] Gold compared the Composers' Collective unfavorably with the Appalachian ballad singers Ray and Lida Auville, who, he said, "write catchy tunes that any American worker can sing and like, and the words of their songs make the revolution as intimate and simple as [the folk tune] 'Old Black Joe.' Is this so little?"[35] Gold's challenge to the communist movement was unequivocal: "Not to see what a step forward it is to find two native musicians of the American people turning to revolutionary themes, converting the tradition to working class uses, is to be blind to progress."[36]

As it turned out, the continued imposition of ideological dogma from on high led even some stalwarts of the Composers' Collective to break with the WML in 1935. By the mid-1930s, with the Popular Front ethos having filtered down into the midst of the collective, there were signs that traditional American music might, after all, have something to offer in the proletarian struggle. In 1934 Adomian followed on from Gold in calling for a reassessment of folk sources: "Negro songs of protest, work songs, railroad songs, cowboy and hill songs . . . would be a colorful addition to our repertoire. Such an approach would carry us a long way toward rooting our work in the tradition of American music. It would give the lie to those who insist that our music is nothing but an importation from the outside."[37] The following year, another of the collective's renegades, Earl Robinson, collaborated with the radical dramatist and poet Alfred Hayes on two songs defiantly drawing on the American folk tradition, "Joe Hill" and "Abraham Lincoln."

The softening of radical attitudes toward folk music in the 1930s was spurred on by the fieldwork of such musicologists as Lawrence Gellert, Benjamin Botkin, Robert Gordon, John and Alan Lomax, and—following his own Pauline conversion to folk—Charles Seeger, who eventually confessed that the Kentucky balladeer Aunt Molly Jackson had been "on the right track and the Composers Collective and the Communist Party the wrong as far as music as a 'weapon in the class struggle' was concerned."[38] The more radical of these collectors (in particular Gellert, Botkin, Seeger, and Alan Lomax) came to see enormous agitprop potential in the ballads and songs of anonymous American workers. Richard Reuss noted this change in the wind by cataloging the new directions of one particular weathervane, the *Daily Worker*: "In one twelve-month period, December 1938 to December 1939, the *Daily Worker* featured a dozen major articles and numerous shorter pieces on such topics as cowboy songs, calypso music, Paul Bunyan, the WPA Folklore Project, W. C. Handy's lectures on Negro blues, Martha Graham's use of native folk themes in her modern dance, the superiority of folk songs to 'pop' tunes, Paul Robeson's appearance in the play *John Henry*, reviews of half a dozen academic and popular folklore books, and announcements and critiques of various folk song concerts."[39] The WML morphed into the American Music League, with one of its declared aims now being to "collect, study and popu-

larize American folk music and its traditions."[40] Siegmeister urged an end
to "the age-old division between learned or art music on the one hand, and
folk or popular music on the other."[41]

These developments still represented, at best, a halfway house between
American folk music and the communist movement in the 1930s. It is true
that the miners' struggles of Harlan County in 1931 had thrown up a musical vanguard represented by Florence Reece (composer of "Which Side Are
You On?"), Aunt Molly Jackson, Jim Garland, and Sarah Ogan; the Gastonia
textile strike of 1929 saw the emergence of the first martyr-balladeer since
Joe Hill in the person of the murdered Ella Mae Wiggins; and radical labor
colleges like Brookwood in New York State, Highlander in Tennessee, and
Commonwealth in Arkansas all anchored folk songs to their curricular and
organizing missions. Claude Williams, A. B. Brookins, and John Handcox,
out of the Southern Tenant Farmers Union, independently wrote some of the
most important foundational ballads of the twentieth-century labor movement. But these developments were slow to impact upon the radical music
circles of New York City. Revolutionary choruses and the theoretical shadow
of Hanns Eisler continued to mark the workings of the American Music
League, and the introduction of Aunt Molly Jackson to the Composers' Collective raised nothing but eyebrows. Charles Seeger recalled having to tell her:
"Molly, they didn't understand you. But I know some young people who will
want to learn your songs."[42] Similarly, when Earl Robinson introduced Lead
Belly at "a progressive summer camp" in 1936, there were arguments, Robinson recalled, about "whether to censure him, or me, or both."[43] However,
two forces would soon combine to inject folk music into the bloodstream of
the communist movement: one was New Deal patronage, and the other—a
force unto himself—was Alan Lomax.

With the advent of the New Deal's Works Progress Administration (WPA)
in 1935, an intense, if brief, cultural-political alliance developed between
radical America and the federal bureaucracy. One of the WPA's most visible
areas of sponsorship was folk culture, which, as R. Serge Denisoff noted, "fed
into the radical subculture of New York City." Thus B. A. Botkin's Folklore
Studies project within the Federal Writers Project, the Folksong and Folklore
Department within the Federal Theater Project, and Charles Seeger's director-
ship of the Federal Music Project all helped to inject "new material into the
radical milieu" that informed much of the New Deal's cultural initiatives.[44]
Seeger's personal conversion to folk champion placed a particularly lasting
stamp on the New Deal, aided by a predilection for folk music (as a channel of
democratic expression) in the highest government circles, including Franklin
and Eleanor Roosevelt, both of whom championed traditional performers.

Seeger's later reflections on the cultural value of folk music, written during his stewardship of the Federal Music Project, amounted to a virtual recantation of his former modernist credo and that of the Composers' Collective: "The folk music of America [has] embodied for well over a hundred years the tonal and rhythmic expression of untold millions of rural and even urban Americans. Contrary to our professional beliefs, the American people at large has had plenty to say and ability to say it, so that a rich repertory has been built up—thousands of tunes each for the dance, for the ballad, the love song, and the religious song. . . . But American songs, hymns and dances were not, and still to practically all musicians and teachers, are not music at all."[45]

In terms of folk-music preservation and promotion, Seeger's chief ally in the New Deal infrastructure was Alan Lomax, to whom Dick Weissman rightly assigned the title—shared with Seeger—of "Cultural Commissar of American Folk Music," given his unparalleled influence in establishing and furthering the careers of radical folk performers.[46] Lomax was both a magnet and a mentor drawing the major figures of what would become the "American folk renaissance" to the centers of cultural power—New York and Washington—in the late 1930s and early 1940s: Aunt Molly Jackson, Josh White, Burl Ives, Sonny Terry, Brownie McGhee, Lead Belly, Lee Hays, Cisco Houston, Pete Seeger, and Woody Guthrie, among others.

Lomax's imprimatur extended into the radio broadcast and recording arenas, through which his protégés first gained their national audiences. As the host of the weekly *School of the Air* programs on CBS (1938–40) and *Back Where I Come From* on CBS and WNYC (1940), Lomax was in a position to establish or further the radio careers of all his singers, including Guthrie, who signed a contract for *Back Where I Come From* within months of meeting Lomax. An encouraging word from Lomax also held sway in the burgeoning folk-music recording industry, influencing the decisions of radical producers such as Eric Bernay (Keynote Records), Robert Harris (Stinson Records), and Moses Asch (Asch, Disc, and Folkways records). In addition, as assistant in charge at the Archives of American Folk Song at the Library of Congress, Lomax was a record producer himself. Consequently, two weeks after the "Grapes of Wrath" benefit, Lomax had Guthrie before his microphone in the basement of the library for his first studio recording session.

Guthrie's recordings for Lomax—reissued under the title *Library of Congress Recordings*—are early case studies in the negotiation of the folksy Guthrie myth, on the one hand, and Guthrie's growing political radicalism on the other. They amplify even further the exaggerated rural persona of Guthrie's KFVD air check of three years before, to the extent that, in his caricature of the Okie rube, Guthrie seems to be deliberately playing upon Lomax's adulation for his most stunning discovery. As Pete Seeger recalled of their first meeting: "When Alan Lomax met Woody in 1940, he exulted—'At last I've met a song*writer,* like the songwriters who wrote the cowboy songs, the railroad songs, the coal mine songs.'"[47] On the recordings, Lomax's awe is indeed palpable—as is his perpetuation of dubious aura and myth—as he introduces his "Dust Bowl Balladeer" over Guthrie's harmonica-and-guitar instrumental "Lost Train Blues": "Woody knows what that lost train means because he's ridden on the red ball train from one end of the country to another. . . . Woody Guthrie is, I guess, about thirty years old, from the looks of him, but he's seen more in those thirty years than most men see before they're seventy. He hasn't sat in a warm house or a warm office to see what he's been interested in looking at; he's gone out into the world, he's looked in the faces of a hundred men and women, he's lived in hobo jungles, he's performed on picket lines and sung his way through every bar and saloon between Oklahoma and California."[48] A number of Lomax's interjections express the open regret that he could not claim as *authentic* a life as Guthrie's, none more so than when he asks Guthrie to repeat a racy drinking toast from Oklahoma:

> GUTHRIE: Well, let's hear you say one, and then I'll be rememberin' mine.
> LOMAX: Oh, well, I wasn't brought up that way, Woody. You see, I didn't grow up in the country. I grew up inside of a brick house. I didn't have that kind of experience—I wish I had.[49]

In at least one place on the recording, Guthrie uncharacteristically sets out to deflate the mythic persona that he and Lomax are otherwise so intent upon building. This is when Guthrie admits to his middle-class origins and the fact that, originally, he inhabited a house similar to the one in which Lomax grew up: "I wasn't in the class that John Steinbeck called 'the Okies' because my dad to start with was worth about thirty-five or forty thousand dollars, and he had everything hunky-dory. Then he started having a little bad luck."[50] (Guthrie's admission here to being the son of a failed real-estate agent and politician also ran counter to the falsehood then being spread on Norman Corwin's CBS radio variety show *The Pursuit of Happiness,* on which Burgess Meredith introduced Guthrie as "one of those Okies who, disposed from their farms, journeyed in jalopies to California.")[51]

Lomax himself signaled his awareness of at least a duplicitous potential in the Guthrie persona when, in a letter of recommendation, he praised Guthrie's abilities at writing "ballads . . . that will fool a folklore expert."[52] Indeed, the myth-making agenda of Lomax's project attracted a degree of skepticism from Moses Asch, who would record more of Guthrie's songs than any other producer. As Asch recalled: "If you listen to those Library of Congress recordings, you can hear all the put-on he wanted to give Alan Lomax. This is the actor acting out the role of the folksinger from Oklahoma."[53]

Nonetheless, and with such caveats established, the *Library of Congress Recordings* are important for their early filtering of Guthrie's political radicalism as he begins to envisage a wider audience than the migrant community tuned in to KFVD. The most significant political narrative underlying the Lomax recordings is the threat of organized rebellion on the heels of the Dust Bowl crisis. "Nobody wants to talk about blood shed and revolution," Guthrie wrote within a year of recording for Lomax; "it's too mean a thing to think about, nobody wants it, not even the rebels. But in the game of football you run over whoever gets in your way. Nobody gets mad. Everybody just whim whams the hell out of each other and the folks all come and pay a buck or two to see out there on the field something that reminds them of something they got in side of 'em. Don't know what it is, maybe, but something out there makes you think of something you done been a thinking for a long time. Fighting. Running and hiding. Pushing and shoving. Trying to get on down the field a little closer to the place you would ruther to be."[54]

While no threats of an Okie revolution are explicitly uttered in the Lomax recordings, Guthrie points to the simmering anger that he assumed would lead to an outpouring of militant activism on the part of the migrants who had been hardly welcomed "with music bands" in California:

> They had a little different kind of band that fitted on your leg. With about thirteen links on it. And they had another kind of orchestra; they called it "The Pea-Patch Papas." . . . If you was out of work, see, of course it was highly unsanitary to be out of work. What I mean by that is, in most towns all over the country it's a jailhouse offence to be unemployed. And in that country they enforced that when they took a notion. In other words, when you come to that country they found different ways of puttin' that vag law on you, and putting you either to working free in some pea patch or garden or washing dishes or something.[55]

Guthrie explicitly likened California to an imperial power on the Lomax recordings, which added a new level of critique to his observations on the LAPD's "bum blockade." Although the blockade—the brainchild of Los Angeles Police Chief James "Two-Gun" Davis—had been dismantled after a few months in 1936, the impact of its audacious illegality had stayed with Guthrie through the writing of "Do-Re-Mi" in 1937 and "This Land Is Your Land" in 1940. He was not so far off the mark with his imperial metaphor; after all, in the midst of the blockade's short tenure, the *Los Angeles Times* had noted in an approving headline: "Queen Elizabeth (Not Our Police) Launched the First War on Bums." The *Times* deprecated, albeit with perceptible regret at their passing, the harsher anti-vagrant measures of sixteenth- and seventeenth-century England (whippings, ear croppings, brandings, hangings), but its writer applauded one surviving Elizabethan legacy: "Not long ago a carload of vagrants rounded up in Los Angeles were 'passed on' through the State of Arizona, and given transportation east on a freight train. This passing on system also had its origin back in the days of the Tudors."[56]

Guthrie of course viewed the "bum blockade"—like the "vag law"—as an affront to the U.S. Constitution. As he told Lomax: "We'd always been taught to believe that these forty-eight states was an absolutely free country and that anytime anybody took a notion to get up and go anywhere in these forty-eight states, that nobody else in these forty-eight states would proceed to ask him a whole bunch of questions or to try to keep him from going where he started out to go."[57] But beyond its illegality, there had been a curious irony in the imposition of the "bum blockade," given that any imperial power's foremost requirement is the availability of a cheap-labor underclass:

> The native Californian sons and daughters, I'll admit, had a lot to be proud of—they had their ancestors there that come in on the old covered wagons a long time ago, and they had discovered oil, they'd discovered gold, they'd discovered silver, they'd discovered all kinds of mines in California, and they'd built up in California quite a wonderful empire. Then, they hadn't built up quite a wonderful *enough* empire. What they needed in California was more and more people to pick their fruit, to gather in their peaches, to pick their extra-select and their select apricots and their prunes, and to gather in their grapes. And they admitted their selves—these people that was born and raised in California—that they'd needed people to do that.[58]

These and other critical observations reflect a distinct muting of any militant agenda that Guthrie may have brought to the basement studio of the Library of Congress. Two months after recording for Lomax, Guthrie was sent to RCA Victor's studios in Camden, New Jersey, on Lomax's recommendation, to record the twelve songs released as *Dust Bowl Ballads,* including "Do Re Mi," "I Ain't Got No Home," "Pretty Boy Floyd," "Tom Joad," and "Vigilante Man." For his part, Guthrie had no doubt over the political significance of *Dust Bowl Ballads,* however much he exaggerated their radicalism. As he wrote in the *Daily Worker* on his last day of recording: "I seem to have been born a shade pink, and didn't have to read many books to be a proletariat, and you can guess that when you hear the records, as I'm sure Victor never done a more radical album."[59] It was perhaps Guthrie's own sense of his developing militancy—or his frustration at being obliged to keep it in check—that led him to misread a Los Angeles *News* review which had merely suggested that *Dust Bowl Ballads* might inspire a serious composer to "make a tone-poem, symphony or suite . . . more American." He spluttered defensively, "An American more American? What the hell do you mean? My dad and my dad's dad was born and raised in this country, and so was my ma and her ma. . . . I ain't out to spread no foreign ideas amongst the people over here, but I have been accused of being a Russian red."[60]

Taken together, the *Library of Congress Recordings* and *Dust Bowl Ballads* are both exercises in insinuation, soft-pedaling the political agitation to which Guthrie was certainly committed upon his arrival in New York. One striking indication of this lies in two versions of his ballad "Jesus Christ" (alternatively, "Jesus Christ Was a Man" or "They Laid Jesus Christ in His Grave"), which, as Guthrie wrote, was one of his earliest New York productions: "I wrote this song looking out of a rooming house window in New York City in the winter of 1940. I saw how the poor folks lived, and then I saw how the rich folks lived, and the poor folks down and out and cold and hungry, and the rich ones out drinking good whiskey and celebrating and wasting handfuls of money at gambling and women, and I got to thinking about what Jesus said, and what if He was to walk into New York City and preach like He used to. They'd lock Him back in jail as sure as you're reading this."[61] While the *Library of Congress Recordings* version of "Jesus Christ" condemns "the rich landlords" and "the soldiers that they hired" for the execution of the Carpenter-Outlaw,[62] no recorded version includes the final verse that Guthrie had already committed to paper:

> When the love of the poor shall turn to hate,
> When the patience of the workers gives away;
> "Twould be better for you rich if you'd never been born"
> For you have laid Jesus Christ in His grave.[63]

This explicit threat of the violent overthrow of capitalism is just one indication of the anger that Guthrie had generally withheld from the recording microphones; indeed, it breaks out unbridled just once in the *Library of Congress Recordings,* when Guthrie tells Lomax: "If people had set and told me that there was hundreds and hundreds and hundreds and hundreds and thousands of families and people living around under railroad bridges, down along the river bottoms in their old cardboard houses, and old rusty beat up houses that they'd made out of tow sacks and old, dirty rags and corrugated iron that they'd got out of the dumps, and old tin cans flattened out, and old orange crates that they'd been able to tear up and get boards out of, I wouldn't believe it."[64]

Thus a more revealing indication of Guthrie's gathering militancy, enthusiastically nurtured by Lomax, is the project in which the unrecorded version of "Jesus Christ" appears, the "angry book"—in Lomax's words—that would not be published until 1967, the year of Guthrie's death, under the title *Hard Hitting Songs for Hard-Hit People*.[65] Although the voice is primarily Guthrie's, the bulk of the material was chosen by Lomax from the Archives of American Folk Song, field trip recordings, migrant newspapers, picket-line broadsides, and "hillbilly" music on the RCA, Columbia, and Decca labels (Lomax was in fact an avid collector of commercial recordings as well as a field worker). The book's eventual publisher Irwin Silber described the project's development: "Lomax next got together with Woody Guthrie . . . to construct the book. They organized it into subjects and chapters. If some subject needed a song that wasn't there, Woody wrote one. Or Woody might write one anyway just being inspired by some particular phrase or idea he got from working on the manuscript. But, most of all, Woody wrote introductions and comments for every song in the book. Somewhere along the way, Pete Seeger came into the project, his work consisting mostly of transcribing tunes from records, from Woody, from other singers."[66]

Guthrie himself was somewhat coy in describing the project's redistributive agenda to an interviewer in 1941 (although the interviewer had been sent by none other than the *Daily Worker*): "The biggest parts of our song collection are aimed at restoring the right amount of land and the right amount of houses and the right amount of groceries to the right amount of working folks."[67] Among the book's thirteen sections, organized under such general headings as "Hard Luck on the Farm," "You're Dead Broke," "So You Got to Hit the Road," and "And You Land in Jail," three sections in particular stand out for their militancy. Section 10—"Detroit Sets Down"—commemorates the early victories of the Congress of Industrial Organizations (CIO) in the 1937 strike waves that led to the unionization of General Motors, through a selection of songs by anonymous strikers as well as some by Maurice Sugar, well known for his compositions "Sit Down" and "The Soup Song." Section 11—"The Farmers Get Together"—is dominated by the songs of the Southern Tenant Farmers Union, particularly those by John Handcox, including "There Is Mean Things Happening in This Land," "Raggedy Raggedy Are We," and "The Planter and the Sharecropper." Section 7—"Hell Busts Loose in Kentucky"—is devoted to the musical record of both the Harlan coal strikes and the Gastonia textile strikes, with Aunt Molly Jackson, Sarah Ogan, Jim Garland, and the murdered Ella Mae Wiggins singing from the pages in uncompromising lyrics such as Ogan's "I Hate the Capitalist System," Garland's "The Murder of Harry Simms," and Jackson's "I Am a Union Woman," along with other songs eulogizing the ILD and the CIO. Guthrie introduces the collection with an autobiographical portrait that, in places, transposes some of his own family tragedies (the incarceration of his mother, the allegedly suicidal impulses of his father) onto other, nameless people he has encountered:

> Nights I slept in jails, and the cells were piled high with young boys, strong men, and old men; and they talked and they sung, and they told you the story of their life, how it used to be, how it got to be, how the home went to pieces, how the young wife died or left, how the mother died in the insane asylum, how Dad tried twice to kill himself, and lay flat on his back for 18 months— and then crops got to where they wouldn't bring nothing, work in the factories would kill a dog, work on the belt line killed your soul, work in the cement and limestone quarries withered your lungs, work in the cotton mills shot your feet and legs all to hell, work in the steel mills burned your system up like a gnat that lit in the melting pot, and—always, always had to fight and argue and cuss and swear, and shoot and slaughter and wade mud and sling blood—to try to get a nickel more out of the rich bosses.[68]

As Lomax recalled, the hiatus of World War II put the project on hold for a few years, but immediately after the war he actively sought to publish: "No publisher would take it then because postwar America was afraid to look reality in the eye."[69] The book's "reality" is its core of anticapitalist anger that translates into Guthrie's explicit call for a socialist revolution. Thus, in introducing Ogan's "I Hate the Capitalist System," Guthrie declares unequivocally: "This song was composed by Sarah Ogan and every word is true."[70] But he does not simply leave the agenda setting to Ogan or to any other songwriter; eventually he comes out with a straightforward call for economic redistribution: "These songs will echo that song of starvation till the world looks level—till the world is level—and there ain't no rich men, and there ain't no poor men, and every man on earth is at work and his family is living as human beings instead of like a nest of rats."[71]

The unambiguous call for economic leveling is only one of the book's main articulations. Another is a mission to build on the successes of the CIO and to perpetuate the struggles of Harlan, Gastonia, and Detroit. "The Banking men has got their Big Union," Guthrie argues, "and the Land Lords has got their Big Union, and the Merchants has got their Kiwanis and Lions Club, and the Finance Men has got their Big Union, and the Associated Farmers has got their Big Union, but down south and out west, on the cotton farms, and working in the orchards and fruit crops it is a jail house offence for a few common everyday workers to form them a Union, and get together for higher wages and honest pay and fair treatment. It's damn funny how all of the big boys are in Big Unions, but they cuss and raise old billy hell when us poor damn working guys try to get together and make us a Working Man's Union."[72] The alternative, Guthrie implies ominously, raises the specter of something much worse for capitalism than simply "a Working Man's Union." The voice he first creates is that of a hard-boiled Wobbly bruiser—perhaps a logger or a longshoreman or any laborer nearing the end of his tether: "Gonna get together and ask him for our share of them eats. Nice way of course. Ain't a gonna hurt him. Don't like to bounce nothing off from his head. Then, we go and ask him. We 'get together' and we go and ask him how about a little stuff to eat and wear and some spare change to tote around in your pocket? And if he don't give it to us, we'll just natural have to take it th' hard way. Dam shore cain't go ragged and hungry."[73]

Guthrie's voice then modulates from this echo of proletarian menace to that of the fiery preachers of Oklahoma's Christian socialism—a hellfire sermon calling down apocalyptic horror on the heads of those carrying out the wholesale rape of the working class: "because in the days to come, and who knows when, the grafters, slave drivers, hate spreaders, and money worshippers will be wiped out and destroyed in the fire of their own damned greed. They will start that fire, and they'll fan it twenty four hours a day and tamper with it and blow it and tease it and then—when it leaps up into a flame as high as the sky—and starts roaring across the pastures, they'll fall back and run and jabber and yell that somebody else caused the whole thing."[74]

Guthrie's eye on the powder keg of deferred justice informs one of his most uncompromising stances in *Hard Hitting Songs for Hard-Hit People*, that concerning the penal system. Categorically he declares: "When any living creature walks out of a jailhouse, I like it. It's wrong to be in it and it's right to be out"[75]—even if, as he writes in his song "Matthew Kimes," a man has "killed some men."[76] Guthrie's declaration is in part driven by a keen perception of the corruption of authority and of the police brutality he witnessed on the road and in California: "This book ain't got no songs in it that was wrote by deputy sheriffs. It ain't got none wrote by company guards, nor cops, nor snitches, nor guys that set fire to the little shacks of the poor folks along the river bottoms."[77] Partly it is driven by sensitivity to desperation and poverty stretched to its limits, as he implies in introducing the selection of what he calls "Prison & Outlaw songs": "These outlaws may be using the wrong system when they rob banks and hijack the rich traveler, and shoot their way out of a gamblin' game, and shoot down a man in a jewelry store, or blow down the pawn shop owner, but I think I know what's on these old boys minds.

Something like this: 'Two little children a layin' in the bed, both of them so hungry that they cain't lift up their head.'"[78]

Ultimately, Guthrie yokes his penal critique to the unequal struggle of workers to gain possession of what is rightfully theirs: "You built that Highway and they can put you in jail for thumbing a ride on it. You built that railroad and they boot you off, shake you down, search your pockets and make you spend your last red cent to buy a ticket into the next town. Then the watchman and cops in the town shove you out. They get you all rounded up like a herd of sheep heading for the sledge hammer and drive you off down the road saying, 'Take warning, boys, and don't ever show yourself in this town again.'"[79] This, in the end, justifies the resistance to—and the tearing down and reconstitution of—the system that links "lousy jails" to "lousy cops," "lousy cops" to "Lousy Governors," and "Lousy Governors" to "Lousy Presidents."[80] *Hard Hitting Songs for Hard-Hit People* is, in the aggregate, testimony to and record of "the working folks [who] have walked bare handed against clubs, gas bombs, billys, blackjacks, saps, knucks, machine guns, and log chains—and they sang their way through the whole dirty mess."[81]

Guthrie's hope and faith in the project was as profound as it was unfulfilled. He wrote to Seeger from Los Angeles: "It'll sweep out acrost the country and mow down whole big wide swaths of tangled grass and sticker weeds—and'll reap the nation's harvest of the songs of the working people, which is just as important as any other crop, and it'll bring new life back to the soil."[82] He told Seeger: "You could be the Johnny Appleseed of Union Folk Songs with this book under your arm strutting from town to town playing your banjo and sowing the good seeds of the big change to come"[83]—as welcome a vote of confidence as any mentor could give his student.

Seeger has discussed Guthrie's formative impact upon him in this period, particularly beginning in mid-May 1940, when, as he recalled, Guthrie told him: "It's a big country out there, Pete, you ought to see it, and if you haven't got money for a ticket, use the thumb."[84] Thus began what Seeger deemed his "education" under Guthrie's tutelage on a cross-country journey (by car rather than thumb) that had the pair encountering Jim Crow segregation firsthand in a Tennessee café, visiting the Highlander Folk School, and singing for oil workers in Oklahoma City.

It was here, at the home of CPUSA organizers Bob and Ina Wood, that Guthrie and Seeger together wrote one of the great anthems of the wartime and postwar labor movement, "Union Maid." Prompted by Ina Wood's urging to Guthrie—"Isn't it about time you wrote a union song for women?"[85]—the pair set about their collaboration, as Guthrie describes in his headnotes to the

"A big part of my education": Pete Seeger and Woody Guthrie,
Oklahoma City, c. 1940. Photographer unknown. Courtesy of Guy
Logsdon via the American Folklife Center, Library of Congress.

song: "Pete and me was fagged out when we got to Oklahoma City, but not
too fagged to plow up a Union Song. Pete flopped out acrost a bed, and I set
over at a Writing Machine, and he could think of one line and me another'n
until we woke up with a great big 15 pound, blue-eyed Union Song, I mean
Union—named the Union Maid."[86]

In spite of Guthrie's admission of a collaboration, Seeger has been content
to credit Guthrie with the sole authorship of "Union Maid," which is how the
song is copyrighted.[87] It has traveled the world in the jaunty, jingly version
first popularized by the Almanac Singers and afterward by Peter, Paul, and

Mary, among others. But there is more to the song's complex history than its collaborative authorship, and more to its voice than the upbeat celebration of the Union Maid who would cheerfully "organize the guys" and "show her card to the National Guard."[88] While the song owes part of its inspiration to Ina Wood, Guthrie pointed to another historical figure with a darker, bloodier tale to tell: "This song was made up in honor of Mrs. Merriweather. She's a woman that was stripped naked and beat up, and then hung to the rafters of the house 'till she was unconscious."[89]

In the manuscript version of what Guthrie calls "Union Maid #1"—which may well be a revision of the original Guthrie–Seeger collaboration (given that it is steeped in a goriness and sexual sadism from which Seeger almost certainly would have recoiled)—Guthrie elaborates: "Mrs. Merriweather was the Union Sharecopper lady that Vaughn Riles and Ralph McQuire stripped naked and beat up, then hung her for dead up to a rafter in the little shack."[90] In a note below the lyrics, Guthrie reproduces the testimony of Annie Mae Meriwether, the African American activist sexually brutalized and nearly lynched for daring to join the radical, interracial Share Croppers Union in Montgomery, Alabama. As she testified for the NAACP sometime between 1927 and 1936 (and as Guthrie quotes her):

> Vaughn Ryles started doubling up the rope and told me to take off all of my clothes. He said, Lay down across the chair. I want naked meat this morning. I lay down across the chair and Ralph McGuire held my head for Ryles to beat me. He beat me about twenty minutes. He was beating me from the hips down. They beat me for about fifteen minutes more. Then Vaughn Ryles put a loop in the rope and put the rope around my neck. One of them said, "Let's carry her out to a damn limb somewhere." Vaughn said, "No, right here in the house will do." Then he threw the rope over the rafters and then he and Ralph McGuire drew me up about two feet from the floor. My sister in law said they kept me there for fifteen or twenty minutes and then let me down. I was unconscious. She said I laid there about twenty minutes and got up.[91]

The chorus of "Union Maid #1" is far more accusatory than the rousing chant of "Oh, you can't scare me, I'm sticking to the Union" in the popular version.[92] Rather, it carries the same promise of biblical vengeance sprinkled throughout the manuscript of *Hard Hitting Songs for Hard-Hit People*, as the Union Maid—Annie Mae Meriwether—turns on her persecutors:

> You have robbed my family and my people,
> My Holy Bible says we are equal,
> Your money is the root of all our evil,
> I know the poor man will win this world.[93]

The aim of Guthrie's "Union Maid #1," in contrast to the simple organizing aim of the popular Almanac Singers version, is above all to illuminate the record of violence that has marked the suppression of the American labor movement, as the final two stanzas make clear (while confusing the names of Meriwether's assailants):

> Now the rich man heard her speech
> And he commenced to itch,
> He hired his thugs to spill her blood
> Along the city streets.
> They whipped her till she bled,
> They hung her up for dead
> In a little old shack one midnight black
> For saying what she said.
>   (Chorus again)
> This bloody crime was done
> Out where the buffalo run,
> By old Bob Ryles
> and Ralph McQuire
> With a knotty rope
> They soaked in blood.
> As this Union girl they beat
> [They] Said, "I want naked meat,"
> They swung her up to a rafter there
> For saying what she said.
>   (Chorus again)[94]

The harrowing "Union Maid #1" notwithstanding, Guthrie was learning about when and when not to reveal the anger and the retributive impulses underlying his activism. He grew increasingly confident in his calculated articulations of Popular Front militancy, through which his vision of the socialist revolution was filtered through the gauze of down-home Americanism. In April 1940, Mike Quin of the *People's World* reviewed one of Guthrie's radio broadcasts, crying: "Sing it, Woody, sing it! Karl Marx wrote it and Lincoln said it and Lenin did it. Sing it, Woody, and we'll all laugh together."[95] On the strength of this joyful accolade, the *Daily Worker* in New York picked up the "Woody Sez" column, not because Guthrie's writings were either "strategic or basic" to the CPUSA agenda—as the *Worker's* feature editor, Sender Garlin, explained—but simply because the Party wanted to demonstrate that it was "interested in people" as well as ideology.[96] Guthrie himself seemed aware of his need to manage the anger driving his writing: "We don't aim to hurt you or scare you when we get to a feeling sorta folksy and make up some folk lore, we're a doing all we can to make it easy on you."[97]

Guthrie's word began to carry some weight in New York's progressive broadcasting circles. He convinced Henrietta Yurchenko, host of the WNYC program *Adventures in Music,* to give Lead Belly a chance on the air. Learning from Lead Belly, Guthrie told her, was "one of New Yorks greatest pleasures"—particularly for his reinforcement of plain speaking and singing in what Guthrie perceived as an overwhelmingly timid and politically evasive broadcasting culture. "Life hasn't been so smooth with Huddie," Guthrie wrote, "and what makes him so good is that he simply wants to sing and tell how it has treated him and what he has learned from it, and he wants to be honest about it, without any pretty put on." In Lead Belly's music, Guthrie saw an entire people and an entire political revolution stirring: "Huddie plays a little old $4 accordion and you can actually hear the sad note of his people singing in the swamps and jungles and echoing in the Louisiana moss. And when you hear it you almost know that it's the sad and lonesome music of a people that can't even vote. But what they have been beat out of by votes they've tried to win back with notes and to my way of thinking they've won it and will keep on winning it." Thus to leave Lead Belly out of the broadcasting mix, Guthrie told Yurchenko, was "like leaving the alcohol out of the wine or leaving the spring out of the clock"; and he took a swipe at Nicholas Ray, the director of *Back Where I Come From* (and future director of the film *Rebel Without a Cause*), who had argued against having Lead Belly share the airtime with Guthrie: "Some radio experts will say that Huddie is too rough and so pass him up but I say that he is just too good and so they cant see it."[98]

Guthrie's influence was such that when he broke with Ray over Lead Belly and walked away from *Back Where I Come From,* Lomax pleaded for him to return: "I wish there was some way you and Nick could get together again. The first program that you failed to appear on just about broke my heart."[99] Lomax arranged a temporary truce, and Lead Belly was soon making periodic appearances on the program. Other conflicts developed, and Guthrie left for good. As Lomax ruefully concluded after the final break, Guthrie's concerns about broadcasting timidity and evasiveness had been justified: "I really miss you a lot on 'Back Where I Come From.' The program has become very 'merry' and 'jolly' since you left us. We don't have anybody who can come out and speak his mind with sincerity and honesty the way you can."[100]

But as his newfound celebrity grew, Guthrie found that he himself was not wholly immune to the pecuniary attractions of commercial broadcasting.

All "sincerity and honesty" notwithstanding, there was a good living to be made from a denuded, sanitized, politically eviscerated folk music amenable to the corporate censor. Commercial radio offers came in quick succession, culminating in a steady contract to host the *Pipe Smoking Time* program on CBS for the Model Tobacco Company. Guthrie confessed to Lomax his giddiness in the face of the monetary seduction, even when offered by a future nemesis such as the munitions giant I. E. Du Pont de Nemours: "I got a call from the Du Pont program Cavalcade of America and they said they had me in view for a ballad telling about the life of Wild Bill Hickock. I said I got you boys in mind for 300 dollars. Then I got a call from Sanka Coffee's program called We the People and I don't know what they want unless it's the people. Our dress rehearsal for Model Tobacco Company went through all right and they are giving me money so fast I use it to sleep under. Handed me fifty bucks the other day just to see how far it would knock me."[101] Thus in November of 1940, for the fee of two hundred dollars a week, Guthrie was briefly seduced as far away as he would ever go from his mission to constitute American folk music as radical agitation. For fear of his *Pipe Smoking Time* contract, he gave up writing his columns for the *People's World* and the *Daily Worker* and butchered his first Dust Bowl ballad, "So Long, It's Been Good to Know Yuh," into a contemptible jingle for Model Tobacco:

> Howdy friend, well it's sure good to know you
> Howdy friend, well it's sure good to know you
> Load up your pipe and take your life easy
> With Model Tobacco to light up your way
> We're glad to be with you today.[102]

This travesty of folk singing continued for a month until, apparently sickened by his self-betrayal and his momentary political weakness, Guthrie uprooted himself and his long-suffering family and fled from "the one and only New York," whose capitalist temptations had finally overpowered the revolutionary potential he had initially celebrated. He returned to Los Angeles with no prospects in sight. (After their divorce, his first wife, Mary, would bitterly declare, "He never should have been involved in politics; he had several job offers and ways to make money.")[103]

In Los Angeles, Guthrie was more than ready to rejoin the political battle. Hearing of the enforced closure of the Commonwealth Labor College after a series of anticommunist raids (in which the college's massive song library was destroyed), he commiserated to its alumnus Lee Hays: "I think it is a god damn lousy low down bastardly shame and insult to the human race to be raided and robbed like this in the name of law and order, or national defense."[104] To Geer he reported being approached by John Steinbeck's literary agents to "turn a bale or two of stuff over to them for possible magazine publication." He bragged: "I can cuss as much as old John or Erskine [Caldwell] either one, me a being borned and raised up in as cuss-fighting a part of the country as they is—and having played music in all of the noisiest honky tonks in said strip of country. Hells Bells Nelly, I can concentrate my mind on a banker for instance, and cuss words just organize into books and plays and manuscripts of ever dam kind under the sun."[105]

By early 1941, of all the topics exercising Guthrie's mind, the drift toward war was the most prominent. Roosevelt's Lend-Lease bill was before the Congress, and on the 27th of February, Guthrie jotted into the margins of his old Pampa songbook his reflections on the "folks" in "superstitious shoes" putting "their faith in witchery":

> And underneath their noses
> Their life is lent and leased
> To wars across the ocean
> To murder o'er the sea—
> To fight and die on foreign soil
> To save—democracy (?)[106]

In a celebration of what he called "the Workers Army," Guthrie appropriated the militaristic imagery increasingly pervading the public discourse. He sought to incite a healthy suspicion of the government's war aims, writing:

> Pretty hard deciding
> Where your enemy's hiding
> But it's by their works you'll know them one and all;
> You fight for the Needy;
> He fights for the Greedy;
> And now the bugle blows the Final Call![107]

And in a moment of inspiration that would return during the Cold War, when he would write his best-known antiwar anthem, "I've Got to Know," Guthrie took the old spiritual "Farther Along" as the basis for a song he performed on "the People's World Radio Program" in Los Angeles:

> Why do the War Ships sail on the ocean?
> Why do the bombs drop down from the sky?
> Why can't we work and have Peace and Plenty?
> . . . We'll understand it all by and by!

Chorus: Farther along we'll know more about it;
     Farther along we'll understand why
     Poor man is poor, and the rich man gets rich-er;
     . . . We'll understand it all by and by![108]

Guthrie knew fully well where he stood on the war: in lockstep with the Party loyalists who had placed the safety of the Soviet Union above all other political considerations, he had amply demonstrated his capacity to blind himself willfully to the realities of Stalinism and to the diabolic nature of the Hitler–Stalin Pact. In this he was no different from many others in the American communist movement; but it was a mistake from which the movement would never recover. In the short term, however, the Party would be helped out of its embarrassing predicament by none other than Adolf Hitler, sharpening his knives in Berlin.

3. Almanac Days

In March of 1941, Guthrie was beginning to sense what Stalin himself still refused to acknowledge, at least openly—that Hitler was preparing to break the nonaggression pact and launch an attack on his Soviet allies in a bid to seize their resources and, eventually, their land. Betrayal was again in the air, as it had been just after Neville Chamberlain's proclamation of "peace for our time" nearly three years earlier. As Guthrie playfully noted to the tune of "Frankie and Johnny":

> Now Hitler started eastward
> But he didn't get so far;
> He saw a light that blinded him
> Was that big red Russian star!
> 　　He was Chamberlain's man, he wouldn't do him wrong!

But having sensed the threat to the Soviet Union, Guthrie was still far from advocating any U.S. intervention, even if it would constitute a de facto military alliance with the socialist homeland:

> And now the rich folks tell us
> To jump into this war—
> For a bunch of thieves and liars
> That ain't worth dyin' for
> 　　Since Hitler and Chamberlain has done 'em wrong![1]

This song had come fresh on the heels of Guthrie's excoriation of Franklin Roosevelt as a duplicitous warmonger—a characterization the president had supposedly revealed at a recent convention of the American Youth Congress in Washington, where thousands of delegates had gathered outside the White

House to protest against the disbursement of war loans to Finland while American workers stood on the breadlines. As Guthrie described it in the manuscript of *Hard Hitting Songs for Hard-Hit People:* "I picked up a noise-paper and it said there that the 6,000 had been over to call on Roosevelt at his Whitehouse—and he called their trip and their stuff that they stood for 'twaddle.' It come up a big soaking rain and he made the kids a 30 minute speech in it. Wrote up this little song about it. . . . Would like to dedicate this song to them 6,000 kids, and about 130 million others in this country that soaked the same day."[2]

The "little song," "Why Do You Stand There in the Rain?" (the title echoing Roosevelt's rhetorical query to the protesters), concludes bitterly:

> Now the guns of Europe roar as they have so oft before,
> And the war lords play the same old game again,
> They butcher and they kill, Uncle Sammy foots the bill,
> With his own dear children standing in the rain.

> Then the President's voice did ring; "Why, this is the silliest thing,
> I have heard in all my fifty eight years of life."
> But it all just stands to reason as he passes another season,
> He'll be smarter by the time he's fifty nine.[3]

As far as Guthrie was concerned, the main battle to be fought was still on the home front. He wrote in his notes to a traditional ballad, "These Old Cumberland Mountain Farms," which was then playing on his mind: "Some landlords make it so hard on us that we can't stand it any longer. Won't let you live, won't let you die. Won't let you eat, won't let you starve, won't let you work, won't let you rest. It's a sorry place to live in."[4] In the original ballad, the tenants are slaves to the bosses and to the thieving company commissary, unluckier than the convicts "found down in prison" or "up in old iron Tennessee."[5] In Guthrie's reworking of the ballad that March, the workers' war was far more significant than the diversionary struggles between Europe's empire builders:

> When you go out to organize these tenants
> You'll hear bullets a whistling in the trees
> And the next thing you know in the sleet and the snow
> You're in jail and you're left there to freeze.

> Well you cain't git no schoolin' it's agin th' bosses rulin'
> If you read about th' C.I.O.;
> If you talk it to your neighbor you're a labor agitator;
> To the Cumberland Mountain Jail you will go.[6]

As he toyed with the ballad in Los Angeles, Guthrie reflected on the meaning of the two separate wars then being fought—the European tempest and the longer struggle playing itself out on the American labor battleground signified by the Cumberland Mountain Farms:

> O' this world is a sight, it's a battle and a fight,
> It's the battle of the rich 'ginst th' poor!
> And it's hard fighting women raises hard fighting men
> And we'll fight for our Cumberland Mountain Farm.[7]

Guthrie thus urged full engagement in one war and strict nonintervention in the other. "Why, hells bells," he had written into the manuscript of *Hard Hitting Songs for Hard-Hit People*, "I'll pitch in with the rest of the boys and

Woody Guthrie playing for a group of migrant laborers at the Shafter Farm Workers Community, California, 1941. Photograph by Seema Weatherwax. Used with permission of the Woody Guthrie Archives.

fight like hell for a good job at honest pay—here at home, and not across the damned ocean."[8] Now, at the top corner of the page on which he refashioned the ballad of the Cumberland Mountain Farms, he wrote himself a reminder: "Songs has got to be poured into the big Peace Battle—every one of us on the side of the working folks has got to out-do about a dozen on the rich side."[9]

Guthrie worked this new preoccupation into letters to his friends back east. To Will and Herta Geer he described his newly rented house, yoking it to the subject of the current war buildup: "This old house had really ought to be jacked up and a new one run under it. But rotten as it is it aint as rotten as this lend lease bill. Reckon that dam thing'll pass?"[10] To Lomax he ruminated on "the war scare" brewing and the state repression that was certain to accompany it: "Just like on any other subject, folks has got something to say about it; they might not let on around the high society ginks, but the people has got just a plenty to say about every little thing that's said and done that's a leading us down this lonesome road to the war—and of course you know how folks always has pretended to be dumb or blank in the presence of officers of the law that they don't trust or like. With every invention of modern times turned against them, the people sing their song just the same as they ever did."[11]

The state repression had already begun; Lomax's beloved *Back Where I Come From* was to be axed—"kicked off the Defense budget," as Guthrie wrote to Pete Seeger—because it was "too honest" (he had apparently forgotten his criticism of Nicholas Ray over Lead Belly).[12] To Lomax he commiserated: "This country's a getting to where it caint hear its own voice," leaving only the lullabies of Broadway to send America "off to sleep and sort of float ½ way between a drink of scotch liquor and a tile shit house."[13]

Guthrie was also engaged in a course of intensive reading as he sought to place the narrative of the Dust Bowl migrants and their ravaged land into a broader frame that could accommodate his disgust over the war buildup. He wrote to the Geers that he was "becoming highly interested" in the issues of soil erosion and land reclamation "after reading a couple of good books on the subject." His prognosis was grim: "I think that 150,000,000 acres of our nation's topsoil is enough to pour down the gutter of a Bankers War in 1918, and if this lend-lease bill goes through and we supply them with stuff to kill each other again, that many more acres will be over-planted, under rotated, unnaturally planted, hurried, rushed, and with no regard to the soil holding qualities of local plants, and this would be just about like giving them the state of Texas two or three times."[14]

The Dust Bowl had come about, Guthrie implied, "because we tried to do the farming for Europe while she killed her farmers off" during the previous war. Now all the signs were that America was on the road to a similar "National Calamity"—just as the West Coast defense industry had begun to absorb the Dust Bowl migrants into its workforce: "And our national soil is rottening as fast as a crew can build a highway, and it winds and crawls, and it throws up all colors of dust, and goes over big mountains, and strikes out down the valleys, and all sorts of hell sets in."[15]

Guthrie went so far as to propose that a conspiracy was afoot between bankers and crop bosses to generate a new cheap agricultural workforce for wartime food production, as he wrote to Millard Lampell: "They're threatening to kick more people who are able to travel off the WPA, in order to force them to become migrants and find a living working in the crops."[16] That done, the more radical, union-minded migrants would have been taught a serious political lesson for the new times:

> The farmers decided that it was a no good gamble a long time before anybody could call them a communist, but they're all a bunch of communists, them farmers that wants a fair, square, and honest deal—imagine that! And the big fat banker, the old son of a bitch, sets back and slobbers, and says, I'll teach you to run away, you god dam toe headed clodhopper! Let your land blow straight to hell! Let your wife and kids starve their guts out! I'll show you who's boss! I'll starve you within an inch of your god dam life,—and when you come back maybe you'll get some of these wild ideas out of your head, and get down and get some work done! Why, you silly hayseed bastard you, don't you know this is for national defense!![17]

He thus issued a stern warning to Franklin Roosevelt, enjoying his "third time around" in the wake of the 1940 election: "If you're sendin' my crops to the dictator wars, / Man, you're on your last time round!"[18]

Guthrie urged Seeger to get his hands on Carey McWilliams's *Factories in the Field,* which he called "the Bible of the record of the crooked titles, deeds, land grants and downright frauds that has bloomed into the capitalist system as she blooms in California."[19] In his 1939 study, McWilliams had set out to expose what he called the "farm fascism" of the California agricultural sector, the "cleverly manipulated exploitation, by large growers," of not only the Dust Bowl migrants but also "a number of suppressed racial minority groups which were imported to work in the fields"—Chinese, Japanese, Mexican, and Filipino.[20] McWilliams, Guthrie argued, would enable Seeger to comprehend the true corruption of "the big land owners controlling hundreds of thousands of acres rolling and rambling around the hacienda, while of course hundreds of thousands of folks are a setting by the side of the road peeking in under the fence and saying all kinds of good old juicy cuss words."

Factories in the Field was "the bible of the migratory working people,"[21] and between its covers, Guthrie advised, progressive singers and actors could find "lots of matter . . . that had ought to be played up in skits, songs etc." His mind was awhirl with the agitprop possibilities offered by McWilliams: "Has the one subject Soil Poverty, its reasons, etc., cause and cure, been used here as the theme for any shows or skits—it is mainly under absentee land lord control, bankerism, etc., that soil is caused to decay through replanting the same crop too much, and not enough attention to different scientific ways of curing the land. Right now the right to vote in the south is more important. Next to that and union organizing, I think Soil Erosion, Rotten Everything, is very good material for a show."[22]

It was in the midst of such scattergun ruminations over "Rotten Everything" that Guthrie casually informed Lampell: "Some feller from the Dept. of Interior is here in town. He just called and said he'd heard my records and wants to come out to the house and talk about a documentary film to be shot up along the Columbia River. Hope he gives me a job. Will let you know."[23] This offhand postscript inaugurates the history of one of Guthrie's most momentous and, at the same time, contradictory projects, his song cycle for the Bonneville Power Administration (BPA) celebrating the Columbia River and the Grand Coulee Dam. It is momentous because of its output and legacy, and contradictory because of the mixed signals it sends about Guthrie's shifting political stance in 1941. The Columbia River cycle illuminates the complex relationship between the waning New Deal and the expanding U.S. war machine, both of which Guthrie viewed with scorn before signing on as their staunchest advocate.

Of the three major Western dam-building projects coming out of the New Deal—Fort Peck, Boulder (subsequently Hoover), and Grand Coulee—it was the Grand Coulee that benefited from the most aggressive promotion, proclaimed by the journalist and future Oregon senator Richard Neuberger "Man's Greatest Structure" and "The Biggest Thing on Earth" (it measured "550 feet from bedrock to quadrant, with a 15-acre spillway").[24] The dam, begun in 1933 and completed in 1941, would generate the electricity for the plants, factories, and towns of Oregon and Washington, and the BPA—established by Congress in 1939—would market the energy via "a triangular grid of power lines that marched up and down over the Cascade range to connect Seattle, Spokane, and Portland with essentially equal-price power."[25]

Helping to inaugurate the BPA on the public-relations front in 1939 was the administration's first public information officer, Steve Kahn, who had written and produced a short promotional film titled *Hydro.* As Kahn recalled over sixty years later, "the vice president took it to Asia, where he had it dubbed into half a dozen languages to show how democracy worked, developing a great river for all its value, for the benefit of all the people."[26] Kahn's BPA superiors next wanted him to produce a feature-length film that would "speak better to 'the common man,'" perhaps including, in the spirit of Popular Front Americanism, a folksinger to "show up in the movie and sing from a cliff or under a tree or something like that."[27] The BPA contacted Lomax at the Library of Congress for "a country singer who can make up some songs and get the people onto our side"; Lomax immediately sent them to Guthrie in Los Angeles.[28]

Having been visited by the "feller from the Dept. of Interior," and with no job secured or contract signed, the Guthrie family headed north to Portland. Kahn recalled Guthrie showing up with his guitar and asking for the job; but, as he explained, there were some problems. "First of all," Kahn told him, "your political background makes it a little difficult to get anything for over one month because it requires Civil Service approval. . . . But we might be able to get you an emergency appointment for one month for a specific job"—as long as Guthrie didn't "express some of his opinions about the inequities of the capitalist system."[29] As Kahn later confessed: "Guthrie's songs indicated he was in the class struggle pretty deep. . . . I didn't want to film anything that would incriminate me."[30] Guthrie apparently held his tongue and signed on the dotted line, truthfully answering "No" to the paranoid question newly imposed by the anticommunist Smith Act: "Do you have membership in any political party or organization which advocates the overthrow of our constitutional form of government in the United States?"[31] For roughly one month, Guthrie was driven in a BPA car up and down the Columbia River for inspiration, and as his daughter Nora later surmised: "The Bonneville Dam project was an incredible release, because someone gave him a frame to fill—'Fill this with everything from A to Z that you can think about a river!'"[32]

Guthrie was in fact looking for an even larger frame to fill, again, one that would encompass both the Dust Bowl migration and the war buildup. As soon as he arrived in Portland, he set off making a series of feverish connections that might account for "the new serious farm labor shortage here now," as he wrote to Lampell: "1. The draft. 2. Higher wages in big towns. 3. Defense Booms. 4. But farm wages are so low that farmers can't attract workers to the fields. 5. Lots of big town industrial workers, etc., are going by the 1000's into the crops, but still not enough. 6. Big aluminium and light metal industries opening up around here every day drains the farms of workers. 7. Guarded freights and patrolled highways make it harder for field workers to travel. 8. Vigilantes and hired thugs have discouraged workers who travel—and fake contractors and crop racketeers have won the hate and distrust of the farming people."[33]

There were thus two different stories now being told: a rosy one for the workers who had abandoned the land to head for flush times in the war factories, and another, more bitter one for those who were determined to remain on the land. Tom Joad may well have gone "off building airplanes" somewhere (as Joe Klein phrases it),[34] but for the remaining agricultural workers, the Pacific Northwest appeared to be offering the same false paradise that California had dangled before the Okies in the previous decade. Guthrie implied that the coming disillusionment could be just as brutal: "Crooked real estate agents have pulled all sorts of thievery deals on the farmers who hit here with a few hundred bucks—no good land—cut over lands—stumplands where the people have worked like slaves with no tractors, no machinery, and by hand, to heave out the big stumps, only to find a dead end: no water. Chemically bad land, and, result, hundreds of vacant houses in the rainy country to almost match the rotten deserted shacks in the dust bowl country."[35] It was *The Grapes of Wrath* and *Factories in the Field* all over again, with misery and poverty in the midst of plenty: "Industries—fish, lumber, wheat, (grain) orchards (cherries, peaches, and delicious apples, + strawberries, melons, and hops, beans, peas, and great flower gardens . . .) for the moneyed folks to look at and smell of while the working people work and stay broke."[36]

Such bitter impressions cast a new and profoundly grimmer light on some of the most celebrated songs of Guthrie's Columbia River cycle. It is true that, to the migrants along Guthrie's Columbia River, "the end of the [Oregon] 'trail' promised rain, excellent crops, no dust or sand, prosperity, and a good life."[37] But if Guthrie's bitter observations as expressed in his letters accurately reflect his impressions, then the migrants to whom he gives such hopeful voice in songs like "Oregon Trail" and "Pastures of Plenty" are already set up for a fall. The farmer "on the flat and windy plains" dreams of a lifetime of work "in that north Pacific land" and decides: "I'm gonna hit that Oregon Trail this comin' fall."[38] The same farmer, in an unrecorded version of "Pastures of Plenty," sings:

> I picked up a rich clod of dirt in my hand,
> I crumble it back into strong fertile land;
> The greatest desire in this world that I know
> Is to work on my land where there's green things to grow.
>
> I think of the Dust and the days that are gone,
> And the day that's to come on a farm of our own;
> One turn of the wheel and the waters will flow
> 'Cross the green growing field, down the hot thirsty row.[39]

When Guthrie's epistolary observations are set alongside the picture of these hopeful migrants, poised on the brink of either salvation or doom, they illuminate the meaning of a note written beneath the lyrics to "Roll On, Columbia": "This song was wrote up by an Oakie passing through your country, and I'm pretty certain that everybody just first a coming into this country has got some such similar song in his or her head, but times is such that they just don't sing it out loud, so you might not hear it."[40] Indeed, the times were "such" that, without a drastic change in the region's labor relations, such hopeful dreams would surely be crushed. As Guthrie diverted his eyes from the awesome grandeur of the Grand Coulee Dam to the state of organized labor in the Pacific Northwest, he was not filled with confidence. He wrote to Lampell: "Portland is a pretty poor union town, full of factional strife."[41]

These considerations do much to undercut the conventional impressions of the Columbia River cycle as a uniformly celebratory body of song character-ized by the odes to the Grand Coulee Dam—whether it be the song of that title, where Guthrie praises "Uncle Sam" for taking "up the challenge in the year of '33 / For the farmer and the factory and for all of you and me,"[42] or the various versions of "The Biggest Thing that Man Has Ever Done," in which Guthrie borrows Richard Neuberger's exaggerated rhetoric to proclaim:

> There's a building in New York that you call the Empire State,
> I rode the rods to Frisco to walk the Golden Gate,
> I've seen every foot of film that Hollywood has run,
> But Coulee is the biggest thing that Man has ever done.[43]

Shadowing this boosterism are scenarios of the migrant farmers condemned to failure and exploitation in the Pacific Northwest's land of plenty. Indeed, Guthrie's most poignant evocation of the migrant's despair, "Ramblin' Round," is one of the twenty-six known songs written during his month on the Co-lumbia River—a song in which the defeated migrant mourns: "My mother prayed that I would be a man of some renown / But I am just a refugee as I go ramblin' round."[44]

In the end, the BPA film that brought Guthrie to the Columbia River was put on hold as the approach of war altered the government's priori-ties. Guthrie was left to record a number of the songs "for possible future use."[45] The question remains: Which songs did he record, and when?—for answering this question would shed further light on Guthrie's shifting politi-cal stance at a pivotal moment. Unfortunately, the murky recording history of the Columbia River project raises more questions than it answers about Guthrie's reaction to the end of the New Deal and the coming world war. The greatest problem lies in the fact that, of the seventeen Columbia River songs known to have been recorded—and there may have been more—the majority of them were recorded in 1944 and 1947, long after Guthrie had fully committed himself to the war effort and revised many of the songs to reflect this shift. In addition, as noted in the fiftieth-anniversary issue of the songs on *Woody Guthrie: The Columbia River Collection* (Rounder, 1987), "the original acetate disc recordings and manuscripts for the songs, made in Portland, disappeared," leaving the producers to collect "copies" from a variety of sources—"former BPA employees, Guthrie fans, scholars, and Woody's family and friends."[46] While the Rounder collection is indeed, as its producers claim, "as complete an edition of Woody singing his Columbia River songs as could be assembled,"[47] the recording dates of all the songs are far from clear. Under such circumstances, it is possible only to speculate over the ambivalence that is surely inscribed into the Columbia River songs.

These songs are often discussed as signals of Guthrie's exhilaration over the social implications and possibilities of the New Deal project and his equation of the Roosevelt government with "the people." Undoubtedly much of Guthrie's subsequent writing indicates that he eventually arrived at this position; but the Columbia River songs suggest that in mid-1941 he still had some way to go. As the two recorded versions of "Talking Columbia" indicate, it is not all that certain that, at this point, Guthrie was quite ready to equate the "government" with "the people." In what appears to be the earlier of the two versions, the talking-blues narrator says:

> Well, the folks need houses and stuff to eat,
> And the folks need metals and the folks need wheat.
> Folks need water and power dams,
> And folks need people and the people need the land.[48]

By "circa 1947," when he recorded the song for Asch,[49] Guthrie's words had changed:

> Uncle Sam needs houses and stuff to eat.
> Uncle Sam needs wool and Uncle Sam needs wheat.
> Uncle Sam needs water and power dams,
> And Uncle Sam needs people and the people need the land.[50]

The possibility that "the folks" had yet to equate with "Uncle Sam" in Guthrie's 1941 estimation is further borne out in *Hard Hitting Songs for Hard-Hit People*, where he writes: "When you say 'government,' you mean the 'people.' You mean the folks that are your friends and your neighbors and guys you see every day. They're the United States Government and not them money mad guys that have managed to beat all of us out of our money. They ain't but a few of them. Just about a couple or three thousand, maybe a few more. They say they are the U.S. Government."[51] But with "them money mad guys" in the seats of power, the government of the day was by implication illegitimate, Franklin Roosevelt—"Labor's Choice"—notwithstanding. In writing his headnote to Bob Miller's "Seven Cent Cotton and Forty Cent Meat," Guthrie made it clear that, as far as he was concerned, the jury was still out on FDR's trustworthiness:

> *Here's another verse made up by folks on one of the first New Deal Resettlement projects. 'Course this here part about Roosevelt can always be changed. It's a matter of personal opinion.*

> We'll raise our cotton, we'll raise our meat,
> We'll raise everything we eat.
> We'll raise our chickens, pigs and corn,
> We'll make you a living just as sure as you're born.
> Farmers getting stronger every year,
> Babies getting fatter all around here.
> No use talking, Roosevelt's the man
> To show the world that the farmer can.[52]

Even more straightforward was Guthrie's introduction to his own song "I'm Looking for that New Deal Now," which rests in the section skeptically titled "So You Hollered for a New Deal," sharing the space with such songs as "NRA Blues," "CWA Blues," "CCC Blues," and "Waitin' on Roosevelt"—all of which imply that some of the heady hopefulness of "back in 19 and 33" had since drained away.[53] Guthrie's disgust is palpable in his headnote: "You was promised a New Deal and you got a Nude Deal. I guess you done know that. Promised a New Deal and got a War Deal. Some 130,000,000 (hundred and thirty million) folks is a lookin' for that New Deal now. The only New Deal that will ever amount to a dam thing will come from Trade Unions."[54]

This is not to suggest that there is no hint of gung-ho nationalism in any of (what appear to be) the earlier versions of the Columbia River songs. There is certainly enough praise for "Uncle Sam," and not merely because of its easy and frequent rhyme with the word "dam." A hefty dose of Popular Front Americanism is precisely what enabled the Washington State Legislature to adopt "Roll On, Columbia" as the "official state folk song" in 1987—in the legislature's words, "to celebrate the river which ties the winter recreation playground of snow capped mountains and the Yakima, Snake, and the Klickitat rivers to the ocean so blue."[55] There was obviously enough pioneer pride to draw on (even if one chose to ignore the ugly history of white conquest in the Columbia River Gorge, from which Guthrie himself did not flinch: "We hung every Injun with smoke in his gun, / So roll on, Columbia, roll on").[56]

There is an intriguing possibility that may account, if only partially, for whatever bullish, nationalist tenor is inscribed into the Columbia River songs, and it may have everything to do with timing. As it is impossible to determine precisely what dates Guthrie recorded his initial versions, or indeed what precise date he left the Pacific Northwest when his BPA contract ran out, it is conceivable that sometime between writing and recording the songs he learned that the Nazis had broken the nonaggression pact with the Soviet Union, launching their invasion of Russia on June 22. As the logic of antifascism dictated, defending the Soviets from Hitler could now—indeed *must* now—be construed as a patriotic American objective.

This, then, may account for the startling gap in the earliest recorded version of "The Biggest Thing that Man Has Ever Done" ("Great Historical Bum")—a gap that is not present on the later, more familiar version of the 1944 Asch recording, in which Guthrie proudly sings:

> There's a man across the ocean and I guess you know him well;
> His name is Adolf Hitler, and damn his soul to hell.
> We'll kick him in the Panzers and we'll put him on the run,
> And that'll be the biggest thing that man has ever done.[57]

On the *Columbia River Collection,* the song clearly finishes with the previous verse. The recording stops—and then it starts again, with the anti-Hitler verse spliced in from what appears to have been a subsequent take. This gap speaks volumes, but it may still never provide a clear answer as to when, precisely, Guthrie committed himself to the war effort. What *is* certain is that, toward the end of June 1941, when a reeking Guthrie climbed down from a transcontinental cattle car and made his way to Seeger's door in New York, he was ready to propose, "Well, I guess we're not going to be singing any more of them peace songs."[58]

There had been significant developments in New York after Guthrie's departure for the West Coast. The previous winter, Seeger and Lee Hays had decided to build on a joint booking at the Jade Mountain Restaurant, where they had earned a grand total of $2.50 between them. Returning to Greenwich Village, the two, along with Hays's roommate, Millard Lampell, had set about forming an agitprop folk group aimed at addressing the socially significant topics of the day—"the structural issues of trade unionism, political machinations in Europe, and the economy."[59] They looked to Guthrie early for their inspiration, on the advice of Alan Lomax, who told them: "What you are doing is one of the most important things that could possibly be done in the field of American music. You are introducing folk songs from the countryside to a new city audience, and you are learning how to do it."[60] Indeed, as Hays later recalled, "The day after Woody left, Millard began writing just like him."[61] Guthrie provided more than passive inspiration; he sent "reams of avuncular advice from the West Coast" along with a name for the group, as Hays recollected: "Well, if you want to know what the weather is going to be, you have to look in your Almanac. And if you want to know when to plant your spuds or what side of the moon to dig 'em in, or when to go on strike, and if you want to know what's good for the itch, or unemployment, or Fascism, you have to look in your Almanac." Hays reckoned that "The Almanac Singers" was "a good name which meant whatever anybody thought it meant."[62]

During a dizzying life span of less than three years, the Almanac Singers would remain in a constant state of flux, both ideologically and in terms of its membership. One of the group's early members, Bess Lomax (sister of Alan), recalled the shifting sands on which the group sometimes recklessly built their political positions: "The Almanacs, like almost every young musical assemblage I have ever known, were inherently unstable, sometimes quarrelsome, and given to large, off-the-cuff pronouncements on matters of policy that later had to change with the times."[63] In addition to Bess Lomax and the three founders (Seeger, Hays, and Lampell), the Almanacs would eventually include the brothers John Peter and Baldwin "Butch" Hawes (the latter of whom would marry Lomax), "Sis" Cunningham, Arthur Stern, and—with his arrival in the summer of 1941—Woody Guthrie; others, including Cisco Houston, would come and go.

Their early mission, the founders declared, was to encourage activists "to write new songs of your own and parodies and poetry, and sing them so loudly that all the warmakers and native fascists and enemies of peace will hear you and tremble in their counting houses. . . . Remember that a singing army is a winning army."[64] The unsolicited "avuncular advice" that Guthrie sent to the Almanacs from Los Angeles went further than the injunction "Stay sober and fight fair, don't get drunk unless you're by yourself or with somebody." He also urged them to stay hungry and keep away from the temptations of Tin Pan Alley: "How's the writers cramps? Making lots of money? It looks like the more money you make the worse it cramps your writing. Same way with singing or anything else. But the way you old boys are set up there in your old loft I imagine there aint no way in the world you could let money cramp you. The more dough you go to making the more you get to run around with the white collars. I hope you don't ever let their ideas soak in on you."[65] The Almanacs, Guthrie warned, could tip either way—into the hearts of the movement or into the lap of the industry: "It was such a good stew that you old boys made and the best time was had right there too. Your songs and the stuff you wrote were worth a lot to either side and will attract

The Almanac Singers: One of many incarnations. Left to right: Agnes "Sis" Cunningham, Cisco Houston, Woody Guthrie, Pete Seeger, Bess Lomax Hawes. Photograph by Gjon Mili, 1943. Time and Life Pictures/Getty Images.

attention for you from both sides. The other side sucks you dry and don't give you nothing. Our side gives you the real stuff you need and whole train loads of good fresh material, but not much money. We aint on the money side and don't fight with money, but we use the Truth and its like a spring of cold water."[66]

Guthrie needn't have worried. The Almanacs were determined at the outset to signal their distance from the popular music industry and its celebrity system. Eschewing the temptations of individual stardom, they made a point of basing their collective identity on the manifesto of the Anonymous Movement, a group of Paris-based poets that included Hays's close friend Walter Lowenfels. This group had resolutely put their emphasis on "that which was written, and not upon the authors' reputation."[67] So it would be with the Almanacs' songs: all titles would be credited to the group, and their individual names would not even be listed on their album covers.

The Almanacs' cherished mission, above all, was to invigorate the American labor movement through song; but, as many in the antifascist Left found, the European war—and, especially, the Hitler–Stalin Pact—had forced them into an ideological double bind: hatred of fascism on the one hand, anti-interventionism on the other. Whatever one's position, it was impossible to remain mute over the drift toward war; hence one of the Almanacs' first efforts, Lampell's "The Ballad of October 16," which threw down the gauntlet in the vein of Guthrie's "Why Do You Stand There in the Rain?," taunting Roosevelt and "his boys on Capitol Hill," who were determined to railroad through "the conscription bill":

> Oh, Franklin Roosevelt told the people how he felt;
> We damn near believed what he said.
> He said, "I hate war, and so does Eleanor,
> But we won't be safe 'til everybody's dead."[68]

Largely on the popularity of this song in the leftist ranks, the Almanacs recorded their first album, *Songs for John Doe,* in mid-March of 1941. It was a mark of political nervousness even among the most die-hard leftists that, after Lomax and Nicholas Ray had convinced Eric Bernay of Keynote Records to record the album, he decided to release it under the hastily constituted label "Almanac Records." Such faintheartedness was unsurprising, given the album's content: a song depicting the sacrifice of the American everyman, John Doe, with "a bayonet sticking in his side," for a "reason" that "no one could say";[69] a song lauding "Billy Boy," the war resister who refuses to die "to defend Republic Steel" or "for Du Pont in Brazil";[70] a song condemning the government's intention to "plow under every fourth American boy" as though he were "no better than a cotton plant."[71]

With the appearance of *Songs for John Doe* to predictably favorable reviews in the *Daily Worker* and *New Masses* and predictably damning reviews in the mainstream press—including the still isolationist *Time* magazine, which grumbled that "honest U.S. isolationists" had received "some help from recorded music that they would rather *not* have received"[72]—the Almanacs awaited the inevitable backlash. Their anti-Roosevelt colors had been nailed so firmly to the mast that even the German-American Bund and Charles A. Lindbergh's America First could claim them as allies. Eleanor Roosevelt heard the record and declared it "in poor taste."[73] Seeger recalled the Librarian of Congress Archibald MacLeish playing it for the president: "And Franklin says,

'Can we forbid this?' And MacLeish says, 'Not unless you want to ignore the First Amendment to the Constitution.' And Roosevelt says, 'Well, only lefties are going to hear it, anyway.' And he was right."[74] In fact, Roosevelt and Seeger were both wrong, for no other record would be so frequently mentioned by wartime red-baiters as *Songs for John Doe*. Seeger recalled how the Almanacs even faced some physical abuse for their anti-interventionist stance: "For example, once [when I'm] singing in a Greenwich Village party about my opinions of Winston Churchill, a tall fellow comes right up to me and says loudly, 'I *like* Winston Churchill.' And he pulls back with a fist and whams me in the face and bangs my head against the brick chimney in back. I was not really hurt very badly. I probably got a black eye. His friends immediately hustled him away before he could rough me up any more."[75]

Quickly on the heels of *Songs for John Doe*, in the spring of 1941, the Almanacs released their second album, *Talking Union*, which showcased an expanded version of Guthrie and Seeger's "Union Maid" alongside a selection of songs that would become union stalwarts, including Florence Reece's "Which Side Are You On?," Jim Garland's "All I Want," and a pair of lyrics written by Lampell, Hays, and Seeger: the Guthrie-inspired "Talking Union" and "Get Thee Behind Me, Satan," the latter of which painted a crude picture of good union men resisting the seductions of nefarious bosses, sham company unions, and scabbing femmes fatales.

But if the release of *Talking Union* augured well for the Almanacs' career, Hitler's invasion of the Soviet Union almost ended it, momentarily leading the group to seriously consider disbanding. Even some of their closest allies in the Left rounded upon them for their strident anti-interventionism. A journalist for the then-progressive *New York Post*, Dorothy Millstone—a great Almanac champion—recalled: "After hearing that Russia had been invaded, I hung up the phone, and the first thing I did was break my Almanac records."[76] As Hays explained, the two previously separate battles—the long class war and the current European war—were no longer so distinct: "Our whole politics took a terrible shift from 'the Yanks ain't coming' to 'the Yanks ARE coming.' All of a sudden it became one war, instead of two, and there was some chance of beating fascism on its own ground, which everybody was for. But it sure knocked hell out of our repertoire."[77] Even the communist-hating Churchill had brought himself to call Russia's danger "our danger and the danger of the United States, just as the cause of any Russian fighting for his hearth and home is the cause of free men and free peoples in every quarter of the globe."[78] Guthrie told Seeger simply: "Churchill's flip-flopped. We got to flip-flop too."[79]

He joined the Almanacs in June 1941 as the Nazis pushed toward Leningrad—and just as the right-wing backlash against *Songs for John Doe* began to gather force. Unbeknownst to any of the Almanacs, they had been the subjects of lively discussion before the House Committee on Un-American Activities (the "Dies Committee") the previous month. The notorious red-baiting informer Hazel Huffman, a former WPA and Federal Theater Project employee, had attended a song-studded Riker's Island rally for the American Peace Mobilization (APM) and cited the Almanacs' "Ballad of October 16" and "Billy Boy"—as well as Guthrie's "Why Do You Stand There in the Rain?"—as examples of the composers' "filthy minds."[80] During her testimony, Huffman conferred a special honor upon Guthrie, singling him out for extensive, if factually incorrect, observation:

> According to reports, Woodie Guthrie, known as "Woodie," is a conscriptee and is now at Camp Dix.
> Now, Woodie Guthrie, a Communist, is a guitar-playing, ballad-singing entertainer, brought to New York by Will Greer [*sic*], also a Communist, and incidentally the grandson-in-law of Ella May Bloor, known as "Mother Bloor," Pennsylvania State secretary of the Communist Party.
> Woodie Guthrie was brought by Will Greer from Oklahoma and advertised as one of the "Joads," or migratory workers.
> During the past 3 or 4 years Woodie Guthrie has become one of the outstanding entertainers in the Communist Party, Communist Party fronts, and other left-wing organization meetings.

Huffman reported that at whatever APM meetings she infiltrated—whether in Lower Manhattan, Harlem, Brooklyn, or Queens—there was always "a great deal of rejoicing over the amount of good that Woodie Guthrie could do now that he was in the camp." She described Guthrie as "an entertainer of the droll, homespun variety that tells tales and plays his guitar. And I have heard him on numerous occasions and it is always with this definite Communist Party tinge, and in his singing and in his talk he has never tried to attempt to conceal the fact that he was the columnist for the *Daily Worker* or that he was a member of the Communist Party and represented it as such."[81]

Outside of the congressional committee room, the most damaging reaction to the Almanacs' output came from the Harvard political theorist Carl Friedrich, who savaged *Songs for John Doe* in a June essay for the *Atlantic Monthly*. In his hatchet job, titled "The Poison in Our System," Friedrich thundered: "These recordings are distributed under the innocuous appeal: 'Sing out for Peace.' Yet they are strictly subversive and illegal. Sung to such familiar tunes as 'Billy Boy,' they ridicule the American defense effort, democracy, and the army"—and he damned the Almanacs as either "Communist or Nazi financed."[82]

These right-wing critics were certainly overstating the case when they labeled the Almanacs a Communist front group. Seeger recalled only a brief flurry of official interest, when the Party had "a nice man come down from the Bronx" to give the Almanacs "a little instruction": "Once a week he'd say, 'What do you think of the news of the week?' We'd give our interpretation. He'd say, 'Well, have you thought of this?' Oh, no, we didn't think of that. 'Well, you should. Marx pointed out the class basis of things.' We met him five or ten times. Now we read the *Worker* every day."[83] Hays also affirmed the Almanacs' independence from the CPUSA: "When it came to shifts and turns in the Party line, I didn't pay any attention to them. I knew what I thought was right, and I wasn't gonna lose sleep over it. I'm sure Pete felt the same way. Woody would have said, 'The Almanacs—why that was just a bunch of old boys sitting around singing.'"[84] However, the Almanacs' output left them tinged with party-line associations regardless of what the Party would or wouldn't do for them.

In fact, CPUSA patronage was less significant to the Almanacs than the following they were quick to acquire from influential cultural figures on the Left. As the word spread of their growing collective, which migrated to a number of Greenwich Village locations before settling in the celebrated "Almanac House" on West 10th Street, radical celebrities such as Dashiell Hammett, Mike Gold, Mother Bloor, Marc Blitzstein, Rockwell Kent, and Walter Lowenfels began to frequent their gatherings. Elizabeth Gurley Flynn, the founding IWW activist eulogized by Joe Hill in his song "Rebel Girl," came to Almanac House to bestow a sacred relic upon the group: a briefcase containing Hill's personal papers—in effect this was "the Wobbly torch" being passed to them.[85] Most important, however, was the record of radical songs that the Almanacs either produced or collected, later described by Guthrie as "the biggest collection of labor and progressive songs in the world, possibly, a file running well past the ten thousand mark."[86]

Almanac House soon became the hub of the American folk revival that sprang from the group's distinctive form of musical gathering, the hootenanny, in which performers and a paying audience (having parted with 35 cents each) would happily mingle under the direction of that particular event's leader. For a time, the Almanacs attempted to survive on their "hoots," but as one close associate, the blues guitarist Brownie McGhee, recalled: "The best we could get was five dollars a night."[87] Guthrie and Seeger had first heard the term *hootenanny* at a Democratic fund-raiser in Seattle—as Guthrie promised, "Pete and me aim to put the world Hootenanny on the market"[88]—but there are conflicting versions of the word's origins. One of the organizers of the Seattle fund-raiser, Terry Pettus, recalled: "It is true that I suggested Hootenanny. I remembered that in my youth in southern Indiana the word Hootenanny was used to designate a party that just seemed to happen as against being planned. We also used metal checks, stamped in the denomination of 'ONE HOOT' which the customers bought and used to pay for food and drink."[89] Gordon Friesen, whose wife, "Sis" Cunningham, joined the Almanacs shortly after Guthrie, recalled a different origin for the word: "*Hootenanny* had been in use in rural America from way back to designate something you didn't know the exact name of. Say, for example, a couple of farm boys in Oklahoma might be overhauling a 'T-bone Ford' out behind the barn with pieces spread all around, and in fitting them back together one might say to the other, 'that thing-a-ma-jig goes here and that hootenanny goes there.'"[90]

Regardless of their nominal origin, the Almanacs' hootenannies immediately acquired a politically subversive association. As Guthrie later exaggerated: "The cops raided several of our first Hoots here because they'd never yet heard anybody hooler so loud outside of Belleview."[91] This subversive association would intensify as the anticommunist backlash gathered force in the 1950s, when prior attendance at an Almanac hoot could well lead to a summons before the House Un-American Activities Committee.

Guthrie's official tenure as an Almanac Singer commenced with a whirlwind of activity. Within two days of his arrival from the West Coast he joined them in recording two albums of traditional ballads and sea chanties before setting off with Seeger, Lampell, Hays, and Pete Hawes in a 1927 Buick sedan on a transcontinental singing tour in the service of the CIO. On the heels of the fascist victory in Spain and the embarrassment of the Hitler–Stalin Pact, the American Left could well do with a boost, and a brief one was provided by the six-year-old CIO, which launched a massive strike wave in 1941 that led to the unionization of Ford's River Rouge plant and the Little Steel firms. From New York and Philadelphia, into the heart of the blue-collar factory belt—Pittsburgh, Cleveland, Detroit, Milwaukee, Chicago, Minneapolis, and on to Denver and San Francisco—the core of the Almanacs traveled (now a quartet, Hawes having dropped out with pneumonia). Against their ideal objective, they found themselves entertaining mostly for middle-class radicals rather than working-class salts of the earth. Guthrie's own recollection of the tour, while fanciful in places, manages to convey the Almanacs' discomfiture: "We learned how hard it is to show a union official acrost a backroom table how much his rank and filers will like our singing. The fights were so hot in those days that the men would toss you out if they didn't like your songs. We got carried out on their shoulders acrost sixteen or eighteen states, and rolled back to NYC, I guess, just about the wisest gang of hungry labor songmakers in the whole 48."[92]

It was on this tour with the Almanacs that Guthrie consciously and conclusively "reconstructed himself as a CIO singer" (in Michael Denning's phrase).[93] Lampell's reflections on the tour bear this out: "Woody had a mystique about working, but he'd never really seen *industrial* workers before. I think it was the first time that Woody—or any of us—saw organized labor with this kind of strength. There was such a sense of excitement and dedication to everything they were doing . . . and the C.I.O. was almost like a religion."[94]

There were indeed some heady moments on the tour, notably an appearance before 100,000 Detroit auto workers and, gratifying to Guthrie especially, a performance for his own future union, the National Maritime Union: "In the big hall of the NMU Convention in Cleveland, the delegates cornered the Almanacs off and said, 'It's mighty high time somebody come that talks our lingo . . . and you guys talk right down our alley . . . and, by god, we aim to see to it that your Union Songs is put on every dam juke box in every single boarding house and beer joint on the Gulf.'"[95] Guthrie's embellishments notwithstanding, his recollections do indicate both the incipient strength of CIO organizing at that moment in American labor history and the official reaction that it inevitably prompted: "We . . . whaled away with 'The Ballad of Harry Bridges,' and the saloon in the basement complained of cement dropping in the beer, nine FBI stinkers dodged behind the depot to duck that Union Train. And the National Maritime Boys sung every chorus a hell of a lot louder than anything Hollywood ever done."[96]

In truth, to the extent that they sought to undermine the Almanacs' propagandist influence (which, as it turned out, was limited in any case), the FBI had some unlikely allies in the labor movement itself. As Seeger recalled: "When we walked down the aisle of a room where one thousand local members of the [San Francisco] longshoremen's union were meeting, we could see some of them turning around in surprise, and even disapproval. 'What the hell is a bunch of hillbilly singers coming in here for? We got work to do.'"[97] The real impact of the Almanac Singers on the consciousness of the labor movement may never be assessed, given that the recollections of the Almanacs themselves vary so widely. On the one hand, Lampell waxed lyrical: "Our *Talking Union* album didn't hit the juke boxes, didn't cause Victor or Columbia any sleepless nights, but it was being distributed by a lot of CIO affiliates. As a wildfire of strikes raged across the country, two and a half million Americans were walking picket lines. It excited us to hear that

['Union Maid'] was being sung by cotton mill workers in North Carolina, by strikers at the International Harvester tractor plant in Minneapolis, by hospital workers in Chicago and aircraft workers in Los Angeles."[98] Seeger, on the other hand, deflates such euphoria: "We had no great fame except in this narrow group of left-wingers; but we sang for a few hundred here and a few hundred there across the country. We stayed in people's homes or the cheapest hotels."[99] (Lampell recalled Guthrie informing him in Pittsburgh: "We're staying at some place Pete found where you pay the cockroach and step on the landlord").[100]

One factor in the group's lukewarm reception was their overly conscious proletarianism, which was certainly an irritation to some within the union movement. Even Seeger's wife Toshi was concerned, telling him: "Look, you're not a working man, you're just pretending. Everybody sees through it."[101] Over two decades later, Seeger himself recalled: "There I was, trying my best to shed my Harvard upbringing, scorning to waste money on clothes other than blue jeans. But Lead Belly always had a clean white shirt and starched collar, well-pressed suit and shined shoes. He didn't need to affect that he was a workingman."[102]

Indeed, in attempting to inaugurate America's first consciously proletarian music movement, the Almanacs were initially compromised by their selective, highly restricted conception of who belonged in the American workforce or even what an American worker looked like. Lampell had declared on behalf of the group: "We are trying to give back to the people the songs of the workers. Their songs have been stolen from them by the bourgeoisie."[103] But as a later member of the group, Arthur Stern, recalled, the Almanacs came in for an abrupt education from "the workers" themselves. On one occasion, dressed according to their idealized conception of proletarian fashion (based on Guthrie's habitual, but hardly exclusive, wardrobe of denim, flannel shirts, and work boots), the Almanacs played a benefit for the Meat Cutters' Union at the Hotel New Yorker, with Stern's parents among the audience:

> The lights lowered and we started to sing our first number, and somewhere in that first number we heard this crash onstage. It was followed by another crash, and then hot and heavy. They were throwing china off the tables, actually skimming plates at us. They were literally doing this. It was because we looked like shit and all these people were in evening clothes. My mother had her hair blued and my father was dressed up, for once in his life, in good clothes. Working-class people dress up and they don't want their entertainers to look worse than they do during the work week, and we were putting on this big romantic, proletarian affectation. They finally told us to get the hell off and leave. They never even paid us.[104]

Bess Hawes recalled a more "kindly" upbraiding from an elderly union man, who told her: "When we go out for an evening, even just to a union meeting, we clean up and dress up a bit so as to present ourselves well. And when you youngsters come in here in jeans and with your hair not combed it makes us feel like you don't think we were worth your dressing up for."[105] Such a revelation, Hawes reflected, was "a shocker" to the group; the issue of dress soon "took up a number of organizing meetings."[106]

With the benefit of hindsight, one can pinpoint other creative and practical pressures that the Almanacs faced. There was the inevitable tension in the collective songwriting and decision-making process—a fact apparently missed by a *People's World* journalist, Don Russell, who sat in on an Almanac creative session in the summer of 1941. As Russell described it, it was as genial as it was free-flowing: "Woody and Pete strummed guitar and banjo. They were organizing a new song. They all contributed—Woody a line, Pete a line, Lee a suggestion. Millard was at a portable typewriter, banging out the lines as they evolved." Gradually, a first draft and some revisions emerged:

> New phrases came from the guitar or banjo, music phrases tossed in, very nonchalantly. Sometimes while Pete talked he strummed his banjo catching at a new line. Almost constantly his fingers plucked lightly at the strings. Woody, leaning back on a couch, suddenly broke out with a brand new verse. He jumped to his feet, sang the words, accompanied himself on the "geetar." The verse went down on the typewriter—and then it was revised.
>
> At the end of about an hour's work, four verses were completed. They got together and sang the completed song.[107]

This jolly description seems to belie the frustrations that Guthrie immediately began to feel upon joining the group—frustrations that he expressed to himself if not to the other Almanacs. In a note jotted below his lyrics to "My Union County Gal," he unburdened himself:

> Almanacs: We've figured out some pretty good songs, and a good many of songs, when you come right down to it. But I've noticed here lately that there is a lot of lost motion. We gang around and sing. Make up new verses, and whole new songs as we go, but we are making a mistake by not taking time out to write these down. This is because we're having such a good time that we just sort of let it ooze over. Nine tenths of this leaks back into the cistern as fast as we draw it out. I think it would work a lot better for you to set down and have regular song writing sessions with your own self, and haul the results in to put before the bunch while they are singing. Even a little start on paper can be added onto, overhauled, fixed up.[108]

Guthrie chafed at the give-and-take of group discussion: "I like talk and speeches about songs, but too much broth spoils the cook. Let most of our theory and lectures be about some one song at a time, while it's wheeling down the assembly line . . . then we'll have songs piling up."[109] In point of fact, none of the Almanacs were overly fond of "theory and lectures," so it is difficult to account for Guthrie's irritation beyond his own native impatience. The atmosphere certainly cannot have been improved by Guthrie's sense of himself as the professional and the others as the amateurs: "Poor day today. Din't write but 3 Union Songs. Oh, well, that'll keep the deputy song writers busy another 6 months."[110]

From this elevated position, Guthrie soon took on the responsibility of instructing his fellow Almanacs in the means and mechanics of building a body of songs that would provide "the answer to Tobacco Road and The Grapes of Wrath"—songs that would reply "not only to the grinding voices of us Oakies, but to the questions of city workers as well."[111] Writing from the West Coast in July of 1941 to Hawes and the others who had stayed behind in New York, he expressed his concerns about the dangers of shoving the political line down the throats of "the People." He described Lampell's attempts at coaching some aspiring young writers in Hollywood's progressive Mobile Theater group: "Mill flew loose at all of their material and put it to a severe, critical, and honest test, as to Political content, composition, etc., (all of them other big long words), and I don't know if any of the We the People Stuff got through or not, I think not; and they had a new ditty or two worked up that they called, Man with a Union Button which wouldn't have passed even any of the tests in an Okie audience on a fast freight."[112]

Beyond issuing his solemn injunction against sermonizing, Guthrie charged the Almanacs with nothing less than the task of modernizing the American folk song: "Our job aint so much to go way back into history, that's already been done, and we caint spare the time to do it all over again. Our job is the Here & now, Today. This week. This month. This year. But we've got to try and include a Timeless Element in our songs. Something that will not tomorrow be gone with the wind. But something that will be as true as it is today. The secret of a lasting song is not the record of current events, but their timeless element which may be contained in their chorus or last line or elsewhere."[113]

Seeger, for one, had confessed to the Almanacs in a moment of insecurity, "I wonder if we really have the right slant on the future of American music— us using so much folk music when jazz is so popular."[114] Guthrie was adamant: "Boys, what I think needs to be done to old time folk songs is not to give over an inch to jazz or swing, as far as the melody goes, but what we've got to do is to bring American Folk Songs up to date. This don't mean to complicate our music a tall, but simply to industrialize, and mechanize the words."[115]

Having thus stubbornly banned consideration of the two most popular forms of American music (unlike songwriters such as "Yip" Harburg and Vern Partlow, the latter of whom declared himself quite happy to use "jive" and "popular stuff" for the radical cause),[116] Guthrie advised feeding the American workers on a steady, Soviet-inspired diet of "wheels, triggers, springs, bearings, motors, engines, boilers, and factories—because these are the things that arm the workers and these are the source of the final victory of Public Ownership."[117] A charitable interpretation might be that Guthrie's intention here was to rescue the Almanacs (if not the wider urban folk revival) from a self-limiting fetish for all things rural. But it was fortunate for the Almanacs— and for Guthrie as an individual songwriter—that neither they nor he ever acted seriously upon his advice, for they could hardly have won the hearts of the American proletariat by singing the praises of "whistles, steam, boilers, shafts, cranks, operators, tuggers, pulleys, engines, and all of the well known gadgets that make up a modern factory."[118] Guthrie himself soon backed away from this suicidally mechanistic program, proposing the next month that the Almanacs consider writing "parodies on popular tunes" such as Irving Berlin's "Blue Skies" (he had never forgiven Berlin for "God Bless America"): "Parodies isn't exactly what I mean, rather, union words."[119]

In spite of such mixed signals, and whatever their petty differences and frictions, Guthrie and his fellow Almanacs were solidly united on the issue of the war, especially now that the Soviet Union had been invaded. America's Hitler-friendly, Roosevelt-hating anti-interventionists fell immediately into Guthrie's newly trained sights, beginning with Charles A. Lindbergh, whose America First organization simply meant, to Guthrie, "America next."[120] In his song "Lindbergh," Guthrie also paints the rabble-rousing, racist demagogue Father Charles Coughlin with "gas on his stomach and Hitler on the brain" and the American Federation of Labor's wavering leader, John L. Lewis, as "sittin' astraddle a fence."[121]

But Guthrie's main target was Hitler, whose capacity for evil initially proved more than a match for Guthrie's powers of description and attack. His earliest anti-Hitler writings were in effect transparent schoolyard taunts:

> O' tell me, Mister Hitler, what's that little thing under your nose?
> O' tell me, Mister Hitler, what's that little thing under your nose?
> That little bit of fuzz won't keep you warm
> When you're among them Moscow snows.[122]

In one scenario, Guthrie has his narrator falling into a New York sewer and conversing with some patriotic rats bent on flushing out the "5th column men"—the "Isolaters," "Hesitaters," and "Long Waiters" among whose number Guthrie himself would have been counted until so recently.[123] Suddenly, full tilt into the lending and leasing that he had so vociferously condemned, Guthrie ventured a promise to "the German workers" who were already, surely, "sick of this war":

> You can hear the Allied factories roar;
> London will have planes. Moscow'll get guns
> To blast the hell out of Hitler's huns.
>   Outstorm the stormtroopers. Lay fascism in its 6x3.[124]

These and other song texts indicate the awkwardness with which Guthrie, in line with the newly interventionist American Left, sought to reflect his abrupt "flip-flop" and bid farewell to the antiwar sentiment that, with the exception of the struggle against Franco, had generally characterized the Left's view of the European war. Guthrie groped to find a credible voice to vent his hatred of Hitler, never really succeeding until he stumbled on a home-grown fascist of whom he could speak with authority. In a direct analogy to Hitler, he drew on a legendary "railroad bull" called "East Texas Red": "This is a song I made up about the stories told to me while I was on the freights down in East Texas and Louisiana. People all up and down the lines, from the Katy Flyer to the S.P., knew about East Texas Red. He chased me out of a box car one day, but I didn't know who he was at the time. East Texas Red was a bully and he thought like a fascist (if they think at all). He lived like a fascist and he died like a fascist."[125] In this ballad, the railroad thug, with "Blackjack and club, brass knuckles and gun," chases away three hungry hoboes from a train yard after kicking over their meager stew pot and faces their revenge a year to the day later, in the same spot:

> Red went to his knees and hollered, Please don't pull that trigger on me;
> I did not get my business fixed—, but he never got his say;
> A gun wheeled out of an overcoat and it played the old one-two,
> And Red was dead as the other two men sat down to eat their stew.[126]

This was a foretaste of the pitiless vengefulness with which Guthrie would treat the Axis powers throughout his wartime imaginings.

Guthrie's growing war fever was ratcheted up on October 31, 1941, when a German U-boat sank the USS *Reuben James,* a convoy escort ship on neutrality patrol off the coast of Iceland; 115 sailors lost their lives. Upon reading of the disaster, Guthrie penned what would be the Almanacs' most rousing and popular war song, "The Sinking of the Reuben James." Guthrie had initially aimed at memorializing each of the drowned sailors before his fellow Almanacs persuaded him that such a catalog of names would make for an interminable song. Collectively they arrived at the chorus that would catapult the group into the American consciousness as war writers: "What were their names, tell me, what were their names? / Did you have a friend on the good *Reuben James?*"[127]

Mike Quin reported in the *Daily Worker* on a trip with Guthrie into the New York subways to hear him sing about the *Reuben James* in November 1941: "It was like a newspaper jumping free of the stale flatness of the page and singing at you." He described "the funniest look [that] came into the faces of those people standing around there. They were half scared and half fascinated":

> People dropped their newspapers and stared at us with that peculiar, half-scared look. Then a lot of them smiled. But their eyes were very thoughtful.
>
> And there we were, banging and scraping and clattering through a tube, with the Hudson River over our heads and tired men and women jammed all around us.
>
> Woody's fingers plunked the strings extra hard and his voice cut through the noise with the story of the Reuben James. Pretty soon other people were joining in on the chorus.
>
> And that night, hundreds of men and women went home with those words ringing over and over in their brains: "Did you have a friend on the good Reuben James?"

Quin concluded with a laudation: "And if anyone should ask me: What's the most effective way of distributing a leaflet? Or if anyone should ask me: what's the best possible way to have a good time? I'd give them both the same answer: Go singing in the subways with Woody Guthrie."[128]

Although Guthrie did warn in "Reuben James" that "our mighty battleships will steam the bounding main," the song, like "Lindbergh," stopped short of actually arguing for military intervention.[129] For now, Guthrie was content to stoke the psychological fires of the war buildup in preparation for the battle that he assumed was inevitable. In November 1941, when he took it upon himself to advise the nightclub impresario Max Gordon on how to stage a Josh White performance at the Village Gate, he argued that "there hadn't ought to be anything [in the program] that would encourage strikes in National Defense Industries, nor to run the morale of the US Army uniform down." He had it all worked out:

Josh could sing songs of how proud he is to be working in Industry to Beat Hitler, how great it is to wear the Uniform of the good old Red White and Blue . . . and in mentioning the Army, or the war, the feeling should be this: Just about the best thing a man can wear is an Army uniform—call for Negro Rights, equal chance, equal pay, equal treatment, but dont run down any branch of the armed service—, because a Uniform and a gun to beat Hitler with is a wonderful thing. A song by Josh about looking for a job in production for Uncle Sam's defense would be a good thing, and even mentioning sending lots of help to everybody, everywhere, of every color, that's fighting to bring old Hitler down . . . this could be worked on.[130]

Guthrie's readiness to provide such unsolicited advice may well have been aggravating; but none could deny that he had been on the mark with "Reuben James." The following month, the Japanese ensured that the song's belligerent threat would be carried out: Uncle Sam's battleships were soon steaming "the bounding main." The attack on Pearl Harbor gave the Almanac Singers—for the briefest of moments—a wider audience than they ever dreamed of.

4. Union War

On the afternoon of Sunday, December 7, 1941, Arthur Stern interrupted the Almanacs' weekly hoot in progress to announce that the Japanese had attacked Pearl Harbor. The stunned silence that hung in the air reflected not only the shock of a nation suddenly thrown from the sidelines into full-scale war. For the Almanacs, it signaled a new strategic dilemma. Lee Hays's rueful observation of six months before was once again apt: events had for a second time "knocked hell" out of the Almanacs' repertoire.[1] The CPUSA president, Earl Browder, swiftly committed the Party to a no-strike pledge intended to last for the war's duration; so on top of the peace songs already lost, the Almanacs were now obliged to put a hold on any "overtly militant class-conscious union songs."[2] All songs—union or not—were now meant to bolster the antifascist war effort and downplay, if not ignore, the unfinished struggle over workers' rights, wages, and conditions. As the Almanacs scrambled to adapt, their previous repertoire remained firmly lodged in the minds of those militant unionists who resisted the Party's shift and continued to call for songs like "Talking Union" and "Get Thee Behind Me, Satan." Meanwhile, the group's reactionary critics continued to cite their prewar lyrics in a gleeful bid to expose them as hypocrites.

Bess Hawes recalled the period as one of "almost never-ending argumentation, debate, and planning meetings" in Almanac House.[3] Guthrie's particular impulse, she said, was to affect amusement over "the curves of history which were wiping out our repertoire."[4] Guthrie's initial response to the U.S. declaration of war on Japan was a self-mocking parody, "New Situation":

I started to sing a song
To the entire population.
But I ain't a-doing a thing tonight
On account of this new situation.

He presented the Almanacs' new predicament as a burlesque love affair:

I fell in love with the prettiest gal
In all this big wide nation.
But her daddy won't let me go with her
In view of the new situation.[5]

Drawing on the scenario of one of his favorite jokes—the one about Mama and Papa Rabbit chased by dogs into a hollow log, determined to "stay here until we outnumber them"[6]—Guthrie concluded the song with the lovers copulating their way to an Allied victory, producing enough children to "outnumber the Axis gang / In view of the new situation."[7]

However, a more serious response underlined Guthrie's awareness that the Almanacs would have some explaining to do, as he attempted to rationalize the second of the group's "flip-flops" in six months: "The world ain't all good or all bad, things happen fast, and change around. . . . Wars break out and folks are first on one side, then on another, because they believe in something, because they hate something, and because they get together with other people that think like they do—and gradually, out of all our isms, new isms, and new songs grow like weeds and flowers."[8] Thus, in Guthrie's reading, the Almanacs' most recent turnabout—far from signaling a failure of nerve or a craven jump to the Party's tune—was a principled stance anchored in fidelity and solidarity. Nonetheless, he was keenly aware of the bizarre swings that his own ideological compass had been obliged to take in a breathtakingly short time. As he joked: "I want to raise the slogan 'Continue In the Highways of Marx and Roosevelt and Free Oklahoma If Possible!'"[9]

For the Almanacs, the only way forward was to write and sing themselves into yet another position consistent with the core values of the movement while, if possible, maintaining their political credibility. Consequently, as Guthrie later recalled: "We made up songs against Hitler and Fascism, homemade and imported. We sang songs about our Allies and made up songs to pay honor and tribute to the story of the trade union workers around the world."[10] As America's war fever coalesced, the Almanacs were catapulted into the national spotlight, aided substantially by such patrons as Alan Lomax and Nicholas Ray, both now attached to the Office of War Information (OWI), and Norman Corwin of CBS. Allied troops overseas were bolstered by the Almanacs singing on shortwave radio; on the home front, 30 million people tuned in to Corwin's prime-time coast-to-coast series *This Is War,* broadcast by all the major networks and starring the Almanac Singers as they belted out "Round and Round Hitler's Grave." The group's "seven months of heatless nights and watery soup" gave way to stylish Sunday hoots covered by the national press (including *Life* magazine) and a raft of industry offers.[11] In the wake of *This Is War* and the rousing broadcast success of "Reuben James," the Almanacs appeared on such radio programs as the U.S. Navy's *The Treasury Hour,* CBS's *We the People,* and NBC's *Labor for Victory,* the latter alternately sponsored by the mutually antagonistic American Federation of Labor (AFL) and the CIO in a gesture of wartime unity foreshadowing their eventual amalgamation. Decca offered the Almanacs a recording contract, the William Morris Agency offered them a management contract (and paid their dues to the American Federation of Musicians), and the exclusive Rainbow Room nightclub atop Rockefeller Center arranged an audition—an event that went well until the suggestion that the group don outlandish barnyard costumes prompted Guthrie, Lampell, and Seeger to improvise a series of disrespectful lyrics about John D. Rockefeller. Even this nose thumbing appeared to work in the Almanacs' favor: the booking was theirs for the taking.

The Almanacs started up a second branch of their outfit in Detroit, where Arthur Stern, Bess Lomax, Butch Hawes, and Charlie Polacheck held forth in song for the United Auto Worker locals in the Plymouth, Dodge, Ford, and Vickers plants. Alan Lomax reported to Guthrie that Eleanor Roosevelt was again listening to Almanac songs. She now "thought that they were swell," Lomax beamed: "She is playing them for her OCD [Office of Civilian Defense] staff, and I think their fame will spread abroad. Besides, the 'News and Special Events' man from BBC was here, and took a copy of [the largely Guthrie-authored] 'Taking It Easy' with the intention of getting it played on their network."[12]

Guthrie invested great hope in the Almanacs' ability to sponsor rural musicians and bring them to a wider audience, in aid of both the proletarian struggle and the war effort. When the Mississippi bluesman Son House accepted an invitation from Lomax to come to New York in February 1942, Guthrie wrote to him on behalf of the Almanacs promising "a railroad ticket, and maybe a few dollars to live on" and offering some unsolicited advice: "Make up a lot of good songs, honest, hard working peoples kind. Make up some good blues that tell all about your part of the country, the crops you grow, weather, the people, what they talk about, and their good and bad times, and the good things in life that they hope for, and how they hope to get them." Guthrie reasserted what he assumed should be House's priority: "The biggest job right now is to beat Hitler, and we're going to have to hear from every part of the United States, and find out how to get every ounce of our strength together. Your songs that talk for your part of the nation, will be a big help, because that is what songs are supposed to do. Good dance tunes, square dances, roadhouse, and church house music, the low down blues, courting songs—get a lot of every kind."[13]

Guthrie also saw great potential in the Almanacs' work on behalf of isolated union locals attempting to forge links with other unions everywhere—another small step on the road to the elusive One Big Union envisaged by the IWW. As he wrote to Marjorie Mazia (soon to become his second wife): "The Teachers Union is buying a series of Sunday Afternoon shows to be put on by the Almanacs, including as Almanacs, Sis, Brownie, Sonny, Lee, and me; and we are going to hire Leadbelly, Bart [van der Schelling], and others to appear regular every Sunday and other singers just once in a while. The Teachers Union wants to weld a solid link of friendship between their own organization and every other level of union members all over the country, so they're planning each Sunday's show to be directed to appeal to a different group of workers and their part in winning the war. I think songs can very well do the job."[14] Lomax agreed with Guthrie's assessment of the Almanacs' importance, writing to his superiors in the Music Division of the Library of Congress: "The group with which Mr. Guthrie is working is continually experimenting with the development and extension of the medium of American folk-song, and the record of their experiments will have much historical significance."[15]

In truth, however, just as such optimistic scenarios were being envisaged, the Almanacs were already on the road to their dissolution. They were to enjoy only the briefest moment of popularity outside of their habitual audience base of diehard leftists, unionists, and New York intellectuals and bohemians. In addition to the loss of various members to the armed forces and civilian agencies, lack of support from the leadership in the communist movement—in particular the CPUSA and the militant trade unions—progressively starved the Almanacs of their income and sapped their energy. Seeger recalled: "We were orphans. . . . There was no organization that really made themselves responsible for us."[16] Consequently, the group often found themselves casting about for both theoretical and practical direction, subjecting themselves to painful self-help sessions on everything from Marxist-Leninist theory to "How to Write a Good Workers' Song."[17]

It is therefore unsurprising that the Almanacs' greatest popular success should have come when they reluctantly narrowed their attention to the war effort. It was as war propagandists that they won their widest audience—and it was as war propagandists that they lost it, helped along by the red-baiting press. Only three days after their acclaimed broadcast on *This Is War,* the New York *World-Telegram* reported that "the Almanac singers have long been the favorite balladeers of the Communists and their official publications, the *Daily Worker* and *New Masses.*"[18] That same day, the *New York Post* sneered, "'Peace' Choir Changes Tune," hearkening back to the strident anti-interventionism of *Songs for John Doe.*[19] The New York *Daily News* joined the chorus, condemning "these lads and lassies who, before Russia went to war against Germany, had nothing but the ugliest things to say about F.D.R., Congress and other things American."[20] For the *Chicago Daily Tribune,* the Almanacs' "anti-this and anti-that" stance was perfectly suited to "the OWI propaganda that life in the good old U.S.A. is just a continuous round of joining unions."[21] All these articles drew heavily on Carl Friedrich's savage *Atlantic Monthly* essay of June 1941.[22]

The Almanacs were in fact fortunate to have withstood the red-baiting for as long as they did, given that they had caught the eye of the Dies Committee as early as May 1941. The FBI was particularly slow on the uptake, although bureau officials had consigned *Songs for John Doe* to a file labeled "GRAMO-PHONE RECORDS OF A SEDITIOUS NATURE" in October 1941. Between the covers of that file it was reported that one Lt. Col. A. R. Bolling (Boston, Mass.) had heard from "an officer on duty in Washington, D.C.," who had himself heard "a group of gramophone records, which while tuneful, were highly seditious" and "were apparently put out by some Communist organization which had its identity under the name of the ALMANAC SINGERS." Bolling went on to advise "that the songs were intended to stir up objection to the Selective Service Act and to the declared policy of all our aid to Britain."[23] In a wild goose chase worthy of the Keystone Kops, the FBI agents scurried after their leads from suspected producers to distributors and back again across three states before storming the office of Keynote Records in mid-1942. There they were informed that the "subversive" recordings they were seeking had already acquired the status of "collectors' items"; the Almanacs had moved on since making that record.[24] (The most entertaining excerpt from the file has J. Edgar Hoover in a flap with his agents over some Almanac records that had been shipped to New Haven as incriminating evidence, only to arrive in pieces. "You should see to it that records and other breakable material are more carefully packed, in order that incidents of this type will not recur," he scolds.)[25] In spite of the slapstick, the red-baiting took its toll, and in swift succession the Almanacs lost their OWI broadcasts, their William Morris and Decca offers, and the Rainbow Room.

Guthrie's own personality and his increasing conflicts with the Almanacs—as well as their close associates—also throw light on the tensions that contributed to their unraveling. Some of these conflicts could simply be attributed to his moodiness, as the composer Earl Robinson recalled: "He could be dull and longwinded, boring to distraction at times. And he could be most cooperative and creative with other folksingers, congenial listeners, and working people. But Woody was an excellent entertainer only when he felt good about himself and his audience. He'd take out his unhappiness on his public, especially if he thought them inattentive, or slick and upper-class. Depending on how he felt at that moment, he could be impossible to work with. I worked and sang with him in all these moods. I have been exhilarated, and frustrated."[26] Robinson found himself picking up the pieces when Guthrie walked away from a collaborative project after a fight with Lampell, leaving him to "scream [Guthrie's] song 'The Great Historical Bum' through a hurting voice" on the opening night of the Lampell and Guthrie review *It's All Yours* (1942).[27] Lampell, for his part, had grown particularly tired of Guthrie's endless lectures on musical authenticity:

> "Leastways I don't write songs about stuff I don't know the first doggone thing about. You never done it, and you never lived it."
>
> "You were never on the *Reuben James* either."
>
> "You're as bad as Bess," Woody snorted, "singing 'House of the Rising Sun' when she's never been within ten country miles of a cathouse."
>
> "Woody, this argument's getting awful damn old."[28]

Guthrie's hypersensitivity certainly got the best of him at times. He complained that the other Almanacs went out of their way to "misunderstand" him, to twist his words into the false assertion that "music and politics don't mix"; consequently, he was "voted down in meetings over and over."[29] At the same time, in spite of his unjust accusation of the Almanacs' obsession with theorizing, Guthrie complained of not *enough* politicization. As the Almanacs "commenced arguing amongst themselves, as to who done what to who," he wrote bitchily, they "let their work drop from a high political level, almost to a low, gossiping personal basis, and it was this tone that discolored even the good work, the memory of the good work that should have given them the drive to pull out of any old rut, and go on down the road to better work."[30]

There were also particular issues that set Guthrie against the collective grain. He wrote to Marjorie complaining of the low musical standards of the Almanacs' hoots and shows: "To yank a girl out of the Bronx and shove a banjo in her hand and say, Come on and play and sing! That's funny, but it's not according to the facts. I don't care how good a Marxist or Leninist she was, Lord knows, I never sing nor play one single word or note that is not for the help of the working classes to know more, feel better, rise up, and to own and control this world they have built, but still, could you take the best Marxist in the country and trot them out onto a stage after two or three rough rehearsals and yell, Dance! It would be just as foolish to grab a dancer off of a stage and walk them into a steel furnace and holler, Blast and fire!"

Almanac performances, he said, had become virtual free-for-alls: "Well, before long, the Almanacs consisted of a lot more people that could not sing than could. I'll read the New Masses and listen to lectures, and give thanks to the farmers and factory workers when I eat a meal or put on my clothes, but when it comes to singing, I want to be on the stage and I want them to be in the audience."[31] This was a particularly hypocritical objection, if Lee Hays is to be believed; he recalled a girlfriend of Guthrie's who could play nothing but a D chord on the guitar: "He used to take her out on bookings, and all of a sudden everything we were playing was in the key of D—and she wasn't even playing the other chords. But every time we'd come around to the D-chord, she'd wham the hell out of it."[32]

Other projects demonstrated Guthrie's awkwardness in collaboration— sometimes with comical results. In late 1941 the Popular Front choreographer Sophie Maslow devised a dance work, *Folksay,* partially based on *Dust Bowl Ballads.* Maslow invited Guthrie to contribute with voice and guitar. As he wrote of their earliest rehearsals: "After she got done with her dances she tried to teach me how to sing these same two songs like they was on the phonograph record. You'd be surprised how hard it was to sing a song the same way twice. . . . I always just run my bluff, and sung them how I felt them."[33] For Maslow, whose dancers naturally relied on a predictable, secure rhythmic and metric pattern for their rehearsals and performances, Guthrie's musical casualness was infuriating. Nora Guthrie recalled what eventually became part of the family lore: "The first rehearsal was a complete disaster, as Woody could/would not play the song the same way as he recorded it. Nor could he even play it through the same way twice. Rushing to get to their places, dancers were bumping into each other, falling all over each other, and being thrown up in the air with no one there to catch them on the way down."[34] Guthrie was initially intransigent. "Well, I'm a folksinger," he sniffed, "and if I want to clear my throat, I play a few chords and do it, and if I want to think of the words for the next stanza, I play some more chords while I am thinking about it, and if I want to leave town, I get up and leave town."[35] As far as he was concerned, if there were any adjustments to be made, it was the dancers who should be making them: "If a song is just the same number of pauses and holds and the same r[h]ythm all of the way through it dont give a dancer much of a chance to show how good a dancer he is."[36]

It was Maslow's desperate appeal to her dance colleague Marjorie Mazia to take Guthrie in hand and force him to sort out his timing that instigated the Guthrie–Mazia courtship. Curiously, Guthrie later told Marjorie: "I know it made several Almanacs pretty sore to see me rehearsing with a dance group"[37]—an odd claim to make, given that the Almanacs had themselves collaborated with Maslow on some dance programs with "a WIN-THE-WAR spirit and theme."[38]

Thus, if the Almanacs were indeed "sore" with Guthrie, the reason lay somewhere beyond his dance collaborations. There was his inflated sense of his proletarian legitimacy, which intensely irritated the Almanacs and others in their circle. Lampell recalled Guthrie rounding on Bess Lomax "for being a pampered, middle-class, college-educated daddy's pet who didn't know what real work meant."[39] Lomax, for her part, would give as good as she got, mocking Guthrie in a parody of his own "Great Historical Bum":

> My name is Woody Guthrie, I'm a great hysterical bum.
> I'm highly saturated with whiskey, rye and rum.
> I've wrote a million pages and I've never read a one.
> And that's about the biggest thing that I have ever done.[40]

Gordon Friesen, Guthrie's fellow Oklahoman, was equally dismissive of Guthrie's proletarian pretensions. "Woody, what on earth are you talking about?" he once jibed. "You never harvested a grape in your life. You're an intellectual, a poet—all this singin' about jackhammers, if you ever got within five feet of a jackhammer it'd knock you on your ass. You scrawny little bastard, you're shitting the public: you never did a day's work in your life."[41] Friesen later recalled: "Once I went with Woody to a bar on the Hudson River frequented by longshoremen. He tried to play and sing for them, but they told us to get the hell out of there. This experience led me to doubt the Guthrie legend that he had played his guitar and sung in bars all over the United States, with the working-class people crowding around him and soaking in his every word along with their boilermakers."[42]

Guthrie's greatest difficulty lay with the Almanacs' credo of anonymity, so at odds with his status as the celebrated Okie bard. It was a tension visibly signaled in his notations to the song "Dig a Hole":

> Song By Woody Guthrie
> Almanac Singers
>
> Woody Guthrie sings
> verses—
> Almanac Singers
>   join chorus[43]

Guthrie himself admitted: "Our hottest arguments came up not so much about the words and the tunes of our Almanac songs, but as to the credits and the notices, the copyrights. I was always highly in favor of keeping the personal name of the Almanac on the credit lines, like, 'Union Maid by Woody Guthrie and the Almanac Singers'. Some of us debated that it ought to be, 'Union Maid by the Almanac Singers.'"[44] Lampell recalled the tension and the increasingly poisoned atmosphere in Almanac House: "Woody would slouch into the meetings with his own agenda, which consisted of mocking anything we wrote that sounded 'citified' and angrily rebelling against attributing the composition of all our songs to The Almanac Singers. 'Hell's fire, when I write a song it damn well ought to have my name stuck to it. If you guys toss in two-three words, that don't mean piss.'"[45] Bess Hawes's backhanded compliment likewise betrays her exasperation with Guthrie's single-minded ambition, which, whenever it surfaced, threatened to cast the collective efforts into the shade: "[His] persona and brilliance and total devotion to getting the world to listen to him none of the rest of us could ever match."[46]

Guthrie's uncertain position vis-à-vis the foreground and background on the Almanac stage was also colored by the preferential patronage of Alan Lomax, who, even as he argued for the significance of the Almanacs as a revolutionary American collective, pushed Guthrie to the forefront of his preservationist mission. "The continuing documentation of this most unusual of American ballad makers," he wrote to his superiors at the Library of Congress, "has a very great importance; and no commercial company's release will provide for us the sort of material which will some day make a study of his repertory and his continued production of new songs possible."[47] While none could deny Lomax's sincerity in his hearty wishes for the Almanacs' success, he was doubly protective of Guthrie, voicing his concerns over the group's prewar reputation as fierce anti-FDR isolationists with the mark of the Kremlin all over them. He told Guthrie: "It's very important, I think, for you to hurry up and change your name, and for heavens sake make it a good old countrified name like 'Oklahoma Rangers' or something of the sort. Your chief point of contact in America is that of the background of the American soil and American folk songs."[48] Guthrie and Lomax had discussed the possibility of "The Headline Singers" as an alternative name, much to the chagrin of Pete Seeger, who viewed any name change as a "sell-out."[49] On mature reflection, however, Lomax advised Guthrie: "Don't become 'Headline Singers,' even though you may be singing the headlines."[50] Contrary and self-promotional as ever, Guthrie promptly outlined to Marjorie his new plans as the Almanacs fell apart:

WOODY GUTHRIE'S
HEADLINE
SINGERS

Woody GUTHRIE–LEADBELLY–SONNY TERRY–BROWNIE MCGHEE

WORK SONGS*WAR SONGS*UNION SONGS*
FOLK SONGS*BALLADS*FOR MEETINGS, PARTIES, RALLIES[51]

(The FBI apparently took a keen interest in Guthrie's new plans, inserting into the Almanacs' file a clipping from the *Daily Worker*—proudly stamped "Clipped at the Seat of Government"—that announced: "Woody Guthrie, perhaps the most talented of all the Almanacs, certainly the most prolific and the most popular, has started his own group, called the Headline Singers.")[52]

The record of Guthrie's conflicts with the Almanac Singers has contributed to the critical speculation that, in the end, he withdrew his labor from the collective project in order to devote his attention—in prima donna fashion—to the completion of his autobiographical novel *Bound for Glory*.[53] At first glance, the Almanacs' recording history would appear to bear out this claim. Before the breaking of the Hitler–Stalin Pact, Guthrie had collaborated on only one Almanac song, "Union Maid"; of the twenty-four sides recorded between June 1941 and the last Almanac recording session in June 1942, only "Reuben James," "Round and Round Hitler's Grave," "Boomtown Bill," "Keep That Oil A-Rollin'," and "Hard, Ain't It Hard" have been identified as Guthrie songs or collaborations. (Guthrie was mistakenly given writing credit for Sarah Ogan's "Babe O' Mine"[54] and sang on the fourteen traditional songs making up the Almanacs' *Deep Sea Chanties and Whaling Ballads* and *Sod Buster Ballads*.)[55] In spite of this appearance of a grudging contribution, however, the archival evidence makes it clear that Guthrie actually devoted enormous energy to a stable of wartime songs, many of which were earmarked for the Almanacs but were never recorded and possibly never performed by them as the various group members dispersed and peeled off into military service or other activities.

More than anything, these songs reveal Guthrie fashioning a conception of the war that would, above all else, embrace the major aims of the American communist movement: antifascism, anticapitalism, anti-imperialism, and international labor solidarity. The war, as he came to see it, would provide the logistics and the battleground for "both armies now doing such loud marchings, the going capitalist, and the coming communist."[56] His strategy was to devise a narrative that could equate the Soviet struggle with that of the American workers. He found it readily: "The first thing that Hitler cracked down on when he took the Nazi Chamber was the Trade Unions. And it will be the Trade Unions that will beat Hitler."[57] Given their common enemy, the American workers' fellowship with their Soviet counterparts was incontestable: "Hitler hates Unions. He hates the Soviet Union, because the USSR is a solid Union Town, and Hitler caint never crack it, let alone take it."[58] Thus Guthrie worked to hammer home the natural fellowship between the singing constituencies of Roosevelt and Stalin:

> The Red Army boys sing about Union Battles and Rich Landlord Battles, and Poor Farmer Fights, Sharecropper Skirmishes, and will stab and cut and fight back at the Nazis as long as there's a pocket knife or club or flint rock handy. The women folks of the USSR will sing in the factories and deliver the goods ahead of time, the young folks and kids will keep the homes and farms grinding out groceries—and it just naturally makes me think of the 6 million CIO folks over here that's putting up the same fight, standing on the side of Britain and the Red Army, and battling for the same thing—a world where everybody's got a good job at honest pay, and nobody can lock a chain around your neck or keep you from voting.[59]

Guthrie's narrative of the war was also bound up in his courtship with Marjorie Mazia—a signal example of the manner in which Guthrie's devotion to the workers' struggle could drive even his most intimate relationships. Antifascism became an obsession that sometimes expressed itself in patronizing lectures that Marjorie gamely tolerated. Guthrie took it upon himself to enlighten her on the seductive power of fascism, which, he explained, had worked such sinister magic on the people of the Axis nations. Fascism, he counseled, could sound "soft and sweet and tender, sentimental, and moody, loving and kind, because fascism feels all of these feelings towards the members of its own family just as free people feel about each other."[60] Against such malignant power there was only one possible bulwark: union, the "higher hope" that would turn every worker "into a vicious anti-fascist soldier." He plotted for Marjorie the chain reaction he envisioned, an antifascist current running from "unions and discussion groups, into meetings and rallies, that turn all at once into armies with firearms and armies with plows and armies with theater stages and armies with dancing shoes on, and armies with cafeteria aprons, warehouse overalls, and lumberjackets, and cotton picking duds on." Guthrie invested his vision with a religious aura, placing Marjorie and himself on a mountaintop as witnesses to a holy creation: "and it's this higher ground that you and me have seen, we know it, we saw it."[61]

For their unborn child—Cathy Ann, who would arrive on February 6, 1943—Guthrie drew the battle lines of the holy war that she would be born to fight: "How come me launching off into a talk about fascism to you—only 4½ months on the way—not even here yet? Because in the whole big world, (out here where your mama and me are, and where you're gonna be one of these days)—fascism and freedom are the only two sides battling—every other early argument, and talk, shades into the fight somewhere."[62] Guthrie even roped in Marjorie's mother, the Yiddish poet Aliza Greenblatt, as a sounding board in his mission to define the proper place for a cultural worker in the midst of such a war: "It is the job of all artists, painters, dancers, writers, singers, sculptors, musicians, critics, actors, everybody everywhere, to join hands with the war workers, and work harder to root out, expose, and kill out the fascist enemy everywhere, at home and abroad. Words must be turned against the Nazis like red hot machine gun bullets and 500 pound bombs, mowing their poor, misled soldiers to the ground like brutes and monsters, blowing their factories and munitions dumps into ten million pieces."[63]

Through Marjorie, Guthrie was drawn deeper into the world of dance, which arena he soon fashioned—as any other—"to fit the cogwheels of the war" (as he wrote in an article for *Dance Observer* magazine): "Production is the job, the main job at home, and work has got to center on turning out more and more of everything. Show folks have a job to do, and that's to see to it that the show business gets its belt line changed just exactly like the Ford Motor plant." The necessary change, he lectured, must be from "the luxury of imitations" (whatever that meant) to "the real fight of beating Hitler." Thus Guthrie presumed to tell Marjorie and her colleagues how to go about their business: "If a dance don't tell you what kind of a fight is going on, and what caused it to break out, and what kind of work you got to do to win out, the goods in your costume are wasted." He had a shrill warning for those dancers who shirked the new responsibilities he set for them: "If the Axis is not wiped off of the map, you'll be doing an ape wobble with a million links of chain around your leg."[64]

Determined to put his preaching into practice, Guthrie launched himself into a tempest of rewriting and new composition. He turned his first Dust Bowl ballad, "So Long, It's Been Good to Know Yuh," into a wartime fable of a young man marching off to fight "Fascists in day time, mosquitos at night."[65] The song "Lindbergh," which had been excoriating the isolationists and America First at the Almanac hoot when Pearl Harbor was attacked, had a new crime hastily written into it: "Hitler said to Lindy, 'Stall 'em all you can. / We're gonna bomb Pearl Harbor with the help of old Japan.'"[66] The Columbia River anthems were revised unambiguously to beef up the efforts on behalf of "Uncle Sam," and Guthrie proclaimed "I'll Fight for the U.S.A." explicitly on behalf of the Almanacs (though no less determined to declare his solo copyright to the song of that title). He was happy to utilize the hackneyed Yankee Doodle Dandy imagery of Tin Pan Alley in rhetoric that would have been unthinkable the previous year:

> Now, I am just a soldier, I've rambled all around;
> I've been to Fort McClelland and other camps around;
> My uniform is spotless, my shoes are shining, too,
> I'm proud to wear the uniform of the old Red, White and Blue.[67]

The cowboy song "Get Along, Little Dogies" became "Get Along, Mister Hitler" ("We'll beat him with bullets; we'll beat him with beef").[68] Against the "Quislings. Lindberghs. Coughlins. Clivedens" and the "breed that sold out France," Guthrie pitted "Our CIO and AF of L," "Our Railroad Brotherhood," "Our NMU, or Miners, too," our "Timber Workers" dropping from the trees, our "Builders" driving the nails, and—to top it all off—Joe Louis in his spanking-new army uniform, ready and able to "free the world from your slave labor jails."[69] Sally, the girl next door, was told "not to grieve after me" by the boyfriend "running down to the army hall," calling over his shoulder with a parting injunction:

> "If a blackout comes to the old home town,
> Sally, won't you pull your curtains down.
> If a shade goes up, then a ship goes down."
> And I told her not to grieve after me.[70]

Home-front knitting circles were encouraged by way of a talking blues, "Talking Hitler to Death," which urged them to "knit one, purl one" but "Purl harder when you think of Pearl Harbor."[71] Guthrie warned against "Reckless Talk" in the song of that name, hectoring his imagined audience in a note typed beneath the lyrics: "This song is a warning to remind you that your loose talk can kill more of your own comrades than bombs, torpedoes, cannons, or incendiary bombs; because all of these things are a hundred times worse when the enemy is guided by the right information."[72]

Children were also drafted into the new war effort:

> Hitler he don't
> Like our doggy;
> Hitler he don't
> Like our doggy;
> Hitler he don't
> Like our doggy;
>   Hitler he's a mean man.[73]

And when not singing and skipping to "Ring around Hitler," the children in Guthrie's imagination recreated the entire civilian–military nexus in their playground boasting: "My daddy rides that ship in the sky"; "My daddy makes planes so they fly through the sky. / That's what keeps your daddy up there so high"; "My daddy works in the place where they land . . . . My dad'll bring your daddy back home again."[74]

By late 1942 Guthrie had written enough songs to propose to Alan Lomax a "project to make America war conscious," a collection of roughly sixty songs to be gathered under the title *War Songs Are Work Songs.*[75] His enumeration of the first tranche of songs for Lomax indicates the prolific degree of his composition and rewriting:

1. Talking Rathole Blues
2. The Girl in the Red, White and Blue
3. Roll On Buddy
4. Gonna Be a Blackout Tonight
5. Bombing of Pearl Harbor
6. I'll Fight for the U.S.A.
7. Open Up That Second Front Today
8. Ice in My Whiskers (Round Up the Nazis an' Bring 'Em In)
9. Let Me Join Your Army
10. Miss Pavlachenko
11. Ship in the Sky
12. Biggest Thing That Man Has Ever Done
13. Takin' It Easy
14. Reuben James
15. Gotta Keep 'Em Sailin'
16. Dig a Hole for the Nazis
17. Take a Tip from Me
18. Certainly Am
19. Reckless Talk
20. Git Along, Mister Hitler
21. You Better Get Ready
22. Sailing Far Over the Sea (Blue Eyes)
23. When I'm Gone Sally Don't You Grieve
24. Goin' Away to Sea[76]

Guthrie's war songs display, among other qualities, a capacity for rhetorical violence that is often astonishing, especially when compared to the pacifism of his prewar writings. In 1940 he had written to his younger sister, Mary Jo: "But worst of all, in a way, was when I got the news that our George had joined the gun-carriers, to go running out shooting and killing and torpedoing, and bombing, other young boys of other countries, whom he had never seen in his life before, nor—that is, they were all rank strangers to one another, the boys on Our side, and the boys on the Other side. That is the business of Murder, that is the art of War, that is the business of Killing. But—all of this for what? I'll tell you for what: All of the Blood must flow because the rich men had an argument."[77] In his "Woody Sez" column, he had declared: "I would like to see every single soldier on every single side, just take off your helmet, unbuckle your kit, lay down your rifle, and set down at the side of some shady lane, and say, nope, I aint a gonna kill nobody. Plenty of rich folks wants to fight. Give them the guns."[78] Now an awful force had been unleashed by "the new situation," as Guthrie grimly promised in his rewriting of "Curly-Headed Baby":

> I'll bomb their towns and bomb their cities,
> Sink their ships beneath the tides.
> I'll win this war, but till I do, babe,
> I could not be satisfied.[79]

He would now gleefully dance on the graves of "the boys on the Other side":

> Way down yonder at the bottom of the hill
>   Raise a rukus tonight
> Fifteen Nazis I done killed
>   Raise a rukus tonight.[80]

Guthrie made no bones about the violence of his rhetoric, fired up, he said in a letter to Marjorie, by "a personal hate so strong that it makes you want to kill in order to keep the people you love from being slaves":

> This is in all of my songs these days. I pour the hate and murder and killing into them by the truck loads. I think of what fascism is trying to do to you and to your relatives, to me and mine, and seeing what they've done and are doing in the nations they've already overrun, it makes me even fuller of hate for them, because if you really love anybody or anything or any principle or any science or belief, you will hate, hate, hate, and keep hating anybody or anything that tries to hurt, or kill or destroy that which you love. Unless love has got this hate, it's not love at all, it's a cave full of mysticism, and one of the most dangerous forms of cowardice.[81]

With his warrior impulse thus released and channeled against an enemy that he could locate, identify, and hate with complete rectitude (and no little relish), he justified his rhetorical savagery in an artistic counterpoint to General Sherman's Civil War declaration that war was "hell" and must be made terrible: "Art is a weapon and as deadly as steel cannons and exploding bombs. Art should not be pacifistic nor mystic, but should send fighting people to the field of battle filled with the clear knowledge of what the real enemy is."[82] None were to shrink from this mission, and all were to enable it; it was "the war job of the men and women that own radio stations or work in them to see to it that you can turn your dial and hear the speeches, operas, songs, orchestras, and plays and comedies that are fighting fascism as hard and fast as you are; and this is what songs are supposed to tell you, to make you vision, see, hear, and 'believe.'"[83] Guthrie imagined more than one scenario in which he would be obliged to defend his violent rhetoric. In an echo of his Shermanesque manifesto, he appended a note beneath the lyrics of "Gonna Be a Blackout Tonight":

> I was walking down the street in New York on Memorial Day. A nice little lady handed me a religious handbill and told me, "If you'll sing songs on the street about Jesus coming, you'll make more money." I said, "I make up war songs, lady, to keep Hitler from getting what little money I've already got." She said, "Oh, no, don't sing about war, sing about the day Jesus is coming down to earth to put an end to all of this killing." I told her, "Well, I feel like I've just got to keep on singing war songs, so we can win this war and fix up a brand new world for Jesus to come down to; he wouldn't feel at home in this one."[84]

Although Guthrie clearly looked forward to peace and the "better world a-comin'" that would be built on the ashes of the war dead, the attack on Pearl Harbor fired him with a vengeful wrath that no humanism or antiwar rhetoric could ameliorate.[85] The fact that this attack came at the hands of the same fascism he had explicitly linked to the plight of the Dust Bowl migrants in California made the prospect of vengeance all the more sweet. The "Axis Japanese" and the "rotten Hitler Vultures" had "fired the first shot, boys, / But we will fire the last," as he vowed in "It Was Down in Old Pearl Harbor."[86] He wrote bullishly to Lomax: "How's the war spirit out there in Washington? High, I hope. I hope everybody's back of me and [longshoremen's leader] Harry Bridges and [maritime union leader] Joe Curran and Franklin D., in this fight to plow Hitler under."[87]

On the first anniversary of the Japanese attack, Guthrie penned the antifascist song for which he is best remembered—"You Fascists Bound to Lose"—a song in which the Russian people shout to the skies, "We killed ten thousand Nazis in just a single day!"; a song in which there are "People of every color fighting side by side / Marching across fields where a million fascists died!"[88] That Guthrie had judged correctly in his assumption that such murderous celebration could ignite the necessary war fever in the hearts of Americans is made clear in the recollection of Joy Doerflinger, the E. P. Dutton editor saddled with the unenviable task of organizing the sprawling manuscript of *Bound for Glory*. In Dutton's in-house newsletter, she described Guthrie and Cisco Houston playing and singing on a subway car hurtling downtown beneath Manhattan: "They began to sing a song Woody had made up: 'You're bound to LOSE, You Fascists, bound to LOSE!' There were many reasons given as to exactly why You Fascists are bound to lose, and each reason was better and funnier than the last. It was a good song. It went on for seven stations. In the last hop, between Rector Street and South Ferry, every single human being in that subway car was singing that song."[89]

Guthrie's unleashed war fever clearly impacted on his drafting of *Bound for Glory*, published in 1943. He would eventually claim: "The later and more progressive, the more political parts of me are not in this book";[90] but on the contrary, he assigned to his younger self within the book's pages a political stance that he did not in fact exhibit until much later in his life. (He also did a great disservice to his fellow Almanac Singers in airbrushing them out of the story completely, as he did to a brother, a sister, and to his first wife and their three children). One of the book's more implausible passages depicts the young Guthrie haranguing his neighbors in Pampa, Texas—in the mid-1930s—in words that he would only have uttered after the German invasion of the USSR. He appears wholly on side with the war buildup that in reality he had resisted until resistance was no longer possible:

> I told them, "Hitler an' Mussolini is out ta make a chain gang slave outta you, outta me, an' outta ever'body else! An' kill ever'body that gits in their road! . . . We gotta all git together an' find out some way ta build this country up. Make all of this here dust quit blowin'. We gotta find a job an' put ever single livin' one of us ta work. Better houses 'stead of these here little old sickly shacks. Better carbon-black plants. Better oil refineries. Gotta build up more big oil fields. Pipe lines runnin' from here plumb ta Pittsburgh, Chicago, an' New York. Oil an' gas fer fact'ries ever'where. Gotta keep an eye peeled on ever' single inch of this whole country an' see to it that none of Hitler's Goddam stooges don't lay a hand on it."[91]

In similar dubious fashion, a closing scene has Guthrie auditioning alone in the Rainbow Room, establishing his incorruptible credentials by improvising the same anti-Rockefeller song that he had actually improvised with the Almanacs. In this version it is Guthrie who contemptuously walks away from the Rainbow Room, cursing "that sentimental and dreamy trash," rather than have the offer withdrawn in a cave-in to the red-baiting press, as had actually happened.[92]

Thus, secondary to its mission of mythologizing the life of Woody Guthrie, *Bound for Glory* is an exercise in propaganda on behalf of the Roosevelt government's war aims. Only once does the narrative betray any reservation over the social fallout from the conversion of the economy into an antifascist war machine; this is when Guthrie has a boxcar-riding hobo telling his story: "'I woiked thirteen years in th' same weave room! Breakout fixer on th' looms! Poil Harbor comes along. Big comp'ny gits alla de war orders. My place is a little place, so what happens? Just like dat! She closes down. An' I'm out on de freights.'"[93] Barring this nod to the misfortunes of those individuals swept aside in the rush for the greater good, *Bound for Glory* celebrates the nation's conversion into the chief Allied power, witnessed, among other places, where Guthrie depicts himself improvising a blues song for a barroom full of sailors:

> I didn't boil myself no coffee
> I didn't boil no tea
> I didn't boil myself no coffee
> I didn't boil no tea
> I made a run for that recruitin' office
> Uncle Sam, make room for me![94]

Guthrie even borrows an unacknowledged phrase from Pete Seeger's "Dear Mr. President" and reworks it into the mouth of a fired-up sailor: "I hope to God that Uncle Sam puts me where I can do those Japs the most damage!"[95]

Although "those Japs" bear the brunt of Guthrie's enmity in *Bound for Glory* (with the necessary distinction being made between the Axis power and the persecuted Japanese-Americans whom Guthrie staunchly defends), and although "Uncle Joe" Stalin and the Red Army are not mentioned, the novel is also an implicit call for the Allies to open up a second front in the European war, the chief aim of the Left's "labor-victory front."[96] In keeping with the clamor for a second front in defense of the embattled Soviet Union, which had begun almost the instant of the Pearl Harbor attack, Guthrie's personal effort in this area had intensified in early 1942, while he was still living and singing with the Almanacs. His song "Gotta Keep 'Em Sailing"—later revised and recorded with minor variations as "What Are We Waiting On?" and "Tear the Fascists Down"—is an early clarion call for the United States to take the heat off the Red Army and to do its part on the European battlefield:

> So I thank the Chinese Vets
> And the mighty Soviets
> And the Allies the whole wide world around

To the battling British, thanks
You will meet 10 million yanks
On a western front to tear old Hitler down.[97]

The second front quickly became Guthrie's own personal obsession, as he readily confessed to Marjorie: "I feel like I'm cursing the fascists to high heaven and red hot hell, and am preaching the Red Army on down to shake hands with the Allies in the middle of main street in Berlin!"[98] His songwriting during this period bears out this sense of urgency:

Cross that channel in one big jump
Stick a bayonet in Hitler's rump
    Gonna open up that second front today
CIO and the AFof L
Gonna blow them Nazis all to hell
    Gonna open up that second front today[99]

In case the channel-jumping threat was lost on anyone, Guthrie reiterated it elsewhere:

I'll make that channel in one big jump
    I'm a fightin' sonofagun
I'll open up me a back and a couple of fronts.
    I'm a fightin' sonfagun![100]

An important strategy of Guthrie's was to highlight the Red Army's sacrifice and heroism, implicitly meant to shame the Americans into a battlefield commitment in Europe. He saw the bitter winter campaign in the Battle of Stalingrad as a singular example of superhuman heroism, deserving an equal share of the awe and reverence attached to the Battle of Britain and the Blitz. Although the narrative voice of Guthrie's "Ice in My Whiskers" carries an American twang, the pre-Normandy winter scenario clearly marks it out as Stalingrad, filtered through the perception of a lone Red Army infantryman:

Icicles hanging down from my chin
I wont thaw them out till I get to Berlin

Chorus: Round up th' Nazis an' bring 'em in
    Round up th' Nazis and bring 'em in.[101]

Guthrie also lionized Lyudmila Pavlichenko, the celebrated Red Army sniper who won the hearts of the Soviets (as well as those of the Roosevelts and a substantial cross-section of the American Left) for her tally of 309 Nazi kills. Pavlichenko's legendary response to Hitler's invasion had been to set aside her books (she was a historian), manicure her nails, don a dress of crepe de chine and a pair of high heels, and burst into the Red Army recruiting office demanding a frontline assignment.[102] Guthrie drew no less on Pavlichenko's well-photographed beauty than on her reputation for sacrifice and deadly skill:

> In summer's heat, or cold winter's snow,
> In all kinds of weather she tracks down the foe;
> Her smile is as bright as the new morning sun,
> But more than three hundred Nazis have fell by your gun![103]

Compared to such sacrifice and heroism as that demonstrated by Pavlichenko and her Red Army colleagues, the sacrifices that Guthrie was simultaneously urging on the U.S. home front were meager indeed, as he implied in yet another redrafting of "So Long, It's Been Good to Know Yuh":

> I'll look in my old coffee cup and I'll dream;
> I'll dream about victory and smell of the steam;
> I'll quit my bad habits and wildest desires;
> I'll kiss "good-bye" to my gas and my tires![104]

Guthrie continued to agitate on paper and in song for a U.S. commitment to a second front, typing "Some other ideas" beneath the lyrics of "Ice in My Whiskers":

1. I'm Gonna Roll Right On to Victory One of These Days
2. You Cain't Win a War Till You Roll into Germany (Biminy Gal)
3. Everytime that I Ride on a Fast Rollin Train
   A Hundred War Songs Roll Through My Brain (Durant Jail)
4. Convoy Song: tune of: "What Did the Deep Sea Say?"[105]

Thus when the "Big Three" finally met in Teheran in November 1943 to agree to an Allied invasion of Europe, Guthrie's euphoria spilled onto the page:

> Well, a union sun was shining
> And November it was ending
> And the year was Nineteen Hundred Forty Three
> They shook hands across the table
> In the city of Teheran
> Joe Stalin! Churchill! and Franklin D!
> > Joe Stalin! Churchill! and Franklin D!
> > Joe Stalin! Churchill! and Franklin D!
> And our new union world was born on that spot.[106]

Dedicated as he was to the opening of the second front, Guthrie sought, as ever, to set the agenda of his own participation. "Writing and singing are the two best things I can do for the war till they call me into a uniform," he wrote to Marjorie in January of 1943, "and even then I would use my gun part of the time, a hand grenade some of the time, a guitar some of the time and a typewriter some of the time to fight with." With his tasks and weapons thus clarified, he declared himself ready to go: "I've been thinking that I might get called. I really feel that tingle, too. I've felt it before. Fight. I like to feel it. I like to fight fascism, and I guess to some people my ways of fighting are a little strange."[107] But the closer he came to his army's call, the more resistant he became to the prospect of conscription. Heading off his induction notice, he and two colleagues, Cisco Houston and Jim Longhi, joined the U.S. Merchant Marine in June. They were destined to make three tours across the Atlantic during a year on the Liberty ships. On the first and third of their voyages, their ship was torpedoed; the only other violence in which Guthrie participated was at the receiving end of a punch in the nose from a right-wing shipmate for shouting, "God bless the Red Army!"[108]

The Merchant Marine experience did much to consolidate Guthrie's perception of his war as a "Union War." His service depended on his joining the National Maritime Union (NMU), just about the country's most radical union and for a time under a Communist leadership; Guthrie carried his NMU card with pride. The long days at sea afforded him the opportunity for prolific thinking and writing. In addition to scores of songs and journal pages he wrote articles—published and unpublished—for the *Daily Worker* and *Sunday Worker* as well as the NMU's magazine, *Pilot*. He conceived of adversaries well beyond the ranks of the Axis powers during his time at sea. As an NMU sailor and shipboard union secretary, he saw himself at war with all the anti-union "goons and gun thugs" and the company-union "fonies" against whom his seafaring predecessors had fought to establish their legitimate union:

> For a clean spoon in y'r coffee cup
> I had to fight the finks
> To win clean sheets and a bar of soap
> I battled with the ginks.
> I marched, I yelled, I fought 'em all,
> I won clean plates f'r yer grub.
> An' f'r every bit ya put in yer mouth
> My head it broke a club.
> Singing: All you fonies bound to lose lose lose
>   All you fonies bound to lose.

For eight hour days an' overtime pay
I battled these comp'ny men,
My old head ached with a thousand knots
A bringing my union in.
My boats was gallery slave ships
With racketeers f'r a crew,
They fit like divils of hell till next
We got our N.M.U.[109]

Guthrie's best-known Merchant Marine song, "Talking Sailor Blues" or, alternatively, "Talking Merchant Marine," extends the war for his particular union into a battle for the soul and safety of the American union at large:

I'm just one of the Merchant crew,
I belong to the union called the N.M.U.
I'm a union man from head to toe,
I'm U.S.A. and C.I.O.
Fightin' out here on the waters
To win some freedom on the land.[110]

Beyond the NMU and the USA, the wide world itself awaited the coming union victory. Inspired by a postage stamp commemorating the proclamation of Roosevelt's "Four Freedoms," Guthrie wrote an essay—never published—that drew the broad outlines of the Union War as he envisaged it:

All kinds and all colors coming together. Minds and brains, hands are coming together. This is Union.
The human race is marching toward this Union. Guns in soldiers' hands win it foxhole by foxhole, hand grenades and shells win it inch by inch, foot by foot. Planes bomb our way clear. Bombs plow our road on ahead. Your silly factories tried to keep the human race from coming to its Union. We are coming into our Union world, inch by inch, clod by clod, weed by weed, tree by tree, field by field, and set our inches end to end, and we are moving toward our Union faster than a falling star.

The enemy in this union war was an undifferentiated army of thugs recruited from the death camps and battlefields of Europe and the Pacific, from beneath the lynching trees of the American South, from the barbed-wire perimeters of the Californian fruit fields, and from the shadowy offices of factory bosses everywhere. Guthrie's words spilled onto the page in a rabid white froth of hatred:

Throw your policemen, your ignorant thugs, your hoodlums, your foney baloneys, your finks, your stooges, spies, rats, and guards at us. Our Union will chew them up and throw them out as manure to make our new flowers grow quicker.

You are called the Axis by some. You are called the Nazis, the Fascists, the Sons of Heaven, the Super Man! Baloney! Horse manure! You are the Ku Klux! You are the Vigilantes! You are those who think that you own us and our labors![111]

In another unpublished essay, Guthrie summarized the activities that had been contributing to his exhilarating political education in the Merchant Marine: "Three invasions, torpedoed twice, but carried my guitar every drop of the way. I washed dishes and fed Fifty gunboys, washed their dirty dishes, scrubbed their greasy messroom, and never graduated up nor down in my whole Eleven months." Musical instruments had become part of the ordnance in the union war: "Two N.M.U. brothers, Jimmie Longhi and Cisco Houston, rode with me on every trip, and we carried a mandolin, a fiddle, and one more guitar, plus a whole armload of new strings which we lent to the troops and sailors on all of these boats." Music making thus dovetailed with other forms of agitation designed to extend the union solidarity into the hearts of the uniformed ranks. Pointedly, Guthrie included those soldiers fighting on the opposing side: "We walked all around over North Africa, the British isles, Sicily, and sung underground songs for underfed fighters. We sung with prisoners of war on both sides, and held meetings on the troopships to get the men to write letters to their congressmen."[112]

Once on shore leave, Guthrie wrote to Pete and Toshi Seeger expressing his certainty that the war in which he was now physically participating was a necessary stage in the fight for union, socialism, and universal liberation: "We had quite a trip and seen a lot of sights, learned a lot more about how terrible and vicious a thing Fascism-Nazism really is. The people of those countries are on their way up the ladder of human freedom, and since all of the conceivable kinds and styles of slavery have already been worn out on them, they certainly can't go back to any of those forms, but only on and on to a world that is owned and operated for everybody."[113]

While Guthrie's days at sea reinforced his enthusiasm for the war effort, they also enabled him to brood dismally on the corruption of the wartime popular music and broadcast industry, for which he reserved a visceral hatred. Here he was in the middle of a war for union and universal uplift—an antifascist war that required the upkeep of morale to its highest pitch—and the industry seemed determined to sap that very morale in a perverse bid to pacify and lull the nation and its forces. He wrote to Marjorie complaining: "There is a pipe organ on the radio. The music is from a church. A lady is singing, 'Sometimes I feel like a motherless child and a long ways from home.' I think the radio songs should be a lot more gutsy than they are and with more of a victorious sound to them. To tell how bad you feel is almost a waste of time these days. Give us reasons for feeling hopeful and good. These are the best sounds you can hear when you're out here on this ocean."[114] Later he recalled with venom: "The maddest I've been in my whole life was when I rode on a troopship with more than three thousand men headed for France and we got about half way out on the ocean and a big storm come up. The ship rocked and rolled and made a lot of us sick. We hadn't been across before. We turned on our radio and a song blubbered out over the loud speaker, 'Born to Lose'!!! Ain't that some hell of a damned song for the United States Army to have poked down its throat on its way into a battle?"[115] Writing against the entire industry, Guthrie sat on his bunk and composed a set of verses as he felt they *should* have been broadcast to the soldiers and sailors taking the fight to the fascists, turning Ted Daffan's 1943 hit "Born to Lose" on its head:

> I had my fun and my troubles
> I had my luck and my blues
> Been up and been down and been sober and drunk
> But I know that I'm not born to lose.
>> Born to win. I know I'm born to win.
>> It's a funny old world that I am in.
>> I'll fight to change it like it ought to be.
>> Born to win. I know I'm born to win.[116]

The broadcast industry was corrupt to the point of treason, Guthrie implied in an unpublished manuscript: "You can tune in your radio and listen to twenty four hours a day, and about twenty two of it will [be] for the business of selling you something instead of making you want to fight and win this war against fascism."[117] For this reason, he told Marjorie, he preferred the state-owned, noncommercial British Broadcasting Company (BBC) to any American broadcaster, because they "don't try to sell you a wild axe handle every few minutes."[118] Broadway, he argued, "didn't get out a good war play for two years after the axis started out to kill all of us. Hollywood was as far behind. And even today you can count the useful movies and plays on your ten toes."[119] Here, Guthrie was rehashing the sentiments he had expressed in a *New York Times* article commissioned on the strength of *Bound for Glory*, in which he blasts the industry for its culpability in sapping the commitment to the war effort: "If you've got war workers playing hooky from the job, I ain't a bit surprised. If you want to smell the rat in his neon-lit hole, take a sniff at this floating, drifting, aimless, pointless, mentally, morally and sexually confusing dope that is drummed into a hundred million ears day and night, day and night, on your pretty nickel phonograph."[120]

Guthrie saw as one alternative to this musical narcotic a project to which he committed himself during the interval between his second and third voyages, the ballad-opera *The Martins and the Coys,* produced by Alan Lomax for the BBC and scripted by his wife, Elizabeth Lyttleton. Certainly one of the Popular Front's hokier wartime projects, the opera drew on the talents of a host of Lomax protégés besides Guthrie—Seeger, Burl Ives, Sonny Terry, Cisco Houston, and Hally Wood, among others—as well as Fiddlin' Arthur Smith and Lily May Ledford. Updating the Appalachian legend of the two feuding families the Hatfields and the McCoys, the Lomaxes presented a scenario in which the families bury the hatchet to join together in the battle against fascism, helped along by the Romeo-and-Juliet subplot uniting Ben Martin and Sary Coy. Sary's brother, Alec (played by Guthrie), joins the army alongside Ben; the two become friends and dedicated antifascists. The opera closes with a celebratory wedding dance to the tune of "Round and Round Hitler's Grave" by way of Guthrie's "You Better Get Ready" and "You Fascists Bound to Lose," as well as Seeger and Hawes's "Deliver the Goods," resurrected from the Almanacs' *Dear Mr. President* album.[121] The fact that Lomax could not secure an American broadcast, while the BBC was happy to commit to the project, only confirmed for Guthrie the reactionary nature of Tin Pan Alley and its stranglehold on the U.S. broadcast industry.

Guthrie's personal war against the industry continued after his return from his third voyage, when he landed a prestigious slot on New York's WNEW radio station. One passage from his first broadcast of December 3, 1944, has since become legendary:

> I hate a song that makes you think that you're not any good. I hate a song that makes you think that you are just born to lose. Bound to lose. No good to nobody. No good for nothing. Because you are either too old or too young or too fat or too slim or too ugly or too this or too that. . . . Songs that run you down or songs that poke fun at you on account of your bad luck or hard traveling.
> I am out to fight those kinds of songs to my very last breath of air and my last drop of blood.[122]

Less frequently reprinted is Guthrie's explicit distancing of himself from the ethos and pecuniary rewards of the broadcast music industry, with just a hint of self-satisfaction over his economic martyrdom:

> I could hire out to the other side, the big-money side, and get several dollars every week just to quit singing my own kind of songs and to sing the kind that

knock you down still farther and the ones that make fun of you even more and the ones that make you think that you've not got any sense at all. But I decided a long time ago that I'd starve to death before I'd sing any such songs as that. The radio waves and your jukeboxes and your movies and your song books are already loaded down and running over with such no-good songs as that anyhow.[123]

If Guthrie perceived any irony in the fact that he had broadcast this speech *on* the radio, and on a commercial station to boot, it was never mentioned. Rather, he presented himself as a musical insurgent undermining the corrupt broadcast agenda from within the belly of the beast.

As he regained his land legs, Guthrie began to reflect on all the destruction he had witnessed in Europe, viewing it pitilessly. He saw the war's military savagery as the bitter but necessary price of a *cultural* dereliction of duty. The fluffy confections of popular music and entertainment had treasonously— disastrously—been diverting the public's attention from the rising tide of fascism since the mid-1930s, and now the world was reaping the whirlwind. "Fascism cannot be dynamited from a nation with ice cream cones," he snarled in an unpublished essay for the *Daily Worker,* writing explicitly of Italy but implicitly referring to any nation with its eyes and ears closed:

No, it takes the bomb. It takes the three inch, the five inch, the twelve and sixteen inch shell. The shell explodes and the shell does not know the difference between the hideout of your enemy or the parlor of your friend. The wreckage must be, now, because we waited so long, it must be. Oh, had we only joined our hands and destroyed Hitlerism on the young battlefields of Spain, France, Poland, then the wreckage would have been ten times less. But we waited until the fascist germ wiggled its way into every street, alley, neighborhood. The cancer of slavery actually found its way into every home.[124]

Guthrie may have forgotten that he had not so long ago condemned any prospect of U.S. intervention on the "young battlefields" of France. He may have forgotten that he had actually construed the Soviet invasion of Poland as a benevolent act on behalf of the Polish farmers. At any rate, by the autumn of 1944 he was fully prepared to bring his union war back to the streets of New York. While walking along the Coney Island boardwalk one September evening, his reflections on the "ninety mile wind" then battering the Eastern Seaboard led him to conclude

that everything bites and fights every other thing
And that hurricanes do blow
And will blow
Some harder than others.[125]

During his wartime explorations of Europe, he had seen "one bombed city" blending into another: "I saw all cities that are bombed and shelled. I think I glimpsed Warsaw, London, Madrid, Stalingrad, Kiev, and all of the others."[126] Now, in similar fashion, he saw the European struggle blending almost seamlessly into a generic labor battleground on the home front:

> They're here, they're here in my city
> These spreaders of greed and of hate
> I'll be friends with all of my comrades
> And fight till we take the last gate.
>
> I'll fight for my field and my factory
> I'll fight for my timber and mine
> I'll fight in a foxhole or jungle
> I'll fight in the front of the line.[127]

Guthrie knew that the election of Franklin Roosevelt to an unprecedented fourth term would be instrumental in the continued prosecution of the union war—long gone were the days of painting FDR as a capitalist stooge. Along with Richard Dyer-Bennett, Sonny Terry, Cisco Houston, Will Geer, and others, he toured twenty-four states as a member of the "Roosevelt Bandwagon," over-optimistically noting that "all along the railroad tracks the trees are turning red."[128] In reading his euphoric reaction to Roosevelt's victory, one might think that 1944 was a good year to be a communist, a badge that now seemed more American than ever in light of the voluntary dissolution of the CPUSA and its reconstitution as the Communist Political Association (CPA). As Earl Browder described the new body, it was now a "non-party organization of Americans which, basing itself upon the working class, carries forward the traditions of Washington, Jefferson, Paine, Jackson, and Lincoln under the changed conditions of modern industrial society."[129] Given the CPA's input into Roosevelt's reelection campaign and its refusal to run any of its own candidates in order to give FDR a clear field, it was characteristic of Guthrie to credit the communist movement with "FDR's Victory and the long list of gains on the Democratic march toward a World Union."[130] Inscribing a gift of Asch's *American Folksay: Ballads and Dances* for his Pampa family, Guthrie wrote gleefully: "You can sing and run and jump and dance and holler and laugh and work and play and grow as big and as smart and as pretty as you want to on account of this is the day after election and F.D.R. got elected again."[131]

Musically and politically energized, Guthrie watched approvingly and lent two songs to the Union Boys, a one-off pickup band put together by Alan Lomax and Moses Asch and featuring Burl Ives, Tom Glazer, Sonny Terry,

Brownie McGhee, Josh White, and Pete Seeger.[132] Their sole recording session afforded Guthrie the opportunity to draw hopeful and generous conclusions about his fellow musicians and their part in rolling the union on: "I think Pete Seeger loves to stand there with his soldier (air corps) uniform on and look away up toward the moon while he yells out to all our fascist minded ones, yes, that I'm a Union man in my fighting clothes. The sound is in his banjo and in his voice. Seeger without the slightest doubt will be one of our very best folk singers. Starting now. I would call him a dialectical Leadbelly."[133]

And with yet no hint of the rancor with which he would later view Ives and White as sellouts to the dollar (and, in Ives's case, to the FBI, as well), Guthrie lauded their hard-core Union commitment: "Josh and Burl. The Union Boys are all here. You hear them on the windward side. But Burl's voice yelps out, comes in there so high and so religious that I said, 'By God, here's a man that believes in some awful big things,' and Burl almost seems to explode in mid air and say, 'Yes. Yessir. And I found the big things not in the spineless AF of L, but here, here in the C.I.O.'"[134]

For all his optimism, Guthrie would soon have cause to revise more than just the words to his songs. Roosevelt may have won the election, but the losers, Thomas Dewey and the Republicans behind him, had begun to smell progressive blood, singling out New Dealers as soft on Communism and laying the groundwork for the worst red scare since 1919–20. It was the dawn of the "Great Fear"—the "Scoundrel Time."[135]

5. Lonesome Radical Soul

Reading through his new copy of Vernon L. Parrington's *Main Currents in American Thought* (inscribed on the inside cover, "Bought with the hard earned money of Woody Guthrie—12–14–44"), Guthrie came across a quote from Daniel Leonard's Loyalist treatise of 1775 arguing that "Rebellion is the most atrocious offence that can be perpetrated by man." "SHIT," he scrawled in the margin.[1] Guthrie was bullish. It was a new year—1945—and it had begun in a blaze of proletarian glory, as Guthrie implied in his reworking of an earlier, nonpolitical composition, "This Morning I Am Born Again":

> I feel this sun against me
> Its rays crawl through my skin
> I breathe the life of Jesus
> And old John Henry in
> I see just one big family
> In this whole big human race
> When the sun looks down tomorrow
> I will be in a union place.[2]

Guthrie was particularly proud of the six songs he recorded for Moses Asch that March, released under the title of *Struggle: Asch Documentary #1,* which included "Ludlow Massacre," "1913 Massacre," and "Union Burying Ground."[3] He was aware that a strong whiff of conservative retrenchment was in the air; it impacted even upon his own program with WNEW. The station executives rejected his song "When I Get Home" for its pinkish insinuations of postwar union muscle—a slight that Guthrie dismissed with a brief splutter: "Their system of censorship protects Franco, Churchill and Hitler, and puts the chains of slavery on the microphones and the legs of the people."[4] He was not all that troubled when the station canceled his program altogether in February. The following month, however, he could not so easily or convincingly hide his dismay over the red baiting that was to keep him from ever sailing again with his beloved NMU. He saw his seaman's papers revoked by Naval Intelligence under the unsubstantiated charge of Communist Party membership (to which Guthrie later claimed to have replied, "If you call me a Communist, I am very proud because it takes a wise and hard-working person to be a Communist").[5] He affected unconcern, declaring: "I thank my God in heaven that I'm on these black lists. If my name wasn't on these lists of Hoover and Dewey and Dies, I don't guess I could enjoy a decent night's sleep."[6]

With his sailing days now over, he was open to the draft. On the day of the German surrender—May 7, 1945—Private Woodrow W. Guthrie donned the uniform of the U.S. Army. Initially assigned to the teletype operators' school, he hoped for a position in the Army Entertainment Section. His application was thrown out:

> I asked them to let me be a singer and they axed me they didn't need no singers and they axed me again to get the hell on back in that classroom and make an honest teletype operator or they would fine me, CM [court martial] me, and put me to chopping weeds which hide flies and bugs that carry more diseases than all of New York State and the City added together. So I knew that I could not stand there and recite my life story three times for every officer, so I retreated worse and faster than Trotsky hoped the Bolsheviks would.[7]

As Guthrie surmised, "They all look at my red background and get afraid to transfer me."[8] Writing to Lomax from his barracks in Scott Field, Illinois, he confessed to his bitterness but put on a defiant face:

> I am jealous and sore, mean and frothing because I didn't get no transfer out of here to work around New York. I had it all cooked up, but you are now gazing at an old dust blower who got used to seeing plans turn tail and blow a long time ago. Of course I know very well that it is my C.I.O. and Communist Party connections that have kept me out of a special service job and I had rather have a smell from a Communist rain cloud than all the pet blessings which any body could shower on me.[9]

He responded with petty, private acts of resistance in his teletype class: "I sang songs to the four-beat exercises . . . and then I imagined that every group of letters was another person joining the Communist party."[10] However, all his subversive efforts came to naught: "I decided that I would just set through every class and fail all of the tests and miss all of the questions and flunk on everything, and get thrown out the window with my guitar. Instead of making it better I convinced every official that I was one of the worlds best typists just goofing off for the fun of it."[11]

From within the army ranks, Guthrie watched with increasing alarm the growing rift in the communist movement between the Browderites struggling to maintain the loosely affiliated CPA and the hard-liners agitating for the reconstitution of the prewar CPUSA. Guthrie argued that with "our Party Principles . . . actually taking a shape at the election booths all over Europe and Asia, we need here in our U.S.A. the most solid form of an elective, politically active, Communist Party." He regretted ever seeing the CPA inaugurated: "Our only prestige is lost when a possible new member asks you, 'If you are so proud of your Party why did it disappear?' Everybody seems to think that everybody else was somehow or another ashamed of the Party":

> I felt when we had our Party that I had found the one organization I could stand up and feel proud of, but I tell you that I have one hell of a time trying to talk these days on the hair split basis of the difference between our CPA and CP. The thing whirls and blows in the mind of the sympathetic outsider. He cannot follow the fancy wing stunts. I use[d] to feel that I could tell you just exactly why you should go down and join your Communist Party in three minutes at most, but bullets fly fast and so do clouds, and so does everybody that are in this war, and I have found it as tough as the devil to explain the ramifications of the CPA in as clear a way as you can tell about the plain old common ordinary every day Communist Party.[12]

Guthrie put his duties as notice-board painter in service of the struggle. He habitually "reword[ed] the news" in order to "throw more weight" against the red-baiting William Randolph Hearst, whom he correctly allied with "fascism and Nazism":[13] "I subtract all of the Randolph Hearst fuzz from every word I paint on my board. I always see that the C.I.O. gets a fair deal, and that the facts of Communist gains are plain."[14] He kept his eyes peeled for news of labor struggles to report: "About a hundred men gang around me while I paint my news board every morning. They chew my rear out as I paint each word and when they curse out 'the god damned strikers' I always say, it's your own wages they're fighting to raise."[15]

In the lull between the German and Japanese surrenders, Guthrie confessed to Moses Asch his decreasing certainty over why his war had been fought at all, given the place where he and the country had arrived and what direction they appeared to be going: "I am a quicker man, hungrier man, healthier man, smarter man in a lot of fine ways, but an awful ignorant man when it comes to knowing what in the hell this war is all about. (No, I kept up with the *Daily Worker*, the N.M.U. *Pilot*, so I know. But I run onto about 50,000 good men here every day that sure as shit don't know.)"[16]

The *Daily Worker* and the *Pilot* were hardly the sturdiest of pegs on which to hang a total conception of the war; in any event, they could not prepare Guthrie for the reality of the 6th and 9th of August, when the first atomic bombs ever deployed in anger fell on Japan. Within a month of the nuclear destruction of Hiroshima and Nagasaki, Guthrie's wartime belligerence turned to intense soul-searching as he imagined the awful awakenings of the *Enola Gay*'s flight crew:

> The jolt was so bad that it shook all the sky
> A cloud sprouted up forty thousand feet high
> The heat flash so bright that it outshined the sun
> We asked one another, "Oh what kind of bomb?"[17]

The atomic bomb had devastated Guthrie's moral landscape just as surely as it had devastated Japan, inaugurating his transformation—while still in army uniform—into the antiwar activist that he would remain for the rest of his life.

It was not so simple or straightforward a transformation. Guthrie viewed the dangers and seductions of the dawning nuclear age with mixed feelings. Atomic power was certainly the most lethal force unleashed in his lifetime— that had been proven; but it was also the most imaginatively captivating power, holding out the promise of beneficent social and technological advancement in the innocent decades before Three Mile Island and Chernobyl. Hence one of Guthrie's most ambivalent sets of lyrics, written less than a month after Hiroshima and Nagasaki, perhaps the basis of a production he envisaged with Marjorie and her dance students. "Freedom Fire" is freighted with equal measures of hypnotic attraction and foreboding. Beginning with a mesmerizing choral chant, it presents a vision of a momentous discovery reaching back to the dawn of time, when the fundamental atomic elements were already in place and patiently awaiting revelation:

> Leader: Radioactive pick and shovel
> Universe on the point of a needle
> Let's break another neutron bottle
> All: Dance around my Freedom Fire.
> Leader: Write down your law of number
> Marriage rings and relativity
> Let's do a little fourth dimension
> All: Dance around my Freedom Fire.
> Leader: Throw on some history pages
> Words of your wits and sages
> On back through your glacial ages
> All: Dance around my Freedom Fire.

As the dance progresses, its imagery and the implied choreography suggest that it has become a dance of death, much in the manner of "Ring around the Rosie" eerily and innocently describing the signs of the Black Plague:

Leader: Dance around my sweet titanium
         Kiss my lips my pretty little helium
         Warm your hands by the flames of nations
All: Dance around my Freedom Fire.

Leader: Whirl round my little atom atom
         Spin around you pretty little neutron
         Dance around and fall down
All: Dance around my Freedom Fire.

Leader: Hug me my goodness gracious
         I'll sing a little song of ages
         Dance around and fall down
All: Dance around my Freedom Fire.

(Fade to whisper):

         Dance around my Freedom Fire
         Dance around my Freedom Fire
            Dance around my Freedom Fire
            Dance around my Freedom Fire[18]

Pandora's nuclear box had been opened, perhaps never to be shut; but there were still other battles to fight in the postwar world—battles that had been set aside only in the interests of Allied victory. The Depression may have played itself out in war, but the struggle for workers' rights was now fully off the back burner and there was no room for ambivalence here. American labor was again on a war footing, with new CIO strike offensives commencing immediately after V-J Day, hitting major cities coast to coast. The Hollywood movie industry was paralyzed. In the South, "Operation Dixie," a massive organizing drive, was launched to extend the militant union struggles of Gastonia and Harlan into the entire region. By January of 1946 the auto workers, steel workers, electricians, and meat cutters were on strike across the country.

That same month, Guthrie had a new assignment. Asch sent him to Boston and Braintree, Massachusetts, to soak up the details of the miscarriage of justice that, in John Dos Passos's estimation, had taken "the clean words our fathers spoke and made them slimy and foul";[19] the verdict and sentence that Katherine Anne Porter called "The Never-Ending Wrong"[20]—the executions of Nicola Sacco and Bartolomeo Vanzetti, two Italian-born anarchists, on trumped-up murder charges in 1927. After this judicial travesty, the notorious hanging judge, Webster Thayer, was heard to boast on a golf course, "Did you see what I did to those anarchist bastards the other day?"[21] The kernel of the prosecution's agenda had been embedded in Thayer's astounding courtroom assertion regarding Vanzetti: "This man, although he may not actually have committed the crime attributed to him, is nevertheless morally culpable, because he is the enemy of our existing institutions."[22] (As Kurt Vonnegut was to marvel: "Word of honor: This was said by a judge in an American court of law.")[23]

Asch wanted Guthrie to write and record a cycle of songs commemorating this episode of political persecution, all the more necessary amid the growing anticommunist backlash. Guthrie vowed: "I'm going to draw back my pencil and pound / Judge Thayers name into ashes":

> Sacco and Vanzetti, to give your heart ease,
>> I'll strike out for Boston, go hungry,
>> Or freeze,
> I'll hitch hike or freight it to see all these
>> Places where you worked and lived with
>> The sun on your faces
> I'll hobo it, cushion it, swing rod or tie,
>> I'll chalk it, I'll walk it, I'll root
>> hog or die[24]

Toward the end of his articulate life, Guthrie would designate *Ballads of Sacco and Vanzetti*—his record about "that frame-up massacre by Judge Webster Thayer"—as "one of the best albums we ever made."[25] The album's twelve songs were, he said, "the most important dozen songs I've ever worked on."[26] However, during their composition, Guthrie confessed to unaccountable difficulties. As he wrote to Asch on one occasion: "I refuse to write these songs while I'm drunk and it looks like I'll be drunk for a long time."[27] The finished product certainly betrays these difficulties.

The ordeal of Sacco and Vanzetti has often been presented as an American Passion. Guthrie himself was not wholly immune to the temptation to depict Sacco and Vanzetti as a pair of holy martyrs—a potentially self-defeating exercise inviting breast-beating rather than steely critical outrage over the blatant corruption of due process. However, *Ballads of Sacco and Vanzetti* is, at its best, an artful collage of responses—irony, outrage, humor, pathos— reflecting the possible range of emotions prompted by the case. There are indeed a number of misfirings, such as the unconvincing inflation of the case's global impact in the opening track, "The Flood and the Storm":

Well the world shook harder on the night they died
Than it was shaken by that great World War.
More millions did march for Sacco and Vanzetti
Than did march for the great warlords.

The song also marks the only instance in which Guthrie adopts—and in the process over-eggs—the storm imagery of Golgotha, tacking perilously close to the holy associations of the Passion:

The zig-zag lighting, the rumbles of the thunder
And the singing of the clouds blowing by,
The flood and the storm for Sacco and Vanzetti
Caused the rich man to pull his hair and cry.[28]

Amid all the messiness, however, there are some very strong moments, such as Guthrie's ruminations on the disappearance of Sacco and Vanzetti from the moral and political landscape of the Land of the Free:

These tourists don't see you, Vanzetti,
The salesmen and gamblers on tour.
Your footprints are dim and your trail has sprung weeds
And their tourist map don't show you there.

The trade union workers, Vanzetti,
Will vacation here and will tour
This Rock and this town and Plymouth around
When statues have souls like yours.[29]

Elsewhere, in a refreshingly comedic engagement (since few, if any, commentators have dared to treat the Passion of Sacco and Vanzetti with humor), Guthrie succeeds in reducing Webster Thayer to a barnyard gangster straight out of a Saturday morning cartoon. As a result, Thayer comes down before all posterity as a bantam thug rather than an awesome grand inquisitor— perhaps a more suitable judgment in the long run:

Well the possum used a big stiff broom
And he polished the new spittoon.
Up did smile a crocodile,
Said, "Here comes the jury down the aisle."
Old Mama Catfish asked the trout,
"What's this trial here all about?"
Little baby suckerfish upped and said,
"The Judge has caught him a couple of Reds."[30]

Strongest of all is the song "Two Good Men," a finely crafted admission of the case's impact on Guthrie as an embattled radical in a time of increasing repression. It is perhaps for this reason that "Two Good Men" has been covered more frequently than any other song from the album, for it is a powerful call to fight the good fight even in the midst of political peril:

> Well, I ain't got time to tell this tale,
> The dicks and bulls are on my trail.
> But I'll remember these two good men
> That died to show me how to live.
>
> Two good men's a long time gone.
> Two good men's a long time gone.
> Two good men's a long time gone.
> Left me here to sing this song.[31]

It is a measure of the project's fitful composition—as well as the postwar political sea change—that *Ballads of Sacco and Vanzetti* was not released by Asch on Folkways until 1964, bearing the inscription "Composed and sung by Woody Guthrie—1946–47."[32] Meanwhile, in the midst of its composition, Guthrie began to formulate other plans. As he had written, singing was "nothing in the world but pure hypnotism," and it could be "used to either put you to sleep or wake you up."[33] Thus he wrote to Asch with an idea for a new wake-up call, "an album of labor martyrs on 4 to 4½ minute records." The subjects would include:

1. Sacco and Vanzetti (one or several songs)
2. Haymarket Bombing (Chicago. Eight men executed)
3. Bloody Sunday (Everett, Wash., Timber workers picnic massacre)
4. Scottsboro Boys (you know this story)
5. Joe Hill (Utah State Copper voted C.I.O. recently)
6. Tom Mooney
7. Mother Bloor
8. Magnus Colorado (Apache Indian bombing)[34]

He also envisaged a new recording of Dust Bowl ballads to supersede the original record, which he had once considered Victor's most "radical album":

> We can do a better job from every point of view if we do a new one, more progressive, bring in the strike songs, spirituals of the migrant workers . . . give it a more organized twist and picture the fights and beatings plainer. We can bring in the big crops, factories, mines, timbers, dams, and building ships and planes, and show how they love you when they need you and hate you when

they don't. I have thought a lot about how different I would do those Victor
Records if I had them to do over again.[35]

Guthrie was also elated to hear that a fan had singled out his *Struggle* album
as a favorite:

> You happen to hit on my pet album, Harry, when you picked out my "Docu-
> mentary Struggle"... Those six songs and ballads in that album, I've always been
> my proudest of. They sound to me like I hope I sound to other folks, and their
> facts are based word for word in the truth of bloody trade union history. There's
> room for several thousand more such songs, chants, ballads, tales, dances, and
> things, to be told and yelled out of the pages of our American labor history, but
> it is a sad thing to see that few schools and few colleges make it socially polite
> to either write up or to sing any such terrible reminders of the good workers
> that have been cut down fighting for a better world for me and you.[36]

There was, however, only so much that an individual songwriter could
achieve. Guthrie looked to the labor movement, which seemed to him obtuse
and blind when it came to utilizing its cultural workers (particularly musicians), causing him—as he confessed—"to weep and to sigh, to tear my hair,
to wave my fists around in this room." He hectored the movement over the
waste of a perfectly good resource: "Lenin said he would like for one out of
every three Communists to play the balalaika. He knew that those little music
notes jumping out of that sound hole would draw the workers, farmers, and
all serious thinkers around in a crowd to sing and to dance and to march
together. Well, our trade union movement did not use its guitar, its mandolin,
its mouth harp, its juice harp, it fiddles, its horns, its woodwinds, and its skin
drums, half as clever and smart as the reactionary side used theirs."[37]

It was in this knowledge that Guthrie cried out to organized labor—in particular, to the CIO—to nurture the cultural potential in its midst: "There is a
thousand neon lit spots all over New York where AFoL nite club performers
draw down good lettuce at a nice easy pace, while the progressive or labor
movement singer is protected by no union and guaranteed no job nor fee,
no set income."[38] (Gone were the days when Guthrie could bring himself to
write a song urging workers to "Go down and join that A.F. of L," as he had
done during the war.[39] Now he was writing to Asch: "They have stayed in
business for Forty Years saying exactly nothing and some days less.")[40] He
pleaded with the CIO to underwrite its cultural workers' efforts: "It is why
we've got to pay our social conscious people at least a fairly decent fee, so that
our good ones will not fall for the sweet lipped baits of the big money side.
We have got to pay our leftwing artists enough so that their soul and body
will remain together long enough for them to perform their greatest good for

the union side instead of for the blackmarket side."[41] This was the only way for the movement to prevent its most articulate and inspiring agents from being lured "off over into the valleys of retreating paradise offered as bait by our lords and masters":

> Just see to it that the average wage and fees of your left wing militant artists climbs up, and up, and up some more, twice or three times what it is today, and then it will commence to figure very nearly as much as a taxi driver, an electrician, a painter, a plumber, or a traveling salesman that buzzes around our highways peddling capitalistic products in a smooth running car. You can no more ask your social conscious artists to do their stuff free than you could ask your butcher, your grocer, your painter, plumber, electrician, to come and bring you their services free. Why this is even expected so often as it is, is something I can't understand, and yet I can understand it very easy.[42]

The situation was aggravated by the reality of the working folk musician's frantic scramble for enough paying jobs to survive. "We do not get a job every night and all are forced to make two or more places over one night's time," Guthrie argued; "and yet, people faint at their fone receivers when a folk singer mentions the word money."[43] Hence Guthrie's oft-quoted response to a woman requesting that he sing for free simply because it was "for a good cause": "Lady, I don't sing for bad causes."[44]

But it was one thing to be aware of such thoughtless exploitation, even if it came at the hands of fellow progressives; it was another thing to devise a strategy to combat it. Guthrie was wrestling with the same dilemma that he and the Almanacs had faced during the war when he told Mike Quin: "We're full of ideas as a dog full of ticks, but somehow or other there comes a time when we feel like the old capitalist system itself—able to produce, but not able to distribute."[45] One part of the strategy must be to reverse the deepening isolation of individual, ideologically committed singers—in a sense, to give them their own union, a union whose mission would be to inspire other unions through music and performance.

Unbeknownst to Guthrie, Pete Seeger had been wrestling with the same ideas while stationed at Saipan, where he and other singers—Mario "Boots" Casetta, Betty Sanders, and Felix Landau—conceived of "a loosely knit organization, some structure where people could get together to exchange and print songs."[46] Meanwhile, in Philadelphia, Lee Hays and Walter Lowenfels had been envisaging a magazine devoted to the mass circulation of labor songs and radical commentary. All this energy suggested to Seeger that "there was a job we could do, intellectually and organizationally. We could make a singing labor movement, take up where Joe Hill left off, and carry the tradi-

tion on."[47] With no sense then of the depths of the conservatism that would
soon wipe out all vestiges of union radicalism—even within the CIO—Seeger
and his colleagues "were convinced that the revival of interest in folk music
would come through the trade unions."[48]

Guthrie described the enthusiasm with which Seeger unveiled to him "the
idea that he had cooked up about People's Songs" (in the process lending
Seeger an improbably Guthriesque voice): "The unions have cried for the
material that we've got, they need our several thousand songs, and they need
new ones made up on the jump as we go along. They have written to me, to
you, to every other songwriter or collector and had to waste time while you
wrote to me and I called somebody else and they chased the next one up
one side and down the other."[49] Guthrie's version of Seeger draws the major
battle lines (while supercharging Seeger's own quiet observation, "We had
the utmost contempt for normal commercial musical endeavors"):[50]

> The bosses and the monopoly folks own their leather lined offices, pay clerks
> big money, pay experts, pay detectives, pay thugs, pay artists to perform their
> complacent crap, pay investigators to try to keep our staff beat down, and the
> earthly way that we can buck against all of this pressure is to all get together
> into one big songwriters and song singers union, and we will call our union
> by the name of Peoples Songs. And if we all stick together, all hell and melted
> teargases can't stop us, nor atoms hold us back.[51]

Years later Seeger ruefully recalled: "How our theories went astray! Most
union leaders could not see any connection between music and porkchops."[52]
Nor, unsurprisingly, was the CPUSA interested. Seeger described how he had
pitched the idea of People's Songs to a Party cultural officer: "He said 'Sure,
fine, great idea, put us on your mailing list'—but he didn't seem to care much
one way or the other."[53] The same lack of interest could not be attributed to
the FBI, which opened its file on People's Songs immediately upon its incor-
poration, eventually amassing a 500-page collection of pilfered documents
and minutes, transcriptions of illegally tapped phone calls, misinformation
from the U.S. Army's *Domestic Intelligence Summary,* and HUAC testimony.[54]
As it happened, the Bureau need not have had such heartfelt concern for the
security of the American way at the hands of People's Songs, for as Seeger
phrased it, the United States was hardly "full of class conscious harmonizing
in those days."[55]

But in the midst of the brief postwar euphoria generated by the CIO's last
great strike wave, Seeger gathered together over thirty musicians, singers,
choral directors, CIO officers, education activists, and at least one FBI stool
pigeon to establish People's Songs, officially incorporated in January 1946 with

Seeger as national director. The board of directors, which included Guthrie and other major folk-revival figures as well as Paul Robeson and the producer John Hammond, presided over a network of activities organized in a tiny office in Times Square. The organization's bulletin, *People's Songs*, was the major source of information dissemination, eventually reaching between two and three thousand subscribers across the United States. The *People's Song Book* soon followed. An auxiliary booking agency, People's Artists, Inc., was set up to arrange and coordinate live performances and—most importantly—to secure payment for radical musicians. (People's Artists would last until 1957, battered by McCarthyism and its own internal conflicts, but having steered radical folk expression through its darkest hours with the organization of hootenannies, the constitution of singing groups, the establishment of the Hootenanny record label, the publication in 1953 of *Lift Every Voice!*—"the only major left-wing songbook of the McCarthy years"[56]—and, in 1950, the founding of *Sing Out!* magazine, to this day its most abiding legacy.)

The first issue of *People's Songs*—published in February 1946—broadcast a manifesto that Seeger drafted, "thinking," he said, "along terms of the Communist movement."[57] Hence the exhortative diction so out of step with the bread-and-butter concerns of the increasingly conservative unions:

> The people are on the march and must have songs to sing. Now, in 1946, the truth must reassert itself in many singing voices.
>
> There are thousands of unions, people's organizations, singers, and choruses who would gladly use more songs. There are many songwriters, amateur and professional, who are writing these songs.
>
> It is clear that there must be an organization to make and send songs of labor and the American people through the land.
>
> To do this job, we have formed PEOPLE'S SONGS, INC.
>
> We invite you to join us.[58]

Seeger appealed first and foremost to the unions themselves:

> Do you want to publish a songbook for your members? Write us for help in putting one together.
>
> Do you want a song composed especially for your union? Would you like to have phonograph records of your own songs for use in your locals?
>
> These are jobs which we are prepared to do.[59]

To individual songwriters he promised that the bulletin would print songs by amateurs and professionals, arrange for further printings in sheet-music form, and ensure "complete copyright and royalty protection"—a significant departure from the Almanacs' "anonymous" credo.[60] A further departure lay in the organization's broadened musical remit. As Seeger wrote in the *New Masses:* "We aim to have People's Songs cover every kind of musical expression which can be of use to musical organizations: folk, jazz, popular, or serious cantatas for union choruses."[61]

People's Songs eventually built up a massive library of labor songs, estimated to contain as many as twenty thousand titles—at the time the largest collection outside of the Library of Congress and the British Museum.[62] They established branches in San Francisco, Hollywood, and Chicago; sent performers out to picket lines and rallies; produced records, filmstrips, and educational material; set up classes on "the use of music for political action" in New York, Boston, Chicago, and Washington; and organized concerts in venues such as New York's Town Hall.[63] They also revived the hootenanny as a source of revenue and visibility. Guthrie's recollection accurately reflects the exponential gain in the hoots' popularity (if not the exact numbers): "The first Peoples Songs Hootenanny was thrown in the Otah home, and Eight people came. The second Hoot was up in Brother's apartment on Thompson Street, and a Hundred and Twelve came. The third was in the Newspaper Guild Hall on East 40th Street, and Three Hundred sang for half a day."[64]

Guthrie treated the People's Songs venture as a godsend in its earliest days. "We are trying not to sell ourselves nor our services over onto the right wing scales and display windows," he wrote. "We are trying to actually fight to rid this world of capitalism amongst artists, performers, and every other place. We are like guns and cannons, we must be polished, oiled, loaded, and loved, to work our best."[65] At last, it seemed, there would be the strength in numbers that had so eluded the Almanacs: "The trouble is lack of organization, the Worlds Worst Illness, and I believe in my soul that 'Peoples Songs' will help a lot."[66]

The buoyant atmosphere among CIO activists contributed to Guthrie's optimism as long as the strike wave lasted. In March of 1946, Seeger, Hays, and Guthrie flew to Pittsburgh to sing at a tumultuous rally for the striking electrical workers at Westinghouse. It appeared to Guthrie that the CIO had finally embraced its folksingers as indispensable resources. His exaggerated recollection of the Pittsburgh rally betrays the sheer euphoria that he, along with other American radicals, felt in the wake of the fascist defeat and at the apparent dawn of labor's new era:

> I saw people throw pages of Peoples Songs out from high buildings to flood the crowd as we sang on the bandstand at the marble steps of the City Hall. . . .
>
> We sang "Solidarity Forever" and the papers said the rally started off with a communist song. Oh. Well. Any song that fights for the case of the workhand is a communist song to the rich folks.

Speakers spoke between our songs. The mayor dished out a nice plate of broad and liberal words into the faces of several Thousand sore and anxious strikers. We sang Two songs made up this day for the situation here at Westinghouse. The crowd roared like the ocean in a rock cavern.

This was the biggest meeting, march, and rally to ever take place here in Pittsburgh. The Iron Town never saw so many troopers nor so many cops nor so many workers in their everyday clothes. The One Hundred Troopers were made so much fun of that I nearly felt sorry for them.[67]

Riding the exhilarating wave of labor militancy, Guthrie rounded on the slightest perceived accommodations with capitalism, even if they came from old activist colleagues such as Jim Garland, whose anthem "All I Want" (recorded by the Almanacs on *Talking Union*) cried plaintively:

> I don't want your millions, mister,
> I don't want your diamond rings;
> All I want is the right to live, mister.
> Give me back my job again.[68]

In a note below the lyrics to his own song "I'm Out to Get," dated April 5, 1946, Guthrie recalled his cross-country tour with the Almanacs in 1941:

> Well, I hated that song and argued about it all across the country and back. I said the workers do want your millions Mister, do want your pleasure yacht, do want your pleasure car, do want your watch and chain, and they do want lots more than, "just the right to live, Mister" or "my old job back again." Well, here it is Three or Four years later and me with my Second wife and Fourth child, and I am just now getting around to half way answering this argument with this song, "I'm Out to Get." I think that the song its own self makes things about as clear as I could by arguing with you any longer.[69]

The "song its own self"—a contemptuous rejoinder to "All I Want"—is both a claim to restitution and a vow of retribution:

> I'm out to get your greenback dollar
> I'm out to get your silver change
> I'm out to get your long black limousine
> You kept me down on my knees too long.

The restitution would come, as ever, through the union solidarity that Guthrie had always championed:

> So brother I'm out to get your excess bacon
> I'm out to get my cut from you
> I'm going to walk and talk and tell all my neighbors
> How they ought to talk right up for their cut too.

It won't be with no gun nor gambling wheel sir
That I will use to relieve your till
It will be in a nice friendly way with all my neighbors
Smelling and barking brother up and down your trail.[70]

Guthrie's bullishness notwithstanding, he was in fact witnessing militant labor's last stand. In May of 1946 the CIO president, Philip Murray, damned the "communistic interference with the affairs of the labor movement," and the following November the CIO passed a sweeping anticommunist resolution.[71] Even Joe Curran, president of Guthrie's own National Maritime Union, joined in the purge, as did Walter Reuther of the United Auto Workers. The intense anticommunist activity on the New York labor front provided a particularly stark microcosm, where the Newspaper Guild, the American Federation of Musicians, and the American Federation of Radio Artists all purged their left-wing leadership. It had not been all that long ago that Guthrie could envision a "Union Train" crewed by the Big Three, who prevent its hijacking by John L. Lewis—in Guthrie's estimation the turncoat who had ditched the CIO (which he had, after all, founded) for the "spineless," conservative AFL:

Johnny Lewis jumped on the coal car
And he says "I'll steal the coal!
I'll steal the fire out of the boiler
So this union train can't roll!"
Churchill touched a lit cigar
To the seat of Lewis's tail
Stalin said to Roosevelt
"Lewis outran the Limited Mail!"[72]

Yet now, with even the CIO turning on the very communist movement that had worked to establish it, Guthrie could not avoid sensing the change in the wind.

It was the beginning of a bitter slide into disillusionment. Guthrie's was an increasingly isolated voice calling from the wilderness for the reconstitution of American society and the destruction of capitalism. He wrote to Asch in July of 1946:

This is the system I would like to see die out. It killed several members of my family, it gassed several and shell shocked several more in the last world war, and in this world war just past, it scattered lots more. It drove families of my relatives and friends by the hundreds of thousands to wander more homeless than dogs and to live less welcome than hogs, sheep, or cattle. This is the system I started out to expose by every conceivable way that I could think of with songs and with ballads, and even with poems, stories, newspaper articles, even by humor, by fun, by nonsense, ridicule and by any other way that I could lay hold on.[73]

Other writings of this period reflect Guthrie's near-bewilderment as he watched the militant labor movement crumble all around him. "The feeling is a crazy mixed up whirl," he wrote in October 1946: "a world of fallen wreckage, a garbage heap, a tangled, wild sort of a salvage yard, a vision called up by a loose blown paper, a curb stone of gum wrappers, struck matches, empty paper cups, the smell of trash cans, the looks on every face, the ways that people hump, stroll, saunter, and crawl along the sidewalks. It comes over me like a mist rising or a fog falling, like a danger bell ringing out here in the channel."[74] Hence the ideological loneliness pervading the lyrics to "Revolutionary Mind," a "Blues: Slow and easy" penned by Guthrie in September 1946:

> Night is here again, Babe,
> I'm stretched out on my bed
> Seeing the years of labor struggles
> Running through my head.
>> I need a progressive woman;
>> I need an awful liberal mama;
>> Aint no reactionary baby
>> Can ease my revolutionary mind.

The song's parodic playfulness does nothing to disguise Guthrie's sense of his own political isolation in the prevailing mood of bourgeois consensus:

> My lonesome soul is radical;
> Yes, I ache and pain and bleed;
> I want you to come here running
> If you blister both your feet.
>> I need a progressive lot mate;
>> I need a liberal understander;
>> Ain't no two party woman
>> Can ease my revolutionary mind.[75]

Guthrie's "radical soul" was made doubly "lonesome" by the postwar musical context, which saw political folksingers elbowed to the margins of society, labeled as naïfs at best and, at worst, "un-American"—a charge being flung about with increasing recklessness. Even the National Maritime Union could no longer find any use for Guthrie as an activist singer. He began to reflect bitterly on the great rift then cleaving the urban folk movement between the commercially successful and the marginalized singers. He made it clear to Asch on which side of the dividing line he stood:

> Not all of us folk and ballad makers stand where I stand. Not all of them see the world as I see it. Some would rather be a "character," and to be fotographed and filmed, broadcast and recorded, and paid big money by the big money side. They would rather occupy a certain social position, to be well known, to play the games of publicity gangsters, and to enjoy the crowds that clap and yell when you tell them directly or indirectly that this old world is okie dokie, she is all right, she is a nice good place to live on, and if you kick or argue, or make too much noise with your mouth, then you are just a native born kicker, and a griper, and you are kicked out by your own inability to "cooperate" with the high moguls.[76]

And then he began to name names: "I can't help wondering about the strange love affairs and all the warm friendships that arise between our big owners and a man, we will say, like Josh White. And when I see this same back patting and hair rubbing going on now between the bosses and Burl Ives, I find my curiosity growing faster than the weeds here in my backyard."[77] Guthrie also had the ballad singer Richard Dyer-Bennett in his sights. These three artists, Guthrie recalled, had "sung for radical rallies and meetings, entertained in homes for left wing causes, sang at cocktail parties where the cause was a revolutionary one, and performed many times among trade union people for the reasons of building the union stronger." Now he compared their output unfavorably with "the more militant works of Earl Robinson, and the others in his same vein," to determine which ones would "walk up the money plank and turn to an oily pile of rope."[78]

It was true that Ives and White in particular were enjoying increasing success in the New York lounge circuit and Hollywood. Both had secured major-label recording contracts. If he was at all envious, Guthrie made no attempt to hide it; rather, he reconstructed his envy as ostentatious martyrdom in order to hammer home the charge of political betrayal:

> Josh, you know how to act the big shoe over in the camping fires of your enemy. But don't forget how us folks are back here where you come from.
> I want me a fast hammer new model Cadillac just like your new Buick.
>
> Burl Ives . . . You got awful tired of singing around with no folding stuff to make your woman snap open and shut. So did I, Burl.
> I want some folding fodder in my long old empty.[79]

He slipped into the self-righteous rhetoric that so often marked his lectures on the pitfalls and corruption of commercial success, assassinating through insinuation and mock indulgence the characters of his former comrades, who not so long ago had been two of his favorite "Union Boys." Against these two flabby, softened sellouts (as Guthrie now painted them), he cast himself as the last of the true musical warriors:

> I just simply took the route I guess you'd call the "Guerrilla Route" with my guitar, while Burl took the padded lounge route to do his own kind of fighting in the kind of scenery that he picked out with his own hand. Josh White took the "Cellar Tavern" Route, the kind of a route that would cramp my tail bone into wild epileptic knots and fits, but Josh would feel just as hogtied and hobbled in my Guerrilla Territory as I feel around his drawing room and parlor crowds. I sing my best down along the waterfront, the Battery, the Bowery, Skid Row, the Back Street, but I can't ask every progressive folksinger to sing his best, nor her best, along the lost streets that inspire my tonsils.[80]

To place these splenetic attacks in some perspective, Guthrie's ire was not driven solely by the fact that a Burl Ives could achieve stardom and riches by singing an anodyne version of "On Top of Old Smoky" for a Hollywood movie. Underlying his puritanical and (especially in the case of White) overstated charges of selling out was a conception of the corporate censor's divisive, reactionary agenda, which, it seemed to Guthrie, went far beyond the simple desire to make money. As he argued: "One of the slickest ways to hush us up is to hire us to perform under their censorship, or to buy us out and put us on their shelf, or to use us in the padded saloons and to pay us enough to scare us away from all of our left wing friends and comrades."[81] Still, Guthrie seemed to forget that Pete Seeger, for one, was happy enough singing "in the padded saloons" and cellar taverns if it meant that People's Songs could benefit from it.

Filtering the Marxist theory increasingly dominating his reading matter, Guthrie began to see menace and obstructions everywhere, spiraling out from "the padded saloons" into the hegemonic and repressive agencies of the capitalist state. There was the hostile right-wing press—"the Hearst papers and the McCormick papers"—ever out to undermine the labor movement ("Yes sir, the money that we give them to use as weapons against us would buy all of us a six room cement house with the very latest plastic furniture, and all pushbuttoned through and through.")[82] There were the music moguls, "buying you and your art out of circulation, to keep you from stirring up your people against their blind owners . . . blocking your hand on every side, or causing you to get all lost and tangled up in a thousand traps of their psychological, emotional, economical, legal and illegal sorts of personal warfare." Behind the moguls was an entire infrastructure of state repression: "But no matter how much he actually pays into your hand, you never get more than a small fraction of what you are worth to him, because he must pay a long line of dicks, guards, deputies, plain clothes men, snoops and stooges, snipers and fonies, that played their parts in rendering you completely harmless."[83]

When Guthrie looked at the political landscape, his fears were only confirmed. November of 1946 brought in the first Republican-dominated Congress in fourteen years; the following year, the Cold War began in earnest, spearheaded in quick succession by the anticommunist Truman Doctrine, the monetary seductions of the Marshall Plan, the anti-union and anticommunist Taft-Hartley Act, and the revival of the House Committee on Un-American Activities, whose first victims would be the Hollywood Ten in the fall of 1947. President Truman's dismissal of Henry Wallace as secretary of commerce marked the final purge of the New Deal spirit from the government. On March 13, 1947, the day after the announcement of the Truman Doctrine, Wallace predicted on national radio "generations of want and war" and the beginning of "a century of fear." America was destined to become "the most hated nation in the world."[84]

The Truman Doctrine, which announced "the policy of the United States to support free peoples who are resisting attempted subjugation by armed minorities or by outside pressures," was America's first statement of Communist containment.[85] It had been sparked by the year-old Greek Civil War in which the Communist-backed Greek National Liberation Front was battling against the monarchy of George II and his government, lately returned from exile in London. The royal government was strongly backed by Britain and the United States. The Truman Doctrine filled Guthrie with fury:

> I'm a Greek working man, and a fighter, too;
> All kinds of bombs and powder I waded through;
> > I've seen my street and my town blowed down,
> And the same black market cops walking all around.
> > Fascists
> > Fought to get rid of them.
> > They didn't even change their uniforms.
> > Still walking my sidewalk.

As far as Guthrie was concerned, the civil war in Greece was no less of an anti-imperialist struggle than the celebrated independence movement shortly to result in Indian and Pakistani nationhood. He poured scorn on Winston Churchill (in spite of the compliment he had conferred in making Churchill an honorary crew member of the "Union Train"—a most curious honor, given

Churchill's lifelong hostility to Britain's trade unions). Churchill remained the defender of empire and was a bitter opponent of both the Greek and Indian resistance movements. Guthrie roundly damned his Greek policy:

> Churchill is in sad company;
> Churchill is in sad company;
> King George of Greece he don't want nobody free;
> And Churchill is in sad company.[86]

As for India, Churchill—while professing *noblesse oblige* for all Britain's imperial subjects—had called Mahatma Gandhi "a seditious Middle-Temple lawyer . . . posing as a fakir" who "dared to parley on equal terms with the representative of the King-Emperor."[87] Guthrie sneered at Churchill's declarations of imperial affection: "The kid from India told me, 'I don't want to see England love our country so much that they send in armies and keep us in cages and feed us less than animals.'"[88]

Guthrie's recharged anti-imperialism drove him even more firmly into the arms of the communist movement (if such a thing were possible); but that movement itself was at the tail end of a poisonous power struggle. In the growing reactionary climate, hard-liners within the movement had launched an offensive that succeeded in nothing but eviscerating the Party's infrastructure through a purge of its reformist membership and a return to prewar orthodoxy. The CPA had been dissolved and the CPUSA formally reconstituted, with its leader, Browder, brutally expelled from the Party in 1946 and replaced by the hard-line William Z. Foster. This fatal rear-guard action was supported by the Party's staunchest defenders, including Guthrie, who argued: "If there is no party, the outsiders get the wrong idea . . . that it had to close its doors like a failed fruit stand, or we are going mysteriously underground."[89] Though he was not a card-carrying member, his loyalty to the CPUSA was unshaken—"Lord knows, I owe them . . . the only guidance and recognition and pay that I've ever tasted"—as was his admiration for Stalin: "The whole world cannot trick Joseph Stalin because he is too scientific for them."[90] (The orthodoxy of Guthrie's jargon at this time could sometimes border on caricature. As he wrote to Asch: "Farm and town are all one word, and work is work, and this has welded the farm scientist and the city scientist together under one name").[91] He kept the faith with the *Sunday Worker,* for which he had begun writing a column shortly after his army discharge, and with the *Daily Worker,* which he defended against all slander. (In one instance, when an acquaintance sneered that he kept a stack of the *Daily Worker* "in the outhouse," Guthrie snapped back: "Some people can't absorb knowledge any other way.")[92]

As if the attacks from reactionaries were not enough, Guthrie began to detect hostility coming from his own comrades in People's Songs—a measure of his increasing hypersensitivity amid the pressures of political backlash. Characteristically, the major issue was censorship—ironically so, given that one of the organization's objectives, as Vivian Howard wrote in *Masses and Mainstream*, was to "free a certain number of artists from the censorship and hampering control of the monopolies."[93] After Seeger and Waldemar Hille gave what they assumed was constructive criticism to a song-in-progress dwelling on the social and sexual squalor of Skid Row, Guthrie fired off an angry letter addressed to "Peoples Songs & Peoples Artists, Pencils and Scissors": "I'm wondering if Winston Churchill, or Heebert Hover, Old Man Taft or Hartley, any or all of them, would not set up just about this same set of moral standards which already chop the heads off of every song and ballad on our radio air waves, recordings, movies, and so forth and so on. I got the blue and red and pink and purpledy pencils shot to my songs so much up at WNEW my 13 Sundays which I was up there, that, well, there wasn't enough left in each of my songs to chase down a drink of liquor with."[94]

The letter hints at a violent break with People's Songs—"I guess I couldn't take it no longer. I give up the crate. I done what you'd call hitting the blue"— and a vow to continue precisely on the path that their criticism discouraged: "I realize that every one of us sings to his or her certain audience and in their own particular tone of word and imagery. But, as for me, I'm just afraid that you have caused me to take another run off down to the slums and to see if I can't write fifty songs, poems, notes, ideas, suggestions, and essays, stories, movies, plots, scenarios, and other kinds of words to make you see these lousy slumjoints as rank and bitter, as sour, as hellish as they really are."[95]

Two weeks later, in a conciliatory letter to Seeger, Guthrie suggested: "I don't think that we'd ought to even use the word sex in analyzing nor criticizing a People's song. No song can contain too much of it, no song can contain too little of it. We're trying to get a big Union set up to where all of us can work and make the money it takes to live a sex life with."[96] The facetiousness of Guthrie's conclusion does not mask the bitterness with which he faced the prospect of censorship, real or perceived, whether at the hands of friends or adversaries.

As was the case with the Almanacs, Guthrie gave to later historians the impression that by 1947 he had withdrawn from the People's Songs project in order to work—yet again—on another novel, *Study Butte* (finally published in 1976 as *Seeds of Man*).[97] But a letter from July 1948 indicates that Guthrie was still active on behalf of People's Songs, reporting to the organization that he had received a note of thanks from a mother in Georgia for sending her a parcel of clothes and the *People's Song Book*: "I got this nice letter in my box a day or so ago, and pass it on to you just to show you that the smaller kids are really a big field for Peoples Songs that say something about something."[98] As was also the case with the Almanacs, whatever energies Guthrie could invest in People's Songs (at about this time a sinister hint of neurological disorder had begun to emerge) he invested according to his greatest strength, which was songwriting rather than bureaucracy.

Union was still his "religion," as he had written while at sea.[99] Now, more than ever, it was a political and spiritual lifeline: "I live union. I eat union. I think union. I see union. I walk it and I talk it. I sing it and I preach it."[100] But everywhere Guthrie looked, the good union fight appeared all but abandoned. In the midst of a tightly typed seven-page prose poem, "Hills of Ithica [sic]," he re-created a moment in a train carriage:

> Every one of you walk up and down my aisle here and you take a goodlong sideglance at the way my guitar case is all painted up. Signs of your own times that say:
> "THIS MACHINE KILLS FASCISTS". "Jim Crow", "Race Hate" and I pasted a little poster across the whole thing that reads: Support the GM Strikers.
> One man tells me, "Take off that GM striker sign; they've won that strike already." I told the man, "No, I'll just leave it on. I'll rub out that GM there and write in that spot: Support ALL your good strikers."[101]

But Guthrie would have to look hard to locate many strikers, thanks to the Taft-Hartley Act and the ongoing union purges. He reached sadly backward to the glory days of Harlan and resurrected its young martyr, Harry Simms, in a ballad made all the more poignant by the current air of surrender:

> I'm crying for a friend of mine that's gone
> I'm crying for a friend of mine that's gone
> A man that studied books to organize us
> He's buried here where my weeping willow sighs.[102]

He could also take, at best, a melancholy pleasure to learn that he was the basis for the character of Woody Mahoney, the fighting, singing union organizer in the 1946 musical *Finian's Rainbow,* by "Yip" Harburg (a fellow People's Songs activist) and Fred Saidy.[103] It was all fine for a fictional union singer to croon out the good fight from the Broadway stage; but as Seeger ruefully recalled, "Which Side Are You On?" was no longer to be heard "in a single miner's union local," however much it was still being sung in the lofts of Greenwich Village.[104]

Guthrie's increasing malaise was thus as much political as it was neurological, and he clung to the struggle as to a life preserver. He wrote to Asch with a

desperately simple formula as a rock on which to stand amid the disintegration of labor militancy: "Everything is a part of the conflict between the boss
man and the work hand."[105] His songs were clearly becoming obsessive, as
Guthrie himself admitted to Asch: "Marjorie seems to think that this piece
preaches too heavy on the Union angle, maybe she's right."[106] His notebook
bristled with expressions of both musical and political need:

> Tune of "Will the Circle Be Unbroken"—will the union stay unbroken.
>   Needed: a sassy tune for a scab song.
>   Need of pointing out in song that you got to rise above simple
>   porkchop unionism.[107]

So it was that in his most harrowing hour of personal desperation, caused
by the death of his daughter Cathy Ann in 1947, Guthrie turned to the union
struggle as a means of making sense of profound tragedy. On February 9,
Guthrie was called to sing for what appeared to be one of the few remaining
radical locals, the United Electrical Workers at the Phelps-Dodge plant in
Elizabeth, New Jersey, who had just concluded an eight-month strike. This
bitter dispute had been marked by police-sponsored strike breaking, violent
clashes between scabs and workers, and the death of union organizer and
father of four Mario Russo, shot on the picket line. When Guthrie returned
home from the rally, he learned that his daughter had been fatally burned
in a fire in their living room. Four months later he was able to send People's
Songs a ballad he had written in honor of Russo, at the top of which he explained: "I wrote up this ballad after I'd sung down there at the rally of the
Phelps Dodge workers in Elizabeth on February the 9th, the day they met to
celebrate their strike was won after 8 months and 3 days. This was the same
Sunday night when I came home with my guitar to find that a copper wire
had shorted out in our front room causing a fire that took the life of our little
four year old daughter, Cathy Ann."[108]

The deaths of Russo and Cathy Ann were soon twinned in Guthrie's mind,
a torturous connection born out of grief and a sense of the cheapness of human life at the mercy of profit and greed. As Guthrie replied to John Lomax's
letter of condolence: "In this case, the spark was caused by a faulty no good
wartime radio wire, which shows that the cheap synthetic imitation products
made for the greedy profits of a manufacturer is still failing in a million ways,
in ship hulls, in brake shoes, in roominghouse and hotel wirings and in the
airplanes that fall down from their upper places to fill our papers and our
radio speakers with only some dim echo of the living eyes and faces that got
marked out in their fall."[109] To his People's Songs colleagues he elaborated on
the connection between these two needless deaths:

One of the main fights in the whole Phelps Dodge stink and mess was that the US Government had found PD guilty of holding back modern scientific inventions and developments that would turn out a better grade of copper wire at a much cheaper price. I can say from the story of this short and fire here in our house which took little Cathy's life, that I know what cheap copper wiring can do.

It is not only the hired gunscabs of the high mucks that shoot and kill our good union souls such as Mario Russo, but also these cheap fraudulent grades of steel, copper, rubber, products of every sort and of every kind that take the lives of our loved ones right in our own house and home.[110]

And, to emphasize the charge of profiteering in the slaughter of innocents, Guthrie lowered Russo's age by ten years in his ballad, so that, like Cathy Ann, he was now a child sacrificed to the greed of the bosses and scabs:

My name is Mario Russo, and seventeen is my age.
I gave my life to write my name on your union history page.
My religion is a union world where you can speak your mind.
Here's how I was shot and killed on that Phelps Dodge picket line.[111]

Eventually, Guthrie channeled his grief into grim resolution as he confronted a ghostly icon of the tragedy that had carried away his daughter:

This is to test the typewriter after it came thru the bath of Cathy's fire. This piece about Blind Sonny was rolled up in my typewriter when I left the house here to sing down in Elizabeth, New Jersey.

I am going ahead now and finish up this letter on this same piece of scorched and smoked paper just to show myself that such a thing as a no good wartime radio wire shorting out and burning little Miss Stackabones to death has not stopped me nor slowed down my thinking, but has made my old bones jump up wider awake to fight against this kind of a greed that sells such dangerous wirings.[112]

His resolve notwithstanding, Guthrie's political loneliness was apparent. Looking backward to what now seemed a golden era—the New Deal that he had initially viewed with suspicion—he thought of the dead Roosevelt as a lost father:

I could tell by the rings
on your voice that your
wife must have brung
you five or six kids
already.

You talked just like my
blacksmith uncle John
plays his fiddle and
he's done won fifty rough
contests and had his
six or seven kids and died last year

I say you and my uncle
John's anvil and fiddle are
two things I could go on
and listen to for twenty
more elections.[113]

He wrote the elegy "Dear Mrs. Roosevelt," praising FDR for his hostility to Wall Street, for the WPA, for his defense of trade unions, and for his instinctive dislike of Churchill. Most importantly, from Guthrie's revisionist angle, Roosevelt had been able to distinguish between the friends and enemies of the international proletariat: "He said he didn't like DeGaulle, nor no Chiang Kai Check; / Shook hands with Joseph Stalin, says: 'There's a man I like!' / This world was lucky to see him born."[114]

Meanwhile, Roosevelt's successor had turned into nothing less than an arch betrayer: "President Truman has proved to me that he don't like my trade unions, don't like organized labor, don't like the Communist Party, don't like the human race."[115] Truman's inauguration of the Cold War quickly led Guthrie to revise whatever hopeful opinions he held about the benefits of atomic power. Returning to "Freedom Fire," he redrafted it as a stark warning now stripped of all ambivalence:

Leader: Healthy lads, my prettiest lasses,
         Nitro and blister gasses,
         A union world or a world of ashes,
All: Dance around my Atom Fire.

Leader: Dancing eyes and dreaming faces
         Down out of my history places
         All of you humanly races
All: Dance around my Atom Fire.

Leader: Warfare is not the settlement,
         Bloodshed is not the element,
         Shake hands and mix all colors
All: Dance around my Atom Fire.[116]

Guthrie now saw only reactionary thugs and gangsters rolling into the centers of political power, scattering the remaining progressives like so many bowling pins. "Show me the party that Hoover hates," he pleaded, "the party that Hearst don't like," and "the party that Pegler fears"—thus forging an unholy trinity of inquisitors (J. Edgar Hoover), media moguls (Hearst), and right-wing yellow journalists (Westbrook Pegler) whose stars appeared in the ascendant. The prospect of a party that could challenge such a rise brought out a desperate vow from Guthrie: "I'll walk these city streets and I will knock on every door / And I'll write my name down in blood red blood."[117]

Guthrie's anxiety was justified, not only on behalf of the nation's progressive forces, but also for those in his closest musical circles. *Life* magazine had singled out Earl Robinson as a degenerate red, while People's Songs invited the charge of "Communist Front" from the yellow press (in particular the *New York Sun* and the *New York World-Telegram*) and the utterly paranoid Tenney Committee of the California State Legislature. California State Senator Jack Tenney and his "State committee investigating Un-American Activities" had been warning all who cared to listen that People's Songs was "directly descended from the Almanac Singers, which prior to World War II published 'songs for the workers' (workers as used by Reds is synonymous with Communists)." Not only was People's Songs "writing songs and plays, promoting choruses and schools for Communist fronts," but it was itself "a vital Communist front in the conduct of the strategy and tactics of the Communist Anti-Imperialist War technique of the Seventh Period of Communist strategy in America"[118]—a bewildering charge that set off a minor epidemic of head scratching across the political spectrum. Even the HUAC was perplexed, calling Tenney to Washington in March 1947 to explain how the "Seventh Period of Communist strategy in America" might have differed from, say, the Sixth or the Fifth or the Fourth. What mattered, Tenney said, was that unless action against such "Communist fronts" was immediately taken, then "you will have the greatest fifth column, the greatest group of traitors, assassins, terrorists, that the world has ever seen, the greatest and most fantastic group of conspirators, saboteurs, and agents of a foreign government the world has ever seen, and America will collapse like an eggshell unless we start doing something in the schools, digging those people out and exposing them to let the people know exactly who they are."[119]

Guthrie was most likely unaware that he was being mentioned by name in the committee rooms of the HUAC. On July 21, 1947, Walter S. Steele, managing editor of the conservative *National Republic* magazine, appeared before congressmen J. Parnell Thomas, Richard Vail, and Richard Nixon, among others, "in the capacity of chairman of the national security committee of the American Coalition of Patriotic, Civic, and Fraternal Societies." Steele cited Guthrie as a director of People's Songs, as a sometime instructor at the "communistic" Jefferson School of Social Science in New York (where various People's Songsters offered ad hoc courses), and as a "staff writer" for the *People's World*.[120] Guthrie's name was almost buried in the sprawling list of "subversives" offered by Steele. More distressing for Guthrie, ultimately, was the attention devoted to Keynote Records, which Steele damned as "another link in the Communist cultural chain": "This outfit propagandizes through recordings. It has recently extended its efforts in issuing albums of records of a Communist propaganda nature. One highly touted album is entitled: 'Six Songs for Democracy.' One of the songs was written by Hans [*sic*] Eisler, brother of Gerhart Eisler, both of whom are German Communists. The latter, it will be recalled, was heard before a congressional committee not long ago, in the course of the hearings he was exposed as a Moscow agent active in Communist Party ranks in this country. Hans [*sic*] Eisler is in Hollywood, writing music for the movies."[121] Nixon's ears pricked up at the mention of Hanns Eisler, whose case he had declared the previous April as "the most important ever to have come before the Committee,"[122] demonstrating to him the sinister chain of Communist subversion that led straight from the door of the Kremlin to Hollywood. Eisler's persecution ended with his deportation from the United States on March 26, 1948, when he voiced his opinion "as an old anti-Fascist" that the HUAC represented "fascism in its most direct form."[123]

Eisler's deportation left Guthrie shaken, prompting a cry of anguish over the prospect of political life in a fascist United States, if not the more immediate possibility of a HUAC summons:

> I don't know what I'll do,
> I don't know what I'll do.
> Eisler's on the come and go and
> I don't know what I'll do.

The world was surely turning upside down if a harmless composer and music instructor could be deemed a threat to "national security" while a much more threatening figure—who had already leveled two Japanese cities and wiped out hundreds of thousands of civilians—could remain with his finger poised over the nuclear button:

> Eisler him write music,
> Eisler him teach school.
> Truman him don't play so good and
> I don't know what I'll do.[124]

It was in such a spirit of hand-wringing and desperation that Guthrie, along with the mass of others in the battered communist movement, looked to the presidential election of 1948 as a last chance to restore the country to its fundamental rights and freedoms of expression, association, thought, and political choice. As Guthrie had written in an annotation to "I'll Write My Name Down in Blood Red Blood":

> If we chase all you fascists
> Out from Washington
> They'd be a world of vacant houses
> For Americans.[125]

As if in answer to a prayer, into the progressive void stepped Henry Wallace, Truman's nemesis and predecessor as Roosevelt's vice president—Wallace, who might now be president had the Democrats seen the wisdom of following him along the road to constructive engagement with the Soviets; instead, they'd convinced FDR to dump him for Truman. Some radical eyes still grew misty at the recollection of Wallace's rejoinder to Henry Luce's arrogant pronouncement of "The American Century," which had cast the United States as a "powerhouse" influencing the world "for such purposes as we see fit and by such means as we see fit." Wallace had declared: "Some have spoken of the 'American Century.' I say that the century on which we are entering—the century which will come out of this war—can be and must be the century of the common man. . . . No nation will have the God-given right to exploit other nations. Older nations will have the privilege to help younger nations get started on the path to industrialization, but there must be neither military nor economic imperialism. The methods of the nineteenth century will not work in the people's century which is now about to begin."[126]

That was in 1942; now, with Hiroshima and Nagasaki destroyed on Truman's orders and the Soviets a year away from unveiling their own atomic bomb, Wallace's conception of "national security" differed starkly from that of the president (who had used that now-sullied phrase to justify not only his military decisions, but also the federal seizure of twenty-six petroleum plants during the CIO strikes of 1945–46).[127] Thus, on both the international and domestic fronts, the last chance for a radical resurgence seemed to lie in the constitution of a third party with Wallace at its helm. This was the birth of America's third short-lived Progressive Party (with its echoes of Theodore Roosevelt's electoral failure in 1912 and Robert La Follette's in 1924). Wallace's Progressives, looking forward to an era of post–Cold War amity, sank their deepest roots in another sepia-toned relic of the 1920s, the Farmer–Labor Party.

Alan Lomax recalled being approached by the Wallace machine to act as the party's "musical consultant" and provided a revealing snapshot of the campaign's idealism (as well as the ridicule and hostility it ultimately invited):

It was my suggestion that the Wallace campaign, like the Lincoln campaign, ought to be a singing movement. We got Peter Seeger on a plane with Wallace and he toured the country. The Wallace meetings were half songs and half oratory. There was one night I remember, in the polo grounds, when, according to the *New York Times,* the united voices of the Wallace party could be heard three miles away in Times Square, singing "It's the Same Old Merry-Go-Round," about the perpetual in-and-outness of the Democratic donkey and the Republican elephant. Another great song of that time was "We are building one big union, the people of this land. We are black and white together, the people of this land"—another of the preludes of the integration movement that was to come. Wallace came back from the south splattered with rotten tomatoes, with fire-breathing Paul Robeson at his right hand.[128]

Lomax invested "Boots" Casetta and People's Songs with responsibility for the musical logistics of the Wallace campaign. After the rousing Progressive convention of July 1948—during which a reporter for the *Nation* "caught a die-hard Republican acquaintance whistling" a Wallace song[129]—Casetta wrote to a friend: "Needless to point out, this is the golden development of People's Songs. The convention once and for [all] convinced the powers that be in the progressive movement that this medium is one of the most vital at their command. The extent to which this has been realized is manifested by Wallace's own decision to make the new party a singing party."[130] In a stunning burst of energy, hundreds of songs were generated across the country and published in *People's Songs;* many more were submitted to Casetta, Seeger, and Irwin Silber and never published. It came to the point where Seeger had to draft a form letter to respond to the rejected songwriters:

> Of course, you may know there is no one official Wallace campaign song. Out of hundreds of good ones that have been sent in, it has been necessary to select a very small number for reprinting in the Wallace song folios and wordbooks which have just gone to press. Although the committee of songleaders and songwriters in charge of editing those folios did not include your song, I hope you will continue to sing it wherever possible and also send us any new campaign songs which you make up, so that they can be considered for future editions.
>
> Thanking you on behalf of Mr. Wallace and the Progressive Party.[131]

While it is true that political campaigns do not tend to produce songs that ring down through the ages, the music of the Wallace campaign is particularly striking as a reflection of both political and rhetorical desperation—and Guthrie contributed more than his fair share to the musical stable, prompting Seeger to tell him, "Christ, the way you keep turning out songs makes me feel very ashamed of myself, sittin' here editing away and not creating much on my own."[132] Guthrie's output for Wallace, while certainly prolific, was inevitably uneven. To the tune of "The Old Chisholm Trail" (or, in Guthrie's word play, "Old Jizzum trail"), "Baking for Wallace" was an awkward curiosity:

> Roll my dough an' put in the pan
> Baking for my Wallace man
>> Come a cake come a roll
>> Come a run to the polls
>> Come Wallace in Forty Eighto[133]

"Bet on Stewball," which Guthrie had recorded joyously with Lead Belly and Cisco Houston, now had a new call:

> You bet on Wallace
> And you might win win win
> And you might win.[134]

The "Streamlined Cannonball" became the "Screwball Cannonball," "tooting for the Mundt and Nixon Bill" and trailing a train of coaches named "The Hearst," "The DuPont," "Hitler's Valley," "Mussolini's Rest," "Franco's Hill," "Lindberg's Cloud," and "Lucy's Boothey"—all chugging along to "their theme song, 'Let's Starve the World to Death'":

> I'll not stand here all my life to give you warning,
> I have got to grab the Wallace Fast Express,
> But when this Screwball Train rolls past your crossing,
> They will jail you if they catch you talking sense.[135]

Another train—the "Farmer–Labor Train" (soon retitled the "Wallace–Taylor Train")—was "rollin' through New England to the West Pacific shore" to the tune of "Wabash Cannonball."[136] Meanwhile, Guthrie advised the voters of 1948:

> If you wanta see what my Democrats done
> Go down to the Bowery
> If you wanta see what the GOP done
> Go down to the slums
> If you want know why we need Wallace
> Go down to the widows and orphans
> Go down to the hungry workers
> Go down and see.

His ear was also tuned to the prevailing mantra of "national security":

> If you wanta see what Truman done
> Go down to the jail.
> When Taft and Hartley kill our union

And you're in th' jug for not being American
And I'm in a cell for singin' this little song,
Go down and see.[137]

In "Henry Wallace Man," Guthrie lauded the Progressive candidate for taking "us out of the Hoover shacks," for seeking "peace with Russians," and—
as Roosevelt's vice president—for having stood up to "the Nazi gang and
fascist[s]" who "tried / To rule this world by hate":

I was glad that Roosevelt lived
To see the haters beat,
And I felt bad when I saw Truman
Drive you from your seat.
The senate bunch and the congress gang
They called you silly names,
Because you worked your fields of peace
And not in their gambling games.

And he took a parting shot at "Hoover's lemony puss" and "Truman's bitter
bark smile."[138]

   Guthrie scrambled to redraft his existing songs, doing Wallace no favors
in confirming the impression of right-wing columnists who claimed that
the Progressive campaign should be "exposed for what it is: an instrument
of Soviet foreign policy":[139]

When I call you on your fone
    My eyes gonna shine
When I walk in at your door
    My eyes gonna shine
When I kick our old black market
And when I kill old Jimmy Crowfus
When Wallace drinks with Joseph Stalin
    My eyes gonna shine.[140]

If Guthrie held any reservations about Wallace's candidacy, he restricted them to
the imaginary musings of his six-month-old son Arlo, for whom he ghost-wrote
to a family friend: "I just wonder, though, if Mr. H. Wallace is half as wise as he
sounds."[141] Otherwise, at a fever pitch of wild and doomed expectations, Guthrie
rededicated his earlier song "I've Got to Know" "to all forty million of us that
are going to run down to those polls and elect Henry Wallace and Glen Taylor
this year, now, here, quick, soon, and fast. Not Fifty Two, but Forty Eight."[142]

   The movement was finished. The HUAC had eviscerated the Progressive
Party, the leadership of the CPUSA had fallen before the indictments of the

Smith Act, and Wallace carried just over a million votes, trailing behind even the segregationist crackpots of Strom Thurmond's third-place Dixiecrat ticket. Guthrie launched into a fury of recrimination against People's Songs, as though the election had been decided by its music:

> How much of the Progressive Party blowup and letdown is due to the failure of our songs? I say that the songs stood at the head of the list in attracting (for close inspection) some of the largest audiences ever ganged together to listen to the words, facts, prophecies, and freedom words of our artists and of our candidates; our songs then, must sure stand up *first* to be counted, first to be taken apart nut by nut and bolt by bolt, first to be looked at under the most critical microscope that we can find to use.

He reeled off a list of faults. The campaigners had failed to capitalize on the depth of religious conviction in America:

> We are not sincerely touching nor blending as much as we should with the several serious deeply religious groups, whose songs so many times are more radical, more deeply convincing, more progressive than (too many) of our own. The song, "Passing Through" for my own money, will keep alive through many coming elections, and as a general pattern to go by, a song of this nature ought to find a home in every issue of our monthly bulletin, instead of once in several months.

Musical sellouts had been treated with too much leniency:

> Anybody who is caught, or who it is proven against, who gives ground, who retreats to the side of the enemy at the simple jingle of a palmful of coins, ought to be suspended and sent over to book out through the gangster agents on the reactionary side of the battle line. When an artist asks his or herself, "How radical can I be today?" they have already strayed from the simple home of their own conscience, and can no more reflect nor clarify nor lead a genuine peoples program than they can kiss a mule in the ass.

People's Songs had failed to rigorously vet its own output:

> How a man with such a long road of sensible travels behind him, Alan Lomax, could expect such a shallow jingly and insincere number as "I Got a Ballot" to touch the heartstrings and conscience of the hardhit masses, is a problem above me. I never did hear a living human being call his "vote" a "magic little ballot." People I have seen call their vote a number of things, none of which are nearly as cutiepie, as highly polite, as flippant, as sissy nor effeminate as this song and its inlaws and outlaws.[143]

And on and on, running to seven closely typed pages.

People's Songs was already on the ropes in any case. Only a handful of unions—the Mine, Mill, and Smelters Union; the Fur and Leather Workers; the United Electrical Workers—still had anything to do with the organization. Brooklyn College banned its own chapter of People's Songs from campus operations in fear of the anticommunist backlash—a reasonable fear given the climate in which Paul Robeson and Hanns Eisler were pilloried by the HUAC. The Wallace campaign had virtually bankrolled the organization throughout 1948; when the Wallace money finally ran out, so did time for People's Songs. It was formally wound up on March 11, 1949—ironically, five days after the *Daily Worker* described it as "a lusty baby of three with a long future."[144] At the final board meeting, Seeger announced the causes of the "lusty baby's" premature death: "continued lack of activity in the labor movement" and "monopoly control of the main channels of communication."[145]

Guthrie was bereft as he viewed the social and political wreckage strewn all around him. While the Democrats celebrated Truman's reelection and the red baiters consolidated their ascendancy in Congress, the winter of 1949 saw Guthrie, during a live performance, ruminating on the mine disaster at Centralia, Illinois, that had killed 111 miners two years previously: "The government mine inspector made several trips down to this mine called Centralia Number 5. As you will remember, the government inspector said that the mine was so full of fumes that it was going to blow up in a day because the miners was working down there with open lights on their caps—on their mining caps. So the mine owner laughed at him and he didn't want to spend the money to put in a cleaning system, and so he said, Well, if you quit sending your inspectors down inside of my mines, you'll quit finding anything wrong with them. So that's the kind of human brains that just so happens to control the lives of several hundred thousand miners—and not in Nazi Germany but right here. A hundred or two miles from here, or less."[146]

And yet one would think that the labor struggle had been won, as the CIO and its union leaders abandoned the picket lines to affably talk "porkchops" with the bosses around polished boardroom tables. Here, in "the one and only New York," an unemployed father could leave his newborn paralyzed baby on the steps of Bellevue Hospital, as Guthrie read in "a true fact story in the Brooklyn Eagle," prompting a somber ballad:

> For nurses and doctors
> We can't even pay;
> For its bed and its drugs
> We still couldn't pay;
> To someone that has

Lots of money, I'll say:
Please, give him the care that he needs.[147]

The "Century of the Common Man," like People's Songs, had been strangled at birth. The victorious "American Century" had begun. It was, supposedly, the "age of affluence," as John Kenneth Galbraith christened it.[148] One would hardly know it to walk the sad streets of Woody Guthrie's New York.

It was a new age of untold technological wonder, economic dominance, and military might for the United States. On an epic cross-country journey in June 1950, Guthrie and his songs came up smartly against the gargantuan military machine, spawning a surreal narrative that foreshadowed Arlo Guthrie's "Alice's Restaurant" of twenty-seven years later. Beating his way from Los Angeles to New York in order "to do a 15 minute antiveedee department of health radio show," the advance payment for which was not enough to buy him a plane ticket, Guthrie took a bus as far as "Saint Louis, Illinois, or Saint Louis, Missouri . . . or maybe it was East Saint Louis." Carrying his "forty pound suitcase full of newmade songs," he found himself hitchhiking as far as "the maingates of the Pennsylvania Turnpike Speedway" outside of Pittsburgh. "So, well, there I was. No shave, no shower, no shampoo, no shoeshine, no razor, no blade, no haircut, no nothing. I commenced to look just about like a pair of mad male porcupines wrastling under a froze drift of thornybrush or stickery weed of some wild sort and flavor." He walked up to the turnpike tollbooth looking, by his own admission, "like a lost scarecrow," and asked "the Luitenant at the gate where was the best spot I could stand on to snag me a ride into Coney Island":

> and the Captain told me, Stand right over here in that lane by that flagpole. I stood by the flagpole awhile till a whole army convoy of some description drove up on an outdoor maneuver. The convoy soldiers ganged around my flagpole so thick that I had to move out of my flagpole lane where all the trucks and pleasure cars were zipping past. The captain of the toll gate and the captain of the convoy both bawled me out for moving out of my lane without their handwave and permit, and asked me to please take up my (forty lb) handbag of balladsongs and turn around and walk back where I'd come from, back down away from the gate, and onto the main highroad #30, to flag the cars and trucks down there at high speeds (where they seldom slowed down to stop). I had to walk right past all of the GIs on their jeeps, cannons, and army trucks, tanks, throwers, tossers, and other machenery of warfare.

As he trudged along the smaller roads, he identified the twitching curtains of Cold War suspicion:

I walked the thirty [highway] ten or fifteen miles that morning, and the Penn-
sylvanya State Patrol Prowlcars got my number from the windows of the neigh-
borhoods I walked past. Everybody saw me trapsing along with nine beards
and ten crops of hair and with my 65 lb songbag dragging my tracks out and
all of them thought I looked like something bad they'd had a nightmare about,
and, too, that I looked exactly like a man out walking up and down this land
stealing all kinds of military secrets.

Thus the citizen who only a decade ago had written, "Nobody living can ever
stop me / As I go walking that freedom highway" was hunted down on the
open roads of Truman's America:

> The first patrol car stopped me and made me open up my bag and I acted as
> friendly as I knew how whilst the patrolman thumbed and hummed around
> through a couple of hundred good and bad ones. He hummed them lots better
> than I ever will. He flipped his dashboard radio on and tuned in the FBI while
> I told him about my songs and my ballads and my job on the antyveedee show
> for the department of health. I was thankful to hear that FBI clerk say under
> that dashboard, No record on Guthrie. That was good news to me. No record.
> No record on me. I made a jillion fonograf records and the FBI never heard a
> single one of them.[149]

(How wrong he was. Earlier that month, an FBI operative had confidently
informed J. Edgar Hoover that one "GUTHRIE . . . previously referred as
(WOODY)" was "a member of the Factionalist Sabotage Group," whose "ultimate purpose" was "sabotage against the United States during war with
Russia.")[150] Guthrie was left with a warning that would be heard with increasing frequency by the long-haired youth of the 1960s counterculture: "The
patrolman told me to pick up my songbag and to move on. He told me to
get myself a shave and a haircut or I'd be stopped and questioned ten dozen
times trying to walk across the whole state of Pennsylvania." The fixation
on his appearance amused him: "Reports about me flooded the entire state
of Pennsylvania. Bushy headed spy nabs convoy seecrits. Is he from a flying
saucer? How come his hairs so long?"[151]

    If only the other absurdities of the Cold War could be laughed away so easily.
Joe McCarthy had begun to smile broadly and with increasing confidence from
his committee-room dais, but it was a reaction that few of his victims would
be able to muster as the decade got under way. American radicals—and many
not even guilty of the charge—would need all the laughs they could get.

6. Long Road to Peekskill

As he gazed upon the radical movement lying apparently in ruins, Guthrie had ample opportunity to reflect on a particular journey that he had taken. If he is to be believed, it must have been quite a miraculous journey, since it actually began in 1911—a year before his birth. That year, in Okemah, Oklahoma, a white policeman named George Loney attempted to arrest a black man named Nelson, supposedly for sheep stealing. Loney went to Nelson's house, only to find his wife, Laura, their thirteen-year-old son Lawrence, and their baby. Thinking that Loney was about to shoot them, young Lawrence grabbed a rifle and shot first, hitting Loney in the leg. The officer bled to death in the Nelsons' front yard, pleading for water. Laura, Lawrence, and the baby were arrested and taken to the jailhouse; a week later, a mob broke into the jail and dragged them all to the Canadian River Bridge. Laura and Lawrence were lynched, and the baby was left crying by the roadside. Some of the good citizens of Okemah were soon selling postcards of the lynching scene to commemorate their handiwork. It is impossible to tell whether one of the grinning white faces in the photographed mob is that of Charley Guthrie, Woody's father; Ed Cray's biography makes no mention of Guthrie's presence, although he refers to the lynching by way of a footnote.[1] Joe Klein's biography is categorical: Charley Guthrie, proud member of the Ku Klux Klan, was part of the lynch mob.[2] (There is in fact no documentary evidence to establish conclusively Charley Guthrie's Klan membership.)[3]

Whatever the biographical discrepancies, historical certainty must recede even further into the haze thanks to Woody Guthrie's headnote to his song "Don't Kill My Baby and My Son," in *Hard Hitting Songs for Hard-Hit People:*

For a year or so my dad was undersheriff of Okemah, Oklahoma, and he used to tell me many a sad tale about that old black jailhouse. I remember one night when I was about eight or nine years old that I was caught out after dark and had to walk through the old dark town after curfew hour—and I was barefooted on the sidewalk—so there wasn't a sound to be heard—except a wild and blood curdling moan that filled the whole town, and it kept getting louder as I walked down the street to the old rock jailhouse. And I heard a Negro lady sticking her head through the jailhouse bars and moaning at the top of her voice.

Given that the Nelson lynching took place a year before he was born, Guthrie's next claim is astounding:

This Negro lady had a right new baby, and a son that was doomed to hang by her dead body with the rise of the morning wind, and my dad told me the whole story.

Several years has gone by and I wrote this song down, because that lady's wail went further, went higher, and went deeper than any sermon or radio broadcast I ever heard.[4]

For some unknown strategic or psychological reason, Guthrie had removed his father from the scene and from any responsibility for the lynching, inserting himself into the historical record as a near-witness to the tragedy. That the Nelson lynching returned to haunt him in later life is indisputable, as a stanza from his poem "High Balladree" makes clear (in the process increasing by one the number of the lynched victims):

A nickel post card I buy off
    your rack
To show you what happens if
    you're black and fight back
A lady and two boys hanging
    down by their necks
From the rusty iron rigs of my
    Canadian Bridge.[5]

Elsewhere, in one of his "Woody Sez" columns, Guthrie reflected on a visit with "a artist and painter by trade" who had painted such "a mighty good picture of a lynching" that it succeeded in silencing entirely the comic voice upon which his column habitually depended: "—and so naturally I caint think up no jokes for today. This painting is so real I feel like I was at a lynching, and it somehow or other just takes all of the fun and good humor and good sport out of you to set here and realize that people could go so haywire as to hang a human body up by a gallus pole and shoot it full of Winchester

rifle holes just for pastime. It reminds me of the postcard picture they sold
in my home town for several years, a showing you a negro mother, and her
two young sons, a hanging by the neck stretched tight by the weight of their
bodies and—the rope stretched tight like a big fiddle string."[6] Again, Guthrie
closed the manuscript of his 1940 song "Slipknot" with a dedication "to the
many negro mothers, fathers, and sons alike, that was lynched and hanged
under the bridge of the Canadian River, seven miles south of Okemah, Okla.,
and to the day when such will be no more."[7]

If it was indeed the pressures of both familial and historical guilt that
caused Guthrie to rewrite himself into the story of a lynching that occurred
a year before his birth, it may help to account for another curious rendering of Guthrie's engagement with what he called "the colored situation."[8] In
Bound for Glory he depicts his moment of racial awakening while a child
encountering a black neighbor named Matilda Walters, who praises him
for his courtesy:

> "You leas'ways sez, yas ma'am an' no ma'am, don' you?"
> "Yes'm."
> "An' me jes' an ol black niggah. Hmmm. Sho' do soun' good."

"A nickel postcard I buy off your rack." The lynching of Laura and Lawrence
Nelson. Photo by G. H. Farnum, 1911. Courtesy of the Research Division of the
Oklahoma Historical Society.

Drawing by Woody Guthrie, c. 1946. Image courtesy of the Ralph
Rinzler Folklife Archives and Collections, with permission from
the Woody Guthrie Archives. © Woody Guthrie Publications, Inc.

"Are you a nigger lady?"
"Whatta I look like, honey?"
"Are you a nigger 'cause you're black?"
"What folks all says."
"What do people call you a nigger for?"

"'Cause they jes' don' know no betta. Don' know what 'niggah' means. Don' know how bad makes ya feel."

"You called your own self that," I told her.

"When I calls my own se'f a niggah, I knows I don' mean it. An' even anothah niggah calls me a 'niggah,' I don' min', 'cause I knows it's most jes' fun. But when a white pusson calls me 'niggah,' it's like a whip cuts through my ol' hide."[9]

The most disturbing thing about this passage is not the hideous minstrel dialect, but rather the implication that Guthrie had been educated out of racism at such a young age. He perpetuated this myth in his interviews with Alan Lomax for the *Library of Congress Recordings,* on which he is plainly uncomfortable in discussing the issue of race. He betrays a lingering tendency toward stereotype as he attempts to present a childhood untainted by racism: "Ever since I was a kid growing up I've always found time to stop and talk to these colored people because I found them to be full of jokes—what I mean, wisdom."[10] On the recordings he juggles his own faux naiveté and the rewriting of his racist childhood with equal awkwardness: "I'd never hardly pass an Indian or a colored boy, because I'm telling you the truth, I learned to like them."[11]

In spite of these protestations, it is clear that when he fled the Dust Bowl in the mid-1930s and landed in California, Guthrie was quite unconcerned about his own racism. His KFVD songbooks indicate that he happily sang about "niggers" in songs like "Little Liza Jane" and "darkies" in "Kitty Wells."[12] Minstrel dialect and caricatures grace the pages of his crude homemade newspaper the *Santa Monica Social Register Examine 'Er* (1937), in which jokes about "Rastus," "coons," "monkeys," "chocolate drops," and "all de Niggahs evahwha" compete with slanderous descriptions of black men at the beach giving off "the Ethiopian smell":

> We could dimly hear their chants
> And we thought the blacks by chance,
> Were doing a cannibal dance
> This we could dimly see.
> Guess the sea's eternal pounding
> Like a giant drum a-sounding
> Set their jungle blood to bounding;
> Set their native instincts free.[13]

Guthrie's merciful comeuppance came at the hands of a member of his KFVD audience on October 20, 1937, after he had introduced and played Uncle Dave Macon's appalling "Run, Nigger, Run" on the air. He received from one Howell Terence a letter so politely incandescent—and he was so shaken by it—that he read it out over the airwaves the next day: "You were getting along quite well in your program this evening until you announced your 'Nigger Blues.' I am a Negro, a young Negro in college, and I certainly resented your remark. No person or persons of any intelligence uses that word over the radio today."[14] Guthrie apologized profusely, dramatically ripped the offending song sheet to shreds before the microphone, and swore that he would never use the word again. He later made the point of repeatedly apologizing to the African American community for all the racist "frothings" that he had uttered.[15]

Having experienced what one historian has called the "liminally white status" of the Dust Bowl migrants in California—where his fellow white Oklahomans had been subjected to eugenicist and race-based attacks similar to those leveled at Mexican, Filipino, Chinese, and African American workers[16]—Guthrie was certainly aware of the ironic kinship implied in the sort of notice that was seen posted outside a Bakersfield movie theater: "Negroes and Okies Upstairs."[17] Indeed, an impression of liminal whiteness appears to have infiltrated Guthrie's own recollections of his life prior to the California migration. The more he began to reflect upon the racism of his Oklahoma childhood, the more the white-based "cowboy angle" of his life "sort of faded out," as he recalled in 1949. "The poor Indians and the poor Negroes had been given the state of Oklahoma by United States treaties of all kinds," he explained to a New Jersey audience, "because [the U.S. government] didn't figure that the land was good enough for anything else." That, he said, had changed "the very minute that everyone found out that there was millions and millions of dollars' worth of oil pools under every acre of land, almost, in Oklahoma." Consequently, "the Indians and poor Negroes that did own the land actually had to be cheated out of it, and fast. A lot of ways was worked to get 'em loose from the land."[18] Thus the experience of dispossession felt on a personal level by the Guthrie family and on a collective level by the Dust Bowl migrants came to dovetail in Guthrie's mind with the dispossession of all the racial minorities with whom he began to empathize in his maturity.

It was this capacity for empathy that ultimately enabled Guthrie to reflect upon American music and upon himself, as a musician, in racial terms—to claim, "We could not tell where our own personal life stopped and Leadbelly's started,"[19] to declare that "the white folks blues quits where the Negro blues starts in,"[20] and to claim that "any talk about American songs, ballads or music has got to first shake hands with the negroes."[21] As he argued in a letter to Max Gordon in 1941: "Victor's two biggest sellers, namely Jimmy Ro[d]gers, the Blue Yodeler, and the Carter Family, blues, ballad, and religious singers, have constantly used the two and three line repeat, with a last line the same. The westerners are singing almost a pure Negro style, while at work or celebrating, and lots of them haven't stopped to think yet that the whole thing traces back to the slaves, the sharecroppers, the big town workers, the chain gangs, and spiritual songs of the Negro People. This is the influence of Negro singing on everybody else in America."[22]

Guthrie's gradually acquired sense of his own "liminally white status" eventually enabled him to associate his Dust Bowl songs with the experiences of oppressed peoples with other histories. Hence his reflections on the song "When the Curfew Blows," about the police harassment of the migrants in California: "This would sound no more out of life, no more disassociated, no more cut off from experience which is truth, than to hear our soap operas and chewing gum symphonies drifting through the weather-leaking walls of 16,000,000 Negroes in the south, yes, and that many more Browns, Whites, and Red Men, to boot."[23]

By the time of his relocation to New York, Guthrie had truly come far from the days when he would consider performing a song called "Run, Nigger, Run" on the radio; and he had further still to go. While Pete Seeger has described the "education" he received under Guthrie's tutelage beginning in 1940,[24] it is clear that Guthrie himself was still being educated about the myriad forms of black oppression. He filtered through verse an experience he shared with Seeger when, in their mutually shared naïveté, they called into a black-owned café in Tennessee during their cross-country travels, to the terror of the waitress:

> I'll just haf to ask you boys to please get up and go.
> Please. Please go now. They'll not say much while you're in here.
> They won't bust in an' tear this old place down long's you're here.
> They won't do nothing that you two boys can see them do.
> They know, so do I know, you boys is come from somewheres else.
> . . . I know you just dropt in here to eat some and be friendly
> But I can't afford to let them see me being friends with you boys
> 'Cause it'll be after you boys gets on out and gone down the line
> They'll catch me an' give me a good fixin'.[25]

The war, too, had enabled Guthrie to integrate race into the struggle for union, which he had envisaged as "a big high rolling train": "I was just thinking, what if somebody in one of the cars was to say, 'I'll unhook this car because a red man, or a green man, or a black or a polka-dotted man made all of this carload, an' I don't like them colors of folks, —so I'll unhook their car'—You'd be doing just perzactly what Adolph would like for you to do."[26] To Marjorie he wrote of "the little things around that add up to make the bigger fights, like killing Jim Crow, Poll Tax, Race discrimination, crook[ed] laws and lawyers, crooked profit makers and profit worshippers, people that put making money ahead of being a human, or people that want to live in idle laziness on the sweat of working peoples backs, all of this, that adds up to the biggest fight of all, the fight against the Axis."[27]

In all its stages, the war enabled this raced-based perception for Guthrie. He articulated it powerfully once during a war bonds benefit in Baltimore, where, after playing with Sonny Terry and Brownie McGhee, he was stung to rage to hear his black colleagues invited to take their meals in the kitchen. As Seeger recalled it: "Woody just shouted out, 'This fight against fascism has got to start right here and now!' And he grabbed the tablecloth and ripped it off, scattering chinaware and silver and glasses all over the floor. He started tipping over tables and shouting; and they finally hustled him out before anybody got arrested."[28]

Later, in his post–Pearl Harbor enthusiasm, Guthrie perceived the righteous sword of the Allied armies being swung in defense of the dispossessed Okies, the dispossessed African Americans and Mexicans, and all other victims of racism. As he wrote to Marjorie: "This will settle the score once and for all, of all kinds of race-hate, and it will give everybody their job doing what they can do best, time for learning, time for rest, and time for fun and singing; nobody can push a man off of a farm, and nobody can make a family live like rats in a filthy dump; nobody can toss a family of kids out onto the streets for the rent."[29] During his final merchant marine voyage, as Jim Longhi recalled, Guthrie defied the segregation still imposed by the U.S. Army, striding into the black quarters to play and sing, only to be upbraided by the battalion commander, who told him to obey the rules—"rules, I might add, that none of us here had anything to do with the making of." As Longhi witnessed it: "Woody stared at the colonel's ribbons and then looked up at him. 'Seems like the rules nobody made are the hardest ones to break.'"[30] After he had exchanged the merchant marine blue for army khaki, Guthrie wrote to Moses Asch from his base at Sheppard Field, Texas: "Jim Crow is here and it is bad. White and Black get together once in a while out on a lecture in the field. Shows are Jim Crow. Prize Fights are segregated. Barracks and chow are Jim Crowed to hell and gone. But both sides are waking up. This is like Prohibition, we are learning at least what we don't want."[31]

Guthrie's conversion from casual, youthful racist to ardent antiracist champion was thus assured by the time he sat down to write his second autobiographical novel, published in 1976 as *Seeds of Man*. Like *Bound for Glory*, it is an exercise in personal revisionism in which Guthrie engages with the forces of his youth, including racism (mostly pertaining to Mexican Americans) and political conflicts with his father. There is no record of Guthrie's knowledge of his father's alleged membership in the Ku Klux Klan, and, in spite of their political differences, he was demonstrably affectionate toward him, inscribing a copy of *Bound for Glory*: "To my papa, as good a dad as a kid ever had. I wrote this book wishing I had more of the stuff that made my dad the best fist fighter in Okfuskee County."[32]

Seeds of Man injects race into the heart of Guthrie's relationship with his father, assigning to both of them a racial awareness and sympathy that neither of them was likely to have held during the years of Guthrie's youth. Guthrie implies in the novel that he countered his father's hostility for socialism with a vague sense of racial wrongs to be righted: "Pap had tried to teach me to hate and despise, and to insult and fight the Socialists in any spot I got the time and chance. I had seen several tribes of good, healthy Indians get cheated, beaten, robbed, doped, rooked, gypped, scared, and tricked out of all their lands and houses, their farms and orchards, pastures, and even their self-respect, their human pride, their natural lives, everything, under the slushy bucket of the rich oil companies. I felt that it was wrong to rob these good, friendly Indians in all of these ways. I felt the same way towards the black folks, and the mixed—bloods."[33]

Given the novel's setting—the Big Bend country of Texas, where Guthrie's Uncle Jerry had supposedly left a gold and silver mine—its overwhelming concern, in terms of race, is the fate of Mexicans on both sides of the border.[34] Hence a harrowing description that prefigures the narrative of the song "Deportee," in which a group of agricultural workers are packed into a truck driven by people smugglers: "In the whining of their motor and above the noises of our own, I did hear the sounds of several people doing some loud talking. Yelling. Some odd whistling. Crying. Wailing. More fast talking. More like begging or pleading. Like it was something between life and death. Like something was gone bad wrong. A truckload of groans."[35]

Amid such misery, Guthrie has his father saying to Rio, a fictional shaman figure with mixed blood and Marxist convictions: "I have a great sympathy for your people, Rio, the Mexicans, the Indians, since I was born and raised with Indian and Spanish folks all around me. There aren't so many Mexicans in my part of Oklahoma. I see you don't have so many blacks down here along your border—a few camp cooks, maybe, and that's about all. I'll have to admit and agree, though, that the poor blacks in Oklahoma live lots better than your people here."[36] This sensitivity does not quite tally with the biographical observation that "because he was able to speak both Creek and Cherokee, Charley became known as especially adept at relieving Indians of their property" in his real estate dealings[37]—a practice Woody Guthrie viewed with contempt, which he expressed during a live performance in 1949: "They used dope, they used opium, they used every kind of a trick to get these Indians to sign over their lands."[38] (He also damned his cousin Jack Guthrie for leaving "the best parts of the whole song" out of his version of "Oklahoma Hills": the names of the "Chickasaw, Choctaw, Cherokee, Creek, and Seminole.")[39]

It would appear that one of Guthrie's main objectives in *Seeds of Man* is to rewrite his father into a man of principles wholly inconsistent with those of white supremacists. He steers clear of allowing his father to express any significant or extensive opinions about African Americans, although in life Charley Guthrie argued vociferously against the Socialist Party not least because (as he sarcastically claimed) it would ensure that "the race problem would be solved by intermarriage"—the main charge in his essay "Socialism Urges Negro Equality."[40] In *Seeds of Man,* Guthrie thus views his youth through the filter of a racially heightened consciousness that, in reality, he began to acquire only after his encounters with antiracist activists in California and New York.[41]

Postwar events had conspired to reaffirm Guthrie's conviction that the "American Century" was a sham and a distraction from the racial injustices blighting America's streets while the occupying forces and the dispensers of Marshall Aid arrogantly strutted across Europe and Japan trumpeting American values. He encapsulated this conviction in one stanza of the song "Madonna on the Curb," in which a poverty-stricken child of three, holding a crying baby, sits on "the curb of a city pavement, by the ash and garbage cans" even while "you're giving millions to Belgian, Pole, and Serb."[42] Guthrie's perception of misplaced American priorities was especially heightened by two cases that occurred in quick succession, both involving returned African American veterans who were brutalized by Jim Crow fascism in spite of their sacrifices in America's war for freedom.

The first, in February 1946, was the case of Isaac Woodard, a veteran of the Pacific War who had returned home to receive his honorable discharge. Woodard had dared to challenge the indignity of Jim Crow and demanded to use a "whites only" washroom at a South Carolina bus stop. He was hauled off the bus and beaten by the police while still in his U.S. Army uniform. He fought back; more police jumped into the fray, dragged him to the jail, and literally beat him blind. Black newspaper editorials argued that the Woodard blinding exposed the "American Century" as "a farce and a fraud": "We have no title to world leadership so long as our own democracy is so counterfeit and bankrupt."[43] By the summer of 1946, the Woodard case was an international cause célèbre, largely through a radio campaign spearheaded by Orson Welles along with a series of rallies and benefits. Guthrie recalled his own participation in a massive benefit held for Woodard at New York's Lewisohn Stadium on August 18, attended by over twenty-five thousand people. "Never seen so many cops in my whole life," he wrote. "Cab Calloway and Fifteen or Twenty big name bands and acts went ahead of me on the program, and for two whole hours I didn't hear nine words of fighting protest"[44]—an exaggeration likely based on Guthrie's ostentatious contempt for commercially successful performers. (In addition to Calloway, Carol Brice, Count Basie, Canada Lee, Louis Jordan, Billie Holiday, and Pearl Bailey—among others—appeared at the Woodard benefit.)[45] For his part, Guthrie sang an eleven-stanza ballad that snowballed toward a final damning couplet: "I thought I fought on the islands to get rid of their kind / But I can see the fight lots plainer now that I am blind."[46]

The same month of Isaac Woodard's blinding, a white policeman in Freeport, New York, shot and killed two African American brothers, Charles and Alfonso Ferguson, who had been refused service in a bus-station café along with two of their other brothers; of the four Fergusons, two were in the armed forces and one was a veteran. An all-white grand jury declined to indict the officer. The case sparked a five-month-long campaign joined by the National Association for the Advancement of Colored People, United Veterans for Equality, the American Labor Party, the Nassau County Communist Party—and Woody Guthrie.[47] In a striking moment of familial identification, Guthrie cast himself as an imaginary fifth Ferguson brother in order to tell their story (although he misnamed Alfonso Ferguson as "Alonzo"):

> The cop turned around and walked back to young Charlie
> Kicked him in the groin and then shot him to the ground;
> The same bullet went through the brain of Alonzo
> And the next bullet laid my brother Joseph down.[48]

On the heels of these tragedies, in 1947 a black sharecropper and mother of twelve, Rosa Lee Ingram, was convicted of murder along with her fourteen- and sixteen-year-old sons by an all-white jury in Georgia. Ingram had fought against her white attacker in an attempted rape and, as she was being beaten "until the blood ran," her sons came to her aid. All three Ingrams were sentenced to death by hanging. (Upon the commutation of their sentences, they would languish in prison until 1959.) In 1949 the National Committee to Free the Ingram Family organized a petition to the United Nations.[49] W. E. B. Du Bois, who authored the petition, set the case in the context of the "American Century" as he appealed to the United Nations to take note of Rosa Lee Ingram. Even as Henry Luce's America was instructing the world on the virtues of capitalist democracy, Du Bois argued: "It may seem a very little thing for fifty-nine nations of the world to take note of the injustice done to a poor colored woman in Georgia . . . yet after all, is it in the end so small a thing to 'do justly, to love mercy and walk humbly' in setting 'this mad world aright'?"[50] A year before the petition was drafted, Guthrie penned "The Ballad of Rosa Lee Ingram," painting a very different picture to that of Luce's American "powerhouse":

> It's four in a bed here in three filthy rooms,
> The children all moaning when Mommy will come:
> Will mother and brothers all hang till they're dead
> For fighting that man that was killing my mom?
>
> The clouds they are storming, the wind's on the blow,
> The branch water's rising, the kids want to know,
> Oh, what can I tell them of courts and laws
> Where you can't use a stick to fight back at a gun?[51]

Guthrie's rage was stoked even hotter when he learned that the military governor of the American sector in Germany, General Lucius Clay, had reduced the life sentence of the notorious Nazi torturer Ilse Koch—the "Beast of Buchenwald"—to four years.[52] Guthrie excoriated Koch in the ballad "Ilsa Koch":

> I see the chimney smoke.
> I see their ashes hauled.
> I see their bones in piles.
> Lamp shades are made from skins.
> I'm choking on the smoke.
> The stink is killing me.
> Old Ilsy Koch was jailed.
> Old Ilsy Koch went free.[53]

The convictions of the Ingram family enflamed Guthrie's outrage against Koch—and against American hypocrisy on the global stage—even further:

> If Rosa Lee Ingram had gassed and burnt
> Five thousand living souls;
> If her two sons had robbed gold teeth
> And stole the corpses clothes,
> If the Ingram boys had cut their shades
> From tattooed human skins,
> Would we cut their time from lifelong terms
> To four little measely years?[54]

Guthrie memorialized other such racist miscarriages of justice after the war, including that of the "Trenton Six," six African American men convicted in 1948 of murdering a white man in New Jersey; it was another internationally known scandal that prompted headlines in London to proclaim: "THEY MUST DIE FOR BEING BLACK."[55] In a pamphlet for the Civil Rights Congress, Dashiell Hammett outlined the features of a case that had "all the earmarks of another Scottsboro frameup":

- No witness reported more than three men at the murder scene. Yet six were convicted.
- The six Negro men were tried by an all-white jury.
- The only evidence against the prisoners consisted of five "confessions" which the police admit were forced. . . .
- None of the Trenton Six fit the witnesses' descriptions of the actual criminals.
- All of the men have proof that they were not anywhere near the scene of the crime.[56]

Guthrie's own version, "Trenton Frameup," filtered the case through the perspective of Bessie Mitchell, sister of one of the defendants. She visits him in the prison where he had been brought by "stormtrooper men" who "laugh at the law":

> Bessie walked to the office, she walked to the door,
> Of Church House, and home, and FBI;
> She begged them in tears, "Save these Six innocent men"
> But, not one did help to save their lives.
>> It was way along in June when this jury got picked;
>> Not a black man allowed to take the box;
>> After Fifty Five days the Six men are found
>> Guilty in the chair to die.[57]

In a second ballad, "Buoy Bells from Trenton," Guthrie suggested that his World War II had been fought, in the end, for nothing. The racist spirit of Judge Webster Thayer, he implied, was alive and well in Trenton, as though the intervening antifascist victory of 1945 had been a mere aberration:

> Old Judge Thayer let Sacco and Vanzetti die;
> He called 'em wops and radical rats
> That same old racial hate
> Ran through the judge and jury's heart, and your death line they signed.[58]

Guthrie amply catalogued these and other instances of black victimization; but this was only one side to his approach. In the same belligerent spirit that had characterized his rhetorical challenges to European fascism during the war, he turned to depictions of militant resistance to Jim Crow (having once—unwisely—lectured African Americans that the blues existed because they "didn't fight and work hard enough to beat" their oppressors).[59] Guthrie had eulogized Joe Louis upon meeting him in 1946, writing to Asch: "Joe is a real champion, a big man in every way, and when he hits at any man out in the ring in front of him, he's hitting at the whole rotten system of decontrol, depression, and degradation."[60]

Another sterling example to Guthrie was Harriet Tubman, the guerrilla fighter born into slavery, who escaped to the North and returned to the South nineteen times under cover to help other slaves escape along the Underground Railroad; the woman whom John Brown had called "General Tubman." Guthrie's Harriet Tubman—in the 1944 ballad of that name—is a veteran of ninety-three years of warfare against the white fascism of antebellum and postbellum America. Guthrie has Tubman pitching righteous violence against terror, state oppression, and vacillating statecraft, culminating in a direct challenge to white power and an appeal to arms:

> Give the black man guns and give him powder,
> To Abe Lincoln this I said.
> You've just crippled the snake of slavery;
> We've got to fight to kill him dead.[61]

Ninety years after John Brown led his men—and Tubman's—against the state power at Harper's Ferry, Guthrie concluded: "The war is so far from won that you can nearly say that we've lost outright to the fascists and lost to those ideas which Hitler, Musso, Horohito, and the reactionary Hooverites seem to believe so dearly in."[62] The combination of racist law and anticommunist repression had convinced him: "Fascism is more closer to you than I can make you see. I'm trying to wake you up to tell you that you're sleeping with something ten times more dangerous than a poison fang snake in your bed"—and he was ready, as ever, to enjoin the battle: "It don't scare me so very much."[63]

Guthrie's brave face was tested during the summer of 1949, when People's Artists secured Paul Robeson as the headline singer at a benefit concert in aid of the Civil Rights Congress. Pete Seeger, Lee Hays, Guthrie, and others from the worlds of folk and classical music would be on hand to support him. The concert was to be held at the Lakeland Acres picnic grounds in Peekskill, New York, on August 27. Robeson never made it to the grounds; he was blocked by massed gangs of white men and women, American Legionnaires and Klansmen in plainclothes, boys and girls, hurling rocks along with antiblack and anti-Semitic chants—duly expressing their distaste for communism, as the *Peekskill Evening Star* had been encouraging them to do for the previous week. Robeson's crime had been to declare it "unthinkable that the Negro people of America or elsewhere in the world could be drawn into war with the Soviet Union."[64] As an African American in the USSR, he said, he had found "new life, not death; freedom, not slavery; true human dignity, not inferiority of status."[65] For this heresy Robeson was greeted with a burning cross towering above the picnic grounds at Peekskill.

For the concertgoers inside the grounds, the situation was even worse, as the novelist Howard Fast recalled in his memoir *Peekskill: USA:*

> They poured down the road and into us, swinging broken fence posts, billies, bottles, and wielding knives. Their leaders had been drinking from pocket flasks and bottles right up to the moment of the attack, and now as they beat and clawed at our lines, they poured out a torrent of obscene words and slogans. They were conscious of Adolf Hitler. He was a god in their ranks and they screamed over and over,
> "We're Hitler's boys—Hitler's boys!"
> "We'll finish his job!"
> "God bless Hitler and f--- you n----- bastards and Jew bastards!"
> "Lynch Robeson! Give us Robeson! We'll string that big n----- up! Give him to us, you bastards!"[66]

Robeson vowed that he would return to Peekskill to sing the following week; as he later said: "I don't get scared when fascism gets near, as it did at Peekskill."[67]

On September 4, Robeson planted himself beneath a massive lonesome oak tree at the Hollow Brook Golf Course and sang, surrounded by a protective ring of sympathetic veterans and union activists prepared to take a bullet in the back from racist snipers reportedly lurking in the trees. The audience comprised tens of thousands of anti-Klan supporters who had been mobilized throughout the week. The concert went ahead with only minor disruption, as Fast recalled: "The great voice of Paul Robeson echoed back from the hills; the music of Handel and Bach was played there; and Pete Seeger and his friends sang those fine old songs of a time when treason and hatred and tyranny were not the most admired virtues of Americans. And the police did what they could. When they saw that they were not able to prevent the concert, they brought in a helicopter and it hovered over our sound truck constantly, swooping down to buzz us again and again, trying to drown out the sound of our music with the noise of its motor."[68]

It was after the singing that the horrors began. The cars of the exiting concertgoers were deliberately directed by the Westchester County Police into an ambush. As Fast described it: "The road that led to the picnic grounds was almost a narrow country lane. All along this road, groups gathered piles of rock and waited. Farther along where the road was crossed by highway bridges, they gathered tons of rocks and waited. Then, when the concert was finished, each car leaving the grounds ran a gauntlet of rocks. Car after car was smashed, windows shattered, cuts, bruises, skull fractures, splinters of glass embedded in eyes—all of this inflicted on the drivers and passengers to such an extent that every hospital in the vicinity was turned into an emergency trauma facility."[69] Seeger would later embed into his chimneybreast the grim memento of a rock hurled through his car window, narrowly missing his son, Danny. As he recalled: "People threw stones at women and children, with intent to kill. At my own family. I had two little kids in the car."[70] One of his passengers, "Boots" Casetta, relived the terror with precision and disgust, describing the mob that had closed around Seeger's car, rocking it violently:

> I was scared to death. I expected any moment that damned car would roll over. Then I heard this terrible noise, a crack. Somebody said, "My God, Greta's been hit." A rock had come through the window and hit her just above the eye.
>
> We got to the end of the turn and there was a clearing. We stopped. Some people were sitting. We asked, "Do you know the nearest hospital?" And they all started laughing and cackling. *Cackling.* I remember one woman rocking back and forth slapping her knees, like she'd heard a good joke. It was unbelievable, like I imagine Nazis would have been in those early street gang days in Berlin. All the way into the Bronx—more than twenty miles—you could see the injured, a long bloody alley.[71]

Lee Hays recalled sitting on a bus with Guthrie in the midst of the attack:

> On the grounds they waited in busses and cars, and all those who had walked in and could not ride out. Negro men and women, and their children—main objects of the fascist attack. All getting ready to run the gauntlet but, like us, not knowing how bad it could be. Troopers had carefully set the beginning of the gauntlet so far down the road from the entrance that "our guys" at the gate could not see or know how furious the attack was.
>
> Woody said, "I've seen a lot, but this is the worst."[72]

As the rocks started to fly, Hays noticed Guthrie pinning up a shirt to prevent the window glass from shattering inward. "Wouldn't you know it," he recalled, "Woody pinned up a red shirt."[73] He noted Guthrie's composure in the face of mob terror: "The people in the busses singing, Woody leading, 'I'm worried now but I won't be worried long!' Our battle song, 'We shall not be moved!' Between songs Woody making fine edgy comments: 'Anybody got a rock? There's a window back here that needs to be opened!'"[74]

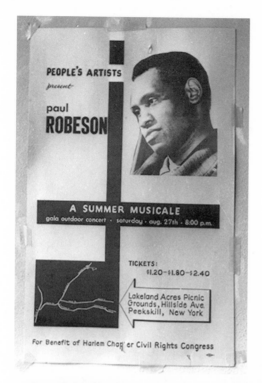

Program for the first Peekskill concert, August 27, 1949. Image courtesy of the Field Library, Peekskill. Colin T. Naylor, Jr. Archives.

Peekskill, USA: The gathering storm. Photographer unknown. Image courtesy of the Field Library, Peekskill. Colin T. Naylor, Jr. Archives, *Evening Star* Photograph Collection.

The Peekskill riots. Photographer unknown. Image courtesy of the Field Library, Peekskill. Colin T. Naylor, Jr. Archives, *Evening Star* Photograph Collection.

"A long, bloody alley." Peekskill ambush road. Photographer unknown. Image courtesy of the Robert F. Wagner Labor Archives, New York University. United Automobile Workers of America, District 65, Photographs Collection.

In the weeks that followed, Guthrie was stung into action, reeling off a series of his angriest, most contemptuous, most defiant songs in a remarkable burst of energy—at least twenty-one songs about Peekskill written within a month. Collected in a makeshift volume titled "Peekskill Songs," they were for the most part parodies of traditional and early country music standards. Thus Jimmie Rodgers's "Blue Yodel #8" ("Muleskinner Blues") became "Peekskill Klookluk Blues":

> Good mornin' Mister Kleagle!
> Klak klak, good morning Klook!
> Good mornin' Mister Kleagle!
> I said, Good morning, Klook!
> Do you need a right good planner
> Out on your Peekskill Road?[75]

Again, Guthrie turned to Rodgers's "Blue Yodel #1" ("T for Texas") for his own "P for Peekskill":

> It was P for People's Artists, P for Paul that day,
> P for People's Artists, P for Paul that day,
> And it was P for Partisanos that waved us on our way.[76]

"Peekskill Golfing Grounds" sets out to transmit the terror and disgust felt by the individual concertgoers:

> I'd never heard such cusswords as they spit from off their lips,
> I just stood and watched their eyes blare as they walked a dozen trips.
> Jew bastard. Wop. Hey nigger. Kike and Commy. And, their lungs
> Sounded like a boiling snake den with a million poison tongues.[77]

"Letter to Peekskillers" speaks the mind of an impressionable teenager from the town seduced into participating in the violence before being arrested by the police in a token gesture of law enforcement. The song is particularly striking for its uncharacteristic endorsement of incarceration—so far from Guthrie's earlier standpoint in *Hard Hitting Songs for Hard-Hit People* ("When any living creature walks out of a jailhouse, I like it. It's wrong to be in it and it's right to be out").[78] His young narrator reflects on the crimes of Peekskill and concludes:

> Nine or ten thugs put on work gangs for nine or ten years
> Would save our fair Peekskill an ocean and river of tears;
> And if nobody here has the guts to start locking them up,
> These crosses will burn till our tears turn to oceans of blood.

On the manuscript, Guthrie typed below his signature: "I was that kid."[79]

Of all the Peekskill songs, it is "My Thirty Thousand" that rings out for its magnificent belligerence.[80] Guthrie's ode to Robeson and the tens of thousands who returned to Peekskill bristles with all the rhetorical violence that he had heaped upon the Nazis during the war:

> Each eye you tried to gouge,
> Each skull you tried to crack,
> Has a thousand thousand friends
> Around this green grass!
> You'll furnish the skull someday
> I'll pass the clubs and guns
> To the billion hands that love
> My Thirty Thousand.
>
> Each wrinkle on your face
> I know it at a glance,
> You cannot run and hide
> Nor duck nor dodge them.
> Your carcass and your deeds
> Will fertilize the seeds
> Of the men that stood to guard
> My Thirty Thousand![81]

Peekskill was the crucible in which anticommunism bled into racism as the dominant expression of postwar American reaction. Its place in U.S. history is double-sided. On the one hand, the revulsion that it prompted from newspapers and commentators across the country bore out the impression of Eleanor Roosevelt, who—after reiterating her political opposition to Robeson—condemned the "lawlessness" at Peekskill with the simple declaration: "This is not the type of thing that we believe in the United States."[82] Lee Hays was nothing less than bewildered by the madness he had witnessed: "What is there in the music of Chopin, Bartok, Mendelssohn, and in the people's songs of Paul Robeson and Pete Seeger and Hope Foye to inspire this savagery, this hatred? Who but beasts are menaced by a culture which brings people together in peace and understanding?"[83]

However, for William L. Patterson of the Civil Rights Congress, these bloody events could be remembered with a degree of pride: "*Peekskill* is a milepost in the great anti-fascist struggles of progressive America. *Peekskill* will also in the future be synonymous with Negro–white unity in struggle. Thereby *Peekskill* becomes more than a name, more than a city; *Peekskill* has become a symbol of progressive America."[84] Hence the decision of "Boots"

Casetta, Tony Schwartz, and Frances Dellorco to incorporate on-site recordings of the violence into an audio documentary, "The Peekskill Story" (1949),
which blended the spoken testimonies of Fast, Seeger, and other participants
with a musical narrative crafted by Seeger and Hays. Against the shouting
of racist epithets ("Jews! Jews! Jews!" and "white niggers!"), Fast is heard to
intone: "That's the sound of Fascism. Not in Germany, but here in America—
remember it!" In between this and other spoken passages, Seeger, Hays,
Ronnie Gilbert, and Fred Hellerman—collectively the nascent folk group
the Weavers—sing "Hold the Line," in which Peekskill becomes a high water
mark of antifascist resistance:

> All across the nation we are telling you this tale;
> You can marvel at the concert and know we have not failed.
> We shed our blood at Peekskill and suffered many a pain,
> But we beat back the fascists and we'll beat them back again.[85]

For Guthrie, Peekskill was as important a personal milestone as it was
a political one. Like the other witnesses who had held the line at Lakeland
Acres and Hollow Brook, he had knowingly put himself in harm's way to
stand up to terror in the name of racial solidarity and antifascism. He had by
then traveled a long road from the casual, thoughtless racism of his youth,
having been painfully educated into a capacity for greater wisdom and racial
empathy. In the process, his journey—a virtual *bildungsroman* in itself—had
proved something uplifting. Racists are not born, but made; and they can
be unmade.

7. The Last Free Place in America

In the weeks and months on either side of the Peekskill riots, Guthrie had been turning his attention to other signs of the deepening Cold War. He continued to play with whimsical settings of nuclear destruction, much as he had done in his mock children's song "Dance Around My Atom Fire." He drafted "Come When I Call You," a cumulative song in the tradition of "Twelve Days of Christmas," with a final verse displaying the accumulated images of his times, both public and personal:

> Ohhh, will you come when I call you? I'll come when you call me.
> I'll call you at half past ten. Ten for the atom bomb loose again.
> Nine for the crippled and the blind. Eight for the eight billion graves.
> Seven for continents blowed up. Six for my cities all wrecked.
> Five for these warplanes that fly. Four for the guns of this war.
> Three for the warships at sea. Two for the love of me and you.
> One for the little pretty baby that's born, born, born & gone away.[1]

He had also taken to writing aggressive, challenging (and probably unsent) letters to public figures whom he held in contempt. Thus to Harry Truman he wrote:

> My dear Mr. Truman
>   If you ever so much as lay a small claim to be a human with a brain, a soul, a heart, a mind, a feeling you could call the warmth of the blood of man, please, good sir, take a good look at these bills you are signing to make more high explosives to blow us all off of the map. Your face will look a whole lot blanker

if the little atoms blow our world away and all of your pals and kinfolks along with the rest of us.

I'm not ready to blow just yet. Your old buddy,

Woody Guthrie[2]

He also slung a catalog of accusations at Truman's attorney general, Tom Clark, over the fearmongering that had stifled political discourse in America—a fearmongering over which Clark, as the nation's senior justice officer, ultimately presided. It was not only the fear of the anticommunist inquisitor that was tearing out the political heart of the nation but also "Useless fears about another war on its bloody way to our streets and fields," "Fears of losing everything you've been building up all of your life," "Fears about taking down sick with no money to pay for medicine nor nurse nor doctor nor hospital."[3] Guthrie thus lay at the attorney general's feet the responsibility for the social wreckage scattered in the whirlwind of the "American Century," both at home and abroad: "If you are full of fears about socialism, sir, then you are surely spreading your killing fears through your own self and through the whole civilized worlds; if you are trying to hold back this only certain cure for all of our hands and our brains (socialism), then you, you see, are one of the causers and one of the spreaders of the fears that are causing all of the sickening diseases that already drown, choke, strangle, and kill the dreams, hopes, the plans, blueprints and struggles of the billion that now stagger sickly around and about."[4]

To Generalissimo Chiang Kai-shek, the anticommunist leader retreating before the advancing forces of Mao Zedong, Guthrie promised a grim retribution for "Each drop of blood spilt" in his war for Chinese "slavery":

You killed my family,
Shy Yang, Shy Yang Kye Check,
With borrowed fire arms,
Shy Yang, Shy Yang Kye Check,
You try to kill me,
Shy Yang, Shy Yang Kye Check,
With borrowed money,
Shy Yang, Shy Yang Kye Check.[5]

Guthrie also turned to the dominant organizations of the Cold War, beginning with NATO, established in April 1949 through the North Atlantic Treaty among the United States, Canada, and the Western European nations. The signatures on the treaty were hardly dry before Guthrie proclaimed: "Just one thing in the world I hate / That's this damned Atlantic Pact! / Take it back, / Take it back, / Yes, take it back!"

> I'll not budge one single inch
> To save that robber gang in Greece. . . .
>
> I'll not march to lose my pants
> For that fascist bunch in France. . . .
>
> I'll not fly one atom bomb
> To blow down the Russian towns. . . .
>
> I'ma gonna build my home in peace;
> Ain'ta gonna start no World War Three!
> Take it back,
> Take it back,
> Yes, take it back![6]

In January 1950, amid all the fireworks celebrating the opening of the United Nations headquarters in New York City, Guthrie balanced his meager hopes against his reservation of judgment (and lurking behind that, once again, the promise of swift retribution for the betrayal of promise):

> First floor is for th' sick an' th' cripple ones;
> Next floor is for th' widows and orphans;
> Top floor's there for th' naked and hungry;
> Y' gonna shine all over this world. . . .
>
> If you heal my sick, I'll bless your buildin;
> If you feed the hungry, I'll pray for your buildin;
> If you forget my people I'll curse you and wreck you
> Y' gonna fall all over this world.

In an explanatory note beneath the manuscript lyrics, Guthrie justified his concluding threat: "I've seen lots of good buildings in my day that forgot all about its main job after it got a highpriced pair of shoes on, and a fancy pair of girdle pants, and a floweredy hat of some kind in its hair, that, well, I just thought we'd ought to have a little song or two made up to make you building owners and building bosses remember and recall that buildings are built by us humans, for us humans, and with money borrowed from a kittybox that belongs to us humans. We can't build humans to fit buildings, but we can raise up buildings to fit a human, to help a human."[7] The invasion of Korea by a multinational force led by the United States—and in the explicit name of the United Nations—finished off Guthrie's already weak faith in the organization's progressive commitment.

In solidarity he nurtured a friendship with the radical activist and Klan in-filtrator Stetson Kennedy, whom he hoped to visit in "them raceyhate Florida jungles" following Kennedy's open invitation to his home at Beluthahatchee.[8] Kennedy had rechristened his home "Poor Boy Estates" as a recuperative colony for beleaguered progressives, advertising in the national press: "The colony is being projected as something of an autonomous republic, where progressives can enjoy all the natural attractions of Florida, and democracy too. The only discrimination practiced at Beluthahatchee will be political; only confirmed progressives need apply."[9] Guthrie had replied to Kennedy: "I think I might like that quick spirit that smolders so friendly down around there in spite of the turpentine bosses and the pineywoods killers and the hooded legions and . . . the longtime landlords which China and Korea are now fighting to rid their camps and pineywoods and redpine timbers of."[10]

Guthrie was soon writing songs in support of Kennedy's doomed cam-paign for the Florida senate on an integrationist ticket. His musical activism on Kennedy's behalf enabled him to hit out at some of his favorite targets, beginning with the Ku Klux Klan:

> Stetson Kennedy, he's that man,
> Walks and talks across our land.
> Talkin' out against the Ku Klux Klan,
> For every fiery cross and note,
> I'll get Kennedy a hundred votes.[11]

Kennedy's opponent, the white supremacist George Smathers, was being bankrolled by the weapons manufacturer I. E. Du Pont de Nemours. Guthrie sang:

> I cain't win out to save my soul,
> Long as Smathers-Dupont's got me in the hole.
> Those war-profit boys are squawkin' and a-balkin',
> That's what's got me outta walkin' and a-talkin'.
> Knockin' on doors and windows,
> Wake up and run down election mornin',
> And scribble in—Stetson Kennedy.[12]

Guthrie shared with Kennedy his barely disguised hopes for a communist victory in Korea, which he increasingly took incorrigible glee in proclaiming outright: "The Korean Reds are sure giving our poor boys a good licking these days. I'm sadly afraid that the news hasn't been as bad nor as sad as the whop-ping we're really taking. The news tales and the news reels back in WW # Two were never as plain and never quite as clear nor as stinky as the real bombed out towns and cities which I saw in North Africa, Sicily, and all over the British Isles. This is why I know that the real news and the blues from Korea is not ½ as good but several times as bad as MacArthur dishes up for us."[13]

These were, of course, dangerous opinions to proclaim, and Guthrie relayed to Kennedy his awareness of the diminishing opportunities for radical expression, musical or otherwise, in the United States. Kennedy had recently helped to draft a petition calling for the indictment of the U.S. government, *We Charge Genocide: The Crime of Government against the Negro People,* which William L. Patterson and Paul Robeson would present to the United Nations in December of 1951 on behalf of the Civil Rights Congress (thus inviting the enmity of the FBI and the State Department). Guthrie wrote to Kennedy:

> I'm already making some might good use of your book, "WE CHARGE GENO-
> CIDE"; I'm thumbing through the pages of it now to make up a long (deep) play-
> ing album of balladsongs of my own making to be printed legally or unlegally
> on one of Moe Asch's labels. Moe told me how scared and how afraid nearly
> all of the big record houses are about recording or printing down anything
> having to do with protests or politicks; but he gets past them by saying this
> is the American scene, this is the American picture, this is what's happening,
> taking place, and what's going on here in this USA of ours; And so, in lots of
> ways Moe is still on the proper beam as far as I'm concerned; and very probably
> one of the few (one or two) houses in this entire recording industry that has
> got the guts to stand up and believe in something somewhere; so many people
> just don't see anything out here to believe in (excepting their bellybutton and
> their bank account).[14]

Guthrie's faith in Asch's political tenacity was compounded by two developments. The Library of Congress—which had been, through Alan Lomax, his first major producer—was increasingly wary of working with him. In 1950 Lomax himself fled the political witch hunts for England, where he would remain for the next eight years. When Guthrie proposed to Duncan Emrich, now in charge of the library's Folklore Section, a further recording of "a few hundred more of my tales, travels, jokes, songs, ballads, and such" to augment the original *Library of Congress Recordings,* he was refused.[15] Emrich had already begun collaborating with the FBI, accusing People's Songs of being "unpatriotic" and voicing his outrage "at the efforts of Communists and Communist sympathizers to infiltrate and gain control of Folksinging."[16]

At the same time, Guthrie watched with bemusement as his old friends Pete Seeger and Lee Hays, along with Ronnie Gilbert and Fred Hellerman, skyrocketed to considerable riches and success at the top of the Hit Parade as the orchestra-laden quartet, the Weavers. As the New York *Daily Compass* reported after the group's first appearance at the Village Vanguard nightclub: "It's hardly what you'd expect in an intimate cafe. Where's the funnyman to give with the clever, satiric verbiage? And where's the thrush, in teasing decollete, to coax patrons with her warble-talk? Instead, four young people, in street clothes attire, harmonizing in high spirits and in unaffected tones. It's showmanship of a kind rarely associated with a night club and the applause that follows the first number assures you that it's paying off."[17]

Guthrie found himself greatly benefiting from the Weavers' commercial appeal, in spite of the high, moral, noncommercial ground he claimed to have occupied: among the Weavers' hits, which included "Kisses Sweeter than Wine," a sanitized version of Lead Belly's "Goodnight, Irene," and the Israeli folk song "Tzena, Tzena," was Guthrie's "So Long, It's Been Good to Know Yuh," feverishly rewritten by Guthrie himself during one of their recording sessions. His new version—a sentimental weepy about two parting lovers— "did sell up into the blue jillions," as he bragged to Marianne "Jolly" Smolens, upon whom he had developed an erotic fixation.[18] To radical colleagues like "Sis" Cunningham, the Weavers' version was a "contemptible garblization,"[19] but that did not stop Guthrie from using it as leverage in a hopeless attempt to impress Smolens: "[It] looks like I've got the goodnews to rolling at long and last on this money front. So Long, alone, from sales of songsheets, records, royalties, performances in all lingoes, (etc etc), will net over unto me and my heirs and assignes and executors (of which I'm the only one of each), not less than Forty to Fifty Thousand Krannkers during these next 2 to 3 years, and by that time I can have several more runs over that grassyback fence, and be grinding down enuff longcabbage to thumb my bellybutton at Gene Autry and Bang Krozby and all of these other armytures."[20]

It was perhaps a mark of Guthrie's envy over the Weavers' success—and a lingering discomfort at having profited by it—that he envisaged a competing group, which he hoped to form with Smolens because her voice could "hit under the highs and over the lows."[21] He cast aside young Tom Paley after brief consideration: "Tom Paley is fine, but me and Cisco have worked around together so many years that it is all second nature with us. If we do have to lose an inch or two in the field of slick fine expert music like Tom's, we'll pick up the difference (and more) in loudness and wild soulness which I love best any way." Thus he arrived at his ideal foursome: himself, Smolens, Cisco Houston, and "Some perty (negroid) girl": "I just dont want our four to look like this Weaverly bunch. I want all four of us to stand up and to even lay down a whole lot pertier than them Weavers ever did or ever can."[22] Guthrie saw that the implicitly radical statement of an interracial group would enable him to distance himself further from the Weavers; but his plans never came to fruition. In November 1951 he turned his back on New York and accepted Kennedy's invitation to Beluthahatchee, where at least one account has him fighting in a pitched gun battle against a mob of Klansmen attacking Kennedy's home.[23]

The year 1952 saw an acceleration of Guthrie's Huntington's disease and a frightening neurological disintegration, witnessed not only in the disoriented, erratic behavior that he and many of his friends and family initially mistook for alcoholism, but also in the marked deterioration of his handwriting and the increasing idiosyncrasy of his wordplay—the "linguistic anarchy" that would mark the rest of his writing.[24] That same year he struck up a brief correspondence with Ken Lindsay, manager of the progressive Collet's International Bookshop in London. In a letter to Lindsay he expressed his keen perception of his political isolation as he considered following Lomax (and, it seemed, scores of the HUAC's victims) to London. "I sure want to do some writings for your papers and mags over there," he told Lindsay, "like I've always done for the Peoples World in Frisco, and the Daily Worker in NYTowne; ass well ass a dozen or so trade union pubbleykations I writ and rotted for." He reiterated his radical and proletarian credentials for a potential British audience: "I never cared to get rich nor financially baronical in or through nor sideways back from any of my gifts and talents which these worker's hands gave to me in my first place. I chatted along a little Will Rogerishly only moreso of the rebel Tom Paineishly; and if you can show me who to shake hands with over there to get my artickels and pieces printed and published for the deepdeep masses, I'll thank you more than just once."[25]

The entire radical wing of American folk music was now openly under siege. The HUAC might claim that Hollywood or the State Department or even the U.S. Army were riddled with communists, but they never went so far as to designate filmmaking or diplomacy or warfare subversive activities by definition. The same could not be said for folk music (the popularity of Harry Belafonte and the growing calypso fad notwithstanding). As the country and western singer Tex Ritter recalled: "At one time I called myself a folk singer. [But] it got to the point there for a few years where it was very difficult to tell where folk music ended and Communism began. So that's when I quit calling myself a folk singer. It was the sting of death if you were trying to make a living."[26] It was thus a fairly surprising feat for Guthrie to have landed a recording contract for the Weavers' label, Decca, in 1952—even with the producer Milt Gabler backing him—since both the political climate and his physical deterioration were against him.[27] He jokingly warned Earl Robinson: "Just don't think that the Decca Recording Company has got me wrapped up around any of their little finger; I was born to be a reddical and the life and death of a reddical is the only kind of a life and a death I'd sign up with."[28]

It is less surprising that both Guthrie and the Weavers lost their Decca contracts as the New York folk scene imploded and folksingers began dropping like sledgehammered cattle before the anticommunist onslaught. On February 6, 1952, Harvey Matusow, a former volunteer for People's Songs, gave 244 names to the HUAC, including those of all the People's Songs associates that he could remember. Guthrie, he lied, was "a member of the cultural division of the Communist Party" as well as "a member of the Brighton section of the party in Brooklyn."[29] Matusow later recanted all of his testimony in his published mea culpa *False Witness* (1955),[30] and as he confessed in 2002: "No, I didn't know Woody was a dues-paying card-carrying member of the Party"; Guthrie's name, he said, was merely "a sideline, a throwaway name."[31] He had stated in closed testimony before the HUAC that "a name I didn't mention before, Woodie Guthrie, who wrote the song So Long, It's Been Good To Know You," was a member of People's Songs and an associate of the Weavers: "They made the song recording of So Long, It's Been Good To Know You; Goodnight Irene; and On Top of Old Smoky; the best-selling records, using their appeal to the young people as a means of getting the young people down to the meetings of the Communist fronts and indoctrinating them with the party line and later recruiting them."[32]

In spite of Matusow's later recantation and his abiding contrition, the damage was done. The anticommunist publications *Red Channels* and *Counterattack* both picked up on and amplified Matusow's testimony with their own insinuations and outright charges, and folksingers willingly beat their way—or were unwillingly dragged—to the doors of the HUAC and Pat McCarran's Senate Internal Security Subcommittee. Friendly witnesses like Burl Ives named names. Some, like Josh White, presented themselves as Communist Party dupes.[33] Some, like Oscar Brand (in informal, closed testimony), fervently affirmed their anticommunism.[34] Some, like Lee Hays, took the Fifth Amendment, and the most hostile—Earl Robinson, Irwin Silber, the actor and singer Tony Kraber, and Pete Seeger among them—refused to cooperate at all. Seeger's First Amendment testimony still rings for its defiance: "I am not going to answer any questions as to my association, my philosophical or my religious beliefs or my political beliefs, or how I voted in any election or any of these private affairs. I think these are very improper questions for any American to be asked, especially under such compulsion as this."[35] He would go to jail before he would name any names: "I decline to discuss, under compulsion, where I have sung, and who has sung my songs, that I have helped to write as well as to sing them, and who else has sung with me, and the people I have known."[36] And he turned upon his inquisitors: "I feel that in my whole life I have never done anything of any conspiratorial nature and I resent very much and very deeply the implication of being called before this committee that in some way because my opinions may be different from yours, or yours, Mr. Willis; or yours, Mr. Scherer; that I am any less of an American than anybody else. I love my country very deeply, sir."[37] For this, Seeger was slapped with a contempt of Congress citation and a ten-year jail sentence; his conviction would not be overturned until 1962, and then only on a technicality.

It remains a mystery as to why Guthrie was never called before the HUAC or the McCarran Committee, given that his FBI file, opened in 1941, was still open. If he was, for the most part, musically inactive thanks to his crippling disease, his opinions were as robust as ever. He wrote to Seeger: "See by the *Daily Punkass* [New York *Daily Compass*] where Burl sung his head off to the F. B. Eye folks. He fell bad into the old and ancient money trap which has been the deaths of whole generations of nations before our times—and will

"I decline to discuss, under compulsion." Pete Seeger stands his ground before the HUAC, 1955. Photographer unknown. Image © Bettmann/Corbis.

be even worser till we get some kind of a planned social (money) system to work by and to live by."[38] He implied his disappointment over Asch's now-evident political nervousness, comparing him unfavorably with Bob Harris of Stinson Records (whom he had once thought "really nervous on the whole idea of even touching a record that said anything that took sides with anybody in any kind of a fight, because his big store outlets called him a red record company").[39] As he told Seeger: "I'm still thinking out a lot of good and bad and mediumsized ideas for longplaying slowspeed record albums for Bob Harris to print, publicize & distribute. Bob is better than Moe Asch I believe for being freer politically about censoring or recordsong ideas. Moe gets a little bit afraid sometimes in spite of his best leftwing intentions and Bob & and his Old Man (Paw) Harris are rebels of the first waters like me; so I dont censor none of their words and they dont censor none of mine; and this is the only sensible way to me it looks like for you to own or to operate a damd record company these days."[40]

In September of 1952, after five months of hospitalization, Guthrie was formally diagnosed with what was still being called Huntington's chorea.[41] Upon discharging himself—and at Marjorie's suggestion, for the good of their children and for his own mental space to face the reality of his disease—Guthrie went to join Will and Herta Geer and other unrepentant leftists banded in solidarity in the politically besieged canyon town of Topanga, California. He purchased a small plot of virtually uninhabitable land, which he envisaged as a haven where "it'll always be against the good law for any citizen to ask you even one question about your whole case history, where you've come from and where you're heading towards."[42] He imagined confronting the McCarthyite witch hunters and winning them over to the side of the angels:

> My tongue is tired of talking more to you. My finger is
> paralyzed here from begging you to break free from your
> killer among them and to come join my builder gang here
> where I'm at this morning.

With the Eisenhower–Nixon ticket drafted in on the strength of anticommunist hysteria, the Korean War in a bloody stalemate, and bellicose, nuclear-tinged rhetoric streaming from politicians and pundits across the country, Guthrie reflected on the recent election:

> When we voted our vote and when we dropped our helpless
> Little ballot vote and when we drowned our freest voice
> Down in the prison acid tanks you call by the name of
> Voting boxes.

> We did go and follow or we did pretend to go and to follow the
>> Words and the deeds and sadist actions and killer pointers
>> Of your deadly fringes by letting this unhuman war keep on
>> Blazing and framing over yonder in sweet old Korealand.[43]

He reflected, too, on his own mental and neurological crisis, which—like "Chorea" and "Korea"—blended into the wider public crisis marked by war, repression, and social neglect. From "Topanga Graveyard Canyon" he wrote:

> I am that psycho raver
> You hear so much talk about
> I raved and drew my G.I. pay
> As long as I held my sight right.
>
> I'm that wild psycho raver.
> I got paid for shooting wild.
> And government check for killing wilder
> As long as I kept my gun clean.
>
> I'm just a skid row raver now
> I rave in my Bellyvue ward
> Nobody sends me a paycheck now
> You tell me I'm raving too loud.[44]

In spite of the breakdown in his motor coordination, which had virtually destroyed his musicianship, Guthrie held on to music as an oasis of sanity, free expression, and political courage. Seeger recalled a visit with him in Topanga, when Guthrie, singing the "Old Settler's Song" ("Acres of Clams"), improvised a verse recounting an FBI interrogation:

> He asked, "Will you carry a gun for your country?"
> I answered the Effbee-eye "Yay!"
> "I *will* point a gun for my country,
> But I won't guarantee you which way!"[45]

Guthrie took to eulogizing the hootenanny as an almost sacred ritual, the last site for singing "to my scared and my nervous cowards / How easy is the union way of life":

> I did help to think up that name, hootinanny
> To mean the place where you could come to and to
> Yell your head off about what's eatin' on you;
> Tell who's beatin' on you, mistreatin' on ya;
> Stoolin' on y', droolin' on ya, tomfoolerin on ya;

So's you'd have a good place to come sing and dance
About whoever it was that done you wrongly and howly.[46]

He lamented the political evisceration of the hootenanny as organizers caved in to the witch hunt and turned the events into harmless entertainments led by celebrity singers such as Burl Ives. As he wrote to Asch: "Mosta the hoots got too danderned smoothyed up to satisfy me & too pleated & plotted & too kleiglighted & too britely polished to suit the workerman spirits Ive got in me."[47] He began to obsess over the subject, writing to Asch again two days later and turning even upon Cisco Houston, who was gracing the hoots with his version of Jim Jackson's "Old Blue": "Jackson teaches me here that Old Blue & Jim both can still teach old Huston a few higher points of doing this here song. Old Huston soups it up & smoothens it up several degrees too damnable smuuuuuthe to suit Mr Me. Cisco is sweetwhining all his laterday songs this same lost way. He'll be pertyneart as smoothy as Mr Sandyburger is if he soups on along at his present rate of Joshua Ives speed. I dont quite plumb believe old Cisco when he or anybody else tryes to runup and to tell me much of anything in his newfound soupysmoothey voice."

Other hootenanny performers earned Guthrie's censure, among them "Erny Lieberman & Laura Duncan & Setty Banders [Betty Sanders] & Hopey Foy & sometimes Petey Seeger"—all of whom were too "sugarsweet" and "sweetylip" for him. He made a portentous, empty vow: "I'll sing all of them Peopledy Artistes right out of them seventy dollar rigs & them brite kleiglights theyre hiding out behind. And I'll give all my stages & my woodfloors & my plattyforms right on back over to my Jim Jackson workhands we've robbed & we've stoled all of our workysongs & our testy protesty songs away from ever since I let my gang of song wreckers & songrapers get in on our union-minded hootenanny stages & to tittysuckle ten damned years too long."[48]

Guthrie also clung to the kindred spirits whose political bravery seemed to fortify his own, none more so than Stetson Kennedy. In March 1953 he and his third wife, Anneke, with Jack Elliott at the wheel of a Model A Ford, sought out Kennedy at his Florida ranch, only to find the Kennedys gone and the property destroyed. As Guthrie wrote to Asch: "Stetson Kennedy and his part negro wife got burned out by the raceyhater gang down here, got his orchard chopped down, his barnsheds smashed, his bushouse broke down, and his book collection, one of the countrys best, stoled and carried out to set the old fascist nazzyheaded flameymatch to."[49] From Kennedy's deserted ranch, Guthrie wrote to Mike Gold on the back of a dust jacket to *The Black Book: The Nazi Crime against the Jewish People,* which had been submitted as evidence at the Nuremberg trials:

I see now that most all of my whole forty and eight I've walked over, Mike, aint washed and cleaned and aint nearly half way as rid of this same deadly kind of super race backtalk that I faced my two torpedoes in my last three invasions of that World War Two we fought and died so hard in to choke that racey hate slavery to death. . . .

Who'ze free?[50]

The Kennedys had gone to London, where Lomax had fled and where Ken Lindsay could still operate an openly progressive bookshop with impunity. From "Stetsin Kennedy Klannrooste," Guthrie wrote wistfully to Lomax: "I'm wanting most of all things now to get us over there to where we can play and sing and keep on making up our stuff around at all of those peacetown rallies and all of them youthful congresses and all of them folks of all colors that wants peace now."[51] To Lindsay, Guthrie boasted desperately about the one thing that he had managed to keep intact as his own body disintegrated along with that of the radical Left—the political integrity of his songs:

> I never did yet cut so much as one little word of my political protest out from one of my jokes or from out of one of my ballads or my songs & I'm too young to give an inch & I'm too damn old to change. People beg me every damn day to come over to some sucha place and to sing out for a big fattyass fee of money but not for me to sing no song that bothers nobody no way & I tell these bat-tyheads just exactly where they can stick their goddamnd bigfat fees (up their big dictatory ass) & that if my balladsongs do bother your thieving robbery soul & conscience that bad . . . you're freely welcome to histe it up and leave. . . . I just cant mark one raddicle word of mine out . . . Just one little word of censor shippery chokes me almost to my death.[52]

While at Kennedy's ranch, a fire that burned his arm from wrist to armpit put an end to Guthrie's guitar playing. At the same time—as his musically productive life was closing—the folklorist John Greenway gave him his first serious scholarly attention in the book that appeared under the miraculous title (miraculous for 1953, with McCarthyism at its height) *American Folk-songs of Protest*. Not that Greenway was immune to the witch hunt: he had excised a perfectly neutral ten-page discussion of People's Songs from the final manuscript.[53] Elsewhere, he appeared to soft-pedal any suggestion of a protest song's subversive potential, arguing for their "ephemeral" nature. "The body of song represented by the selections in this collection," he claimed, "will not survive"; the majority would "lose their meaning when the events for which they were composed are forgotten, or displaced by greater crises."[54] Among these supposedly "ephemeral" songs were Guthrie's "Tom Joad," "Plane Wreck at Los Gatos" ("Deportee"), "Pretty Boy Floyd," and "Jesus Christ" (in its most militant version)—all of which Greenway reproduced in full. He neglected to mention Guthrie's writings for the *People's World* and the *Daily Worker* and skated over his involvement with the Almanacs.

The Guthrie whom Greenway presents through interviews and correspondence is bitter and defensive: "'Everybody tells me how good I am,' he says, 'but I can't make a living for my wife and kids.'"[55] At one point, responding to what Greenway admits is "a somewhat ill-considered criticism of the psychology" used by Guthrie "to convey his political philosophy," Guthrie snaps back with withering sarcasm: "I fall on the rim of my table of grief and cry because you have ripped aside the cloudy blanket of my soul and shown me that I am too far to the left of the center, too radical in my political views, and, sad to tell, too unpleasant even in my class relationships."[56] In spite of his apparent determination to diminish the oppositional potential of Woody Guthrie or any protest-song writer in the long term, Greenway concluded his discussion with a claim to Guthrie's "real importance as a man and as a symbol."[57] Conceivably, Greenway's aim was to protect Guthrie as much as himself. As Seeger later said, referring to Greenway's book: "I don't trust political analys[e]s when they're made at the height of the Cold War and you can't speak the truth without getting someone in serious trouble."[58]

Guthrie may well have been thinking of all such nervous accommodations when he wrote the following year: "I can't help but hate to see all of us wiggling around in rooms like McCarthys trying to suit & satisfy his dictatorial mind when he cuts off all of our most gifted and our highest talented minds and he keeps them from being useful to the rest of us."[59] He turned his hatred against a whole fellowship of reactionaries—particularly racists—in a white-hot burst of typing in mid-1955, inflamed by the aggressive symptoms of Huntington's disease:

> YA DAMNDAMN SHITTYHEEL BASTERDSCAB
> YA LOWLYLIFE SONOFABITCHHYSCAB
> YA GADDAMND NOGOODY PI[S]TOLPRICK
> YA BASSTARDYY ONERY SCAB
> YA RACEYHATER'N ASSUHOLE
> YA JIMMY KROWED FUCK'RDUP STOOLE
> YA TENCENTER TWOBITTY LYINMOUTH FROTHER
> Y' DAMN KRAZEY LOCOEDY FOOLE . . .
>
> YA FIXER YA KLUXER YA RACEYMAD HOODERM'N
> YA HOODLUM YA KLOOXSTER YA HOOD HIDIN COWERDYASS
> YA SLUGGERD YA MUGGER'D YA BLACKSOUL'D BRAGGERBOY
> YA GANGER Y' HANGER YA THUGGERD YA BUGGERD[60]

He attempted a reworking of Lead Belly's "Titanic," in which the boxer Jack Johnson is refused passage on the doomed ship because of his race. Lead Belly's song concludes:

> Black man oughta shout for joy
> Never lost a girl or either a boy
> Cryin', "Fare thee, Titanic, fare thee well."[61]

In Guthrie's hands, the relief over the unintentional saving of black lives is inflated to outright rejoicing over the destruction of the liner guided by "Old Jimmy Krow": "Gladdest news I ever heard / Titanick's crack'd onna big icey-berg."[62] A further reworking amplified this glee to hysterical proportions:

> I JUST LAFF TA HEAR Y'R GODDAMND BOAT SUNK DOWN
> I JUST LAFF TA SEE Y'R HATEYFUL SHIP SINK DOWN
> GOD HE LAFFS TA SEE Y'R BIGGYPROUD BOAT SINKYDOWN
> GOD HE LAFFS TA SEE Y'R OLD HATE SHIP GO DOWN
> MY GOD LAFFS TA HEAR Y'R BADSAD BOAT SUNK DOWN
> MY GOD LAFFS TA HEAR Y'R BADSAD BOAT SUNK DOWN[63]

And, on the unnamed "Mister" to whom Jim Garland once pleaded in "All I Want" ("I Don't Want Your Millions, Mister"), the disgusted Guthrie vented the hatred that had been welling up since he first heard the song:

> I'LL NOT BAG YOU F'R MY OLDEY JOB MIST'R
> TA HALFFFYWAYS FEEDE MY KIDS AN' WYFEEYYY
> I'LL NEVER BEG YOU ONE REDDY PENNYE
> Y'BASTERD Y' STOLED IT ALL FRUM ME[64]

As Guthrie spewed his remaining oaths of defiance onto paper, FBI Director J. Edgar Hoover received a memo from a field operative dated June 3, 1955: "In view of the subject's health status and the lack of reliable firsthand information reflecting Communist Party membership in the last five years, it is believed that his name should be deleted from the Security Index."[65] Thus was Guthrie's surveillance terminated (although his file remained open even after his death). He watched from the sidelines as the witch hunt continued; Joe McCarthy's censure by the Senate in 1954 had not signaled the end of the persecution of Americans for their political beliefs and associations. Pete Seeger was still looking at ten years in jail.

In May of 1956—two months after his canonization in the live concert performance "Bound for Glory: A Musical Tribute to Woody Guthrie" at New York's Pythian Hall—the new patron saint of American folk music was committed to the Greystone Park Psychiatric Hospital in Morris Plains,

New Jersey. When his friends Harold Leventhal and Fred Hellerman visited and asked after him, he told them: "You don't have to worry about me. I'm worried about how *you* boys are doing. Out there, if you guys say you're communists, they'll put you in jail. But in here, I can get up there and say I'm a communist and all they say is 'Ah, he's crazy.' You know, this is the last free place in America."[66]

To Seeger he commiserated: "Hal and Freddy told me when they visited me here a few little weeks ago how you mite not have to go to jail for another two or more years for refusing to testify before my unnamerican committee theyre all a big bunch of the very unnnamericanistic people I ever did hear of. . . . To me you are just another goody martyr Pete over on my side of gods eternal love since I never did ever even hear you speakout actout nor so much as even breathe out one little breathe of hateyful hatreds of no earthy sort my crazy committee to me are always my very worst sorts of haters always anyways."[67]

A month before the 1956 presidential election, Guthrie wrote to Marjorie from his hospital bed: "Eisenhower can't be my big chiefy bossyman till he makes alla my United States alla my races all equal. . . . I vote for my communist candidates anyhow that'll be the only ones ta ever even partways tryta give birth ta my racey equality."[68] He was going down, but he was going down fighting.

By the end of the year, he had written his last letter. Eisenhower was ensconced in his second term, groping toward the sinister conception of what he himself would name the "military–industrial complex." The courts and congressional committee rooms were still clogged with scores of Americans awaiting conviction, acquittal, sentencing, or appeal for their political activities and beliefs. In Montgomery, Alabama, the yearlong bus boycott sparked by Rosa Parks had ended with the desegregation of the city's buses. The Hungarian revolt had been crushed and flattened beneath the treads of Soviet tanks, the Communist Party was banned in West Germany, and Fidel Castro with his eighty-one fighters had landed on Cuban shores to commence the revolution. There was still plenty to sing about—in Washington Square Park and at the Village Gate in New York; at the Purple Onion and the hungry i in San Francisco; at the Gate of Horn in Chicago; and at countless universities, coffeehouses, folk clubs, and lakeside gatherings across the country where guitars were being tuned, banjos were being strung, and the second American folk revival stirred in its infancy, in the shadow of the dying Woody Guthrie.

Conclusion

The Miners and the Mill

In late 1959 or early 1960, a transplanted Californian couple, Bob and Sidsel (Sid) Gleason, learned that Woody Guthrie was confined to the Greystone Park Psychiatric Hospital, not far from their home in East Orange, New Jersey. Sid Gleason remembered Guthrie from his KFVD broadcasts, and soon they were offering him a weekly respite, taking him to their apartment where his friends, family, and an ever-growing number of acolytes could meet, talk, and sing for him. The Gleasons also took it upon themselves to answer the burgeoning pile of fan letters that had begun to flow in. In August of 1960, Sid Gleason answered a letter from an English admirer, Bob Brough, who had written to Guthrie from Liverpool. She described the weekly sessions:

> Our apartment is never silent on Sunday. Next week, Ralph Rinzler, Logan and Barbara English will be here. Last week it was a boy Stan Appel from England. And Barbara Appelman from New York City. So it goes. Never a dull moment. And Woody loves every minute of it. . . .
>
> Just recently Woody, Pete Seeger & Cisco Huston were all together for the first time in 12 years. That, my friends, was a day. Such picking and singing. Logan was here too. And Woody's children [and] their mother Marjorie. Pete & Logan's wives, Tóshi Seeger and Barbara. Margo Mayo a teacher of folk music and dance.

She reported that a film script of *Bound for Glory* was circulating around somewhere: "So if the public interest increases, then we will see the Woody Guthrie story 'Bound for Glory' in a movie. If they do make a movie of it, Jack Elliott should play Woody. They are the same size. And Jack can do Woody as no one else can. However he isn't the handsome devil Woody

A circle of acolytes. Left to right: Ralph Rinzler, Ellen Kossoy, Woody Guthrie, Irene Kossoy, Oscar Brand, New York City, 1959. Photograph by Photo-Sound Associates, J. Katz, A. Rennert, R. Sullivan. Image courtesy of Ron Cohen.

Ellen Kossoy, Woody Guthrie, Irene Kossoy, New York City, 1959. Photograph by Photo-Sound Associates, J. Katz, A. Rennert, R. Sullivan. Image courtesy of Ron Cohen.

was at that age." And she confided: "We are hoping Jack will come home soon. We all miss him."[1]

Elliot Charles Adnopoz had come into Guthrie's life early in 1951. The son of a Brooklyn surgeon, he had visited Guthrie in the hospital, introducing himself as the guitar-playing, ballad-singing "Buck" Elliott and slipping quite easily into the Guthrie family circle. In another three months he had changed his name to "Jack." He spent a year and a half as a virtual member of the Guthrie household. As Nora Guthrie later told Elliott's daughter, Aiyana: "It was a strange moment in time when my dad was losing it, and I think in some way he knew it—he was losing his life. I think he was very grateful to have a protégé right there. There was some kind of very wonderful thing that happened in that moment when he was losing his life and here was this young guy saying 'Howja do this? Howja do that? What are you doin'?' And I think that, in one way, my dad was so happy to hand over everything he knew, and everything about himself that he could pass on. Because he knew he didn't have time."[2] Elliott—a "perfect mimic," as he called himself—had set himself a single-minded task: to play "Woody Guthrie songs exactly the way that Woody did."[3] Guthrie was already on record as having discouraged such an approach, writing to a young fan, Harry St. Amand, in 1946: "I'm not saying that my kind of traveling, Harry, is good for you. You know best what you want to see and learn. I can't dictate to you, coax you, lure you, nor bait you to go and do like I done. You would just be imitating Woody Guthrie and we sure don't want that. It is good to learn all you can from everybody you see, but it is bad to think that you are imitating me or anybody else every step you take."[4] Thus, while he was flattered by Elliott's admiration, amused by his mimicry, and indeed "grateful to have a protégé right there," his own observation—"He sounds more like me than I do"—had a double edge to it.[5]

There was even less ambivalence in the Guthrie family's initial reaction. Nora Guthrie recalled her mother's distress when she saw Elliott—and later, his own disciple, Bob Dylan—performing Guthrie's songs: "They heard Huntington's, the slur when singing, talking. In Elliott, Dylan, you hear early Huntington's."[6] Pete Seeger was concerned enough about the growing tendency to mimic his old mentor that he issued a public warning in 1960:

Beware of trying to imitate Woody's singing too closely—it will sound fake and phony.
 1. Don't try to imitate his accent.
 2. Don't try and imitate his flat vocal quality.
 3. In short, be yourself.[7]

Elliott, for his part, could imitate everything from Guthrie's "accent" and his "flat vocal quality" to his idiosyncratic guitar runs and the way he "dra-

"Howja do this? Howja do that?" Ramblin' Jack Elliott and Woody Guthrie, 1961.
Photograph by John Cohen. Hulton Archive / Getty Images.

matically lifted his cigarette to his lips in a swooping 'S curve'."[8] As his early
musical colleague Eric Von Schmidt recalled, Elliott had been "casting about
for a persona. He finally met Woody Guthrie and he didn't have to look any
farther."[9] But one thing that nobody heard in Elliott's mimicry was any advocacy of Guthrie's political radicalism. Elliott later admitted, "I was . . . much
more interested in the cowboy thing than the politics of Woody Guthrie."[10]
Nonetheless, Guthrie and his radical champions owed a substantial debt to
Elliott, in particular for his part in spreading the Guthrie oeuvre throughout
Britain and continental Europe.

In 1955, Elliott began a six-year sojourn abroad, basing himself primarily
in London. Before then, Guthrie's work was known to a relatively small cross-
section of radical British musicians (some of whom could perhaps recall the
Martins and the Coys broadcast or Guthrie's brief appearance on the BBC's
Children's Hour during a London shore leave in 1944). As early as 1946, John
Hasted, a founder of the Oxford University Communist Party and a future
leading light in Britain's Campaign for Nuclear Disarmament (CND), had
heard the Almanacs' *Talking Union* and immediately began practicing the
flattop guitar. Around 1950 he hooked up with an expatriate American banjo
player, Jean Butler, who had known Guthrie and the Almanacs (it was Butler
who first publicly performed a number of Guthrie's lesser-known songs in

Britain, including the complete "Tom Joad").[11] Hasted was also a friend of Alan Lomax's British counterpart, the musicologist A. L. "Bert" Lloyd: "One day, I asked Bert if he would like to help me organise an Almanacs-style group. To my astonishment, his voice dropped about an octave and he said, very quietly . . . 'passionately'! Jean Butler came in and suggested we call ourselves the Ramblers, after Woody's song *As I Go Rambling Round*—and that was one of the first songs we learned."[12] Meanwhile, Lomax continued to champion Guthrie from his base in London, where he ensured that his old protégé was heard from time to time on his BBC radio broadcasts.

Elliott's arrival marked a sea change in the British reception of Woody Guthrie. Through his live performances and recordings, Elliott drove Guthrie's songs further into the public consciousness, entrancing the audiences at the Roundhouse, the Blue Angel, and other London music clubs, either solo or with his banjo-playing partner, Derroll Adams. Bob Watson, a Roundhouse organizer, recalled that Elliott "was like a visiting lecturer": "He didn't just introduce his songs, he used to weave in these fantastic stories, so you could never be sure about what was truth and what was fiction. His playing was very influential too: he would manage to combine chording with single string runs, which gave a lot of variety to what he did. . . . He was a very skilful musician, even then."[13]

In London, shortly after his arrival, Elliott made his first records for the Topic label, then the recording arm of the Workers' Music Association. A 78 of Guthrie's "Talking Miner Blues" (the first commercial recording of this song) backed with "Pretty Boy Floyd" was followed by the 8-inch LP *Woody Guthrie's Blues,* which included versions of "Talking Columbia Blues," "Hard Travelin'," "1913 Massacre," "Ludlow Massacre," "Talking Dust Bowl Blues," and "Talking Sailor." These were highly influential recordings that helped to fuel the British base of the Anglo-American folk revival, as did Elliott's subsequent Topic recording *Jack Takes the Floor* and Topic's distribution of the Folkways tribute album *Bound for Glory* (both in 1958). In spite of Elliott's own downplaying of a political dimension, the fact of his releases on the Topic label ensured that Guthrie's radicalism would be perceived by those in Britain who sought that avenue—a factor causing a curious bout of irritation to the blues scholar Paul Oliver, who complained of *Woody Guthrie's Blues:* "The disc has been issued by the Workers Music Association and one cannot help but feel that there has been a somewhat deliberate use of this feature of Woody's work and Jack's admiration for the man, in the selection that has been made."[14]

The energetic atmosphere of the British folk revival—and the impact of both Elliott and Guthrie on it—were evocatively captured in the reminiscences between Dave Arthur, Bert Lloyd's biographer, and Mike Paris, biographer of

On the streets of London: Cover image of Jack Elliott's EP record, *Kid Stuff* (1960). Image provided by Hank Reineke, courtesy of EMI Records.

Jimmie Rodgers.[15] Both writer-musicians were on the ground in London at the start of the revival, and as Arthur recalled for Paris: "A couple of [Topic's] earliest 78s were of Jack Elliott, before he did the Woody Guthrie Talking Blues 8-inch album that you introduced me to back in the Kings' Road days around '57 or '58. And, of course, once the skiffle craze got going everyone was singing either Guthrie or Leadbelly material. Then after the skiffle thing you had people like Wizz Jones, Les Weston (with his fake Gretsch), Pete Stanley, Alex Campbell, you and me! playing Guthrie songs around Soho, and in Paris, and on the N7 down to the south of France, and down at St. Ives."[16]

Sid Gleason may well have been speaking for all of Guthrie's purist colleagues (and to some extent, Elliott) when she dismissed British skiffle, with its tea-chest basses and washboards, as "a type of abortion called music";[17]

but it was a major vehicle for lodging Guthrie's songs (and Elliott's versions of them) into the broader popular sphere. Even Lomax had a go with skiffle, forming a London-based group with Ewan MacColl, Peggy Seeger, and Shirley Collins, also called (in an echo of Butler's echo of Guthrie) the Ramblers. Hasted started up the 44 Skiffle and Folksong Group, named for the 44 Skiffle Club in London, where the group held forth. He recalled Elliott's guest performances there: "He was our most welcome visitor; not just a Brooklyn cowboy but a genuine travelling singer. He had a great influence on skiffle."[18]

Other skiffle bands utilizing Guthrie's songs in their repertoires—either directly or through Elliott's versions—included Dick Bishop and His Sidekicks, the Vipers, the Livewires, the 2.19 Skiffle Group, and Ken Colyer's Skiffle Group. None of them would ever capture the popularity of the self-styled "King of Skiffle," Lonnie Donegan (a minor nemesis of Elliott's), who notoriously attempted to claim cowriting credit for several of Guthrie's songs, including "Dead or Alive," "Gamblin' Man," and "Grand Coolie [*sic*] Dam."[19] (Donegan, in turn, would never attain the popularity of the Liverpool-based skiffle band the Quarrymen, following their reconstitution as the Beatles—and as Paul McCartney would tell Harold Leventhal: "I love Woody Guthrie and really admire the kind of songs he writes.")[20] Looking back on what became known as the "skiffle craze," the guitarist Wizz Jones nailed down the central positions of Elliott and Guthrie, both as models and as alternatives: "Skiffle was in at the time and strangulated versions of Woody Guthrie songs appeared in the charts while in the back rooms of smoky pubs Jack Elliott showed us how they should be sung."[21] By 1958 the craze was fairly well spent. Hasted accurately predicted: "When skiffle dies down, it will split in two directions: rock 'n' roll and folk music. When that happens, we shall have a legacy of serious singer/guitarists to develop."[22]

Sometime in the early 1960s, one of those budding "singer/guitarists" sent a letter to his hero in the Brooklyn State Hospital:

Dear Woody,

I am writing to you to tell you that I have sung your songs in Franco's Spain. I have your picture inside my guitar case.

Yours sincerely with huge admiration, Ralph May.

He was thrilled to receive a letter in reply:

Dear Ralph,

Thank you for writing. Keep singing, signed Marjorie Guthrie.[23]

Decades later, after he had adopted the name "Ralph McTell," May recalled Guthrie's formative influence on him, particularly with regard to the world of work. He wrote of the series of "mundane, undemanding" jobs he had taken in his youth: "People often asked me what I was doing with my life working in these places. I tried to explain that I knew what I was doing and that I was enjoying a kind of freedom of the soul. Also, I would like to have had as many jobs as Woody Guthrie."[24] He became a kitchen porter in a Bournemouth hotel: "I had become fascinated by the life of Woody and his praise of the workingman and in order to rightly claim my place alongside all working heroes, I felt it necessary to try as many different jobs as I could."[25] He worked through "a nightmare of boredom" at the dismal Philips electrical factory in Croydon: "I was perpetually being docked wages for timekeeping. I hated the clock which we had to use to punch our times in and out of work. Woody Guthrie once made a drawing of a fist smashing into the face of a time clock as a reward for its passive tyranny. That's what I felt like doing."[26] When May took off for continental Europe, he packed some of the Guthrie mystique into his rucksack: "I wrote to Woody Guthrie from Fascist Spain, telling my dying hero that I was playing his songs to the working people. Which I was, in a way, sitting by the side of the road waiting for rides, but also in towns and villages whenever we stopped."[27] In his maturity, McTell confessed to having taken his emulation of Guthrie—or whatever proletarian authenticity Guthrie signified to him—a bit too far: "Later on, when I read George Orwell's account of his life as a plongeur in Paris, I realised I was not the only one who had slightly patronised the workers by accepting menial jobs below his ability."[28]

Such was Guthrie's influence on the British folk consciousness in the late 1950s and early 1960s—an influence with such great commercial potential that Topic Records had Elliott signing an agreement that he would not "record any of the Guthrie material for another UK label for a period of seven years."[29] Elliott was thus inextricably linked to Guthrie—a linkage that persisted after Elliott returned to the United States in 1960, when Sid Gleason cornered him in a recorded conversation:

SID GLEASON: Well, one of the reasons we wanted Jack to come home, one of the biggest reasons is, of course, because Woody wanted him to come home. And another of the reasons is because so much of Woody's music is not—

BOB GLEASON: It's in Woody's head.

SID: Yeah. And it's going to take somebody like you, Jack, who has the patience to sit down and listen—

BOB: And get it on tape before it's gone completely.

SID: Because Marjy doesn't even know some of the tunes. But Woody can sort of half hum them . . . he sort of half hums them, and you can pretty well get an idea now—he did that for John Cohen, and John got the right tune.[30]

It was not only the loss of the music in Guthrie's head that had become worrisome by 1960; it was also the loss of some of the most radical verses he had committed to paper. "This Land Is Your Land" had been circulating so freely in its politically eviscerated version that it attracted a savage parody from Lawrence Block in *The Bosses' Songbook* edited by Dave Van Ronk and Dick Ellington in 1958:[31]

> This land is their land, it is not our land
> From their rich apartments to their Cadillac carland
> From their Wall Street office to their Hollywood Starland
> This land is not for you and me.[32]

(Guthrie got off relatively lightly in comparison to Seeger, who was parodied as a CPUSA stooge in Roy Berkeley's "The Ballad of Pete Seeger"—judiciously retitled "Ballad of a Party Folksinger" in the songbook's 1959 reprinting.)[33]

Guthrie's deradicalization had come at a particularly fraught period in the history of the American folk revival, which was experiencing a cleavage between the commercial and the activist singers similar to that perceived by Guthrie in the previous generation. On the one hand there were the Weavers-inspired folk groups such as the Kingston Trio, the Limeliters, the Tarriers, the Chad Mitchell Trio, the Highwaymen, and the Brothers Four, many of whom kept Guthrie's name and his better-known "standards" circulating, among them "Deportee," "Pastures of Plenty," "Hard Travelin'," "Reuben James," and the stripped-down "This Land Is Your Land." Some of these clean-cut, smartly dressed groups were derided as "button-down" songsters representing "an apolitical and nontraditional music culture"—in some respects an unfair charge.[34] They were at least keeping some of Guthrie's songs from falling below the cultural radar as the folk revival took on an increasingly commercial and mass-market dimension. But they were positively innocuous when compared with the efforts of the activists taking folk music into the front line of the civil rights movement.

At the forefront of this activist fellowship was Guy Carawan, who had traveled south with Elliott in 1953 "in search of American folk music," as their road buddy Frank Hamilton recalled (both Carawan and Hamilton having also known Guthrie in Topanga Canyon).[35] Among their stops was the Highlander Folk School in Monteagle, Tennessee, which Guthrie and Seeger had visited on their 1940 tour. Instantly devoted to the school and its musically activist mission, Carawan had returned in 1959 to succeed the deceased Zilphia Horton as musical director. He began to implement an ambitious program of publications, recordings, festivals, and workshops, resulting in such ventures as the April 1960 Highlander Folk School College Workshop, which introduced "We Shall Overcome" to the civil rights movement, and the August 1960 "Sing for Freedom" workshop, which gathered together such musical warriors as Seeger, Gil Turner, Bill McAdoo, Ethel Raim, Waldemar Hille, Hedy West, and Ernie Marrs, the latter of whom would lay claim to having been the first to sing the complete version of "This Land Is Your Land" on the air the same year.[36] The earliest lunch-counter sit-ins in the metropolitan South—in Nashville in 1960—were also influenced by the Highlander mission, largely through Carawan and the Nashville Quartet, who introduced other songs that would go on to define the movement—"Sit at the Welcome Table," "Hold On," "This Little Light of Mine," "We Shall Not Be Moved," and "Oh Freedom" among them. Following the Nashville sit-ins, the Freedom Rides of 1961, and the Albany integration movement of 1961–62, the Freedom Singers took the songs from Highlander further into the consciousness of the nation.

Meanwhile, in the small New York apartment of "Sis" Cunningham and Gordon Friesen, Guthrie's old colleagues were taking note of musical developments across the Atlantic, where the Campaign for Nuclear Disarmament (with Hasted as its musical director) had been putting jazz and protest songs at the heart of their marches and rallies. Cunningham recalled: "I wanted to work very much on a topical song paper whether we got it out ourselves or worked with somebody else on it. What I think made me decide that if possible it had to be done was it was being said around that all these topical songs were coming out of Great Britain, and in this country none were being written. I just didn't go along with that. I figured that a lot of topical songs were being written, and just didn't have any way of getting out."[37]

Seeger and Malvina Reynolds, another People's Songs veteran, had been sensing the same thing and encouraged Cunningham and Friesen to act on their impulses. Thus was born *Broadside,* the "topical" folk song magazine that emerged in February 1962 from the Freisens' hand-cranked mimeograph machine, offering a forum for new songwriters whose songs were no longer being introduced in the increasingly up-market *Sing Out!* Over the next few years, *Broadside* would introduce—either in print or through concerts and its Broadside Ballads album series—Reynolds's "Little Boxes" and "What Have They Done to the Rain?"; Bob Dylan's "Blowin' in the Wind," "Talking John Birch," and "Masters of War"; Phil Ochs's "Links on the Chain" and "Hazard, Kentucky"; Peter La Farge's "Ballad of Ira Hayes" and "As Long as the Grass Shall Grow"; Janis Ian's "Society's Child," and Tom Paxton's "What Did You Learn in School Today?," among many others.[38]

It was through contrast with these examples that Josh Dunson proposed in *Freedom in the Air* (1965)—the first major study of the 1960s protest song movement—that the majority of New Left songwriters (particularly college students and dropouts) had turned to Guthrie more for style than for substance. It was a tendency that he could actually trace to "the years 1960 and 1961," when, he said, "the pronoun 'I' replaced 'we' in topical songs." Dunson looked sadly upon the apparent introspection of the new generation: "The young songwriters, as Woody Guthrie used to do, give their reactions in the first person, but, unlike him, they seldom notice others to their left or to their right. They write their songs while riding in subway cars, while waiting out in the cold for one or two hours, while trying to 'bum' a ride, while sitting in a bar drinking, while alone in a room thinking."[39] While not providing any particular examples to back up his claim, Dunson perceived in the "young songwriter today" an inverse relationship between the appeal of Guthrie's mannerisms and an appreciation of his politics: "The new songs reflected Guthrie's marked influence. There were many dropped final 'g's,' and the songs were sung in highly personal form. Since the students had little interest in social systems or basic change, the subject matter of these songs was specific and immediate. The use of terms that punctuated Left literature of the 1930's and 1940's, like 'fascist,' 'counter-revolutionary,' 'capitalist,' or labor terms like 'scab,' 'strike' and 'organize' did not appear in the new songs."[40] Dunson suggested that the problem was a generational one, in which Guthrie—as songster of the Old Left—was, in spite of his hard-travelin' appeal, considered an outdated spokesman for the political sensibilities of the New Left: "The young song writer today is sparked by disillusionment and anger. Often he has gone through the hardship of rejecting the values of his parents and those he had considered infallible during childhood. His rejection of segregation, war and exploitation often grows into a conviction that none of the older people knew what they were doing when they made or tried to remake the world. He has little faith in their organizations even when their goals may have been and still are similar."[41]

Dunson's broad generalizing did not take into account (for instance) the musical activism of the Berkeley Free Speech Movement, which in 1964 produced the *Free Speech Songbook* and, in Lee Felsenstein's "Put My Name Down," drew upon Guthrie's "Hard Travelin'" to recruit students to the cause—in Felsenstein's words, to "set up more tables and [give] the Deans more names than they could handle":[42]

> We're going to break the rules, I thought you knowed,
> Yes we're going to talk and think, 'way down the road,
> What do we want, why the mess,
> The Constitution, nothing less,
> I'm going to put my name down.[43]

Such exceptions aside, Dunson was tapping into a prevailing sense that the younger generation "did not think in terms of ideology" even as they embraced Guthrie. While they were certainly "concerned with what injustices they saw and felt," they avoided a decision as to "how the evil should be removed."[44]

Some Old Leftists, like Lee Hays, saw such strategic evasiveness as amounting to a wholesale flight from political responsibility. He recalled being asked by a "young waiter in an Adirondack resort" how Guthrie was faring in the hospital. "Why are you so interested in him at your age?" Hays asked him. The young man replied: "Woody represents freedom, the ability to just pick up and go anywhere you want to, whenever you take a mind to. Just get up and go and not be responsible to any living soul, absolute freedom." Hays kept his concluding thoughts to himself: "Of course, in picking up and taking off whenever he wanted to he had to leave behind people, more often than not, that he should have stayed with and taken care of, people that needed him. But if he took a notion to go somewhere, that came first, and it didn't matter what he owed anybody."[45]

The charge of betraying Guthrie's radical spirit was flung with the greatest intensity at the embattled Bob Dylan, who—at least to some people on either side of the Atlantic—could never seem to do the right thing. One the one hand, he had taken his emulation of Guthrie too far and much too selectively. Ralph McTell recalled having to defend him against the accusation that he had "crawled over the dying body of Woody Guthrie to success."[46] (For McTell, Dylan's emulation was simply "respect and humility at source and the effect was profoundly moving to those who loved Woody's work and were growing to love Bob."[47] Dylan's style was in any case "based more on Jack Elliott than Woody Guthrie.")[48] Dylan himself confessed that he had begun by "writing like I thought Woody would write";[49] but some saw him going much further, channeling Guthrie to an unsavory degree. Consequently, he appalled not only the Guthrie family (Nora Guthrie: "Dylan didn't even know the real person. Woody was mythology in his own mind"),[50] but also friends like John Cohen, who recalled Dylan's earliest appearances in the New York clubs: "It's interesting—he was visiting Woody Guthrie, and I was visiting Woody at that time also. . . . I had known Woody five or six, maybe eight years by then, and you could see all that jerky stuff starting to happen in his body. And then when Bob stood up to the microphone and started jerking around, tilting his head this way, and making these moves—I'd never seen anything like that except in Woody. When I first saw him, I said, 'Oh, my God, he's mimicking Woody's disease.'"[51] John Greenway was perhaps the most vituperative, slandering not only Dylan, but also his followers en masse: "Bobby Dylan, the idol of the unlaved student Existentialists, never knew

Guthrie when his mind was whole, but imitated the incoherent, rambling, pseudo-mystical lines of Guthrie's last letters on the edge of his insanity. Somehow Dylan has convinced a few *avant garde* critics that on the basis of these synthetic effusions he is America's most promising young poet."[52]

At the same time—again, on both sides of the Atlantic—Dylan apparently wasn't trying hard *enough* to channel Guthrie. Martin Carthy recalled that in 1962, when Dylan was being touted in Britain as "the new Woody and all that," he came up against the censure of the more doctrinaire wing of the British folk revival—led by Ewan MacColl and Peggy Seeger—for his failure to target political adversaries as Guthrie had done. This was one year before Dylan incorrigibly dismissed politics as "trivial" at the Tom Paine Award dinner (where he also announced that he "used to have an idol, Woody Guthrie");[53] it was two years before he declared to Nat Hentoff that he was finished with "finger-pointing songs" like "The Lonesome Death of Hattie Carroll" and that he would no longer "write *for* people anymore."[54] As Carthy recalled: "Ewan and Peggy insisted that if you're going to write protest songs—if you want to call them that—then you should name names. Bob never did. So he would sing 'Masters of War' and he wouldn't name anybody. And they didn't like that; they didn't think that it made any kind of sense. It was in those days a question of pointing the finger in the right direction, as far as Ewan and Peggy were concerned. Especially Ewan."[55]

In the United States, Irwin Silber led the charge against Dylan in his scathing "Open Letter to Bob Dylan" in 1964, condemning his supposed fondness for "the paraphernalia of fame," his "inner-directed," "innerprobing," self-conscious," "maudlin," and "cruel" songwriting, his rejection of "protest songs," and—pointedly—his failure to live up to the equation with Guthrie that *Sing Out!* had been only too happy to perpetuate: "SING OUT! was among the first to respond to the new ideas, new images, and new sounds that you were creating. By last count, thirteen of your songs had appeared in these pages. Maybe more of Woody's songs were printed here over the years, but, if so, he's the only one."[56] Years later, a more conciliatory Silber explained:

He was the most exciting person I'd heard since Woody Guthrie, and he combined a great artistic feel with a political sense that was poetic, that moved people. And now, to find him turning his back on it . . . .

Remember, I wrote that open letter in '64. This is when the civil rights movement is at its height, the beginnings of the protest against the Vietnam War, and so on. Politics, after the '50s, was *really* resurging in a big way. [With] the New Left and people who were not stuck in the framework of the Communist Party and Trotskyism and so on, there was a whole new sense of politics. And

"The new Woody and all that." Bob Dylan at the Troubadour, London, 1962. Left to right: Ethan Signer, Martin Carthy, Richard Fariña, Dylan, Eric von Schmidt. Photograph by Alison Chapman McLean. Image courtesy of the photographer.

to have Dylan deliberately, consciously, moving away from it at that time—well, I really felt bad about that.[57]

Guthrie was still alive while these arguments over the betrayal of his political legacy raged. In the early to mid-1960s, as he languished in hospital or made his increasingly difficult appearances in public parks and the living rooms of those who brought him home for a change of scene—and with "This Land Is Your Land" being sung across the country by the most patriotic of schoolchildren and their parents—American folk music was monolithically and laughably being caricatured as "subversive" by the far Right, even as those in the Old Left mourned the passing of its radical edge personified by, above all others, Woody Guthrie. The years 1963–67 demonstrated this curious paradox, beginning with the right-wing attacks on school "songbooks [that] can subvert," such as the *Fireside Book of Folk Music,* which Edith Kermit Roosevelt condemned for its supposed glorification of "the U.S.S.R., the Ukrainian communist guerrilla fighters and the Red Chinese Workers."[58] That same year, 1963, something calling itself the "Los Angeles Fire and Police

Research Association" mobilized to block a concert by Pete Seeger and the Freedom Singers by naming folk music a "tool of Communist psychological or cybernetic warfare to ensnare and capture youthful minds"[59]—an attempt that even had a Republican senator, Kenneth Keating, noting "the absurd lengths to which the amateur ferrets of the radical right will go in their quixotic sallies against the Communist menace."[60]

Not long afterward, Jere Real of the John Birch Society raised the hue and cry in the organization's journal, *American Opinion:* "Along with the handclapping, the guitar strumming, the banjo-picking, the shouting and the howling, comes a very subtle but highly effective presentation of standard Communist Party propaganda. Not since the 1930s have so many young people of the United States been so directly, so cleverly, deceived into a widespread parroting of the Communist line."[61]

In 1965, William Steuart McBirnie, senior minister of the United Community Church of Glendale, California, published (under the imprint of the "Voice of Americanism") *Songs of Subversion,* which drew largely upon Dunson's *Freedom in the Air* (in McBirnie's opinion, the Communist horse's mouth, since it was published by International Publishers, the Marxist-Leninist press). Among McBirnie's targets were Lead Belly (whose songs "degrade our nation"), Carawan (and Highlander, the "public nuisance"), Dylan (whose words are "barely intelligible through his assumed dialect"), Joan Baez (who has "starred at so many communist-infiltrated gatherings that it would be difficult to list them all"), and Guthrie ("For further information regarding Guthrie see House Committee on UnAmerican Activities reports: 8463; s 38, 43, 49, 102; da 3288, 3313; dm 71").[62]

The following year, a former FBI agent named Herbert Philbrick wrote of how the Communists were "Subverting Youth with Folksinging" (as his article in Kenneth Ingwalson's alarmist anthology *Your Church—Their Target* was titled).[63] Philbrick's ideological kinsman David Noebel argued in *Christian Crusade* that the "Communist infiltration into the subversion of American music has been nothing short of phenomenal and in some areas, e.g. folk music, their control is fast approaching the saturation point under the able leadership of Pete Seeger, *Sing Out!,* Folkways Records and Oak Publications, Inc."[64]

To the right-wing accusers, *hootenanny* was a word to conjure up fear and loathing in equal measure. It signified and encapsulated the depths of Communist subversion as no other word (besides *Communism* itself) could do. The Fire and Police Research Association argued: "It is becoming more and more evident that certain of the 'hootenannies' and other similar youth gatherings and festivals, both in this country and in Europe, have been used to *brainwash and subvert,* in a seemingly innocuous but actually covert and deceptive manner, vast segments of young people's groups."[65]

Yet if anything captured the extent of the mass-market appropriation of harmless, politically anodyne "folk music," it was that same word, *hootenanny,* that in 1963–64 was used by the ABC network as the title of their popular variety show, feeding into a memorable commercial craze reflected, among other places, in the astounding jump in *Sing Out!*'s circulation, from one thousand in 1960 to twenty thousand in 1964.[66] Hootenanny-themed songbooks, magazines, chocolate bars, paper dolls, bath gels, powder mitts, and pinball machines flooded the market. The craze produced a rash of strange musical hybrids as nonfolk labels jumped on the bandwagon to produce such titles as *Hot Rod Hootenanny, Kiddie Hootenanny, Soul Meeting Saturday Night Hootenanny Style,* and *Jazz Meets the Folk Song.* Car salesmen flogged their latest models "with a Hootenanny Sale at which local folk performers sang while sitting on the hoods of cars"; the American Dairy Association produced "a full-page newspaper advertisement that depicted a young housewife in her kitchen, strumming a guitar. The headline asked, 'Wish you could write a protest song about your family's eating habits?'"[67]

Moviegoers thrilled to Jack O'Connell's *Greenwich Village Story* ("Birthplace of the Hootenanny," where "THEY LIVE . . . AND LOVE AS THEY PLEASE") and tested the reviews from the *New York Times* ("A TALE OF YOUNG LOVE AND DESIRE . . . ROAMING THE BARS, THE CAVERNS, THE PADS AND LOFTS AND THE CLANGOROUS CONFINES OF THE EXTROVERTS, INTROVERTS, AND PERVERTS!") and the *Herald Tribune* ("Greenwich Village life—its folk songs, its marijuana-soaked parties, its artists in creative turmoil and youth in revolt, let alone extra-marital passions").[68] Or, if they wanted to "C'mon get with it" in a more wholesome fashion, they went to see Maury Dexter's *The Young Swingers* for "THAT BRAND NEW SOUND . . . AND THAT NEW KIND OF FUN THAT'S SWEEPING THE COUNTRY!" (including "These Hand-Clapping Hits!"—"Greenback Dollar," "Elijah," and "You Pass Me By").[69] For those too young to appreciate these films—or Gene Nelson's *Hootenanny Hoot* (which featured Sheb Wooley, Johnny Cash, the Brothers Four, the Gateway Trio, and Ronald Reagan's daughter, Maureen, calling the male lead "the squarest")[70]—there were comic books such as *Love Diary,* with its episode "Hootenanny Heel" ("Oh, Ritchie, how can anyone who sings and plays as beautifully as you do be so . . . so cruel!"),[71] and even *Batman,* "guest-starring The HOOTENANNY HOTSHOTS!," in which a guitar-strumming Robin enlightens a perplexed (square) Batman: "Hootenanny folk-singing is the big *rage* nowadays!" (Batman: "If you can spare a little time from your *Hootenannying* I'd like to clear up that 'secret business' I've been on").[72]

Those seeking a more active engagement could order a "Hootenanny Party Kit" from the makers of the Orange Crush soft drink, containing a 45-rpm sing-along record of "Greensleeves," "Michael, Row the Boat Ashore," and "The Gray Goose"; preprinted invitations promising "a Hootin' good time"; helpful suggestions on how to decorate your party-room walls with hootenanny motifs; a list of games to play (including charades with folk-song titles and characters); and suggested prizes such as a guitar pick, a banjo string, or a song sheet.[73] For those who aspired to the ultimate—becoming hootenanny performers themselves!—the "beautifully boxed" Elektra Folk Song Kit included a "★Complete guitar instruction course for beginners!★Special long-playing 12″ record with step-by-step instructions—and recorded examples of 20 favorite folk songs★Illustrated 52 page instruction manual★Spirited survey of American folk music by Lee Hays★Extensive data, bibliographic material and photographs"—all for the "Special Price" of $5.95.[74]

One of the first decisions made by ABC's *Hootenanny* executives was to ban Pete Seeger and the Weavers from appearing, in spite of Seeger's part in establishing the institution and in spite of the fact that the Weavers—not least through their *Weavers at Carnegie Hall* album (1957)—had signaled the partial emergence of folksingers from the prison house of McCarthyism and virtually introduced a new generation to the genre. Harold Leventhal, Seeger's manager, issued a press statement to the effect that "the American Broadcasting Company would 'consider Pete Seeger' for the ABC Hootenanny Show if he would sign a 'loyalty oath affidavit.'" He quoted Seeger's response: "I have just finished fighting a seven year court battle to prove the principle that such oaths are unconstitutional and I was acquitted and vindicated."[75] Seeger later recalled: "I won't even call it a folk music show. And it was thirty minutes of 'pow!' Clap your hands, and smile, and don't ever rock the boat, folks. Matter of fact, not only would they not have me on it unless I was going to sign an anti-communist oath . . . but they wouldn't take a quartet that had two white and two black in it. They would take an all black or an all white, but not mixed. . . . In six months, ABC just about ruined the poor word 'hootenanny' and it's hardly been the same since. And it gave me a good lesson in the power of the mass media. I wasn't the only person they wouldn't have hired—I don't think they would have hired Woody if he'd been around at that time."[76]

Seeger's sentiments were shared by Nat Hentoff, writing in 1964: "Today, the television show *Hootenanny* has refused to allow Seeger to appear on the program because some of the groups for which he sang in the past do not meet the network's political criteria. Also excluded from *Hootenanny* are The Weavers, whose 1951 recording of 'So Long, It's Been Good to Know You' was Guthrie's first popular hit. And it is almost certain that if Woody himself were able to sing, he too would be barred from *Hootenanny*."[77]

Guthrie was thus caught between two poles—implicated and damned, on the one hand, for his radicalism, and celebrated, on the other, for what seemed to be a patriotism that bordered on jingoism. In between, of course, was the reality of his songs, the vast amount of which were unknown to the public and to many of Guthrie's closest friends. Millard Lampell's somewhat dramatic assessment contains a grain of truth: "Nobody knows just how many songs Woody made up. A collector claims to have counted over a thousand. But that would only be the ones Woody took the trouble to write down. It wouldn't include the songs that slipped away in the dusty wind, the ones that vanished in the clank and rattle of a fast freight crossing through the hills in the darkness."[78] Lampell's mention of "a collector" almost certainly referred to Greenway, who had written: "Not all of Guthrie's compositions are songs of overt protest. Of an estimated one thousand songs in his manuscript collection, I found only about 140 whose basic theme was one of protest; the remainder fell into conventional folksong categories—love, humor, crime, ballads of disaster, tragedies, and war, non-protest labor songs, and even nursery songs."[79] Greenway's assessment clearly reflected his determination to downplay the significance of protest music in the midst of the McCarthy era; but more to the point, his curious distinction between songs of "overt protest" and other song categories made his assertion untenable (as though songs of "crime, ballads of disaster, tragedies, and war" might not also be protest songs). In fairness to Greenway, he should not be blamed for his drastic underestimation of the number of Guthrie's compositions, for of the roughly three thousand songs now housed in the Woody Guthrie Archives and other repositories, many would have come to light after his book was published.

But there is more to the deradicalization of Woody Guthrie than Greenway's good intentions or the fact of Guthrie's publicly unknown output, which by any account swamps his published output. There is, of course, the recording career cut short by Huntington's disease, resulting in a meager legacy of fourteen years' worth of sporadically recorded songs, some of which have never been released. There is the fact that the great bulk of Guthrie's printed songs, which greatly outnumber his recorded songs, are contained in a variety of songbooks that have either gone out of print or have been restricted to relatively small selections. Certainly taking its toll has been the continued popularity of the politically denuded "This Land Is Your Land"—a popularity so enduring that in January 2009, when Seeger and Bruce Springsteen sang a restored version for Barack Obama's inaugural concert, it was notewor-

"Like Woody wrote it." Pete Seeger and Bruce Springsteen teach America the restored "This Land Is Your Land." Obama inaugural concert, January 2009. Photograph by Justin Sullivan. Getty Images.

thy enough for newspapers to comment on the song "Like Woody Wrote It."[80] During the globally broadcast performance, on the steps of the Lincoln Memorial and in the face of American power, Springsteen introduced what he called "the greatest song ever written about our home," with its outright condemnation of "private property," its empathy for the victims of capitalism lining up "by the relief office," and its challenge to the authoritarian state along the "freedom highway."[81]

This performance was in some respects the culmination of a fight-back most fully articulated by Seeger for the *Village Voice* in 1971, when he described the three protest verses desperately taught by Guthrie to his son Arlo toward the end of his life. "I and others have started singing them," Seeger wrote. "We feel that there is a danger of this song being misinterpreted without these new / old verses being added. The song could even be co-opted by the very selfish interests Woody was fighting all his life." He singled out one example, the "Washington big wheel Clark Clifford," who had addressed "the wealthy businessmen at Chicago's Executive Club" in 1950 with the following words: "The people have to feel that their small share of this country is as much theirs as it is yours and mine." As Seeger argued, "With only half of Woody's verses, 'This Land Is Your Land' falls right into Mr. Clifford's trap.

In other words, 'Let people go ahead and sing the song. Meanwhile you and I know who really controls the country.'"[82]

Seeger was hardly alone in reasserting Guthrie's radical challenge in the midst of his deradicalization. In the mid-1980s, the guitarist and singer Ry Cooder reflected on the enduring power of one particular song in his repertoire, Guthrie's "Vigilante Man," a song rooted in the violent struggles between the migrant workers and the Associated Farmers of the San Joaquin Valley in the 1930s but taking on new associations in the succeeding decades. As Cooder recalled: "Wherever I sang that song, especially in the '60s when Vietnam was a problem, the dope culture was staking its claim and the youth culture was stating its case, it was well received, like any song that's about the revolt against the institutional order. These songs have a life because of that, and I still get a lot of requests for that song today, because there's always someone who's the vigilante, and someone else who's getting their head beat open, wherever you may be."[83]

A wide coalition of progressive musicians on both sides of the Atlantic have continued to actively champion Guthrie's "revolt against the institutional order," taking up the baton from those in the first generation of "Woody's Children" (Dylan, Baez, Paxton, Ochs, et al.). A microscopic sample of these later champions would include Cooder, Ralph McTell, Joe Strummer, Country Joe McDonald, Dick Gaughan, Christy Moore, Andy Irvine, Bruce Springsteen, Emmylou Harris, Steve Earle, John Mellencamp, Bono and U2, Ani DiFranco, Jimmy LaFave, Joel Rafael, Tom Morello, and the Indigo Girls, among many others. The extent of this fellowship certainly prompts a raised eyebrow over Nora Guthrie's claim that in the 1990s the English songwriter Billy Bragg was "the only singer [she] knew taking on the same issues as Woody." Still, her sense that her father's "icon thing" was "really holding him back" was certainly justified, as was her conclusion: "And it really pisses me off."[84]

Hence the groundbreaking projects through which Guthrie's unpublished lyrics have been put to music and recorded by contemporary singers, beginning with Bragg and Wilco's *Mermaid Avenue,* Volume 1 (1998) and Volume 2 (2000).[85] With such songs as "Christ for President," "Eisler on the Go," and "The Unwelcome Guest" on Volume 1 and "Stetson Kennedy," "Aginst th' Law," and "All You Fascists" on Volume 2, the *Mermaid Avenue* releases go far toward "dragging [Guthrie] out of the Dust Bowl" and reaffirming his political radicalism.[86] (As of this writing, Nora Guthrie has engaged Son Volt's Jay Farrar for *New Multitudes,* another volume of previously unreleased songs).[87] Other collaborations between contemporary musicians and Guthrie from beyond the grave include Eliza Gilkyson's "Peace Call,"[88] Janis Ian's "I Hear You Sing Again,"[89] Ellis Paul's "God's Promise,"[90] Anti-Flag's "Post-War Breakout,"[91] the Dropkick Murphys' "Gonna Be a Blackout Tonight,"[92] Slaid

Cleaves's "This Morning I Am Born Again,"[93] the Red Dirt Rangers' "Cadillac Eight,"[94] the Autumn Defense's "Revolutionary Mind,"[95] and entire albums by Jonatha Brooke,[96] Joel Rafael,[97] and the Klezmatics.[98] Various artists have recorded new versions of Guthrie's unreleased children's lyrics, including those on Sarah Lee Guthrie and Family's *Go Waggaloo*[99] and the many collaborating musicians on *Daddy-O Daddy!*[100]

The global dimension to Guthrie's musical and political legacy has also been attracting increased scrutiny. The British connection has long been established, but latterly, scholars and musicians have explored Guthrie's impact in non-Anglo circles (perhaps taking up the mantle of Eric Bye, who as early as 1958 had impressed Jack Elliott with his translations of Guthrie's lyrics "into Norwegian slang, successfully capturing the nuances and spirit of the songs").[101] Jorge Arévalo Mateus's 2007 multimedia exhibition *Global Woody* charts the connections between such varied personages as the Ojibwa musician Keith Secola, the Beijing postpunk band PK 14, and the Brooklyn funk/soul band Sharon Jones and the Dap Kings, all of whom have claimed Guthrie as an influence. Secola's Ojibwa language version of "This Land Is Your Land" responds to the predicament of Pete Seeger and Jimmy Collier singing it at the Resurrection City protest camp in 1968, when the Oglala Sioux activist Henry Crow Dog challenged them: "Hey, you're both wrong. It ["this land"] belongs to me."[102] Allied to Secola's project is that of the radical Native American (or "alter-Native") punk-rock band Blackfire, whose versions of Guthrie's "Mean Things Happenin' in This World" and "~~Indian~~ Corn Song" (with the word "Indian" pointedly crossed out) take on such issues as war profiteering, land theft, political corruption, and the moral poverty of capitalism.[103] In a 2002 single, Jones and the Dap Kings paired their own "What If We All Stopped Paying Taxes" with "This Land Is Your Land" as a protest against the Iraq War.[104] Subsequently, their version of "This Land," with the words "welfare office" replacing Guthrie's original "relief office," was aptly chosen for the main title theme of Jason Reitman's film *Up in the Air* (2009), in which George Clooney plays a corporate agent whose job is to fire people in downsized businesses all across the country.[105] While PK 14 have not recorded any Guthrie songs, their lead vocalist, Yang Haisong, claims an inheritance specifically from "Woody Guthrie, Bob Dylan, Phil Ochs, and a whole generation of protest musicians"[106]—a list pregnant with meaning in post-Tiananmen China. The German metal band Z-Joe and the Dustbowlers has reinterpreted Guthrie's songs in a markedly new fashion—as a "Woody Zombie Hootenanny."[107] In addition to these musicians, Germany's Hans-Eckardt Wenzel and Denmark's Esben Langkniv have recorded Guthrie's songs in their respective languages—Wenzel with a risky career of East German dissidence behind him,[108] and Langkniv with an established repertoire of historical, social, and financial criticism in song.[109]

Among all the efforts to establish Guthrie's global significance, one by the London-based Alabama 3 (A3)—a "punk rock, blues and country techno situationist crypto-Marxist-Leninist electro band"[110]—deserves special attention. Known by many for having contributed the theme tune to the television series *The Sopranos*, A3 released a song titled "Woody Guthrie" on their 2002 CD *Power in the Blood*. The song's references spiral outward from the crisis-ridden American heartland to the global sphere of rampant labor exploitation—from the alienated midwestern "psychopath . . . loading up another round," to the "baby in Afghanistan cryin' for its mama now" (it could be an Afghan baby or a terrified American soldier), to the exhausted Indonesian mother "in some free-trade compound where they work you 'til you're dead." The most intriguing aspect of the song is the fact that Guthrie is not mentioned once. The inescapable conclusion is that, through the song's title, Guthrie's political sensibility is invoked for a new era of globalized capital and the oppressed labor that feeds it. Nothing cements that invocation more firmly than the repeated refrain implicitly linking the Dust Bowl migration to the neglect of those for whom the global market can find no use—the "asylum seeker" and "the frightened baby on some foreign beach," exhausted and in search of their "safe harbor."[111]

In an intense, undated moment of introspection, Woody Guthrie sat down and confessed on paper: "I loved so many people everywhere I went. / Some too much, others not enough."[112] He was certainly aware of his own faults: "You don't hate me any worse than I do. You don't bawl me out any more than I do."[113] But he uttered the quiet hope that whatever happened to him personally—whether he went "down or up or anywhere"—his "scribbling might stay."[114] On the eve of his centenary, his words are still being sung for all the hard-hit and the hard traveling who have yet to reach their "safe harbor"—those of whom Bharati Mukherjee writes so eloquently in her novel *Jasmine*: "We are the outcasts and deportees, strange pilgrims visiting outlandish shrines, landing at the end of tarmacs, ferried in old army trucks where we are roughly handled and taken to roped-off corners of waiting rooms where surly, barely wakened customs guards await their bribe. We are dressed in shreds of national costumes, out of season, the wilted plumage of intercontinental vagabondage. We ask only one thing: to be allowed to land; to pass through; to continue."[115] Guthrie's words are still being sung, too, against the "system" by which these millions are even now made to "wander more homeless than dogs and to live less welcome than hogs, sheep, or cattle" (as he had written to Asch in 1946)[116]—the "system," call it "capitalism," that earned his undying hatred.

Notes

Archival Abbreviations

AFC   Archive of Folk Culture, American Folklife Center, Library of Congress, Washington, D.C.
ALC   Alan Lomax Collection, American Folklife Center, Library of Congress, Washington, D.C.
BJOC   Barry and Judy Ollman Collection, Greenwood Village, Colorado.
RCC   Ronald Cohen Collection, Gary, Indiana.
WGA   Woody Guthrie Archives, Mount Kisco, New York.
WGMC   Woody Guthrie Manuscript Collection, American Folklife Center, Library of Congress, Washington, D.C.
WGP   Woody Guthrie Papers, Moses and Frances Asch Collection. Ralph Rinzler Archives, Center for Folklife and Cultural Heritage, Smithsonian Institution, Washington, D.C.

Introduction

1. Will Kaufman, "Voice of the Other America," *Times Higher Education Supplement,* September 28, 2007: 16–17 (p. 16).

2. Woody Guthrie, "I've Got to Know," in *Woody Guthrie Folk Songs* (New York: Ludlow Music, 1963), 168.

3. Secretary of the Interior Stuart Udall to Guthrie, April 6, 1966. WGP, Correspondence: By and about Woody Guthrie, Box 4, Folder 4/5.

4. Silber quoted in Ed Cray, *Ramblin' Man: The Life and Times of Woody Guthrie* (New York: Norton, 2004), 389.

5. Unknown constituent to Senator Mark Hatfield, September 7, 1967. Reproduced in Woodrow W. Guthrie FBI files. WGA, Personal Papers, Box 2, Folder 48.1.

6. This quote is reproduced on the back cover of Ed Robbin, *Woody Guthrie and Me* (Berkeley, Calif.: Lancaster-Miller, 1979). I have been unable to locate the original source.

7. Arlo Guthrie quoted in Cray, 389n.

8. John Lennon to Marjorie Guthrie, March 26, 1975. WGA, Woody Guthrie Correspondence, Series 2, Box 2, Folder 2.1.

9. Woody Guthrie, *Woody Sez*, comp. and ed. Marjorie Guthrie et al. (New York: Grosset and Dunlap, 1975), xix.

10. David Marc, *Comic Visions: Television Comedy and American Culture* (Oxford: Blackwell, 1997 [1989]), 158.

11. See http://www.woodyguthrie.org/Lyrics/Dear_Mrs_Roosevelt.htm.

12. Woody Guthrie, "This Land Is Your Land." WGA, Songs 1, Box 3, Folder 27.

13. Guthrie, "This Land Is Your Land," on Woody Guthrie, *The Asch Recordings*, Vol. 1: *This Land Is Your Land* (Smithsonian Folkways, 1999), Track 14.

14. Guthrie, "This Land Is Your Land," *Ten of Woody Guthrie's Twenty-Five Cent Songs* (c. 1945), WGP, Box 2, Folder 1.

15. Arlo Guthrie quoted in Joe Klein, *Woody Guthrie: A Life* (New York: Delta, 1999 [1980]), xii.

16. Notable among these general studies are R. Serge Denisoff, *Great Day Coming: Folk Music and the American Left* (Baltimore: Penguin, 1973); Michael Denning, *The Cultural Front: The Laboring of American Culture in the Twentieth Century* (London: Verso, 1998 [1996]); Bryan K. Garman, *A Race of Singers: Whitman's Working-Class Hero from Guthrie to Springsteen* (Chapel Hill: University of North Carolina Press, 2000); John Greenway, *American Folksongs of Protest* (New York: A. S. Barnes, 1953); Wayne Hampton, *Guerrilla Minstrels* (Knoxville: University of Tennessee Press, 1986); Peter La Chapelle, *Proud to Be an Okie: Cultural Politics, Country Music, and Migration to Southern California* (Berkeley: University of California Press, 2007); Robbie Lieberman, *"My Song Is My Weapon": People's Songs, American Communism, and the Politics of Culture, 1930–50* (Urbana and Chicago: University of Illinois Press, 1995); and Richard Reuss with JoAnne C. Reuss, *American Folk Music and Left-Wing Politics, 1927–1957* (Lanham, Md.: Scarecrow Press, 2000). The major academic studies devoted to Guthrie are Martin Butler, *Voices of the Down and Out: The Dust Bowl Migration and the Great Depression in the Songs of Woody Guthrie* (Heidelberg: Universitätsverlag Winter, 2007); Mark Allan Jackson, *Prophet Singer: The Voice and Vision of Woody Guthrie* (Jackson: University Press of Mississippi, 2007); John S. Partington, ed., *The Life, Work, and Thought of Woody Guthrie: A Critical Assessment* (Aldershot: Ashgate, 2011); and Robert Santelli and Emily Davidson, eds., *Hard Travelin': The Life and Legacy of Woody Guthrie* (Hanover, N.H.: Wesleyan University Press, 1999).

17. James N. Gregory, *American Exodus: The Dust Bowl Migration and Okie Culture in California* (New York: Oxford University Press, 1989), 154.

18. All the arguments attempting to establish Guthrie's Communist Party membership can be traced back to two of his associates, Agnes "Sis" Cunningham and Gordon Friesen, who claimed that he had joined the Party in 1941–42. No documentary evidence has emerged to confirm his membership. See Cray, 446 (note 322) and Ronald D. Cohen, "Woody the Red?" in Santelli and Davidson, eds., *Hard Travelin': The Life and Legacy of Woody Guthrie*, 138–52.

19. Woody Guthrie, "Curly-Headed Baby." Typed manuscript of "War Songs Are Work Songs." ALC, AFC 2004/004, Woody Guthrie Manuscripts, Box 33.02, Folder 16.

20. Steven Brower and Nora Guthrie, eds., *Woody Guthrie Artworks* (New York: Rizzoli, 1995), 194–95.

21. Jonatha Brooke on NPR Radio, *Weekend Edition Sunday,* November 16, 2008.

22. Norman Pierce quoted in Cray, 143.

23. Heidi Slettedahl Macpherson, *Women's Movement: Escape as Transgression in North American Feminist Fiction* (Amsterdam: Rodopi, 2000), 2.

24. Jack Elliott quoted in Hank Reineke, *Ramblin' Jack Elliott: The Never-Ending Highway* (Lanham, Md.: Scarecrow Press, 2010), xviii–xix.

25. Ellen Steckert, "Cents and Nonsense in the Urban Folk Movement: 1930–66," in Neil V. Rosenberg, ed., *Transforming Tradition: Folk Music Revivals Examined* (Urbana and Chicago: University of Illinois Press, 1993): 84–106 (p. 90).

26. Woody Guthrie, "Song about Tipping." WGA, Songs 1, Box 3, Folder 24.

27. Woody Guthrie, "Socialismo." WGA, Songs 1, Box 3, Folder 24.

28. Woody Guthrie, "The Unwelcome Guest." WGA, Songs 1, Box 3, Folder 28. See also Billy Bragg and Wilco, *Mermaid Avenue,* Vol. 1 (Electra, 1998), Track 15.

Chapter 1: Awakenings

1. Woody Guthrie, "More War News." WGA, Songs 2, Notebook 5, 95.

2. Al Richmond, *A Long View from the Left: Memoirs of an American Revolutionary* (New York: Delta, 1972), 280.

3. Ibid., 283, 284.

4. Fraser M. Ottanelli, *The Communist Party of the United States from the Depression to World War II* (New Brunswick, N.J.: Rutgers University Press, 1991), 167.

5. Judy Kutulas, *The Long War: The Intellectual People's Front and Anti-Stalinism, 1930–1940* (Durham, N.C.: Duke University Press, 1995), 79.

6. Woody Guthrie and Maxine Crissman, *Woody and Lefty Lou's Favorite Collection of Old Time Hill Country Songs: Being Sung for Ages, Still Going Strong* (Gardena, Calif.: Spanish American Institute Press, 1937), n.p. WGP, Box 2, Folder 4.

7. Guthrie quoted in Ed Robbin, *Woody Guthrie and Me* (Berkeley, Calif.: Lancaster-Miller, 1979), 28.

8. Jack Guthrie quoted in Ed Cray, *Ramblin' Man: The Life and Times of Woody Guthrie* (New York: Norton, 2004), 100.

9. Woody Guthrie, "Skid Row." KVFD air check recording (1937), Track 3. Unlabeled CD, Ralph Rinzler Archives, Smithsonian Institution, Center for Folklife and Cultural Heritage.

10. Woody Guthrie, "Big City Ways," on ibid.

11. Peter La Chapelle, *Proud to Be an Okie: Cultural Politics, Country Music, and Migration to Southern California* (Berkeley: University of California Press, 2007), 53–54.

12. Ibid., 59.

13. Ibid.

14. Woody Guthrie, "Poor Girl's Prayer," in *Songs of Woody Guthrie* (manuscript). WGMC, Box 1, Folder 13.

15. Woody Guthrie, "If You Aint Got the Do Re Mi." WGA, Songs 1, Box 1, Folder 7.

16. Guthrie, notes to ibid.

17. Woody Guthrie, "Talkin' Dustbowl Blues." WGP, Song Texts, Box 1, Folder 8.

18. Fan letters quoted in Joe Klein, *Woody Guthrie: A Life* (New York: Delta, 1999 [1980]), 93, 100.

19. Burke quoted in ibid., 114.

20. Guthrie to Marjorie Mazia, April 12, 1942. WGA, Woody Guthrie Correspondence, Series 1, Box 1, Folder 43.

21. Woody Guthrie, "Hooversville." WGP, Song Texts, Box 1, Folder 4.

22. Donald Worster, *Dust Bowl: The Southern Plains in the 1930s* (Oxford: Oxford University Press, 1982), 61.

23. Woody Guthrie, *Bound for Glory* (London: Penguin, 2004 [1943]), 39, 40.

24. Woody Guthrie, "My Life," in Woody Guthrie, *American Folksong*, ed. Moses Asch (New York: Oak Publications, 1961), 2–3.

25. Worster, *Dust Bowl*, 50–51.

26. Woody Guthrie, "I Was There and the Dust Was There," on *The Live Wire Woody Guthrie* (Woody Guthrie Foundation, 2007), Track 3.

27. Woody Guthrie, "Dust Storm Disaster," on Woody Guthrie, *Library of Congress Recordings* (Rounder Records, 1988), Disc 3, Track 2.

28. Woody Guthrie, "Boll Weevil Blues," *Library of Congress Recordings*, Disc 1, Track 8.

29. Woody Guthrie, "Dusty Old Dust," on Woody Guthrie, *Dust Bowl Ballads* (Buddha Records, 2000), Track 4.

30. See Mark Allan Jackson, *Prophet Singer: The Voice and Vision of Woody Guthrie* (Jackson: University Press of Mississippi, 2007), 4; and Studs Terkel, *And They All Sang* (London: Granta, 2005), 212.

31. Milton Cantor, *The Divided Left: American Radicalism, 1900–1975* (New York: Hill and Wang, 1978), 31; Garin Burbank, *When Farmers Voted Red: The Gospel of Socialism in the Oklahoma Countryside, 1910–1924* (Westport, Conn.: Greenwood Press, 1976), 7.

32. Charley Guthrie quoted in Cray, *Ramblin' Man*, 10.

33. Burbank, *When Farmers Voted Red*, 7.

34. Cantor, *The Divided Left*, 28.

35. Debs quoted in Cantor, *The Divided Left*, 24.

36. Socialist Party platforms quoted in Burbank, *When Farmers Voted Red*, 9, 44.

37. Michael Denning, *The Cultural Front: The Laboring of American Culture in the Twentieth Century* (London: Verso, 1998 [1996]), 125.

38. Burbank, *When Farmers Voted Red*, 4–5.

39. Sulpher *New Century* quoted in ibid., 60.

40. Okemah *Sledge Hammer* quoted in ibid., 50.

41. Sentinel *Sword of Truth* quoted in ibid., 57–58.

42. C. E. Guthrie, *Kumrids: A Discussion of Scientific Socialism* (Okemah, Okla.: Ledger Printing, 1912).

43. Cantor, *The Divided Left*, 23.

44. Sulpher *New Century* quoted in Jim Bissett, *Agrarian Socialism in America: Marx, Jefferson, and Jesus in the Oklahoma Countryside, 1904–1920* (Norman: University of Oklahoma Press, 1999), 94.

45. McClanahan quoted in Burbank, *When Farmers Voted Red*, 37–38.

46. Guthrie quoted in Cray, *Ramblin' Man*, 147.

47. Moses Asch, interview with Guy Logsdon, July 1974. Logsdon, "Introduction," liner notes to Woody Guthrie, *The Asch Recordings*, Vol. 3: *Hard Travelin'* (Smithsonian Folkways, 1999), 15.

48. Woody Guthrie, "Jesus My Doctor." WGA, Songs 1, Box 2, Folder 14.

49. Woody Guthrie, "No Disappointment in Heaven," in *Songs of Woody Guthrie* (manuscript). WGMC, Box 1, Folder 13.

50. WCU literature quoted in Burbank, *When Farmers Voted Red*, 145, 148.

51. Farm-Labor Union declaration quoted in ibid., 168.

52. IWW, *Message to the Oil Workers*, quoted in Nigel Anthony Sellars, *Oil, Wheat, and Wobblies: The Industrial Workers of the World in Oklahoma, 1905–1930* (Norman: University of Oklahoma Press, 1998), 71–72.

53. *Oklahoma Pioneer* quoted in ibid., 27.

54. Woody Guthrie, "Some from the Old Wobblies," in Alan Lomax, Woody Guthrie, and Pete Seeger, eds., *Hard Hitting Songs for Hard-Hit People* (New York: Oak Publications, 1967), 87.

55. *I.W.W. Songs: To Fan the Flames of Discontent* (Chicago: Industrial Workers of the World, 1923).

56. Joe Hill quoted in Gibbs Smith, *Joe Hill* (Layton, Utah: Peregrine Smith, 1969), 19.

57. Joe Hill quoted in ibid.

58. Woody Guthrie, "Joe Hillstrom," in Woody Guthrie, *American Folksong*, ed. Moses Asch (New York: Oak Publications, 1961), 23.

59. Woody Guthrie, "Going Down the Road Feeling Bad," *Library of Congress Recordings*, Disc 3, Track 1.

60. Woody Guthrie, "California California." WGA, Songs 1, Box 1, Folder 5.

61. Guthrie, *Bound for Glory*, 223.

62. Woody Guthrie to Marjorie Mazia, October 3, 1945. Reprinted in Woody Guthrie, *Pastures of Plenty*, ed. Dave Marsh and Harold Leventhal (New York: HarperPerennial, 1990), 140–41.

63. Robbin, *Woody Guthrie and Me*, 30–31.

64. Richmond, *A Long View*, 280.

65. Woody Guthrie, "Dust Bowl Refugee," *Library of Congress Recordings*, Disc 3, Track 6.

66. Woody Guthrie, *Woody Sez* (New York: Grosset and Dunlap, 1975), xix.

67. Ibid., 2.

68. Ibid., 5.

69. Ibid., 14.

70. "Political Books Owned by Woody Guthrie," n.d., p. 1. WGA, Personal Papers, Box 2, Folder 49.

71. Ibid., p. 2.

72. Guthrie, *Woody Sez*, 17.

73. Robbin, *Woody Guthrie and Me*, 99.

74. Will Geer quoted in ibid., 109.

75. Woody Guthrie, "High Balladree." WGA, Manuscripts 1, Box 7, Folder 4.

76. Nelson A. Pichardo, "The Power Elite and Elite-Driven Countermovements: The

Associated Farmers of California during the 1930s," *Sociological Forum* 10, no. 1 (March 1995): 21–49 (p. 25).

77. "The Old Wop" quoted in Cray, *Ramblin' Man,* 156–57.

78. "The Old Wop" quoted in ibid., 158.

79. Woody Guthrie, "Poor, Hard-Working Man Blues," *Songs of Woody Guthrie* (manuscript). WGMC, Box 1, Folder 13.

80. Woody Guthrie, "Story That's Never Been Told," in ibid.

81. Woody Guthrie, "Death Valley Scotty," in ibid.

82. Woody Guthrie, "Roosevelt-Olson," in *Songs of Woody Guthrie* (manuscript). WGMC, Box 1, Folder 13.

83. Guthrie, *Woody Sez,* 42.

84. Ibid., 162.

85. Woody Guthrie, "Capital City Cyclone," in *Songs of Woody Guthrie* (manuscript). WGMC, Box 1, Folder 13.

86. Ibid., 26.

87. Woody Guthrie, "Ham and Eggs Is Marching On," in *Songs of Woody Guthrie* (manuscript). WGMC, Box 1, Folder 13.

88. Guthrie, *Woody Sez,* 40.

89. Richmond, *A Long View,* 230.

90. Mary E. Glantz, *FDR and the Soviet Union: The President's Battles over Foreign Policy* (Lawrence: University Press of Kansas, 2005), 21.

91. Don Mitchell, *The Lie of the Land: Migrant Workers and the California Landscape* (Minneapolis: University of Minnesota Press, 1996), 127, 134.

92. James N. Gregory, *American Exodus: The Dust Bowl Migration and Okie Culture in California* (New York: Oxford University Press, 1989), 155–60.

93. Mitchell, *The Lie of the Land,* 125.

94. La Chapelle, *Proud to Be an Okie,* 64–65.

95. Woody Guthrie, "California Blues," *Library of Congress Recordings,* Disc 3, Track 5.

96. H. L. Mencken, "The Dole for Bogus Farmers," *American Mercury* 39 (December 1936): 400–408 (p. 404).

97. La Chapelle, *Proud to Be an Okie,* 28, 31.

98. Woody Guthrie, "I Ain't Got No Home." KVFD air check recording (1937), Track 4. Unlabeled CD, Ralph Rinzler Archives, Smithsonian Institution, Center for Folklife and Cultural Heritage.

99. Buck Owens quoted in Cray, *Ramblin' Man,* 134.

100. Katherine Archibald quoted in Gregory, *American Exodus,* 179.

101. Woody Guthrie, "I Ain't Got No Home." WGP, Song Texts, Box 1, Folder 1.

102. Woody Guthrie, annotation to "Do Re Mi." WGP, Typescripts: Woody Guthrie Songs, Box 2, Folder 3.

103. Woody Guthrie, "Dust Bowl Refugee," *Library of Congress Recordings,* Disc 3, Track 6.

104. Guthrie, annotation to "I Aint Got No Home in This World Any More." WGP, Song Texts, Box 1, Folder 4.

105. Kenneth Crist, "Career Men—in Relief," *Los Angeles Times Sunday Magazine,* May 14, 1939, 4–5, 81.

106. Guthrie, *Woody Sez,* 29, 30.

107. Woody Guthrie, "Pretty Boy Floyd." WGA, Songs 1, Box 2, Folder 21.

108. Woody Guthrie, "The Unwelcome Guest." WGA, Songs 1, Box 3, Folder 28.

109. Woody Guthrie, "Jesus Christ," in Woody Guthrie, *Woody Guthrie Folk Songs* (New York: Ludlow Music, 1963), 12; Woody Guthrie, "A Hard Working Man Was Jesus." WGA, Songs 1, Box 1, Folder 11.

110. Guthrie, annotation to "Pretty Boy Floyd." WGA, Songs 1, Box 2, Folder 21.

111. Woody Guthrie, "Vigilante Man," *Woody Guthrie Folk Songs,* 28.

112. Woody Guthrie, "Woody Sez That Okies Haven't Given Up the Fight," *Daily Worker,* April 23, 1940, 7.

113. Pete Seeger on *Pete Seeger at 90,* prod. Vincent Dowd. BBC Radio 4, first broadcast May 1, 2009.

114. Woody Guthrie, "This Land Is Your Land." WGA, Songs 1, Box 3, Folder 27.

115. Woody Guthrie, "This Land Is Your Land," *Ten of Woody Guthrie's Twenty-Five Cent Songs* (c. 1945), WGP, Box 2, Folder 1.

Chapter 2: Hard-Hitting Songs for Hard-Hit People

1. Gordon Friesen in Agnes "Sis" Cunningham and Gordon Friesen, *Red Dust and Broadsides: A Joint Biography,* ed. Ronald D. Cohen (Amherst: University of Massachusetts Press, 1999), 207.

2. Guthrie's KFVD business card, BJOC.

3. Millard Lampell, "Hard Travelin'," in Millard Lampell and Hally Wood, eds., *A Tribute to Woody Guthrie* (New York: Ludlow Music in association with Woody Guthrie Publications, 1972): 1–3 (p. 2).

4. Michael Denning, *The Cultural Front: The Laboring of American Culture in the Twentieth Century* (London: Verso, 1998 [1996]), 16.

5. Woody Guthrie, *Woody Sez* (New York: Grosset and Dunlap, 1975), 116.

6. Ibid., 105.

7. Ibid., 107.

8. Ibid., 114.

9. Ibid., 114.

10. Ibid., 105–6.

11. Ibid., 106.

12. Ibid., 115.

13. Woody Guthrie, "My Name Is New York," in Guthrie, *New Found Land* (c. 1941). Typed manuscript, ALC, AFC 2004/004. Woody Guthrie Manuscripts, Box 33.02, Folder 20.

14. Woody Guthrie, annotation to "Wheelbarrow Pusher." WGP, Typescripts: Woody Guthrie Songs, Box 2, Folder 3.

15. Guthrie, "Wheelbarrow Pusher." WGP, Typescripts: Woody Guthrie Songs, Box 2, Folder 3.

16. Guthrie to "Dear Everybody at April Farms" (Almanac Singers), n.d., n.p. WGA, Woody Guthrie Correspondence, Series 1, Box 1, Folder 3.

17. Guthrie to Almanac Singers from Los Angeles, n.d. (but March 1941). WGA, Woody Guthrie Correspondence, Series 1, Box 1, Folder 3.

18. Woody Guthrie, "The Bowery and Me," *Sunday Worker,* January 26, 1947, reprinted in Guthrie, *Pastures of Plenty,* ed. Dave Marsh and Harold Leventhal (New York: HarperPerennial, 1990), 189.

19. Woody Guthrie, "Manifesto on Wage Slaves, Sleep Walking, and Jesus," n.d. ALC, AFC 2004/004, Box 33.03, Folder 03.

20. Woody Guthrie, "I'll Not Beg." WGA, Songs 1, Box 2, Folder 12.

21. Guthrie, annotation to "I'll Not Beg." WGA, Songs 1, Box 2, Folder 12.

22. Robbie Lieberman, *"My Song Is My Weapon": People's Songs, American Communism, and the Politics of Culture, 1930–50* (Urbana and Chicago: University of Illinois Press, 1995), 50–51.

23. "Lead Belly"—as opposed to "Leadbelly"—was the form preferred by Ledbetter and his family. It has become the accepted standard in writing about Ledbetter.

24. Lomax quoted in David King Dunaway, *How Can I Keep from Singing? The Ballad of Pete Seeger* (New York: Villard Books, 2008 [1981]), 69. Wayne Hampton does little to challenge Lomax's overstatement in claiming that "it marked the beginning of a proletarian renaissance in American popular music." Hampton, *Guerrilla Minstrels* (Knoxville: University of Tennessee Press, 1986), 108. David Dunaway, with his inclusion of Lead Belly, also approaches Lomax's hyperbole: "If an observer from another world had trained his eye on a two-mile-square area bounded by Greenwich Village to the south and Times Square to the north, with the participants drawing together from Louisiana, New York, and Oklahoma's Dust Bowl, he would have witnessed an art form—the modern protest song—in the making." Dunaway, 65.

25. Seeger quoted in Dunaway, *How Can I Keep from Singing?,* 67.

26. R. Serge Denisoff, *Great Day Coming: Folk Music and the American Left* (Baltimore: Penguin, 1973), 40.

27. Seeger quoted in David K. Dunaway, "Charles Seeger and Carl Sands: The Composers' Collective Years," *Ethnomusicology* 24, no. 2 (May 1980): 159–68 (p. 162).

28. Carl Sands (Charles Seeger), "A Program for Proletarian Composers," *Daily Worker,* January 16, 1934, 5.

29. Cowell quoted in Anon., "Cowell Performs Own Compositions in Piano Recital," *Daily Worker,* November 21, 1933, 5.

30. Workers Music League, *Red Song Book* (New York: Workers Library Publishers, 1932), 3.

31. Denisoff, *Great Day Coming,* 39.

32. Lieberman, *"My Song Is My Weapon,"* 29.

33. Seeger quoted in Dunaway, "Charles Seeger and Carl Sands," 163.

34. Mike Gold, "What a World," *Daily Worker,* October 19, 1933, 5.

35. Mike Gold, "Change the World!" *Daily Worker,* January 2, 1933, 5.

36. Ibid.

37. Lan Adomian, "What Songs Should Workers' Choruses Sing?" *Daily Worker,* February 7, 1934, 5.

38. Seeger quoted in Shelly Romalis, *Pistol Packin' Mama: Aunt Molly Jackson and the Politics of Folk Song* (Urbana and Chicago: University of Illinois Press, 1999), 101.

39. Richard A. Reuss, with JoAnne C. Reuss, *American Folk Music and Left-Wing Politics, 1927–1957* (Lanham, Md.: Scarecrow Press, 2000), 131.

40. American Music League manifesto quoted in Denisoff, *Great Day Coming,* 45.

41. Elie Siegmeister, *Music and Society* (New York: Critics Group Press, 1938), 58–59.

42. Charles Seeger quoted in Reuss, *American Folk Music,* 53. Seeger was certainly thinking of his son, Pete, who was told by Jackson at their first meeting: "We're going to make a new world for you to grow up and fight in." Pete Seeger recalled in Jackson's voice "the combination of soprano saxophone, oboe, and bassoon." Jackson and Pete Seeger quoted in Romalis, *Pistol Packin' Mama,* 101.

43. Earl Robinson quoted in Reuss, *American Folk Music,* 138.

44. Denisoff, *Great Day Coming,* 62, 64.

45. Charles Seeger, "Grass Roots for American Composers" (1939), quoted in Lieberman, 37.

46. Dick Weissman, *Which Side Are You On? An Inside History of the Folk Music Revival in America* (New York: Continuum, 2006), 43.

47. Pete Seeger, letter to Will Kaufman, February 28, 2010.

48. Lomax on Woody Guthrie, "Lost Train Blues," *Library of Congress Recordings* (Rounder Records, 1988), Disc 1, Track 1.

49. "Rye Whiskey," on Guthrie, *Library of Congress Recordings,* Disc 1, Track 3.

50. Guthrie, "Beaumont Rag," *Library of Congress Recordings,* Disc 1, Track 5.

51. Burgess Meredith quoted in Joe Klein, *Woody Guthrie: A Life* (New York: Delta, 1999 [1980]), 161.

52. Lomax quoted in Ed Cray, *Ramblin' Man: The Life and Times of Woody Guthrie* (New York: Norton, 2004), 168.

53. Moses Asch, interview with Guy Logsdon, July 1974, in Logsdon, "Introduction," notes to Woody Guthrie, *Hard Travelin': The Asch Recordings,* Vol. 3 (Smithsonian Folkways Recordings, 1999).

54. Guthrie to Almanac Singers, n.d. (but March 1941). WGA, Woody Guthrie Correspondence, Series 1 Box 1, Folder 3.

55. Guthrie, "Talking Dust Bowl Blues," *Library of Congress Recordings,* Disc 1, Track 10.

56. David West, "Queen Elizabeth (Not Our Police) Launched the First War on Bums." *Los Angeles Times,* March 1, 1936: 5, 26 (p. 5).

57. Guthrie, "Dust Bowl Refugee," *Library of Congress Recordings,* Disc 3, Track 6.

58. Ibid.

59. Guthrie, "Tom Joad in American Ballad," *Daily Worker,* May 3, 1940, 7.

60. Los Angeles *News* and Guthrie quoted in Klein, *Woody Guthrie: A Life,* 170.

61. Guthrie, introductory notes to "Jesus Christ Was a Man," in Alan Lomax, Woody Guthrie, and Pete Seeger, eds., *Hard Hitting Songs for Hard-Hit People* (New York: Oak Publications, 1967), 336.

62. Guthrie, "They Laid Jesus Christ in His Grave," *Library of Congress Recordings,* Disc 2, Track 3.

63. Guthrie, "Jesus Christ Was a Man," *Hard Hitting Songs for Hard-Hit People,* 337.

64. Guthrie, "California Blues," *Library of Congress Recordings,* Disc 3, Track 5.

65. Alan Lomax, "Compiler's Postscript," *Hard Hitting Songs for Hard-Hit People,* 366.

66. Irwin Silber, "Publisher's Foreword," *Hard Hitting Songs for Hard-Hit People,* 12.

67. George Lewis, "America Is in Their Songs," *Daily Worker,* March 24, 1941, 7.

68. *Hard Hitting Songs for Hard Hit People,* 15.

69. Lomax, "Compiler's Postscript," in ibid., 366.

70. *Hard Hitting Songs for Hard-Hit People,* 164.

71. Ibid., 17.

72. Ibid.

73. Ibid., 294.

74. Ibid., 99.

75. Ibid., 116.

76. Guthrie, "Matthew Kimes," *Hard Hitting Songs for Hard-Hit People,* 116.

77. *Hard Hitting Songs for Hard-Hit People,* 236.

78. Ibid., 18.

79. Ibid., 62.

80. Ibid., 74.

81. Ibid., 16.

82. Guthrie to Pete Seeger, March 19, 1941. WGA, Woody Guthrie Correspondence, Series 1, Box 3, Folder 23.

83. Guthrie to Pete Seeger, n.d. WGA, Woody Guthrie Correspondence, Series 1, Box 3, Folder 23.

84. Guthrie quoted in Dunaway, *How Can I Keep from Singing?,* 69.

85. Ina Wood quoted in ibid., 74.

86. *Hard Hitting Songs for Hard-Hit People,* 324.

87. Millard Lampell has been increasingly credited for his additional verse.

88. Almanac Singers, "Union Maid," on *Songs for Political Action: Folk Music, Topical Singers and the American Left, 1926–1953,* comp. Ronald D. Cohen and Dave Samuelson (Bear Family Records, 1996), Disc 3, Track 12.

89. Woody Guthrie, *Woody Guthrie Songbook,* ed. Harold Leventhal and Marjorie Guthrie (New York: Grosset and Dunlap, 1976), 236.

90. Guthrie, annotation to "Union Maid #1." WGA, Songs 1, Box 3, Folder 28.

91. Ibid. For a brief account of the Meriwether case, see the introduction to Mary Robinson, *Moisture of the Earth,* ed. Fran Leeper Buss (Ann Arbor: University of Michigan Press, 2009), 14.

92. Almanac Singers, "Union Maid," *Songs for Political Action,* Disc 3, Track 12.

93. Guthrie, "Union Maid #1." WGA, Songs 1, Box 3, Folder 28.

94. Ibid.

95. Mike Quin, "Double Check," *People's World,* April 25, 1940, 5.

96. Sender Garlin quoted in Cray, *Ramblin' Man,* 171.

97. Guthrie to Alan Lomax, September 19, 1940. WGA, Woody Guthrie Correspondence, Series 1, Box 1, Folder 39.

98. Guthrie to "Mrs. 'Chenko" (Henrietta Yurchenko), October 3, 1940. BJOC.

99. Lomax quoted in Klein, *Woody Guthrie: A Life,* 177.

100. Lomax to Guthrie, February 4, 1941. AFC, AFC 1940/004, Woody Guthrie Manuscript Collection, Box 1, Folder 7.

101. Guthrie to Lomax, September 17, 1940. WGA, Woody Guthrie Correspondence, Series 1, Box 1, Folder 39.

102. *Pipe Smoking Time* theme quoted in Klein, *Woody Guthrie: A Life,* 179.

103. Mary Guthrie Boyle quoted in Cray, *Ramblin' Man,* 161.

104. Guthrie to Almanac Singers, March 1941. WGA, Woody Guthrie Correspondence, Series 1, Box 1, Folder 3.

105. Guthrie to Will and Herta Geer, February 27, 1941. WGA, Woody Guthrie Correspondence, Series 1, Box 1, Folder 18.

106. Guthrie, handwritten addendum to *Alonzo M. Zilch's Own Collection of Original Songs and Ballads.* WGMC, AFC 1940/004, Box 1, Folder 9.

107. Guthrie, "The Final Call." WGA, Songs 1, Box 1, Folder 9.

108. Guthrie, "Farther Along." WGA, Songs 1, Box 1, Folder 9.

Chapter 3: Almanac Days

1. Guthrie, "Adolph and Nevilline," in Guthrie, *Pastures of Plenty,* ed. Dave Marsh and Harold Leventhal (New York: Harper Perennial, 1990), 56.

2. Guthrie, notes to "Why Do You Stand There in the Rain?," in Alan Lomax, Woody Guthrie, and Pete Seeger, eds., *Hard Hitting Songs for Hard-Hit People* (New York: Oak Publications, 1967), 362.

3. Guthrie, "Why Do You Stand There in the Rain?," in Lomax, Guthrie, and Seeger, eds., *Hard Hitting Songs,* 363.

4. Guthrie, notes to "These Old Cumberland Mountain Farms" in Lomax, Guthrie, and Seeger, eds., *Hard Hitting Songs,* 29.

5. "These Old Cumberland Mountain Farms" in Lomax, Guthrie, and Seeger, eds., *Hard Hitting Songs,* 29.

6. Guthrie, "Cumberland Mountain Farms." WGA, Songs 1, Box 1, Folder 5.

7. Ibid.

8. *Hard Hitting Songs for Hard-Hit People,* 32.

9. Guthrie, annotation to "Cumberland Mountain Farms." WGA, Songs 1, Box 1, Folder 5.

10. Guthrie to Will and Herta Geer, February 27, 1941. WGA, Woody Guthrie Correspondence, Series 1, Box 1, Folder 18.

11. Guthrie to Alan Lomax, February 15, 1941. WGMC, AFC 1940/004, Box 1, Folder 3.

12. Guthrie to Pete Seeger, n.d. WGA, Woody Guthrie Correspondence, Series 1, Box 3, Folder 23.

13. Guthrie to Alan Lomax, February 20, 1941. WGA, Woody Guthrie Correspondence, Series 1, Box 1, Folder 39.

14. Guthrie to Will and Herta Geer, February 27, 1941. WGA, Woody Guthrie Correspondence, Series 1, Box 1, Folder 18.

15. Ibid.

16. Guthrie to Millard Lampell, n.d. (but 1941). WGA, Woody Guthrie Correspondence, Series 1, Box 1, Folder 34.

17. Guthrie to Will and Herta Geer, February 27, 1941. WGA, Woody Guthrie Correspondence, Series 1, Box 1, Folder 18.

18. Woody Guthrie, "He's on His Third Time Round," *Songs of Woody Guthrie* (manuscript). WGMC, Box 1, Folder 13.

19. Guthrie to Pete Seeger, March 19, 1941. WGA, Woody Guthrie Correspondence, Series 1, Box 3, Folder 23.

20. Carey McWilliams, *Factories in the Field: The Story of Migratory Farm Labor in California* (Berkeley: University of California Press, 2000 [1939]), 104–5.

21. Guthrie to Pete Seeger, March 19, 1941. WGA, Woody Guthrie Correspondence, Series 1, Box 3, Folder 23.

22. Guthrie to Seeger, n.d., n.p. WGA, Woody Guthrie Correspondence, Series 1, Box 3, Folder 23.

23. Guthrie to Millard Lampell, April 9, 1941. WGA, Woody Guthrie Correspondence, Series 1, Box 1, Folder 34.

24. Carl Abbott, "The Federal Presence," in Clyde A. Milner II et al., eds., *The Oxford History of the American West* (New York: Oxford University Press USA, 1996): 469–500 (480).

25. Ibid.

26. Steve Kahn in Michael Majdic and Denise Edwards, prods. and dirs., *Roll On Columbia: Woody Guthrie and the Bonneville Power Administration*, documentary video (Eugene: University of Oregon, Knight Library Media Services and School of Journalism and Communication, 2000).

27. Bill Murlin, BPA Public Information Officer, in ibid.

28. Pete Seeger in ibid.

29. Steve Kahn in ibid.

30. Kahn quoted in Ed Cray, *Ramblin' Man: The Life and Times of Woody Guthrie* (New York: Norton, 2004), 208–9.

31. Guthrie's signed oath for the Department of the Interior, May 1941, reproduced in Guthrie, *Pastures of Plenty,* 26.

32. Nora Guthrie in Majdic and Edwards, *Roll On Columbia.*

33. Guthrie to Millard Lampell, n.d. (but 1941). WGA, Woody Guthrie Correspondence, Series 1, Box 1, Folder 34.

34. Joe Klein, *Woody Guthrie: A Life* (New York: Delta, 1999 [1980]), 185.

35. Guthrie to Millard Lampell, n.d. (but 1941). WGA, Woody Guthrie Correspondence, Series 1, Box 1, Folder 34.

36. Ibid.

37. Guy Logsdon and Jeff Place, notes to Woody Guthrie, *Hard Travelin': The Asch Recordings, Vol. 3* (Smithsonian Folkways Recordings, 1999), 22–23.

38. Guthrie, "Oregon Trail," on Woody Guthrie, *The Columbia River Collection* (Rounder Records, 1987), Track 1.

39. Guthrie, "Pastures of Plenty," alternate manuscript version. WGP, Song Texts, Box 1, Folder 6.

40. Guthrie, annotation to "Roll On Columbia, Roll On." WGP, Song Texts, Box 1, Folder 7.

41. Guthrie to Millard Lampell, September 9, 1941. WGA, Woody Guthrie Correspondence, Series 1, Box 1, Folder 34.

42. Guthrie, "Grand Coulee Dam," *Columbia River Collection,* Track 13.

43. Guthrie, "The Biggest Thing that Man [Has] Ever Done." WGP, Song Texts, Box 1, Folder 1.

44. Guthrie, "Ramblin' Round," *Columbia River Collection,* Track 15.

45. Klein, *Woody Guthrie: A Life,* 205.

46. Anon., notes to Guthrie, *The Columbia River Collection.*

47. Ibid.

48. Guthrie, "Talking Columbia." *Columbia River Collection,* Track 4.

49. Logsdon and Place, notes to Guthrie, *Hard Travelin',* 24.

50. Guthrie, "Talking Columbia." *Hard Travelin',* Track 14.

51. *Hard Hitting Songs for Hard-Hit People,* 254.

52. Ibid., 39.

53. Ibid., 192.

54. Guthrie, notes to "I'm Looking for that New Deal Now," *Hard Hitting Songs for Hard-Hit People,* 206.

55. Revised Code of Washington, Title 1, Chapter 20, Section 073. 1987 c 526 § 4.

56. Guthrie, "Roll On, Columbia," *Columbia River Collection,* Track 2.

57. Guthrie, "The Biggest Thing That Man Has Ever Done," *This Land Is Your Land,* Track 17.

58. Guthrie quoted in Cray, *Ramblin' Man,* 215. Klein has Guthrie saying, "I guess we won't be singing 'Why Do You Stand There in the Rain' anymore, will we?" Klein, *Woody Guthrie: A Life,* 205.

59. R. Serge Denisoff, *Great Day Coming: Folk Music and the American Left* (Baltimore: Penguin, 1973), 73.

60. Lomax quoted in Pete Seeger, "History of the Almanac Singers, 1941–42" (in form of a letter to Millard Lampell, dictated October 1, 1987). RCC.

61. Hays quoted in Klein, *Woody Guthrie: A Life,* 191.

62. Lee Hays, *Sing Out, Warning! Sing Out, Love: The Writings of Lee Hays,* ed. Robert S. Koppelman (Amherst: University of Massachusetts Press, 2004), 86. Pete Seeger has an alternative version of the group's naming: "I took out the manuscript for 'Hard-hitting Songs' and started leafing through it, trying to find ideas for a name for this trio. I came to the word, 'almanac.' Lee was sprawled out on another bed twelve feet away, and he says, 'Wait a minute; wait a minute. You know, back in Arkansas there were really two books that a poor farmer might know about: the Bible would help him get through the next world, but the Almanac would help him through this world. And we have an Almanac too, of sorts, although not everybody knows how to read it. And why don't we call ourselves the Almanac Singers.' Mill and I must have agreed pretty quickly. I don't remember there being much argument." Pete Seeger, "History of the Almanac Singers, 1941–42." RCC.

63. Bess Lomax Hawes, *Sing It Pretty: A Memoir* (Urbana and Chicago: University of Illinois Press, 2008), 41.

64. Almanac manifesto quoted in Denisoff, *Great Day Coming,* 77.

65. Guthrie to Millard Lampell, April 9, 1941. WGA, Woody Guthrie Correspondence, Series 1, Box 1, Folder 34.

66. Ibid.

67. Anonymous Movement manifesto, quoted in Richard A. Reuss, with JoAnne C. Reuss, *American Folk Music and Left-Wing Politics, 1927–1957* (Lanham, Md.: Scarecrow Press, 2000), 158.

68. Almanac Singers, "Ballad of October 16th," on *Songs for Political Action: Folk Music, Topical Songs and the American Left, 1926–1953,* comp. Ronald D. Cohen and Dave Samuelson (Bear Family Records, 1996), Disc 3, Track 6.

69. Almanac Singers, "The Strange Death of John Doe," on ibid., Disc 3, Track 1.

70. Almanac Singers, "Billy Boy," on ibid., Disc 3, Track 2.

71. Almanac Singers, "Plow Under," on ibid., Disc 3, Track 7.

72. "Music: June Records," *Time*, June 16, 1941. Online *Time* archive: http://www.time.com/time/magazine/article/0,9171,765744,00.html.

73. Eleanor Roosevelt quoted in Klein, *Woody Guthrie: A Life*, 198.

74. Pete Seeger on Paul Sexton, *The Times They Are A-Changing*, radio documentary, BBC Radio 2, first broadcast January 3, 2009.

75. Pete Seeger, "History of the Almanac Singers, 1941–42." RCC.

76. Dorothy Millstone quoted in David King Dunaway, *How Can I Keep from Singing? The Ballad of Pete Seeger* (New York: Villard Books, 2008 [1981]), 91.

77. Lee Hays quoted in Doris Willins, *Lonesome Traveler: The Life of Lee Hays* (Lincoln: University of Nebraska Press, 1993), 69.

78. Winston Churchill quoted in Williamson Murray, MacGregor Knox, and Alvin H. Bernstein, *The Making of Strategy: Rulers, States, and War* (Cambridge: Cambridge University Press, 1996), 412.

79. Guthrie quoted in Cray, *Ramblin' Man*, 215.

80. United States House of Representatives, *Investigation of Un-American Propaganda Activities in the United States. Hearings before a Special Committee on Un-American Activities, House of Representatives, Seventy-Seventh Congress, First Session, on H. Res. 282*, Volume 14 (Washington, D.C.: United States Government Printing Office, 1941), 8427.

81. Ibid., 8463. Huffman was portrayed with neurotic intensity by Joan Cusack in Tim Robbins's film *Cradle Will Rock* (1999).

82. Carl J. Friedrich, "The Poison in Our System," *Atlantic Monthly* 167, no. 6 (June 1941): 661–72 (p. 668).

83. Pete Seeger quoted in Dunaway, *How Can I Keep from Singing?*, 99.

84. Lee Hays quoted in Robbie Lieberman, *"My Song Is My Weapon": People's Songs, American Communism, and the Politics of Culture, 1930–50* (Urbana and Chicago: University of Illinois Press, 1995), 56.

85. Wayne Hampton, *Guerilla Minstrels* (Knoxville: University of Tennessee Press, 1986), 115.

86. Guthrie, "The Almanacs and Me," 2, n.d. WGA, Manuscripts 2, Box 1, Folder 2.

87. Brownie McGhee quoted in Denisoff, *Great Day Coming*, 79.

88. Guthrie quoted in Klein, *Woody Guthrie: A Life*, 213.

89. Terry Pettus quoted in Peter Tamony, "'Hootenanny': The Word, Its Content and Continuum," *Western Folklore* 22, no. 3 (July 1963): 165–70 (pp. 167–68).

90. Friesen in Agnes "Sis" Cunningham and Gordon Friesen, *Red Dust and Broadsides: A Joint Biography*, ed. Ronald D. Cohen (Amherst: University of Massachusetts Press, 1999), 211.

91. Guthrie, "The Almanacs and Me," 1.

92. Ibid.

93. Michael Denning, *The Cultural Front: The Laboring of American Culture in the Twentieth Century* (London: Verso, 1998 [1996]), 280–81.

94. Lampell quoted in Klein, *Woody Guthrie: A Life*, 209–10.

95. Guthrie, "Hard Hitting Songs by Hard Hit People," n.d. WGA, Manuscripts 1, Box 1, Folder 11.

96. Guthrie, "Almanacs Almanac: With the NMU Boys in Cleveland," n.d. WGA, Manuscripts 1, Box 1, Folder 10.

97. Seeger quoted in Dunaway, *How Can I Keep from Singing?*, 95.

98. Lampell quoted Ronald D. Cohen, *Work and Sing: A History of Occupational and Labor Union Songs in the United States* (Crockett, Calif.: Carquinez Press, 2010), 104.

99. Seeger quoted in ibid., 104.

100. Guthrie quoted in Lampell to Seeger, December 19, 1987. RCC.

101. Toshi Seeger quoted in Dunaway, *How Can I Keep from Singing?*, 108.

102. Seeger, "Leadbelly," in *The Leadbelly Songbook: The Ballads, Blues, and Folksongs of Huddie Ledbetter,* ed. Moses Asch and Alan Lomax (New York: Oak Publications, 1962), 7.

103. Almanac Singers, "Songs of Work, Trouble, Hope," *People's World,* October 28, 1941, 5.

104. Stern quoted in Klein, *Woody Guthrie: A Life,* 222–23.

105. Unidentified union member quoted in Hawes, *Sing It Pretty,* 42

106. Hawes, *Sing It Pretty,* 42.

107. Don Russell, "They Sing the Hard Hitting Songs That Belong to America's Workers," *People's World,* August 14, 1941, 7.

108. Guthrie, annotation to "My Union County Gal." WGP, Song Texts, Box 1, Folder 6.

109. Ibid.

110. Guthrie, *Woody Sez* (New York: Grosset and Dunlap, 1975), 138.

111. Guthrie to Almanac Singers, July 8, 1941. WGA, Woody Guthrie Correspondence, Series 1, Box 1, Folder 3.

112. Guthrie to "Dear Everybody at April Farms" (Almanac Singers), n.d., n.p. WGA, Woody Guthrie Correspondence, Series 1, Box 1, Folder 3.

113. Guthrie to Almanac Singers, July 8, 1941.

114. Seeger quoted in Denning, *The Cultural Front,* 284.

115. Guthrie to Almanac Singers, July 8, 1941.

116. Partlow quoted in Cohen, *Work and Sing,* 127.

117. Guthrie to Almanac Singers, July 8, 1941.

118. Ibid.

119. Guthrie to Lampell, September 9, 1941. WGA, Woody Guthrie Correspondence, Series 1, Box 1, Folder 34.

120. Guthrie, "Lindbergh," on Woody Guthrie, *This Land Is Your Land,* Track 6.

121. Ibid.

122. Guthrie, "Beat Hitler Blues." WGP, Song Texts, Box 1, Folder 1.

123. Guthrie, "Talking Rat Hole Blues." WGMC, Box 1, Folder 15 ("Wartime Songs, 1940–42 and undated").

124. Guthrie, "Talking Hitler's Head Off Blues." WGA, Songs 1, Box 3, Folder 26.

125. Guthrie, annotation to "East Texas Red." WGP, Typescripts: Woody Guthrie Songs, Box 2, Folder 2.

126. Guthrie, "East Texas Red." WGP, Typescripts: Woody Guthrie Songs, Box 2, Folder 2.

127. Almanac Singers, "Reuben James," *Songs for Political Action,* Disc 4, Track 6.

128. Mike Quin, "Way Down East," *Daily Worker,* November 21, 1941, 7.

129. Almanac Singers, "Reuben James."

130. Guthrie to Max Gordon, November 27, 1941. BJOC.

Chapter 4: Union War

1. Lee Hays quoted in Doris Willens, *Lonesome Traveler: The Life of Lee Hays* (Lincoln: University of Nebraska Press, 1993), 69.

2. Richard Reuss with JoAnne C. Reuss, *American Folk Music and Left-Wing Politics, 1927–1957* (Lanham, Md.: Scarecrow Press, 2000), 167.

3. Bess Lomax Hawes, *Sing It Pretty: A Memoir* (Urbana and Chicago: University of Illinois Press, 2008), 43.

4. Bess Lomax quoted in David King Dunaway, *How Can I Keep from Singing? The Ballad of Pete Seeger* (New York: Villard Books, 2008 [1981]), 93.

5. Guthrie, "New Situation." WGA, Songs 2, Notebook 3, p. 72.

6. Arlo Guthrie, "Going Back to Coney Island," in Robert Santelli and Emily Davidson, eds., *Hard Travelin': The Life and Legacy of Woody Guthrie* (Hanover, N.H.: Wesleyan University Press, 1999): 34–41 (p. 40).

7. Woody Guthrie, "New Situation."

8. Guthrie, "Big Guns (By the Almanac Singers)," in Woody Guthrie, *Pastures of Plenty,* ed. Dave Marsh and Harold Leventhal (New York: HarperPerennial, 1990), 78.

9. Guthrie to Marjorie Mazia, April 3, 1942. WGA, Woody Guthrie Correspondence, Series 1, Box 1, Folder 43.

10. Guthrie, *American Folksong,* ed. Moses Asch (New York: Oak Publications, 1961), 6.

11. Dunaway, *How Can I Keep from Singing?,* 110.

12. Lomax to Guthrie, January 21, 1942. WGMC, AFC 1940/004, Box 1, Folder 7.

13. Guthrie to Son House, February 27, 1942. Letter from the Richard Reuss Collection, University Archives, Indiana University, Bloomington, Indiana. Copy held in RCC.

14. Guthrie to Marjorie Mazia, n.d. (but between September and December 1942). WGA, Woody Guthrie Correspondence, Series 1, Box 1, Folder 44.

15. Lomax to Harold Spivacke, January 26, 1942. WGMC, AFC 1940/004, Box 1, Folder 7.

16. Seeger quoted in Reuss, *American Folk Music,* 174.

17. Reuss, *American Folk Music,* 174.

18. "Singers on New Morale Show Also Warbled for Communists," New York *World-Telegram,* February 17, 1942, p. 3.

19. Robert J. Stephens, "'Peace' Choir Changes Tune," *New York Post,* February 17, 1942, 1, 4.

20. Art Smith, "OWI's Face Is Red as Its Own Hill Billies," New York *Daily News,* January 5, 1943, pp. 2, 12 (p. 2).

21. "U.S. Defamers Yodel for OWI," *Chicago Daily Tribune,* January 5, 1943, 1.

22. Carl J. Friedrich, "The Poison in Our System," *Atlantic Monthly* 167, no. 6 (June 1941): 661–72.

23. FBI file on the Almanac Singers. RCC.

24. Dunaway, *How Can I Keep from Singing?,* 119

25. FBI file on the Almanac Singers. RCC.

26. Earl Robinson with Eric A. Gordon, *Ballad of an American: The Autobiography of Earl Robinson* (Lanham, Md.: Scarecrow Press, 1998), 142.

27. Ibid., 143.

28. Lampell, "Home Before Morning." Unpublished ms., 224. RCC.

29. Guthrie to Marjorie Mazia, n.d., quoted in Joe Klein, *Woody Guthrie: A Life* (New York: Delta, 1999 [1980]), 254.

30. Notes typed on the reverse of lyrics to Guthrie, "In Washington." WGP, Transcripts: Woody Guthrie Songs, Box 2, Folder 3.

31. Guthrie to Marjorie Mazia, November 17, 1942. WGA, Woody Guthrie Correspondence, Series 1, Box 1, Folder 44.

32. Hayes quoted in Dunaway, *How Can I Keep from Singing?*, 118.

33. Guthrie, "Acting and Dancing," notebook written for Marjorie Mazia, n.d. (but Jan. 1943). BJOC. Parts of this notebook appeared as an article under the title "Singing, Dancing and Teamwork" for *Dance Observer*, November 1943.

34. Nora Guthrie, "Sophie Maslow and Woody Guthrie," *Monthly Review*, November 7, 2006. Online version at http://mrzine.monthlyreview.org/2006/guthrie110706.html.

35. Guthrie quoted in Ed Cray, *Ramblin' Man: The Life and Times of Woody Guthrie* (New York: Norton, 2004), 245–46.

36. Guthrie, "Acting and Dancing," notebook written for Marjorie Mazia, January 1943. BJOC.

37. Guthrie quoted in Klein, *Woody Guthrie: A Life*, 254.

38. Ellen Graff, *Stepping Left: Dance and Politics in New York City, 1928–1942* (Durham: University of North Carolina Press, 1997), 156.

39. Millard Lampell, "Home Before Morning." Unpublished ms, 236. RCC.

40. Bess Hawes quoted in Cray, *Ramblin' Man*, 229. In one instance Hawes credits Lee Hays with the authorship of this parody; see Cray, *Ramblin' Man*, 434n229. Elsewhere she credits Pete Seeger; see David King Dunaway and Molly Beer, *Singing Out: An Oral History of America's Folk Music Revivals* (New York: Oxford University Press USA, 2010), 54.

41. Friesen quoted in Klein, *Woody Guthrie: A Life*, 222.

42. Friesen in Agnes "Sis" Cunningham and Gordon Friesen, *Red Dust and Broadsides: A Joint Biography*, ed. Ronald D. Cohen (Amherst: University of Massachusetts Press, 1999), 224.

43. Guthrie, annotation to "Dig a Hole." WGA, Songs 1, Box 1, Folder 6.

44. Guthrie, "The Almanacs & Me." WGA, Manuscripts 2, Box 1, Folder 2.

45. Lampell, "Home Before Morning," 209–10.

46. Hawes, *Sing It Pretty*, 40.

47. Lomax to Harold Spivacke, January 26, 1942. WGMC, AFC 1940/004, Box 1, Folder 7.

48. Lomax to Guthrie, January 21, 1942. WGMC, AFC 1940/004, Box 1, Folder 7.

49. Dunaway, *How Can I Keep from Singing?*, 106.

50. Lomax to Guthrie, January 21, 1942. WGMC, AFC 1940/004, Box 1, Folder 7.

51. Guthrie to Marjorie Mazia, n.d. (but between September and December 1942). WGA, Woody Guthrie Correspondence, Series 1, Box 1, Folder 4.

52. Copy of "The 'Almanacs' Part, But Keep On Singing," *Daily Worker*, January 8, 1943, 7, in FBI file on the Almanac Singers. RCC.

53. See Reuss, *American Folk Music*, 171.

54. "When Sarah next saw him, she pretended to be angry, grabbing him by his long hair and saying, 'Woody, you curly-headed son of a sea cook! I am going to beat the tar out of you. Why did you record my song without asking me?' Woody answered her,

'Oh hell, Sarie, that is a good song that needed recording, and you never would have done nothing with it.'" Jim Garland, *Welcome the Traveler Home: Jim Garland's Story of the Kentucky Mountains,* ed. Julia S. Ardery (Lexington: University Press of Kentucky, 1983), 185.

55. "The Almanac Singers Sessionography," in Ronald D. Cohen and Dave Samuelson, companion text to *Songs for Political Action: Folk Music, Topical Songs and the American Left, 1926–1953* (Hambergen, Germany: Bear Family Records, 1996), 82–83.

56. Guthrie, "My Secret," in Woody Guthrie, *Born to Win,* ed. Robert Shelton (New York: Collier, 1967), 174.

57. Guthrie, "Big Guns (By the Almanac Singers)," *Pastures of Plenty,* 80, 82.

58. Guthrie, "To a Union Show Troup" (written on behalf of the Almanac Singers), c. 1941. WGA, Manuscripts 1, Box 1, Folder 12.

59. Guthrie, "Woody Says." WGA, Manuscripts Box 1, Folder 13.

60. Guthrie to Marjorie Mazia, December 9, 1942. WGA, Woody Guthrie Correspondence, Series 1, Box 1, Folder 44.

61. Ibid.

62. Guthrie, *Pastures of Plenty,* 105.

63. Guthrie to Aliza Greenblatt, July 9, 1942, in ibid., 93.

64. Guthrie, "People Dancing," manuscript, March 15, 1942, BJOC. A version of this article was published in *Dance Observer,* December 1943.

65. Guthrie, "So Long, It's Been Good to Know Yuh." WGP, Song Texts, Box 1, Folder 7.

66. Guthrie, "Lindbergh," on Woody Guthrie, *This Land Is Your Land: The Asch Recordings,* Vol. 1 (Smithsonian Folkways Recordings, 1999), Track 6.

67. Guthrie, "I'll Fight for the U.S.A." WGMC, AFC 1940/004, Box 1, Folder 15 ("Wartime Songs, 1940–42 and undated").

68. Guthrie, "Get Along, Mister Hitler." WGA Songs 1, Box 1, Folder 10.

69. Guthrie, "A Letter to A. Hitler from a Good Union Worker." WGP, Song Texts, Box 1, Folder 5.

70. Guthrie, "Sally, Don't You Grieve," on Woody Guthrie, *Hard Travelin': The Asch Recordings,* Vol. 3 (Smithsonian Folkways Recordings, 1999), Track 16.

71. Guthrie, "Talking Hitler to Death." WGP, Song Texts, Box 1, Folder 8.

72. Guthrie, annotation to "Reckless Talk." WGP, Song Texts, Box 1, Folder 7.

73. Guthrie, "Ring around Hitler." WGP, Song Texts, Box 1, Folder 7.

74. Guthrie, "Ship in the Sky," on Guthrie, *Hard Travelin',* Track 4.

75. Guthrie to Alan Lomax, November 29, 1942. ALC, AFC 2004/004, Woody Guthrie Manuscripts, Box 33.02, Folder 16.

76. Ibid.

77. Guthrie to Mary Jo Guthrie, n.d. (but 1940), reprinted in *Pastures of Plenty,* 29–30.

78. Guthrie, *Woody Sez* (New York: Grosset and Dunlap, 1975), 71.

79. Guthrie, "Curly-Headed Baby." Typed manuscript of "War Songs Are Work Songs." ALC, AFC 2004/004, Woody Guthrie Manuscripts, Box 33.02, Folder 16.

80. Guthrie, "Raise a Rukus Tonight." WGA, Songs 1, Box 2, Folder 23.

81. Guthrie to Marjorie Mazia, November 17, 1942. WGA, Woody Guthrie Correspondence, Series 1, Box 1, Folder 44.

82. Guthrie to Aliza Greenblatt, July 9, 1942, in *Pastures of Plenty,* 91.

83. Guthrie, "War Songs and Work Songs." WGA, Manuscripts 1, Box 3, Folder 22.

84. Guthrie, annotation to "Gonna Be a Blackout Tonight." WGP, Song Texts, Box 1, Folder 3.

85. Guthrie, "Better World A-Comin'," *Hard Travelin'*, Track 7.

86. Guthrie, "It Was Down in Old Pearl Harbor." WGA, Songs 1, Box 2, Folder 13.

87. Guthrie to Alan Lomax, June 7, 1942. WGA, Woody Guthrie Correspondence, Series 1, Box 1, Folder 39.

88. Guthrie, "You Fascists Bound to Lose," in typed manuscript of "War Songs Are Work Songs." ALC, AFC 2004/004, Woody Guthrie Manuscripts, Box 33.02, Folder 16.

89. Doerflinger quoted in Klein, *Woody Guthrie: A Life,* 262.

90. Guthrie to Marianne "Jolly" Smolens, January 12, 1951. BJOC.

91. Woody Guthrie, *Bound for Glory* (London: Penguin, 2004 [1943]), 188–89.

92. Ibid., 299.

93. Ibid., 26.

94. Ibid., 261.

95. Ibid., 261. In his lyrics, Seeger sings to FDR:

> I guess you know best, just where I can fight
> All I want to be is situated right
> To do the most damage.

Almanac Singers, "Dear Mr. President," on *Songs for Political Action,* Disc 4, Track 1.

96. Michael Denning, *The Cultural Front: The Laboring of American Culture in the Twentieth Century* (London: Verso, 1998 [1996]), 24.

97. Guthrie, "Gotta Keep 'Em Sailin.'" WGMC, AFC1940/004, Box 1, Folder 15 ("Wartime Songs, 1940–42 and undated"); Guthrie, "What Are We Waiting On?" *Hard Travelin'*, Track 18; Guthrie, "Tear the Fascists Down," on Woody Guthrie, *My Dusty Road* (Rounder, 2009), Disc 3 (*Woody the Agitator*), Track 8.

98. Guthrie to Marjorie Mazia, n.d. (but January 1943). WGA, Woody Guthrie Correspondence, Series 1, Box 1, Folder 45.

99. Guthrie, "Open Up That Second Front Today." WGMC, AFC 1940/004. Box 1, Folder 15 ("Wartime Songs, 1940–42 and undated").

100. Guthrie, "Fightin' Sonofagun." WGA, Songs 1, Box 1, Folder 9.

101. Guthrie, "Ice in My Whiskers." WGMC, AFC 1940/004, Box 1, Folder 15 ("Wartime Songs, 1940–42 and undated").

102. Kazimiera Janina Cottam, "Lyudmila Pavlichenko," *Women in War and Resistance: Selected Biographies of Soviet Women Soldiers* (Newburyport, Mass.: Focus Publishing/R. Pullins, 1998), 208–13 (p. 208).

103. Guthrie, "Miss Pavlachenko." WGMC, AFC 1940/004, Box 1, Folder 15 ("Wartime Songs, 1940–42 and undated").

104. Guthrie, "So Long, It's Been Good to Know Yuh." WGP, Song Texts, Box 1, Folder 7.

105. Guthrie, annotation to "Ice in My Whiskers." WGMC, AFC 1940/004, Box 1, Folder 15 ("Wartime Songs, 1940–42 and undated").

106. Guthrie, "Ballad of Teheran." WGA, Songs 1, Box 1, Folder 2.

107. Guthrie to Marjorie Mazia, January 25, 1943. WGA, Woody Guthrie Correspondence, Series 1, Box 1, Folder 45.

108. Guthrie quoted in Jim Longhi, *Woody, Cisco and Me: With Woody Guthrie in the Merchant Marine* (New York: ibooks, 2004 [1997]), 110.

109. Guthrie, "All You Fonies." WGP, Song Texts, Box 1, Folder 1.

110. Guthrie, "Talking Sailor Blues," on Guthrie, *Hard Travelin'*, Track 7.

111. Guthrie, "Postage Stamp." WGA, Manuscripts 1, Box 4, Folder 6.

112. Guthrie, "People's Songs and Its People." WGA, Manuscripts 1, Box 4, Folder 25.

113. Guthrie to Pete and Toshi Seeger, October 30, 1943. WGA, Woody Guthrie Correspondence, Series 1, Box 3, Folder 23.

114. Guthrie to Marjorie Mazia, January 20, 1944. WGA, Woody Guthrie Correspondence, Series 1, Box 1, Folder 49.

115. Guthrie, annotation to "Born to Win." WGA, Songs 1, Box 1, Folder 4.

116. Guthrie, "Born to Win." WGA, Songs 1, Box 1, Folder 4.

117. Guthrie, "War Songs and Work Songs." WGA, Manuscripts 1, Box 3, Folder 22.

118. Guthrie to Marjorie Mazia, n.d. (but July 1944). WGA, Woody Guthrie Correspondence, Series 1, Box 1, Folder 50.

119. Guthrie to "Dear Friends" at an unnamed magazine, July 18, 1944. WGA, Manuscripts 1, Box 4, Folder 6.

120. Guthrie, "America Singing," *New York Times,* April 4, 1943, reprinted in *Pastures of Plenty,* 115.

121. *The Martins and the Coys,* the Alan Lomax Collection (Rounder CD, 2000).

122. Guthrie, "WNEW," in Guthrie, *Born to Win,* 224.

123. Ibid., 224–25.

124. Guthrie, "Sicily Will Rise from Its Ruins," unpublished essay for the *Daily Worker,* reprinted in *Pastures of Plenty,* 134.

125. Guthrie, "Ninety Mile Wind." WGA, Songs 1, Box 2, Folder 19.

126. Guthrie, "Sicily Will Rise from Its Ruins," *Pastures of Plenty,* 135.

127. Guthrie, "I'll Fight." WGA, Songs 1, Box 2, Folder 12.

128. Guthrie quoted in Klein, *Woody Guthrie: A Life,* 294.

129. Browder quoted in Maurice Isserman, *Which Side Were You On? The American Communist Party during the Second World War* (Champaign: University of Illinois Press, 1993), 1–2.

130. Guthrie to Will and Herta Geer, November 12, 1944. WGA, Woody Guthrie Correspondence, Series 1, Box 1, Folder 18.

131. Record inscription "to Mary and Teeny and Sue and Bill and to Everybody that Hears it!" from "Woody and Marjorie and Cathy and Coney Island," November 8, 1944. BJOC.

132. The Union Boys had only one recording session, on March 11, 1944. See Ronald D. Cohen and Dave Samuelson, "The Union Boys Sessionography," in their companion text to *Songs for Political Action,* 103. Guthrie's songs were "Sally, Don't You Grieve" and "All You Fascists Bound to Lose."

133. Guthrie, "Songs for Victory: music for political action." WGA, Manuscripts 1, Box 4, Folder 8.

134. Ibid.

135. David Caute, *The Great Fear: The Anti-Communist Purge under Truman and Eisenhower* (New York: Simon and Schuster, 1978); Lillian Hellman, *Scoundrel Time* (Boston: Little Brown, 1976).

Chapter 5: Lonesome Radical Soul

1. Guthrie's copy of Vernon Louis Parrington, *Main Currents in American Thought* (New York: Harcourt, Brace, 1930), 1:209. Woody Guthrie Collection, Center for Folklife and Cultural Heritage, Smithsonian Institution.

2. Guthrie, "This Morning I Am Born Again" (revised version), in Guthrie, *Pastures of Plenty,* ed. Dave Marsh and Harold Leventhal (New York: HarperPerennial, 1990), 141.

3. Woody Guthrie, *Struggle: American Documentary, Vol. 1* (Asch Recordings, 1945); re-released as *Struggle* (Smithsonian Folkways, 1998).

4. Guthrie quoted in Joe Klein, *Woody Guthrie: A Life* (New York: Delta, 1999 [1980]), 300.

5. Guthrie quoted in Klein, *Woody Guthrie: A Life,* 303.

6. Guthrie, "Union Labor or Slave Labor." WGA, Manuscripts 1, Box 4, Folder 16.

7. Guthrie to Sophie Maslow and Ben (Max) Blatt, August 21, 1945. BJOC.

8. Guthrie quoted in Klein, *Woody Guthrie: A Life,* 309.

9. Guthrie to Alan Lomax, October 14, 1945. ALC, AFC 2004/04. Box 33.02, Folder 02.

10. Guthrie quoted in Klein, *Woody Guthrie: A Life,* 310.

11. Guthrie to Sophie Maslow and Ben (Max) Blatt, August 21, 1945. BJOC.

12. Guthrie to Moses Asch and Marian Distler, July 4, 1945. BJOC.

13. Guthrie to Alan Lomax, October 14, 1945. ALC, AFC 2004/004. Box 33.02, Folder 02.

14. Guthrie to Sophie Maslow and Ben (Max) Blatt, November 5, 1945. BJOC.

15. Guthrie to Alan Lomax, October 14, 1945. ALC, AFC 2004/004. Box 33.02, Folder 02.

16. Guthrie to "Moe, Marian, Harris, and all," June 17, 1945. WGP, Correspondence: By and about Woody Guthrie. Box 4, Folder 1/5.

17. Guthrie, "What Kind of Bomb?" WGA, Songs 1, Box 3, Folder 30.

18. Guthrie, "Freedom Fire." WGP, Song Texts, Box 1, Folder 3.

19. John Dos Passos, *U.S.A.* (New York: Literary Classics of the United States, 1996 [1936]), 1157.

20. Katherine Anne Porter, *The Never-Ending Wrong* (Boston: Little, Brown, 1977). On August 23, 1977, Massachusetts governor Michael Dukakis issued an official proclamation declaring that "any stigma and disgrace should be forever removed from the names of Nicola Sacco and Bartolomeo Vanzetti." Dukakis quoted in Bruce Watson, *Sacco and Vanzetti: The Men, the Murders, and the Judgment of Mankind* (New York: Penguin, 2008), 365.

21. Thayer quoted in Watson, *Sacco and Vanzetti,* 252.

22. Thayer quoted in Nicholas N. Kittrie and Eldon D. Wedlock Jr., eds., *The Tree of Liberty: A Documentary History of Rebellion and Political Crime in America* (Baltimore: Johns Hopkins University Press, 1998), 543.

23. Kurt Vonnegut, *Jailbird* (New York: Delta, 1999 [1979]), 235.

24. Guthrie, "To Give Your Heart Ease." WGP, Song Texts, Box 1, Folder 8.

25. Guthrie, comments on Sacco and Vanzetti project, May 10, 1960. CD number 569: Reel to Reel Transfers, Track 16. Ralph Rinzler Archives, Center for Folklife and Culture Heritage, Smithsonian Institution.

26. Guthrie quoted in Klein, *Woody Guthrie: A Life,* 327.

27. Guthrie quoted in ibid.

28. Guthrie, "The Flood and the Storm," *Ballads of Sacco and Vanzetti* (Smithsonian Folkways Recordings, 1996), Track 1.

29. Guthrie, "Vanzetti's Rock," ibid., Track 8.

30. Guthrie, "Old Judge Thayer," ibid., Track 7.

31. Guthrie, "Two Good Men," ibid., Track 2.

32. Woody Guthrie, *Ballads of Sacco and Vanzetti* (Folkways FH5485, 1964).

33. Guthrie, daybook entry for November 3, 1942, in *Pastures of Plenty*, 95.

34. Guthrie to Moses Asch and Marian Distler, January 2, 1946. WGP, Correspondence: By and about Woody Guthrie, Box 4, Folder 1/5.

35. Ibid.

36. Guthrie to Harry St. Amand, July 10, 1947. BJOC.

37. Guthrie, "Singing High Balladree." WGA, Manuscripts 1, Box 4, Folder 46.

38. Guthrie, "On Ballad Singers." WGA, Manuscripts 1, Box 4, Folder 26.

39. Guthrie, "Join that A.F. of L." WGA, Songs 1, Box 2, Folder 14.

40. Guthrie to Moses Asch and Marian Ditsler, n.d. WGA, Woody Guthrie Correspondence, Series 1, Box 1 Folder 6.

41. Guthrie, "Singing High Balladree."

42. Ibid.

43. Guthrie, "On Ballad Singers."

44. Guthrie quoted in Robbie Lieberman, *"My Song Is My Weapon": People's Songs, American Communism, and the Politics of Culture, 1930–50* (Urbana and Chicago: University of Illinois Press, 1995), 78.

45. Guthrie quoted in Mike Quin, "Coast to Coast," *Sunday Worker*, January 4, 1942, Section 2, 4.

46. Mario "Boots" Casetta quoted in David K. Dunaway, *How Can I Keep from Singing? The Ballad of Pete Seeger* (New York: Villard Books, 2008 [1981]), 127.

47. Seeger quoted in Lieberman, *"My Song Is My Weapon,"* 62.

48. Seeger, "Foreword," in *Reprints from the People's Songs Bulletin, 1946–1949*, ed. Irwin Silber (New York: Oak Publications, 1961), 3.

49. Seeger quoted in Guthrie, "Peoples Songs and Its People." WGA, Manuscripts 1, Box 4, Folder 25.

50. Seeger, "Foreword," 3.

51. Seeger quoted in Guthrie, "Peoples Songs and Its People."

52. Seeger, "Foreword," 3.

53. Seeger quoted in Dunaway, *How Can I Keep from Singing?*,134.

54. Dunaway, *How Can I Keep from Singing?*, 143–44.

55. Seeger, "Whatever Happened to Singing in the Unions?" *Sing Out!* 15:2 (May 1965): 28–31 (p. 29).

56. Richard Reuss with JoAnne C. Reuss, *American Folk Music and Left-Wing Politics, 1927–1957* (Lanham, Md.: Scarecrow Press, 2000), 244.

57. Seeger quoted in Ed Cray, *Ramblin' Man: The Life and Times of Woody Guthrie* (New York: Norton, 2004), 293.

58. *Reprints from the People's Songs Bulletin*, 1.

59. Ibid.

60. Ibid.

61. Seeger, "People's Songs and Singers," *New Masses*, July 16, 1946, 9.

62. R. Serge Denisoff, *Great Day Coming: Folk Music and the American Left* (Baltimore:

Penguin, 1973), 102. The People's Songs Library collection is now housed in the Walter P. Reuther Library of Labor and Urban Affairs at Wayne State University, Detroit. The inventory is available online at http://www.reuther.wayne.edu/files/LR000452.pdf.

63. Ibid., 103.

64. Guthrie, "Peoples Songs and Its People."

65. Guthrie, "Singing High Balladree."

66. Guthrie, "On Ballad Singers."

67. Guthrie, *Pastures of Plenty*, 174.

68. Almanac Singers, "All I Want," on *Songs for Political Action: Folk Music, Topical Songs and the American Left, 1926–1953*, comp. Ronald D. Cohen and Dave Samuelson (Bear Family Records, 1996), Disc 3, Track 13.

69. Guthrie, annotation to "I'm Out to Get." WGA, Songs 1, Box 2, Folder 13.

70. Guthrie, "I'm Out to Get." WGA, Songs 1, Box 2, Folder 13. Jim Garland recalled: "Woody Guthrie told me he didn't like my song, 'I Don't Want Your Millions, Mister,' saying that indeed he did want that money. But we can make money out of rattails. If the corporations could just be satisfied with the wealth they have thus far accumulated, I would let them keep it. I just ask that they don't take what working people will create from here on out in new wealth." Jim Garland, *Welcome the Traveler Home: Jim Garland's Story of the Kentucky Mountains*, ed. Julia S. Ardery (Lexington: University Press of Kentucky, 1983), 201.

71. Murray quoted in Robert H. Zieger, *The CIO, 1935–1955* (Chapel Hill: University of North Carolina Press, 1997), 270.

72. Guthrie, "Union Train." WGA, Songs 1, Box 3, Folder 28.

73. Guthrie to Moses Asch, July 15, 1946. WGA, Woody Guthrie Correspondence, Series 1, Box 1, Folder 6.

74. Guthrie, "The Debt I Owe," *Pastures of Plenty*, 86.

75. Guthrie, "Revolutionary Mind." WGP, Song Texts, Box 1, Folder 7.

76. Guthrie to Moses Asch, July 15, 1946. WGA, Woody Guthrie Correspondence, Series 1, Box 1, Folder 6.

77. Ibid.

78. Ibid.

79. Guthrie, *Pastures of Plenty*, 200.

80. Guthrie, "Singing High Balladree." The feeling was mutual as far as Josh White was concerned: "Woody Guthrie and I came up together. Let's face it. He's got his bag, and it's a great bag he's in." White quoted in Elijah Wald, *Josh White: Society Blues* (London: Routledge, 2002), 264. "'He had a chip on his shoulder,' Ives would later say. 'His mind worked so fast that you couldn't keep up with him, and sometimes I just felt like decking him, but Woody was so small and delicate that it just didn't seem fair.'" Klein, *Woody Guthrie: A Life*, 137.

81. Guthrie, "On Ballad Singers."

82. Guthrie, annotation to "What Shall It Profit a Man." WGP, Song Texts, Box 1, Folder 9.

83. Guthrie to Moses Asch, July 15, 1946.

84. Henry A. Wallace quoted in J. Samuel Walker, *Henry A. Wallace and American Foreign Policy* (Westport, Conn.: Greenwood Press, 1976), 168.

85. Truman Doctrine quoted in Howard Jones, *"A New Kind of War": America's Global*

Strategy and the Truman Doctrine in Greece (New York: Oxford University Press USA, 1997), 43.

86. Guthrie, "Talking News Blues," in Guthrie, *New Found Land,* typed manuscript, ALC, AFC 2004/004, Woody Guthrie Manuscripts, Box 33.02, Folder 20.

87. Churchill quoted in Martin Gilbert, *Winston S. Churchill: The Prophet of Truth, 1922–1939* (New York: Houghton Mifflin, 1977), 618.

88. Guthrie, annotation to "Go and Leave Me." WGP, Song Texts, Box 1, Folder 3.

89. Guthrie quoted in Klein, *Woody Guthrie: A Life,* 332.

90. Guthrie quoted in ibid.

91. Guthrie to Moses Asch, n.d. (but probably 1947). WGA, Woody Guthrie Correspondence, Series 1, Box 1, Folder 8.

92. Conversation quoted in Cray, *Ramblin' Man,* 307n.

93. Vivian Howard quoted in Denisoff, *Great Day Coming,* 14.

94. Guthrie to "People's Songs and People's Artists, Both . . . ," April 16, 1948. WGA, Woody Guthrie Correspondence, Series 1, Box 3, Folder 18.

95. Ibid.

96. Guthrie to Pete Seeger, May 1, 1948. WGA, Woody Guthrie Correspondence, Series 1, Box 3, Folder 24.

97. See Dunaway, *How Can I Keep from Singing?,* 139, and Denisoff, *Great Day Coming,* 107.

98. Guthrie to People's Songs, July 24, 1948. WGA, Woody Guthrie Correspondence, Series 1, Box 3, Folder 18.

99. Guthrie, "Union's My Religion." WGA, Songs 1, Box 3, Folder 28.

100. Guthrie, "Union Labor or Slave Labor." WGA, Manuscripts, Box 4, Folder 16.

101. Guthrie, "Hills of Ithica [*sic*]." WGA, Songs 1, Box 1, Folder 11.

102. Guthrie, "His Name Was Harry Simms." WGA, Songs 1, Box 1, Folder 11.

103. E. Y. Harburg and Fred Saidy, *Finian's Rainbow: A Musical Satire* (New York: Random House, 1946), 21–22.

104. Seeger, "Foreword," *Reprints from the People's Songs Bulletin,"* 3.

105. Guthrie to Moses Asch, July 15, 1946.

106. Guthrie to "Asch Outfit," n.d. WGP, Correspondence: By and about Woody Guthrie. Box 4, Folder 1/5.

107. Guthrie quoted in Klein, *Woody Guthrie: A Life,* 330–31.

108. Guthrie to "Dear Peoples Singers," June 29, 1947. WGP, Correspondence: By and about Woody Guthrie. Box 4, Folder 2/5.

109. Guthrie to John A. Lomax, March 6, 1947. ALC, AFC 2004/04, Woody Guthrie and Carl Sandburg Correspondence, Box 33.02.

110. Guthrie to "Dear People's Singers."

111. Guthrie, "Mario Russo." WGP, Song Texts, Box 1, Folder 5.

112. Guthrie quoted in Klein, *Woody Guthrie: A Life,* 350.

113. Guthrie, "To F.D.R.," *Pastures of Plenty,* 186.

114. Guthrie, "Dear Mrs. Roosevelt," *Woody Guthrie Folk Songs* (New York: Ludlow Music, 1963), 249–50. "There is a discernable flow to Roosevelt's messages to Stalin. Roosevelt is determinedly friendly. He compliments, flatters, sometimes at Churchill's expense. As the war progresses and he distances himself from Churchill, he soothes Stalin, long-

distance." Susan Butler, "Introduction," *My Dear Mr. Stalin: The Complete Correspondence of Franklin D. Roosevelt and Joseph V. Stalin* (New Haven, Conn.: Yale University Press, 2005), 5. Roosevelt saw De Gaulle as "an apprentice dictator." See Olivier Wieviorka, *Normandy: The Landings to the Liberation of Paris,* trans. M. B. DeBevoise (Cambridge, Mass.: Harvard University Press, 2008), 301. FDR publicly called Chiang an "unconquerable man . . . of great vision [and] great courage," but—according to Joseph Stilwell—he said privately, "If you can't get along with Chiang . . . get rid of him once and for all. You know what I mean." FDR and Stilwell quoted in Jonathan Fenby, *Chiang Kai-Shek: China's Generalissimo and the Nation He Lost* (Cambridge, Mass.: Da Capo Press, 2005), 411, 412.

115. Guthrie, *Pastures of Plenty,* 173.

116. Guthrie, "Dance around My Atom Fire." WGP, Song Texts, Box 1, Folder 2.

117. Guthrie, "I'll Write My Name Down in Blood Red Blood." WGA, Songs 1, Box 2, Folder 12.

118. Tenney Committee quoted in Denisoff, *Great Day Coming,* 115–16.

119. Testimony of Senator Jack Tenney, *Investigation of Un-American Propaganda Activities in the United States: Hearings before the Committee of Un-American Activities, House of Representatives, Washington, D. C., March 24, 25, 26, 27, 28, 1947* (Washington, D.C.: United States Government Printing Office, 1947), 249.

120. United States House of Representatives, Committee on Un-American Activities, *Testimony of Walter S. Steele Regarding Communist Activity in the United States* (Washington, D.C.: United States Government Printing Office, 1947), 1, 38, 43, 48, 102.

121. Ibid., 112.

122. Richard Nixon quoted in Albrecht Betz, *Hanns Eisler: Political Musician,* trans. Bill Hopkins (Cambridge: Cambridge University Press, 2006), 199.

123. Hanns Eisler quoted in ibid., 207.

124. Woody Guthrie, "Eisler on the Go." WGA, Songs 1, Box 1, Folder 8. See also Billy Bragg and Wilco, *Mermaid Avenue,* Vol. 1 (Elektra Records, 1998), Track 12.

125. Guthrie, annotation to "I'll Write My Name Down in Blood Red Blood." WGA, Songs 1, Box 2, Folder 12.

126. Henry Luce and Henry Wallace quoted in John C. Culver and John Hyde, *American Dreamer: A Life of Henry A. Wallace* (New York: Norton, 2001), 277.

127. Culver and Hyde, *American Dreamer,* 409.

128. Alan Lomax on *Pete Seeger at 90* (radio documentary, prod. Vincent Dowd), BBC Radio 4, 2009.

129. The *Nation* quoted in Mario "Boots" Casetta, "How Did You Like the Singing at the Convention?," Progressive Party leaflet, RCC.

130. Casetta to "Shirl," August 19, 1948. Mario "Boots" Casetta file, RCC.

131. Seeger to "Dear Friends," August 7, 1948. RCC.

132. Seeger to Guthrie, August 23, 1948. Mario "Boots" Casetta file, RCC.

133. Guthrie, "Baking for Wallace." WGP, Song Texts, Box 1, Folder 1.

134. Guthrie, "Bet on Wallace." WGP, Song Texts, Box 1, Folder 1.

135. Guthrie, "Screwball Cannonball." WGP, Song Texts, Box 1, Folder 1.

136. Guthrie, "Farmer–Labor Train," on Woody Guthrie, *Hard Travelin': The Asch Recordings, Vol. 3* (Smithsonian Folkways Recordings, 1999), Track 2.

137. Guthrie, "Go Down and See." WGP, Song Texts, Box 1, Folder 3.

138. Guthrie, "Henry Wallace Man," People's Songs Library Collection, Walter P. Reuther Library of Labor and Urban Affairs, Wayne State University, Detroit. Copy in RCC.

139. Stewart Alsop quoted in Culver and Hyde, *American Dreamer,* 459.

140. Guthrie, "My Eyes Gonna Shine." WGA, Songs 1, Box 2, Folder 18.

141. "Arlo Davy Guthrie" to Natanya Newman, January 12, 1948. BJOC.

142. Guthrie, "I've Got to Know." WGP, Song Texts, Box 1, Folder 5.

143. Guthrie, "My Ideas about the Use of Peoples Songs in the Progressive Party Movement to Elect Henry Wallace and Glen Taylor." WGA, Manuscripts 1, Box 7, Folder 17.

144. Dunaway, *How Can I Keep from Singing?,* 150.

145. Seeger quoted in Ronald D. Cohen, *Work and Sing: A History of Occupational and Labor Union Songs in the United States* (Crockett, Calif.: Carquinez Press, 2010), 129.

146. Guthrie, "Quit Sending Your Inspectors," *The Live Wire Woody Guthrie* (Woody Guthrie Foundation, 2007), Track 13.

147. Guthrie, "Doorstep Baby." WGA, Songs 1, Box 1, Folder 7.

148. John Kenneth Galbraith, *The Affluent Society* (New York: Houghton Mifflin, 1998 [1958]), 52.

149. Guthrie to "Geo. W. [George Wilhelm], KGIL, Everybody," June 30, 1950. BJOC.

150. SAC, Los Angeles to Director, FBI, June 2 1950. Woodrow W. Guthrie FBI Files. WGA, Personal Papers Box 2, Folder 48.1.

151. Guthrie to "Geo. W. [George Wilhelm], KGIL, Everybody," June 30, 1950. BJOC.

Chapter 6: Long Road to Peekskill

1. Ed Cray, *Ramblin' Man: The Life and Times of Woody Guthrie* (New York: Norton, 2004), 8n.

2. "A week passed, presumably time enough for everyone to calm down. But then a mob burst into the jail one night—a mob composed of many of Okemah's finest citizens, including Charley Guthrie—and dragged Laura Nelson, her son, and her baby to the bridge over the Canadian River about six miles west of town, where she and Lawrence were lynched and the baby left crying helplessly by the side of the road. The Okemah *Ledger* reported the news rather huffily: 'It is generally thought the negroes got what would have been due them under due process of law.' The *Ledger* also published a grisly photo of the lynched bodies, which later was reprinted as a postcard and became a popular novelty item in local stores." Joe Klein, *Woody Guthrie: A Life* (New York: Delta, 1999 [1980]), 10.

3. Jorge Arévalo Mateus, "Beluthahatchee Blues: An Interview with Stetson Kennedy," in Chris Green, Rachel Rubin, and James Smethurst, eds., *Radicalism in the South since Reconstruction* (New York: Palgrave Macmillan, 2006), 211–26 (p. 216).

4. Guthrie in Alan Lomax, Woody Guthrie, and Pete Seeger, eds., *Hard Hitting Songs for Hard-Hit People* (New York: Oak Publications, 1967), 334.

5. Guthrie, "High Balladree," in Woody Guthrie, *Pastures of Plenty,* ed. Dave Marsh and Harold Leventhal (New York: HarperPerennial, 1990), 25.

6. Guthrie, *Woody Sez* (New York: Grosset and Dunlap, 1975), 166.

7. Guthrie, *Pastures of Plenty,* 37.

8. Guthrie, "Lost Train Blues," on Woody Guthrie, *Library of Congress Recordings* (Rounder CD, 1988), Disc 1, Track 1.

9. Guthrie, *Bound for Glory* (London: Penguin, 2004 [1943]), 63.

10. Guthrie, "Lost Train Blues," *Library of Congress Recordings,* Disc 1, Track 1.

11. Guthrie, "Railroad Blues," *Library of Congress Recordings,* Disc 1, Track 2.

12. Guthrie, "Little Liza Jane," KFVD Songbook, WGA Microfilm; Guthrie, "Kitty Wells," Songs of Woody Guthrie, WGMC, Box 2.

13. Guthrie, *Santa Monica Social Register Examine 'Er* (1937), WGA Microfilm.

14. Howell Terence to Woody Guthrie, October 20, 1937. WGA Microfilm.

15. Guthrie, draft introduction to *American Folksong.* WGP, Box 3, Folder 6.

16. Peter La Chapelle, *Proud to Be an Okie: Cultural Politics, Country Music, and Migration to Southern California* (Berkeley: University of California Press, 2007), 23.

17. Carey McWilliams, "California Pastoral," *Antioch Review* 2, no. 1 (March 1942): 103–21 (p.116).

18. Guthrie, "How Much, How Long?" *The Live Wire Woody Guthrie* (Woody Guthrie Foundation, 2007), Track 1.

19. Guthrie, *American Folksong,* ed. Moses Asch (New York: Oak Publications, 1961), 10.

20. Guthrie to Max Gordon, November 27, 1941. BJOC.

21. Guthrie, *Pastures of Plenty,* 78.

22. Guthrie to Max Gordon, November 27, 1941. BJOC.

23. Guthrie, annotation to "When the Curfew Blows." WGA, Songs 1, Box 3, Folder 30.

24. Pete Seeger quoted in David King Dunaway, *How Can I Keep from Singing? The Ballad of Pete Seeger* (New York: Villard Books, 2008 [1981]), 67.

25. Guthrie, "Low Levee Café." WGA, Manuscripts Box 4, Folder 55.

26. Guthrie, "War Songs and Work Songs." WGA, Manuscripts Box 3, Folder 22.

27. Guthrie to Marjorie Mazia, Jan 25 1943. WGA, Woody Guthrie Correspondence, Series 1, Box 1, Folder 45.

28. Seeger quoted in Cray, *Ramblin' Man,* 261.

29. Guthrie to Marjorie Mazia, n.d. (but January 1943). WGA, Woody Guthrie Correspondence, Series 1, Box 1, Folder 45.

30. Jim Longhi, *Woody, Cisco and Me: With Woody Guthrie in the Merchant Marine* (New York: ibooks, 2004 [1997]), 236.

31. Guthrie to "Moe, Marian, Harris, and all," June 17, 1945. WGP, Correspondence: By and about Woody Guthrie. Box 4, Folder 1/5.

32. Guthrie quoted in Cray, *Ramblin' Man,* 266.

33. Guthrie, *Seeds of Man* (New York: Pocket Books, 1977 [1976]), 197.

34. "The other races all have their troubles, but I would judge that the Mexicans catch the roughest end of it all. They are allowed to come in, make their trip north, and then are herded back out as aliens and undesireables every year as the birds fly; only the birds are lots more welcome and fed better." Guthrie to Moses Asch and Marian Distler, June 21, 1946. WGA, Woody Guthrie Correspondence, Series 1, Box 1, Folder 6.

35. Guthrie, *Seeds of Man,* 159.

36. Ibid., 206.

37. Klein, *Woody Guthrie: A Life,* 11.

38. Guthrie, "How Much, How Long?" *The Live Wire Woody Guthrie,* Track 1.

39. Guthrie, annotation to "Oklahoma Hills," dated "March, 1951." BJOC.

40. Charley Guthrie quoted in Klein, *Woody Guthrie: A Life,* 12.

41. Nora Guthrie maintains: "I don't think he ever heard the word 'That's racism,' until he heard it from Will Geer." Again: "It was Lead Belly . . . who really educated him mentally and emotionally and psychologically about the black movement and about oppression." Nora Guthrie quoted in Mark Allan Jackson, *Prophet Singer: The Voice and Vision of Woody Guthrie* (Jackson: University Press of Mississippi, 2007), 139, 140.

42. Guthrie, "Madonna on the Curb." WGA, Songs 1, Box 2, Folder 17. See also Jonatha Brooke, *The Works* (Bad Dog Records, 2008), Track 5.

43. The *New York Age,* July 27, 1946, quoted in Martha Biondi, *To Stand and Fight: The Struggle for Civil Rights in Postwar New York City* (Cambridge, Mass.: Harvard University Press, 2006), 61.

44. Guthrie, annotation to "The Blinding of Isaac Woodward" [*sic*]. WGP, Song Texts, Box 1, Folder 1.

45. Biondi, *To Stand and Fight,* 67.

46. Guthrie, "The Blinding of Isaac Woodward." WGP, Song Texts, Box 1, Folder 1.

47. Biondi, *To Stand and Fight,* 62.

48. Guthrie, "The Ferguson Brothers' Killing," in John Greenway, *American Folksongs of Protest* (New York: A. S. Barnes, 1953), 118.

49. Carol Elaine Anderson, *Eyes off the Prize: The United Nations and the African American Struggle for Human Rights, 1944–1955* (New York: Cambridge University Press, 2003), 160.

50. W. E. B. Du Bois, *Against Racism: Unpublished Essays, Papers, Addresses, 1887–1961,* ed. Herbert Aptheker (Amherst: University of Massachusetts Press, 1985), 265. "Because Ingram was a black-woman-sharecropper in Georgia, no less, the State Department believed that this was a tailor-made case for the Soviet propaganda mill and that there was a 'likelihood that the USSR may raise the Ingram case in the General Assembly.'" Anderson, *Eyes off the Prize,* 160.

51. Guthrie, "The Ballad of Rosa Lee Ingram." WGP, Song Texts, Box 1, Folder 1.

52. "The trail at Dachau condemned Ilse Koch to life imprisonment (she was spared the death penalty because, however improbably, she had gotten pregnant while in her cell). A year later, in 1948, her sentence was reduced by American Army officials to a four-year term, occasioning a spasm of outrage in the United States. (The stated reason for the reduction was that the prosecution of Koch had relied too heavily upon hearsay . . .)." Lawrence Douglas, "The Shrunken Head of Buchenwald: Icons of Atrocity at Nuremburg," *Representations,* no. 63 (Summer 1998): 39–64 (pp. 62–63n75).

53. Guthrie, "Ilsa Koch." WGA, Songs 1, Box 2, Folder 12.

54. Guthrie, "Lucius Clay & Ilsa Koch," *Pastures of Plenty,* 214.

55. Unidentified London newspaper quoted in Gerald Tomlinson, *Murdered in Jersey* (Piscataway: Rutgers University Press, 1994), 76.

56. Dashiell Hammett, "Public Letter," March 1, 1949, reprinted in *Selected Letters of Dashiell Hammett, 1921–1960,* ed. Richard Layman with Julie M. Rivett (Washington, D.C.: Counterpoint, 2002), 507. "In June 1949 the New Jersey State Supreme Court ordered a new trial, and four of the Trenton Six were found not guilty in 1951. A second successful

Notes to Pages 157–65

appeal on behalf of the two found guilty in 1951 led to a third trial at which one of the remaining accused was found not guilty. The other defendant died of a heart attack before the third trial." Hammett, 508n1.

57. Guthrie, "Trenton Frameup." WGP, Song Texts, Box 1, Folder 8.

58. Guthrie, "Buoy Bells for Trenton," in *Woody Guthrie Folk Songs* (New York: Ludlow Music, 1963), 165.

59. Guthrie, "Blues," *Pastures of Plenty*, 207.

60. Guthrie to "Disc Co of America," December 9, 1946. WGP, Correspondence: By and about Woody Guthrie, Box 4, Folder 1/5.

61. Guthrie, "Harriet Tubman's Ballad," on Woody Guthrie, *Long Ways to Travel: The Unreleased Folkways Masters, 1944–1949* (Smithsonian Folkways, 1994), Track 4.

62. Guthrie to Harry St. Amand, July 10, 1947. BJOC.

63. Guthrie, "Bloody Run." WGA, Manuscripts Box 7, Folder 9.

64. Paul Robeson, *Paul Robeson Speaks* (New York: Citadel Press, 1978), 209.

65. Ibid., 147.

66. Howard Fast, *Peekskill: USA* (New York: Civil Rights Congress, 1951), 33.

67. Robeson, *Paul Robeson Speaks*, 234.

68. Fast, *Peekskill: USA*, 83.

69. Howard Fast, *Being Red: A Memoir* (Armonk, N.Y.: M. E. Sharpe, 1994), 238.

70. Seeger quoted in Dunaway, *How Can I Keep from Singing?*, xxx.

71. Mario "Boots" Casetta quoted in ibid., 13–14.

72. Lee Hays, *Sing Out, Warning! Sing Out, Love: The Writings of Lee Hays*, ed. Robert S. Koppelman (Amherst: University of Massachusetts Press, 2004), 97.

73. Lee Hays quoted in Steve Courtney, "So Long to Lee Hays," *North County News* (Yorktown Heights, N.Y.), 2–8 September, 1981. Online at http://www.bencourtney.com/hays.

74. Hays, *Sing Out, Warning!*, 98–99.

75. Guthrie, "Peekskill Klookluk Blues." WGA, Songs 1, Box 2, Folder 21.

76. Guthrie, "P for Peekskill." WGA, Songs 1, Box 2, Folder 21.

77. Guthrie, "Peekskill Golfing Grounds." WGA, Songs 1, Box 2, Folder 21.

78. Guthrie in Alan Lomax, Woody Guthrie, and Pete Seeger, eds., *Hard Hitting Songs for Hard-Hit People* (New York: Oak Publications, 1967), 116.

79. Guthrie, "Letter to Peekskillers." WGA, Songs 1, Box 2, Folder 16.

80. See Billy Bragg and Wilco, "My Thirty Thousand," on *Way Over Yonder in the Minor Key* (Rhino/Elektra, 2006), Track 2.

81. Guthrie, "My Thirty Thousand." WGA, Songs 1, Box 2, Folder 18.

82. Eleanor Roosevelt, "My Day," September 7, 1949. Online at the Eleanor Roosevelt Papers Project, George Washington University, http://www.gwu.edu/~erpapers/myday/displaydoc.cfm?_y=1949&_f=md001378.

83. Lee Hays quoted in Ronald D. Cohen, *Rainbow Quest: The Folk Music Revival and American Society, 1940–1970* (Amherst: University of Massachusetts Press, 2000), 63.

84. William L. Patterson, Introduction to Fast, *Peekskill: USA*, 7.

85. Howard Fast and the Weavers, "The Peekskill Story," *Songs for Political Action*, Disc 8, Track 22.

Chapter 7: The Last Free Place in America

1. Woody Guthrie "Come When I Call You." WGA, Songs 1, Box 1, Folder 5. See also the Klezmatics, *Wonder Wheel* (Jewish Music Group, 2006), Track 1.

2. Guthrie to Harry Truman, July 31, 1949. WGA, Woody Guthrie Correspondence, Series 1, Box 3, Folder 27.

3. Guthrie to Attorney General Thomas C. Clark, 12 January 1949. WGA, Woody Guthrie Correspondence, Series 1, Box 1, Folder 11.

4. Ibid.

5. Guthrie, "Shy Yang Kye Check." WGA, Songs 1, Box 3, Folder 24.

6. Guthrie, "I Don't Like Your 'Lantic Pact." WGA, Songs 1, Box 2, Folder 12.

7. Guthrie, "UN Building Song." WGA, Songs 1, Box 3, Folder 28.

8. Guthrie to Moses Asch, August 26, 1953. WGA, Woody Guthrie Correspondence, Series 1, Box 1, Folder 9.

9. Kennedy quoted in Margaret Anne Bulger, "Stetson Kennedy: Applied Folklore and Cultural Advocacy" (PhD dissertation, University of Pennsylvania, 1992), 266.

10. Guthrie to Stetson Kennedy, August 15, 1950. WGA, Woody Guthrie Correspondence, Series 1, Box 1, Folder 32.

11. Guthrie, "Kennedy, He's That Man," quoted in Bulger, 263.

12. Guthrie, "Stetson Kennedy," quoted in ibid. See also Billy Bragg and Wilco, *Mermaid Avenue*, Vol. 2 (Elektra Records, 2000), Track 7.

13. Guthrie to Stetson Kennedy, August 15, 1950. WGA, Woody Guthrie Correspondence, Series 1, Box 1, Folder 32.

14. Ibid.

15. Guthrie quoted in Ed Cray, *Ramblin' Man: The Life and Times of Woody Guthrie* (New York: Norton, 2004), 337.

16. Emrich quoted in David K. Dunaway, *How Can I Keep From Singing? The Ballad of Pete Seeger* (New York: Villard Books, 2008 [1981]), 155.

17. Jay Russell, "How the Weavers Break Night Club Ice," *Daily Compass*, January 27, 1950, 20.

18. Guthrie to Marianne "Jolly" Smolens, January 12, 1951, BJOC. In 1954 Smolens would give birth to the future disco singer, Vicki Sue Robinson.

19. "Sis" Cunningham quoted in Cray, *Ramblin' Man*, 448n.

20. Guthrie to Marianne "Jolly" Smolens, January 12, 1951. BJOC.

21. Guthrie to Marianne "Jolly" Smolens, January 22, 1951. BJOC.

22. Guthrie to Marianne "Jolly" Smolens, March 31, 1951. BJOC.

23. "Guthrie, at the first alarm, tumbled from his hammock. In his excitement he dashed across the hot coals in the barbeque pit, Springfield in hand, to blaze away at the marauding night riders." Cray, *Ramblin' Man,* 343–44. Klein maintains that the "attack" was a practical joke on Guthrie staged by Kennedy and his friend, Gerald Hart. Joe Klein, *Woody Guthrie: A Life* (New York: Delta, 1999 [1980]), 383.

24. Klein, Woody Guthrie: A Life, 379. "I feel slowly better every day I steer away clear from alcohol But I sure do take some dizzy spells of craving it several times a day." Guthrie to Ken Lindsay, September 30, 1952. AFC, AFC 2005/06, Ken Lindsay Collection of Woody Guthrie Correspondence, Folder 18.

25. Guthrie to Ken Lindsay, September 31, 1952. AFC, AFC 2005/06, Ken Lindsay Collection of Woody Guthrie Correspondence, Folder 20.

26. Ritter quoted in Richard A. Reuss with JoAnne C. Reuss, *American Folk Music and Left-Wing Politics, 1927–1957* (Lanham, Md.: Scarecrow Press, 2000), 253.

27. Two dates have been given for Guthrie's final recording session. Guy Logsdon cites the Decca recording session of January 7, 1952: "The Decca recordings were not and should not be issued, for the debilitating symptoms of Huntington's disease are evident in his enunciation." Guy Logsdon, Introduction to *Long Ways to Travel*, 3. Jeff Place refers to a final Asch session of January 18, 1954 with Guthrie, Sonny Terry, Brownie McGhee, Jack Elliott, and Alonzo Scales: "The disease is apparent in Woody's voice, a situation not helped by the drinking going on in the studio." Jeff Place, "Woody Guthrie's Recorded Legacy," in Robert Santelli and Emily Davidson, eds., *Hard Travellin': The Life and Legacy of Woody Guthrie* (Hanover, N.H.: Wesleyan University Press, 1999), 57–68 (p. 67).

28. Guthrie quoted in Cray, *Ramblin' Man*, 345.

29. Matusow quoted in Cray, *Ramblin' Man*, 346.

30. Harvey Matusow, *False Witness* (New York: Cameron and Kahn, 1955). See also Robert M. Lichtman and Ronald Cohen, *Deadly Farce: Harvey Matusow and the Informer System in the McCarthy Era* (Urbana and Chicago: University of Illinois Press, 2004).

31. Matusow quoted in Cray, *Ramblin' Man*, 346.

32. Matusow in *Communist Activities among Youth Groups (Based on Testimony of Harvey M. Matusow). Hearings before the Committee on Un-American Activities, House of Representatives, Eighty-Second Congress, Second Session, February 6 and 7, 1952.* (Washington, D.C.: United States Government Printing Office, 1952), 3288, 3289. Copy held in BJOC.

33. Josh White, "I Was a Sucker for the Communists," *Negro Digest* (December 1950): 26–31.

34. Brand appeared only in private session, and has always maintained that he never cooperated with the HUAC, citing his hatred of blacklisting "by both the left and the right." However, as he declared: "When it was demonstrated that my anti-Communism predated that of most of the blacklisters, the doors were again opened to me." Oscar Brand, *The Ballad Mongers: Rise of the Modern Folk Song* (New York: Minerva Press, 1962), 135, 137.

35. Seeger in *Investigation of Communist Activities, New York Area—Part VII (Entertainment), Hearings before the Committee on Un-American Activities, House of Representatives, Eighty-Fourth Congress, First Session, August 17 and 18, 1955* (Washington, D.C.: United States Government Printing Office, 1955), 2449.

36. Ibid., 2456.

37. Ibid., 2449.

38. Guthrie to Seeger, September 27, 1952. WGA, Woody Guthrie Correspondence, Series 1, Box 3, Folder 24.

39. Guthrie to Harry St. Amand, July 10, 1947. BJOC.

40. Guthrie to Pete Seeger, n.d. WGA, Woody Guthrie Correspondence, Series 1, Box 3, Folder 24.

41. "Chorea is the most frequent movement problem seen in Huntington's Disease. Chorea is not the only movement disorder that can be recognized, and as the emotional and behavioural aspects can be more of a difficulty for the patient and the family, the

term 'Huntington's Disease' has become fashionable in recent times." Oliver W. J. Quarrell, *Huntington's Disease: The Facts* (New York: Oxford University Press USA, 2008), 2.

42. Guthrie quoted in Klein, *Woody Guthrie: A Life,* 404.

43. Guthrie, "B W Breakdown," *Pastures of Plenty,* 240.

44. Guthrie, "Psykoe Raver," *Pastures of Plenty,* 243.

45. Guthrie quoted in Pete Seeger, *The Incompleat Folksinger* (New York: Simon and Schuster, 1972), 49.

46. Guthrie, "My Hootenanny." WGP, Correspondence: By and about Woody Guthrie, Box 4, Folder 3/5.

47. Guthrie to Moses Asch, December 12, 1953. WGA, Woody Guthrie Correspondence, Series 1, Box 1, Folder 9.

48. Guthrie to Moses Asch and Marian Distler, December 15, 1953. BJOC.

49. Guthrie to Moses Asch, May 27, 1953. WGA, Woody Guthrie Correspondence, Series 1, Box 1, Folder 9.

50. Guthrie to Mike Gold, June 1, 1953. WGA, Woody Guthrie Correspondence, Series 1, Box 1, Folder 21.

51. Guthrie to Alan Lomax, April 1953 (no date specified). ALC, AFC 2004/004, Woody Guthrie and Carl Sandburg Correspondence, Box 33.02.

52. Guthrie to Ken Lindsay, September 16, 1953. AFC, AFC 2005/06, Ken Lindsay Collection of Woody Guthrie Correspondence, Folder 29.

53. R. Serge Denisoff, *Sing a Song of Social Significance* (Bowling Green, Ky.: Bowling Green State University Popular Press, 1983), 42.

54. John Greenway, *American Folksongs of Protest* (New York: A. S. Barnes, 1953), 4, 6.

55. Ibid., 275.

56. Ibid., 287.

57. Ibid., 288. Greenway and Guthrie had begun to collaborate on a performance program titled "Songs of Struggle and Protest," with a cast of characters including "Woody," "Sonny Terry," "Negro Lady," and "Anny." Script deposited in WGA, Manuscripts 2, Box 1, Folder 28.

58. Seeger to Josh Dunson, n. d. Letter in "Sis" Cunningham papers, RCC.

59. Guthrie, "The Atom and Me," reprinted in *Pastures of Plenty,* 245.

60. Guthrie, "Cussss sin Skabby Song." WGA, Songs 1, Box 1, Folder 5.

61. Leadbelly, "The Titanic," on Leadbelly, *The Titanic,* Vol. 4 (Rounder, 1994), Track 13.

62. Guthrie, "Tytanick." WGA, Songs 1, Box 3, Folder 27.

63. Guthrie, "Sad Ship." WGA, Songs 1, Box 3, Folder 24.

64. Guthrie, "I'm Goin ta Git." WGA, Songs 1, Box 2, Folder 13.

65. Woodrow W. Guthrie FBI Files. WGA, Personal Papers, Box 2, Folder 48.1.

66. Guthrie quoted in Cray, *Ramblin' Man,* 378.

67. Guthrie to Seeger, n.d. (but 1956). WGA, Woody Guthrie Correspondence, Series 1, Box 3, Folder 24.

68. Guthrie quoted in Klein, *Woody Guthrie: A Life,* 436.

Conclusion: The Miners and the Mill

The phrase used for the title of this chapter is borrowed from David Dunaway, who writes: "Woody was awfully rich ore, but without the miner and the mill, many would never have seen the gold." David K. Dunaway, *How Can I Keep from Singing? The Ballad of Pete Seeger* (New York: Villard Books, 2008 [1981]), 73.

1. Sid Gleason to Bob Brough, August 17, 1960. Letter courtesy of Bob Brough.

2. Nora Guthrie in *The Ballad of Ramblin' Jack*, dir. Aiyana Elliot (Plantain Films, 2000).

3. Elliott quoted in Ed Cray, *Ramblin' Man: The Life and Times of Woody Guthrie* (New York: Norton, 2004), 142.

4. Guthrie to Harry St. Amand, June 5, 1946. BJOC.

5. Guthrie quoted in Joe Klein, *Woody Guthrie: A Life* (New York: Delta, 1999 [1980]), 381.

6. Nora Guthrie quoted in Cray, *Ramblin' Man*, 384.

7. Seeger, "An Introductory Note about the Man and His Music," in Millard Lampell, Irwin Silber, et al., eds., *California to the New York Island* (New York: Guthrie Children's Trust Fund, 1960), 4.

8. Hank Reineke, *Ramblin' Jack Elliott: The Never-Ending Highway* (Lanham, Md.: Scarecrow Press, 2010), 36.

9. Eric Von Schmidt quoted in ibid., 33.

10. Jack Elliott quoted in ibid., 40.

11. Pete Frame, *The Restless Generation: How Rock Music Changed the Face of 1950s Britain* (London: Rogan House, 2007), 108.

12. John Hasted quoted in ibid., 108.

13. Bob Watson quoted in ibid., 100.

14. Paul Oliver quoted in Reineke, *Ramblin' Jack Elliott*, 73.

15. Dave Arthur, *Bert: The Life and Times of A. L. Lloyd* (forthcoming); Mike Paris and Chris Comber, *Jimmie the Kid: The Life of Jimmie Rodgers* (Cambridge, Mass.: Da Capo Press, 1981).

16. Dave Arthur to Mike Paris, May 28, 2008. Email provided courtesy of Dave Arthur and Mike Paris.

17. Sid Gleason to Bob Brough, August 17, 1960.

18. Hasted quoted in Frame, *The Restless Generation*, 111.

19. Frame, *The Restless Generation*, 136, 234, and 295.

20. Paul McCartney quoted in Robert Santelli, "Beyond Folk: Woody Guthrie's Impact on Rock and Roll," in Robert Santelli and Emily Davidson, eds., *Hard Travelin': The Life and Legacy of Woody Guthrie* (Hanover, N.H.: Wesleyan University Press, 1999), 45–56 (p. 48).

21. Jones quoted in Reineke, *Ramblin' Jack Elliott*, 264.

22. Hasted quoted in Frame, *The Restless Generation*, 244.

23. Ralph McTell, *As Far as I Can Tell* (London: Leola Music, 2008), 540.

24. Ibid., 451.

25. Ibid., 374.

26. Ibid., 408.

27. Ibid., 388.

28. Ibid., 374.

29. Reineke, *Ramblin' Jack Elliott*, 104.

30. Bob and Sid Gleason in conversation with Jack Elliott and Andy Irvine, June 1960.

Smithsonian Institution, Center for Folklife and Cultural Heritage, CD number 45: Martins and Coys/Woody Guthrie Dubs, Track 11.

31. Dave Van Ronk to Ronald Cohen, June 1996. RCC.

32. Lawrence Block, "This Land Is Their Land," in Dave Van Ronk and Dick Ellington, eds., *The Bosses' Songbook: Songs to Stifle the Flames of Discontent* (New York: Bosses Artists Press, 1958), 28.

33. Roy Berkeley, "The Ballad of Pete Seeger," in ibid., 24. "I was told on good authority that Pete was thinking of suing us, and for our second printing we changed the title of 'The Ballad of Pete Seeger' to 'Ballad of a Party Singer.' (Dick Ellington remembered this quite differently. He heard that Pete found the song funny and actually performed it a few times, and as proof presented Pete's order for three songbooks.)" Dave Van Ronk with Elijah Wald, *The Mayor of MacDougal Street: A Memoir* (Cambridge, Mass.: Da Capo Press, 2005), 70.

34. Wayne Hampton, *Guerrilla Minstrels* (Knoxville: University of Tennessee Press, 1986), xi.

35. Frank Hamilton quoted in Ronald D. Cohen, *Rainbow Quest: The Folk Music Revival and American Society, 1940–1970* (Amherst: University of Massachusetts Press, 2002), 4.

36. Ernie Marrs, "The Rest of the Song," *Broadside* no. 8 (January 1968); 8–9.

37. "Sis" Cunningham quoted in Josh Dunson, *Freedom in the Air: Song Movements of the Sixties* (New York: International Publishers, 1965), 56.

38. *The Best of Broadside, 1962–1988,* produced, compiled, and annotated by Jeff Place and Ronald D. Cohen, 5 vols. (Smithsonian Folkways Recordings, 2000).

39. Dunson, *Freedom in the Air,* 33, 46–47.

40. Ibid., 46.

41. Ibid., 47–48.

42. Lee Felsenstein quoted in David Lance Goines, *The Free Speech Movement: Coming of Age in the 1960s* (Berkeley: Ten Speed Press, 1993), 713.

43. Lee Felsenstein, "Put My Name Down," in ibid., 720.

44. Dunson, *Freedom in the Air,* 48.

45. Lee Hays, *Sing Out, Warning! Sing Out, Love: The Writings of Lee Hays,* ed. Robert S. Koppelman (Amherst: University of Massachusetts Press, 2004), 150–51.

46. McTell, *As Far as I Can Tell,* 563.

47. Ibid., 466.

48. Ibid., 465.

49. Dylan quoted in Sy Ribakove and Barbara Ribakove, *Folk-Rock: The Bob Dylan Story* (New York: Dell, 1966), 24.

50. Nora Guthrie quoted in Cray, *Ramblin' Man,* 384.

51. John Cohen quoted in David Hajdu, *Positively 4th Street* (London: Bloomsbury, 2001), 72.

52. John Greenway, "Woody Guthrie: The Man, the Land, the Understanding," in David A. DeTurk and A. Poulin Jr., eds., *The American Folk Scene: Dimensions of the Folksong Revival* (New York: Dell, 1967), 184–202 (p. 199).

53. Dylan quoted in Robert Shelton, *No Direction Home: The Life and Music of Bob Dylan* (Cambridge, Mass.: Da Capo Press, 1997), 200–201.

54. Dylan quoted in Nat Hentoff, "The Crackin', Shakin', Breakin' Sounds," *The New Yorker* 40, no. 36 (October 24, 1964): 64–90 (p. 65).

55. Martin Carthy on *Bob Dylan's Big Freeze,* produced by Katrina Fallon and Patrick Humphries. BBC Radio 2, broadcast November 25, 2008.

56. Irwin Silber, "An Open Letter to Bob Dylan," *Sing Out!* 14, no. 5 (November 1964): 22–23.

57. Silber quoted in Richie Unterberger, *Turn! Turn! Turn!: The '60s Folk-Rock Revolution* (San Francisco: Backbeat Books, 2002), 97.

58. Edith Kermit Roosevelt quoted in R. Serge Denisoff, *Great Day Coming: Folk Music and the American Left* (Baltimore: Penguin, 1973), 143.

59. *When Is Folk Music NOT Folk Music?* (Los Angeles: Fire and Police Research Association, 1963), n.p.

60. Kenneth B. Keating, "Mine Enemy, the Folksinger," in De Turk and Poulin Jr., eds. *The American Folk Scene,* 103–10 (p. 110).

61. Jere Real, "Folk Music and Red Tubthumpers," *American Opinion* 7 (December 1964): 19–24 (pp. 19–20).

62. William Steuart McBirnie, *Songs of Subversion* (Glendale, Calif.: Voice of Americanism, 1965), 36–39. Copy held in RCC.

63. Herbert Philbrick, "Subverting Youth with Folksinging," in Kenneth W. Ingwalson, ed., *Your Church—Their Target: What's Going On in the Protestant Churches* (Arlington, Va.: Better Books, 1966): 167–77.

64. David Noebel quoted in Richard A. Reuss with JoAnne C. Reuss, *American Folk Music and Left-Wing Politics, 1927–1957* (Lanham, Md.: Scarecrow Press, 2000), 12.

65. *When Is Folk Music NOT Folk Music?,* n.p.

66. Mikiko Tachi, "Commercialism, Counterculture, and the Folk Music Revival: A Study of *Sing Out!* Magazine, 1950–1967," *Japanese Journal of American Studies* 15 (2004): 187–211 (p. 192).

67. Hajdu, *Positively 4th Street,* 192–93.

68. Press kit for *Greenwich Village Story,* dir. Jack O'Connell (Shawn International, 1963), RCC.

69. Press kit for *The Young Swingers,* dir. Maury Dexter (Associated Producers, 1963), RCC.

70. *Hootenanny Hoot,* dir. Gene Nelson (MGM, 1963).

71. *Love Diary* (Charlton Comics Group, September 1966), cover, RCC.

72. *Batman,* no. 164 (DC Comics, June 1964), 2. Copy held in RCC.

73. Orange Crush "Hootenanny Party Kit," RCC.

74. Elektra Folk Song Kit advertisement reproduced in Tachi, "Commercialism, Counterculture," 199.

75. Press release, Harold Leventhal Management, Inc., September 6, 1963. RCC. One positive outcome of the *Hootenanny* banning was that it eventually led Seeger to host his own resolutely down-market television series *Rainbow Quest* for the multilingual UHF television station WNJU, in 1965–66.

76. Seeger on untitled program, University of Tulsa radio, February 3, 1976. CD no. 43: Pete Seeger in Tulsa, Part 2 / Acetate Dubs. Smithsonian Institution, Center for Folklife and Cultural Heritage.

77. Nat Hentoff, "The Odyssey of Woody Guthrie: The Rebel Who Started the Folk-Song Craze," *Pageant* (March 1964): 102–8 (p. 108).

78. Millard Lampell, "Hard Travelin'," in Millard Lampell and Hally Wood, eds., *A Tribute to Woody Guthrie* (New York: Ludlow Music in association with Woody Guthrie Publications, 1972): 1–3 (p. 3).

79. John Greenway, *American Folksongs of Protest* (New York: A. S. Barnes, 1953), 282.

80. Tommy Stevenson, "'This Land Is Your Land' Like Woody Wrote It," *Tuscaloosa News*, January 18, 2009. Online version: http://politibits.blogs.tuscaloosanews.com/10068/this-land-is-your-land-like-woody-wrote-it/.

81. Bruce Springsteen and Pete Seeger, "This Land Is Your Land," Obama Inaugural Celebration Concert, HBO Television. First broadcast January 18, 2009.

82. Pete Seeger, "Portrait of a Song as a Bird in Flight," *Village Voice*, July 1, 1971; reprinted with amendments in Seeger, *Where Have All the Flowers Gone: A Singalong Memoir* (New York: Norton, 2009 [1993]), 143.

83. Ry Cooder quoted in Fred Metting, *The Unbroken Circle: Tradition and Innovation in the Music of Ry Cooder and Taj Mahal* (Lanham, Md.: Scarecrow Press, 2001), 131.

84. Nora Guthrie quoted in Greg Kot, *Wilco: Learning How to Die* (New York: Broadway Books, 2004), 143.

85. Strictly speaking, on the heels of Martin Hoffman's musical setting of Guthrie's poem "Deportee" in the late 1950s, Country Joe McDonald deserves credit for inaugurating the practice of putting music to Guthrie's unreleased lyrics with "Woman at Home" in 1975. See various artists, *A Tribute to Woody Guthrie* (Warner Brothers / WEA CD, 1989), Track 18.

86. Nora Guthrie quoted in Phil Milstein, "Emily's Illness: Diagnosis of a Song," *Ugly Things*, no. 19 (Summer 2001), online at http://www.spectropop.com/NoraGuthrie/index.htm.

87. Nora Guthrie to Will Kaufman, January 19, 2010. See also Sean Michaels, "Jay Farrar Continues Woody Guthrie Album Series," *The Guardian* (September 18, 2009), online at http://www.guardian.co.uk/music/2009/sep/18/jay-farrar-woody-guthrie-album.

88. Eliza Gilkyson, "Peace Call," *Land of Milk and Honey* (Red House, 2004), Track 10.

89. Janis Ian, "I Hear You Sing Again," *Billie's Bones* (Oh Boy, 2004), Track 5.

90. Ellis Paul, "God's Promise," *The Speed of Trees* (Philo, 2002), Track 11.

91. Anti-Flag, "Post-War Breakout," *The Terror State* (Fat Wreck Chords, 2003), Track 3.

92. Dropkick Murphys, "Gonna Be a Blackout Tonight," *Blackout* (Hellcat Records, 2003), Track 5.

93. Slaid Cleaves, "This Morning I Am Born Again," *Broke Down* (Philo, 2000), Track 8.

94. Red Dirt Rangers, "Cadillac Eight," *Rangers Command* (Lazy S.O.B. Records, 1999), Track 4.

95. The Autumn Defense, "Revolutionary Mind," *The Green Hour* (Broadmoor Records, 2001), Track 3.

96. Jonatha Brooke, *The Works* (Bad Dog Records, 2008).

97. Joel Rafael, *Woodyboye* and *Woodeye*, combined in Rafael, *The Songs of Woody Guthrie*, Vols. 1 and 2 (Inside Recordings, 2008).

98. The Klezmatics, *Wonder Wheel* (Jewish Music Group, 2006) and *Woody Guthrie's Happy Joyous Hanukah* (Jewish Music Group, 2006).

99. Sarah Lee Guthrie and Family, *Go Waggaloo* (Smithsonian Folkways, 2009).

100. Various artists, *Daddy-O Daddy!* (Rounder, 2001).

101. Reineke, *Ramblin' Jack Elliott*, 96.

102. Henry Crow Dog quoted in Seeger, *Where Have All the Flowers Gone*, 144. See also Keith Secola, "This Land," on Keith Secola, *Native Americana* (Akina Records, 2005), Track 12.

103. Wilhelm Murg, "Blackfire: Guthrie Poems Set to Music," *Indian Country Today* (October 2, 2003), online at http://www.indiancountrytoday.com/archive/28179879.html. Blackfire's 2004 EP *Woody Guthrie Singles* is out of print. "Mean Things Happenin' in This World" and "Indian Corn Song" can be accessed at www.blackfire.net.

104. Sharon Jones and the Dap Kings, "What If We All Stopped Paying Taxes" / "This Land Is Your Land" (Daptone Records DAP-1019, 2002).

105. Sharon Jones and the Dap Kings, "This Land Is Your Land," on *Up in the Air: Music from the Motion Picture* (Rhino CD, 2009), Track 1.

106. Yang Haisong quoted in Lara Day, "Asia's Best Bands: 5 Asian Acts to Watch in 2008," *Time Asia* (January 17, 2008), online at http://www.time.com/time/specials/2007/article/0,28804,1704856_1704855_1704828,00.html.

107. Z-Joe and the Dustbowlers, *A Woody Zombie Hootenanny* (Safety Records, 2003).

108. Neda Ulaby, "A German Twist on Woody Guthrie," *NPR Music* (April 5, 2003), online at http://www.npr.org/templates/story/story.php?storyId=1220190. See also Wenzel, *Ticky Tock* (Conträr Musik, 2003).

109. See Esben Langkniv, *Iørefaldende Anonym* (Intermusic CD, 2003).

110. Alabama 3 official website, http://www.alabama3.co.uk/en/general_articles/about.

111. Alabama 3, "Woody Guthrie," on Alabama 3, *Power in the Blood* (One Little Indian, 2003), Track 4.

112. Guthrie, "Another Man Done Gone." WGA, Songs 1, Box 1, Folder 1. See also Billy Bragg and Wilco, *Mermaid Avenue*, Vol. 1 (Elektra, 1998), Track 14.

113. Guthrie quoted in Greenway, *American Folksongs of Protest*, 275.

114. Guthrie, "Another Man Done Gone."

115. Bharati Mukherjee, *Jasmine* (New York: Grove Press, 1989), 101.

116. Guthrie to Moses Asch, July 15, 1946. WGA, Woody Guthrie Correspondence, Series 1, Box 1, Folder 6.

Sources

Printed Sources

Abbott, Carl. "The Federal Presence." In Clyde A. Milner II et al., eds., *The Oxford History of the American West*, 469–500. New York: Oxford University Press USA, 1996.

Adomian, Lan. "What Songs Should Workers' Choruses Sing?" *Daily Worker*, February 7, 1934, 5.

Almanac Singers. "Songs of Work, Trouble, Hope." *People's World*, October 28, 1941, 5.

"The 'Almanacs' Part, But Keep On Singing." *Daily Worker*, January 8, 1943, 7.

Anderson, Carol Elaine. *Eyes off the Prize: The United Nations and the African American Struggle for Human Rights, 1944–1955*. New York: Cambridge University Press, 2003.

Arévalo Mateus, Jorge. "Beluthahatchee Blues: An Interview with Stetson Kennedy." In Chris Green, Rachel Rubin, and James Smethurst, eds., *Radicalism in the South since Reconstruction*, 211–26. New York: Palgrave Macmillan, 2006.

Betz, Albrecht. *Hanns Eisler: Political Musician*. Trans. Bill Hopkins. Cambridge: Cambridge University Press, 2006.

Biondi, Martha. *To Stand and Fight: The Struggle for Civil Rights in Postwar New York City*. Cambridge, Mass.: Harvard University Press, 2006.

Bird, Brian. *Skiffle: The Story of Folk Song with a Jazz Beat*. London: Robert Hale, 1958.

Bissett, Jim. *Agrarian Socialism in America: Marx, Jefferson, and Jesus in the Oklahoma Countryside, 1904–1920*. Norman: University of Oklahoma Press, 1999.

Brand, Oscar. *The Ballad Mongers: Rise of the Modern Folk Song*. New York: Minerva Press, 1962.

Bray, Thelma. *Reflections: The Life and Times of Woody Guthrie*. Pampa, Texas: Bray, 2001.

Brocken, Michael. *The British Folk Revival, 1944–2002*. Aldershot: Ashgate, 2003.

Bulger, Margaret Anne. "Stetson Kennedy: Applied Folklore and Cultural Advocacy." PhD dissertation, University of Pennsylvania, 1992.

Burbank, Garin. *When Farmers Voted Red: The Gospel of Socialism in the Oklahoma Countryside, 1910–1924*. Westport Conn.: Greenwood Press, 1976.

Butler, Martin. *Voices of the Down and Out: The Dust Bowl Migration and the Great Depression in the Songs of Woody Guthrie.* Heidelberg: Universitätsverlag Winter, 2007.

Butler, Susan, ed. *My Dear Mr. Stalin: The Complete Correspondence of Franklin D. Roosevelt and Joseph V. Stalin.* New Haven, Conn.: Yale University Press, 2005.

Cantor, Milton. *The Divided Left: American Radicalism, 1900–1975.* New York: Hill and Wang, 1978.

Cantwell, Robert S. *When We Were Good: The Folk Revival.* Cambridge, Mass.: Harvard University Press, 1997.

Caute, David. *The Great Fear: The Anti-Communist Purge under Truman and Eisenhower.* New York: Simon and Schuster, 1978.

Civil Rights Congress. *We Charge Genocide: The Historic Petition to the United Nations for Relief from a Crime of the United States Government against the Negro People.* New York: Civil Rights Congress, 1951.

Cohen, Ronald D. *Folk Music: The Basics.* London: Routledge, 2006.

———. *Rainbow Quest: The Folk Music Revival and American Society, 1940–1970.* Amherst: University of Massachusetts Press, 2002.

———. *Wasn't That a Time! Firsthand Accounts of the Folk Music Revival.* Lanham, Md.: Scarecrow Press, 1995.

———. "Woody the Red?" In Robert Santelli and Emily Davidson, eds., *Hard Travelin': The Life and Legacy of Woody Guthrie,* 138–52. Hanover, N.H.: Wesleyan University Press, 1999.

———. *Work and Sing: A History of Occupational and Labor Union Songs in the United States.* Crockett, Calif.: Carquinez Press, 2010.

Cohen, Ronald D., and Dave Samuelson. *Songs for Political Action: Folk Music, Topical Songs and the American Left, 1926–1953.* Hambergen, Germany: Bear Family Records, 1996.

Communist Activities among Youth Groups (Based on Testimony of Harvey M. Matusow). Hearings before the Committee on Un-American Activities, House of Representatives, Eighty-Second Congress, Second Session, February 6 and 7, 1952. Washington, D.C.: United States Government Printing Office, 1952.

Cottam, Kazimiera Janina. "Lyudmila Pavlichenko." In *Women in War and Resistance: Selected Biographies of Soviet Women Soldiers,* 208–13. Newburyport, Mass.: Focus Publishing/R. Pullins, 1998.

Courtney, Steve. "So Long to Lee Hays." *North County News.* (Yorktown Heights, N.Y.), 2–8 September, 1981. Online at http://www.bencourtney.com/hays.

"Cowell Performs Own Compositions in Piano Recital." *Daily Worker,* November 21, 1933, 5.

Cray, Ed. *Ramblin' Man: The Life and Times of Woody Guthrie.* New York: Norton, 2004.

Crist, Kenneth. "Career Men—in Relief." *Los Angeles Times Sunday Magazine,* May 14, 1939, 4–5, 81

Culver, John C., and John Hyde. *American Dreamer: A Life of Henry A. Wallace.* New York: Norton, 2001.

Cunningham, Agnes "Sis," and Gordon Friesen. *Red Dust and Broadsides: A Joint Biography.* Ed. Ronald D. Cohen. Amherst: University of Massachusetts Press, 1999.

Daniel, Cletus E. *Bitter Harvest: A History of California Farmworkers, 1870–1941.* Ithaca, N.Y.: Cornell University Press, 1981.

Day, Lara. "Asia's Best Bands: 5 Asian Acts to Watch in 2008." *Time Asia* (January 17, 2008), online at http://www.time.com/time/specials/2007/article/0,28804,1704856_1704855_1704828,00.html.

Denisoff, R. Serge. *Great Day Coming: Folk Music and the American Left.* Baltimore: Penguin, 1973.

———. *Sing a Song of Social Significance.* Bowling Green, Ky.: Bowling Green State University Popular Press, 1983.

Denning, Michael. *The Cultural Front: The Laboring of American Culture in the Twentieth Century.* London: Verso, 1998.

DeTurk, David A., and A. Poulin Jr., eds. *The American Folk Scene: Dimensions of the Folksong Revival.* New York: Dell, 1967.

Dewe, Mike. *The Skiffle Craze.* Aberystwyth: Planet, 1998.

Dickstein, Morris. *Dancing in the Dark: A Cultural History of the Great Depression.* New York: Norton, 2009.

Dos Passos, John. *U.S.A.* New York: Literary Classics of the United States, 1996.

Douglas, Lawrence. "The Shrunken Head of Buchenwald: Icons of Atrocity at Nuremburg." *Representations,* no. 63 (Summer 1998): 39–64.

Du Bois, W. E. B. *Against Racism: Unpublished Essays, Papers, Addresses, 1887–1961.* Ed. Herbert Aptheker. Amherst: University of Massachusetts Press, 1985.

Dunaway, David K. "Charles Seeger and Carl Sands: The Composers' Collective Years." *Ethnomusicology* 24, no. 2 (May 1980): 159–68.

Dunaway, David K. *How Can I Keep from Singing? The Ballad of Pete Seeger.* New York: Villard Books, 2008.

Dunaway, David K., and Molly Beer. *Singing Out: An Oral History of America's Folk Music Revivals.* New York: Oxford University Press USA, 2010.

Dunson, Josh. *Freedom in the Air: Song Movements of the Sixties.* New York: International Publishers, 1965.

Ericson, Edward E. *Feeding the German Eagle: Soviet Economic Aid to Nazi Germany, 1933–1941.* Westport, Conn.: Praeger, 1999.

Farrell, James J. *The Spirit of the Sixties: Making Postwar Radicalism.* London: Routledge, 1997.

Fast, Howard. *Being Red: A Memoir.* Armonk, N.Y.: M. E. Sharpe, 1994.

———. *Peekskill USA.* New York: Civil Rights Congress, 1951.

Fenby, Jonathan. *Chiang Kai-Shek: China's Generalissimo and the Nation He Lost.* Cambridge, Mass.: Da Capo Press, 2005.

Filene, Benjamin. *Romancing the Folk: Public Memory and American Roots Music.* Chapel Hill: University of North Carolina Press, 2000.

Frame, Pete. *The Restless Generation: How Rock Music Changed the Face of 1950s Britain.* London: Rogan House, 2007.

Freeman, Joshua B. *Working-Class New York: Life and Labor since World War II.* New York: The New Press, 2001.

Friedrich, Carl J. "The Poison in Our System." *Atlantic Monthly* 167, no. 6 (June 1941): 661–72.

Galbraith, John Kenneth. *The Affluent Society.* New York: Houghton Mifflin, 1998.

Garland, Jim. *Welcome the Traveler Home: Jim Garland's Story of the Kentucky Mountains.* Ed. Julia S. Ardery. Lexington: University Press of Kentucky, 1983.

Garman, Bryan K. *A Race of Singers: Whitman's Working-Class Hero from Guthrie to Springsteen.* Chapel Hill: University of North Carolina Press, 2000.

Gilbert, James Burkhart. *Writers and Partisans: A History of Literary Radicalism in America.* New York: John Wiley and Sons, 1968.

Gilbert, Martin. *Winston S. Churchill: The Prophet of Truth, 1922–1939.* New York: Houghton Mifflin, 1977.

Gioia, Ted. *Work Songs.* Durham, N.C.: Duke University Press, 2006.

Glantz, Mary E. *FDR and the Soviet Union: The President's Battles over Foreign Policy.* Lawrence: University Press of Kansas, 2005.

Goines, David Lance. *The Free Speech Movement: Coming of Age in the 1960s.* Berkeley, Calif.: Ten Speed Press, 1993.

Gold, Mike. "Change the World!" *Daily Worker,* January 2, 1933, 5.

———. "What a World" *Daily Worker,* October 19, 1933, 5.

Goldsmith, Peter D. *Making People's Music: Moe Asch and Folkways Records.* Washington, D.C.: Smithsonian Institution Press, 1998.

Graff, Ellen. *Stepping Left: Dance and Politics in New York City, 1928–1942.* Durham: University of North Carolina Press, 1997.

Gregory, E. David. "Lomax in London: Alan Lomax, the BBC, and the Folk-Song Revival in England, 1950–1958." *Folk Music Journal* 8, no. 2 (2002): 136–69.

Gregory, James N. *American Exodus: The Dust Bowl Migration and Okie Culture in California.* New York: Oxford University Press, 1989.

Green, Archie. "Woody's Oil Songs." In Archie Green, ed., *Songs about Work: Essays in Occupational Culture for Richard A. Reuss,* 208–20. Bloomington: Folklore Institute, Indiana University, 1993.

Green, James R. *Grass-Roots Socialism: Radical Movements in the Southwest, 1895–1943.* Baton Rouge: Louisiana State University Press, 1978.

Greenway, John. *American Folksongs of Protest.* New York: A. S. Barnes, 1953.

———. "Woodrow Wilson Guthrie (1912–1967)." *Journal of American Folklore* 81, no. 319 (January–March, 1968): 62–65.

———. "Woody Guthrie: The Man, the Land, the Understanding." In David A. DeTurk and A. Poulin, Jr., eds., *The American Folk Scene: Dimensions of the Folksong Revival,* 184–202. New York: Dell, 1967.

Guthrie, Arlo. "Going Back to Coney Island." *Hard Travelin': The Life and Legacy of Woody Guthrie,* ed. Robert Santelli and Emily Davidson, 34–41. Hanover, N.H.: Wesleyan University Press, 1999.

Guthrie, C. E. *Kumrids: A Discussion of Scientific Socialism.* Okemah, Okla.: Ledger Printing, 1912.

Guthrie, Woody. *American Folksong.* Ed. Moses Asch. New York: Oak Publications, 1961.

———. *Born to Win.* Ed. Robert Shelton. New York: Collier, 1967.

———. *Bound for Glory.* London: Penguin, 2004.

———. *Pastures of Plenty.* Ed. Dave Marsh and Harold Leventhal. New York: HarperPerennial, 1990.

———. *Seeds of Man.* New York: Pocket Books, 1977 [1976].

———. "Tom Joad in American Ballad." *Daily Worker,* May 3, 1940, 7.

———. *Woody Guthrie Artworks.* Ed. Steven Brower and Nora Guthrie. New York: Rizzoli, 1995.

———. *Woody Guthrie Folk Songs.* New York: Ludlow Music, 1963.

———. *Woody Guthrie Songbook.* Ed. Harold Leventhal and Marjorie Guthrie. New York: Grosset and Dunlap, 1976.

———. *Woody Sez.* New York: Grosset and Dunlap, 1975.

———. "Woody Sez That Okies Haven't Given Up the Fight." *Daily Worker,* April 23, 1940, 7.

Guthrie, Woody, and Maxine Crissman. *Woody and Lefty Lou's Favorite Collection of Old Time Hill Country Songs: Being Sung for Ages, Still Going Strong.* Gardena, Calif.: Spanish American Institute Press, 1937.

Hajdu, David. *Positively 4th Street.* London: Bloomsbury, 2001.

Halker, Clark D. *For Democracy, Workers, and God: Labor Song-Poems and Labor Protest, 1865–95.* Urbana and Chicago: University of Illinois Press, 1991.

Hammett, Dashiell. *Selected Letters of Dashiell Hammett, 1921–1960.* Ed. Richard Layman with Julie M. Rivett. Washington, D.C.: Counterpoint, 2002.

Hampton, Wayne. *Guerrilla Minstrels.* Knoxville: University of Tennessee Press, 1986.

Harburg, E. Y., and Fred Saidy. *Finian's Rainbow: A Musical Satire.* New York: Random House, 1946.

Hawes, Bess Lomax. *Sing It Pretty: A Memoir.* Urbana and Chicago: University of Illinois Press, 2008.

Hays, Lee. *Sing Out, Warning! Sing Out, Love: The Writings of Lee Hays.* Ed. Robert S. Koppelman. Amherst: University of Massachusetts Press, 2004.

Hellman, Lillian. *Scoundrel Time.* Boston: Little, Brown, 1976.

Hentoff, Nat. "The Crackin', Shakin', Breakin' Sounds." *New Yorker* 40, no. 36 (October 24, 1964): 64–90.

———. "The Odyssey of Woody Guthrie: The Rebel Who Started the Folk-Song Craze." *Pageant* (March 1964): 102–8.

Hille, Waldemar, ed. *The People's Songbook.* New York: Boni and Gaer, 1948.

Investigation of Communist Activities, New York Area—Part VII (Entertainment), Hearings before the Committee on Un-American Activities, House of Representatives, Eighty-Fourth Congress, First Session, August 17 and 18, 1955. Washington, D.C.: United States Government Printing Office, 1955.

Isserman, Maurice. *Which Side Were You On? The American Communist Party during the Second World War.* Champaign: University of Illinois Press, 1993.

I.W.W. Songs: To Fan the Flames of Discontent. Chicago: Industrial Workers of the World, 1923.

Jackson, Mark Allan. *Prophet Singer: The Voice and Vision of Woody Guthrie.* Jackson: University Press of Mississippi, 2007.

Jones, Howard. *"A New Kind of War": America's Global Strategy and the Truman Doctrine in Greece.* New York: Oxford University Press USA, 1997.

Kaufman, Will. "Voice of the Other America." *Times Higher Education Supplement,* September 28, 2007: 16–17.

———. "Woody Guthrie and the Cultural Front." In John S. Partington, ed., *The Life,*

248 *Sources*

Work, and Thought of Woody Guthrie: A Critical Assessment. Aldershot: Ashgate, 2011: in press.

Keating, Kenneth B. "Mine Enemy, the Folksinger." *The American Folk Scene: Dimensions of the Folksong Revival*, ed. David A. DeTurk and A. Poulin Jr., 103–10. New York: Dell, 1967.

Kittrie, Nicholas N., and Eldon D. Wedlock Jr., eds. *The Tree of Liberty: A Documentary History of Rebellion and Political Crime in America.* Baltimore: Johns Hopkins University Press, 1998.

Klein, Joe. *Woody Guthrie: A Life.* New York: Delta, 1999.

Kot, Greg. *Wilco: Learning How to Die.* New York: Broadway Books, 2004.

Kutulas, Judy. *The Long War: The Intellectual People's Front and Anti-Stalinism, 1930–1940.* Durham, N.C.: Duke University Press, 1995.

La Chapelle, Peter. *Proud to Be an Okie: Cultural Politics, Country Music, and Migration to Southern California.* Berkeley: University of California Press, 2007.

Lampell, Millard, and Hally Wood, eds. *A Tribute to Woody Guthrie.* New York: Ludlow Music in association with Woody Guthrie Publications, 1972.

Lampell, Millard, Irwin Silber, et al., eds. *California to the New York Island.* New York: Guthrie Children's Trust Fund, 1960.

Lankford, Ronald, Jr. *Folk Music USA: The Changing Voice of Protest.* London: Omnibus Press, 2006.

Ledbetter, Huddie. *The Leadbelly Songbook: The Ballads, Blues, and Folksongs of Huddie Ledbetter.* Ed. Moses Asch and Alan Lomax. New York: Oak Publications, 1962.

Lewis, George. "America Is in Their Songs." *Daily Worker,* March 24, 1941, 7.

Lichtman, Robert M., and Ronald Cohen. *Deadly Farce: Harvey Matusow and the Informer System in the McCarthy Era.* Urbana and Chicago: University of Illinois Press, 2004.

Lieberman, Robbie. *"My Song Is My Weapon": People's Songs, American Communism, and the Politics of Culture, 1930–50.* Urbana and Chicago: University of Illinois Press, 1995.

Lomax, Alan. *Assistant in Charge: The Library of Congress Letters, 1935–1945.* Ed. Ronald D. Cohen. Jackson: University Press of Mississippi, 2010.

Lomax, Alan, Woody Guthrie, and Pete Seeger, eds. *Hard Hitting Songs for Hard-Hit People.* New York: Oak Publications, 1967.

Longhi, Jim. *Woody, Cisco and Me: With Woody Guthrie in the Merchant Marine.* New York: ibooks, 2004.

Macpherson, Heidi Slettedahl. *Women's Movement: Escape as Transgression in North American Feminist Fiction.* Amsterdam: Rodopi, 2000.

Malone, Bill C. *Don't Get above Your Raisin': Country Music and the Southern Working Class.* Urbana and Chicago: University of Illinois Press, 2006.

Marrs, Ernie. "The Rest of the Song." *Broadside* no. 8 (January 1968): 8–9.

Matusow, Harvey. *False Witness.* New York: Cameron and Kahn, 1955.

McBirnie, William Steuart. *Songs of Subversion.* Glendale, Calif.: Voice of Americanism, 1965.

McTell, Ralph. *As Far as I Can Tell.* London: Leola Music, 2008.

McWilliams, Carey. "California Pastoral." *Antioch Review* 2, no. 1 (March 1942): 103–21.

———. *Factories in the Field: The Story of Migratory Farm Labor in California.* Berkeley: University of California Press, 2000 [1939].

Mencken, H. L. "The Dole for Bogus Farmers." *American Mercury* 39 (December 1936): 400–408.

Michaels, Sean. "Jay Farrar Continues Woody Guthrie Album Series." *The Guardian* (September 18, 2009), online at http://www.guardian.co.uk/music/2009/sep/18/jay-farrar-woody-guthrie-album.

Milstein, Phil. "Emily's Illness: Diagnosis of a Song." *Ugly Things*, no. 19 (Summer 2001), online at http://www.spectropop.com/NoraGuthrie/index.htm.

Mitchell, Gillian. *The North American Folk Music Revival: Nation and Identity in the United States and Canada, 1945–1980*. Aldershot: Ashgate, 2007.

Mitchell, Don. *The Lie of the Land: Migrant Workers and the California Landscape*. Minneapolis: University of Minnesota Press, 1996.

Mukherjee, Bharati. *Jasmine*. New York: Grove Press, 1989.

Murg, Wilhelm. "Blackfire: Guthrie Poems Set to Music." *Indian Country Today* (October 2, 2003), online at http://www.indiancountrytoday.com/archive/28179879.html.

Murray, Williamson, MacGregor Knox, and Alvin H. Bernstein. *The Making of Strategy: Rulers, States, and War*. Cambridge: Cambridge University Press, 1996.

"Music: June Records." *Time*, June 16, 1941. Online *Time* archive: http://www.time.com/time/magazine/article/0,9171,765744,00.html.

Ottanelli, Fraser M. *The Communist Party of the United States from the Depression to World War II*. New Brunswick, N.J.: Rutgers University Press, 1991.

Paris, Mike, and Chris Comber. *Jimmie the Kid: The Life of Jimmie Rodgers*. Cambridge, Mass.: Da Capo Press, 1981.

Parrington, Vernon Louis. *Main Currents in American Thought*. New York: Harcourt, Brace, 1930.

Partington, John S., ed. *The Life, Work, and Thought of Woody Guthrie: A Critical Assessment*. Aldershot: Ashgate, 2011.

Perone, James E. *Mods, Rockers, and the Music of the British Invasion*. London: Praeger, 2008.

Philbrick, Herbert. "Subverting Youth with Folksinging." In Kenneth W. Ingwalson, ed., *Your Church—Their Target: What's Going On in the Protestant Churches, 167–77*. Arlington, Va.: Better Books, 1966.

Pichardo, Nelson A. "The Power Elite and Elite-Driven Countermovements: The Associated Farmers of California during the 1930s." *Sociological Forum* 10, no. 1 (March 1995): 21–49.

Place, Jeff. "Woody Guthrie's Recorded Legacy." *Hard Travelin': The Life and Legacy of Woody Guthrie*, ed. Robert Santelli and Emily Davidson, 57–68. Hanover, N.H.: Wesleyan University Press, 1999.

Porter, Katherine Anne. *The Never-Ending Wrong*. Boston: Little, Brown, 1977.

Quarrell, Oliver W. J. *Huntington's Disease: The Facts*. New York: Oxford University Press USA, 2008.

Quin, Mike. "Coast to Coast." *Sunday Worker*, January 4, 1942, Section 2, 4.

———. "Double Check." *People's World*, April 25, 1940, 5.

———. "Way Down East." *Daily Worker*, November 21, 1941, 7.

Redding, Arthur. *Turncoats, Traitors, and Fellow Travellers: Culture and Politics of the Early Cold War*. Jackson: University Press of Mississippi, 2008.

Real, Jere. "Folk Music and Red Tubthumpers." *American Opinion* 7 (December 1964): 19–24.

Reineke, Hank. *Ramblin' Jack Elliott: The Never-Ending Highway.* Lanham, Md.: Scarecrow Press, 2010.

Reuss, Richard A. *Woody Guthrie: A Bibliography.* New York: The Guthrie Children's Trust Fund, 1968.

Reuss, Richard A., with JoAnne C. Reuss. *American Folk Music and Left-Wing Politics, 1927–1957.* Lanham, Md.: Scarecrow Press, 2000.

Ribakove, Sy, and Barbara Ribakove. *Folk-Rock: The Bob Dylan Story.* New York: Dell, 1966.

Richmond, Al. *A Long View from the Left: Memoirs of an American Revolutionary.* New York: Delta, 1972.

Robbin, Ed. *Woody Guthrie and Me.* Berkeley, Calif.: Lancaster-Miller, 1979.

Roberts, Geoffrey. *Stalin's Wars: From World War to Cold War, 1939–1953.* New Haven, Conn.: Yale University Press, 2008.

Robeson, Paul. *Paul Robeson Speaks.* New York: Citadel Press, 1978.

Robinson, Earl, with Eric A. Gordon. *Ballad of an American: The Autobiography of Earl Robinson.* Lanham, Md.: Scarecrow Press, 1998.

Robinson, Mary. *Moisture of the Earth.* Ed. Fran Leeper Buss. Ann Arbor: University of Michigan Press, 2009.

Rodnitzky, Jerome L. *Minstrels of the Dawn: The Folk-Protest Singer as a Cultural Hero.* Chicago: Nelson Hall, 1976.

Romalis, Shelly. *Pistol Packin' Mama: Aunt Molly Jackson and the Politics of Folk Song.* Urbana and Chicago: University of Illinois Press, 1999.

Rosemont, Franklin. *Joe Hill: The IWW and the Making of a Revolutionary Workingclass Counterculture.* Chicago: Charles H. Kerr, 2003.

Rosenberg, Neil V., ed. *Transforming Tradition: Folk Music Revivals Examined.* Urbana and Chicago: University of Illinois Press, 1993.

Russell, Don. "They Sing the Hard Hitting Songs That Belong to America's Workers." *People's World,* August 14, 1941, 7.

Russell, Jay. "How the Weavers Break Night Club Ice." *Daily Compass,* January 27, 1950, 20.

Santelli, Robert, and Emily Davidson, eds. *Hard Travelin': The Life and Legacy of Woody Guthrie.* Hanover, N.H.: Wesleyan University Press, 1999.

Seeger, Charles ("Carl Sands"). "A Program for Proletarian Composers." *Daily Worker,* January 16, 1934, 5.

Seeger, Pete. "Foreword." In *Reprints from the People's Songs Bulletin, 1946–1949,* ed. Irwin Silber, 3. New York: Oak Publications, 1961.

———. *The Incompleat Folksinger.* New York: Simon and Schuster, 1972.

———. "People's Songs and Singers." *New Masses,* July 16, 1946, 9.

———. "Whatever Happened to Singing in the Unions?" *Sing Out!* 15:2 (May 1965): 28–31.

———. *Where Have All the Flowers Gone: A Singalong Memoir.* New York: Norton, 2009.

Sellars, Nigel Anthony. *Oil, Wheat, and Wobblies: The Industrial Workers of the World in Oklahoma, 1905–1930.* Norman: University of Oklahoma Press, 1998.

Shelton, Robert. *No Direction Home: The Life and Music of Bob Dylan.* Cambridge, Mass.: Da Capo Press, 1997.

Siegmeister, Elie. *Music and Society.* New York: Critics Group Press, 1938.

Silber, Irwin. "An Open Letter to Bob Dylan." *Sing Out!* 14, no. 5 (November 1964): 22–23.

———, ed., *Lift Every Voice! The Second People's Songbook.* New York: Oak Publications, 1953.

———, ed. *Reprints from the People's Songs Bulletin, 1946–1949.* New York: Oak Publications, 1961.

Silber, Irwin, and Fred Silber, eds. *Folksinger's Wordbook.* New York: Oak Publications, 1973.

"Singers on New Morale Show Also Warbled for Communists." New York *World-Telegram,* February 17, 1942, 3.

Songs for Wallace: People's Songs 4, no. 1 (June 1948).

Smith, Art. "OWI's Face Is Red as Its Own Hill Billies." New York *Daily News,* January 5, 1943, 2, 12.

Smith, Gibbs. *Joe Hill.* Layton, Utah: Peregrine Smith, 1969.

Steckert, Ellen. "Cents and Nonsense in the Urban Folk Movement: 1930–66." In Neil V. Rosenberg, ed., *Transforming Tradition: Folk Music Revivals Examined,* 84–106. Urbana and Chicago: University of Illinois Press, 1993.

Stephens, Robert J. "'Peace' Choir Changes Tune." *New York Post,* February 17, 1942, 1, 4.

Stevenson, Tommy. "'This Land Is Your Land' Like Woody Wrote It." *Tuscaloosa News,* January 18, 2009. Online version: http://politibits.blogs.tuscaloosanews.com/10068/this-land-is-your-land-like-woody-wrote-it/.

Szwed, John. *Alan Lomax: A Biography.* New York : Viking Adult, 2010.

Tachi, Mikiko. "Commercialism, Counterculture, and the Folk Music Revival: A Study of *Sing Out!* Magazine, 1950–1967." *Japanese Journal of American Studies* 15 (2004): 187–211.

Tamony, Peter. "'Hootenanny': The Word, Its Content and Continuum." *Western Folklore* 22, no. 3 (July 1963): 165–70.

Terkel, Studs. *And They All Sang.* London: Granta, 2005.

Tomlinson, Gerald. *Murdered in Jersey.* Piscataway, N.J.: Rutgers University Press, 1994.

Ulaby, Neda. "A German Twist on Woody Guthrie," *NPR Music* (April 5, 2003), online at http://www.npr.org/templates/story/story.php?storyId=1220190 .

United States House of Representatives. *Investigation of Un-American Propaganda Activities in the United States. Hearings before a Special Committee on Un-American Activities, House of Representatives, Seventy-Seventh Congress, First Session, on H. Res. 282,* Volume 14. Washington, D.C.: United States Government Printing Office, 1941.

United States House of Representatives, Committee on Un-American Activities. *Testimony of Walter S. Steele Regarding Communist Activity in the United States.* Washington, D.C.: United States Government Printing Office, 1947.

Unterberger, Richie. *Turn! Turn! Turn!: The '60s Folk-Rock Revolution.* San Francisco: Backbeat Books, 2002.

"U.S. Defamers Yodel for OWI." *Chicago Daily Tribune,* January 5, 1943, 1.

Van Ronk, Dave, with Elijah Wald. *The Mayor of MacDougal Street: A Memoir.* Cambridge, Mass.: Da Capo Press, 2005.

Van Ronk, Dave, and Dick Ellington, eds. *The Bosses' Songbook: Songs to Stifle the Flames of Discontent.* New York: Bosses Artists Press, 1958.

Van Ronk, Dave, and Richard Ellington, eds. *The Bosses' Songbook: Songs to Stifle the Flames of Discontent.* New York: Richard Ellington, 1959.

Vonnegut, Kurt. *Jailbird.* New York: Delta, 1999.

Wald, Elijah. *Josh White: Society Blues.* London: Routledge, 2002.

Walker, J. Samuel. *Henry A. Wallace and American Foreign Policy.* Westport, Conn.: Greenwood Press, 1976.

Warren, Frank A. *Liberals and Communism: The "Red Decade" Revisited.* New York: Columbia University Press, 1993.

Watson, Bruce. *Sacco and Vanzetti: The Men, the Murders, and the Judgment of Mankind.* New York: Penguin, 2008.

Weissman, Dick. *Which Side Are You On? An Inside History of the Folk Music Revival in America.* New York: Continuum, 2006.

When Is Folk Music NOT Folk Music?. Los Angeles: Fire and Police Research Association, 1963.

White, Josh. "I Was a Sucker for the Communists." *Negro Digest* (December 1950): 26–31.

Wieviorka, Olivier. *Normandy: The Landings to the Liberation of Paris.* Trans. M. B. DeBevoise. Cambridge, Mass.: Harvard University Press, 2008.

Wilkinson, Alec. *The Protest Singer: An Intimate Portrait of Pete Seeger.* New York: Knopf, 2009.

Willens, Doris. *Lonesome Traveler: The Life of Lee Hays.* Lincoln: University of Nebraska Press, 1993.

Winkler, Allan M. *"To Everything There Is a Season": Pete Seeger and the Power of Song.* New York: Oxford University Press, 2009.

Workers Music League. *Red Song Book.* New York: Workers Library, 1932.

Worster, Donald. *Dust Bowl: The Southern Plains in the 1930s.* Oxford: Oxford University Press, 1982.

Yurchenko, Henrietta. *A Mighty Hard Road: The Life of Woody Guthrie.* New York: McGraw-Hill, 1970.

Zieger, Robert H. *The CIO, 1935–1955.* Chapel Hill, N.C.: University of North Carolina Press, 1997.

Audio Sources

Alabama 3. *Power in the Blood.* One Little Indian, 2003.

Anti-Flag. *The Terror State.* Fat Wreck Chords, 2003.

The Autumn Defense. *The Green Hour.* Broadmoor Records, 2001.

The Best of Broadside, 1962–1988. Prod., comp., and annot. by Jeff Place and Ronald D. Cohen. 5 vols. Smithsonian Folkways Recordings, 2000.

Blackfire. *Woody Guthrie Singles:* "Mean Things Happenin' in This World" and "Indian Corn Song." www.blackfire.net.

Bob Dylan's Big Freeze. Radio documentary, Katrina Fallon and Patrick Humphries, prod. Whistledown Productions, BBC Radio 2. First broadcast November 25, 2008.

Bragg, Billy, and Wilco. *Mermaid Avenue,* Vols. 1 and 2. Elektra Records, 1998 and 2000.

———. *Way Over Yonder in the Minor Key.* Rhino/Elektra, 2006.

Brooke, Jonatha. *The Works*. Bad Dog Records, 2008.

Cleaves, Slaid. *Broke Down*. Philo, 2000.

Dropkick Murphys. *Blackout*. Hellcat Records, 2003.

Elliott, Jack. *Jack Takes the Floor*. Topic Records, 1958.

———. "Talking Miner Blues" / "Pretty Boy Floyd." Topic Records, 1956.

———. *Woody Guthrie's Blues*. Topic Records, 1956.

Gilkyson, Eliza. *Land of Milk and Honey*. Red House Records, 2004.

Guthrie, Sarah Lee, and Family. *Go Waggaloo*. Smithsonian Folkways, 2009.

Guthrie, Woody. *The Asch Recordings*. 4 vols. Smithsonian Folkways, 1999: Vol. 1, *This Land Is Your Land*; Vol. 2, *Muleskinner Blues*; Vol 3., *Hard Travelin'*; Vol. 4, *Buffalo Skinners*.

Guthrie, Woody. *Ballads of Sacco and Vanzetti*. Folkways Records, 1964.

———. *Ballads of Sacco and Vanzetti*. Smithsonian Folkways, 1996.

———. *The Columbia River Collection*. Rounder Records, 1987.

———. *Dust Bowl Ballads*. Buddha Records, 2000.

———. *Library of Congress Recordings*. Rounder Records, 1988.

———. *The Live Wire Woody Guthrie*. Woody Guthrie Foundation, 2007.

———. *Long Ways to Travel: The Unreleased Folkways Masters, 1944–1949*. Smithsonian Folkways, 1994.

———. *My Dusty Road*. 4 discs. Rounder Records, 2009: Disc 1, *Woody's "Greatest" Hits*; Disc 2, *Woody's Roots*; Disc 3: *Woody the Agitator*; Disc 4: *Woody, Cisco, and Sonny*.

———. *Struggle*. Smithsonian Folkways, 1998.

———. *Struggle: American Documentary, Vol. 1*, Asch Recordings, 1945.

Ian, Janis. *Billie's Bones*. Oh Boy, 2004.

Jones, Sharon, and the Dap-Kings. "What If We All Stopped Paying Taxes" / "This Land Is Your Land." Daptone Records, 2002.

The Klezmatics. *Wonder Wheel*. Jewish Music Group, 2006.

The Klezmatics. *Woody Guthrie's Happy Joyous Hanukah*. Jewish Music Group, 2006.

Langkniv, Esben. *Iørefaldende Anonym*. Intermusic CD, 2003.

The Martins and the Coys. The Alan Lomax Collection. Rounder Records, 2000.

Paul, Ellis. *The Speed of Trees*. Philo, 2002.

Pete Seeger at 90. Radio documentary. Prod. Vincent Dowd, BBC Radio 4. First broadcast May 1, 2009.

Rafael, Joel. *The Songs of Woody Guthrie*, Vols. 1 and 2. Inside Recordings, 2008.

Red Dirt Rangers. *Rangers Command*. Lazy S.O.B. Records, 1999.

Secola, Keith. *Native Americana*. Akina Records, 2005.

Songs for Political Action: Folk Music, Topical Songs and the American Left, 1926–1953. Comp. Ronald D. Cohen and Dave Samuelson. Bear Family Records, 1996.

The Times They Are A-Changing. Radio documentary. Prod. Paul Sexton, BBC Radio 2. First broadcast January 3, 2009.

Various artists. *The Best of Broadside, 1962–1988: Anthems of the American Underground from the Pages of Broadside Magazine*. 5 discs. Smithsonian Folkways, 2000.

Various artists. *Daddy-O Daddy!* Rounder, 2001.

Various artists. *Ribbon of Highway, Endless Skyway: The Woody Guthrie Tribute Tour*. Music Road Records, 2008.

Various artists. *'Til We Outnumber 'Em: Woody Guthrie*. Righteous Babe Records, 2000.

Various artists. *A Tribute to Woody Guthrie*. Warner Brothers / WEA CD, 1989.

Wenzel, Hans-Eckardt. *Ticky Tock*. Conträr Musik, 2003.

Video Sources

Arena: Woody Guthrie. Dir. Paul Lee. BBC, 1988.

The Ballad of Ramblin' Jack. Dir. Aiyana Elliot. Plantain Films, 2000.

Bound for Glory. Dir. Hal Ashby. MGM, 1976.

Greenwich Village Story. Dir. Jack O'Connell. Shawn International, 1963.

Hootenanny Hoot. Dir. Gene Nelson. MGM, 1963.

Man in the Sand. Dir. Kim Hopkins. Palm Pictures, 2001.

Roll on Columbia: Woody Guthrie and the Bonneville Power Administration. Prod. and dir. Michael Majdic and Denise Edwards. University of Oregon, Knight Library Media Services and School of Journalism and Communication, 2000.

A Vision Shared: A Tribute to Woody Guthrie and Leadbelly. Dir. Jim Brown. CBS/Sony DVD, 1991.

Woody Guthrie: Ain't Got No Home. Writ. and dir. Peter Frumkin. PBS, American Masters Series, 2007.

Woody Guthrie: This Machine Kills Fascists. Writ. and dir. Stephen Gammond. Snapper Music, 2005.

The Young Swingers. Dir. Maury Dexter. Associated Producers, 1963.

In addition to all Woody Guthrie correspondence and untitled writings copyrighted by Woody Guthrie Publications, Inc., I gratefully acknowledge permission to quote from the following prose and lyric writings (all words by Woody Guthrie, © copyright Woody Guthrie Publications, Inc., all rights reserved, used by permission):

"Acting and Dancing," "A Hard Working Man Was Jesus," "A Letter to A. Hitler from a Good Union Worker," "All You Fonies," "Almanacs Almanac: With the NMU Boys in Cleveland," "Another Man Done Gone," "Baking for Wallace," "Ballad of Teheran," "Beat Hitler Blues," "Bet on Wallace," "Big City Ways," "Bloody Run," "Born to Win," "California California," "Capital City Cyclone," "Come When I Call You," "Cumberland Mountain Farms," "Curly-Headed Baby," "Cussss sin Skabby Song," "Dance Around My Atom Fire," "Death Valley Scotty," "Dig a Hole," "Doorstep Baby," "Do Re Mi," "East Texas Red," "Eisler on the Go," "Farther Along," "Fightin' Sonofagun," "Freedom Fire," "Get Along, Mister Hitler," "Go and Leave Me," "Go Down and See," "Gonna Be a Blackout Tonight," "Gotta Keep 'Em Sailin'," "Ham and Eggs Is Marching On," "Hard Hitting Songs by Hard Hit People," "Henry Wallace Man," "He's On His Third Time Round," "High Balladree," "Hills of Ithica," "His Name Was Harry Simms," "Hooversville," "How Much, How Long?" "I Ain't Got No Home," "I Ain't Got No Home in This World Anymore," "Ice in My Whiskers," "I Don't Like Your 'Lantic Pact," "If You Ain't Got the Do Re Mi," "I'll Fight," "I'll Fight for the U.S.A.," "I'll Not Beg," "I'll Write My Name Down in Blood Red Blood," "Ilsa Koch," "I'm Goin ta Git," "I'm Out to Get," "It Was Down in Old Pearl Harbor," "I've Got to Know," "I Was There and the Dust Was There," "Jesus My Doctor," "Join that A.F. of L.," "Kennedy, He's That Man," "Letter to Peekskillers," "Low Levee Café," "Madonna on the Curb," "Manifesto on Wage Slaves, Sleep Walking, and Jesus," "Mario Russo," "Miss Pavlachenko," "More War News," "My Eyes Gonna Shine," "My Hootenanny," "My Ideas about the Use of Peoples Songs in the Progressive Party Movement to Elect Henry Wallace and Glen Taylor," "My Name Is New York," "My Thirty Thousand," "My Union County Gal," "New Situation," "Ninety Mile Wind," "No Disappointment in Heaven," "On Ballad Singers," "Open Up That Second Front Today," "Pastures of Plenty," "Peekskill Golfing Grounds," "Peekskill Klookluk Blues," "People Dancing," "People's Songs and Its People," "P for Peekskill," "Political Books Owned by

Woody Guthrie," "Poor, Hard-Working Man Blues," "Poor Girl's Prayer," "Postage Stamp," "Pretty Boy Floyd," "Quit Sending Your Inspectors," "Raise a Rukus Tonight," "Reckless Talk," "Revolutionary Mind," "Ring Around Hitler," "Roll On Columbia, Roll On," "Roosevelt-Olson," "Sad Ship," *Santa Monica Social Register Examine 'Er*, "Screwball Cannonball," "Shy Yang Kye Check," "Singing High Balladree," "Skid Row," "Socialismo," "Song About Tipping," "Songs for Victory: music for political action," "Stetson Kennedy," "Story That's Never Been Told," "Talkin' Dust Bowl Blues," "Talking Hitler's Head Off Blues," "Talking Hitler to Death," "Talking News Blues," "Talking Rat Hole Blues," "The Almanacs and Me," "The Ballad of Rosa Lee Ingram," "The Biggest Thing that Man Ever Done," "The Blinding of Isaac Woodward," "The Final Call," "The Unwelcome Guest," "This Land Is Your Land," "To a Union Show Troup," "To Give Your Heart Ease," "Trenton Frameup," "Tytanick," "UN Building Song," "Union Labor or Slave Labor," "Union Maid # 1," "Union's My Religion," "Union Train," "War Songs and Work Songs," "What Kind of Bomb?" "What Shall It Profit a Man," "Wheelbarrow Pusher," "When the Curfew Blows," "Woody Says," and "You Fascists Bound to Lose."

Index

Note: Page references in *italics* indicate illustrations.

to Almanac Singers' *Songs for John Doe,*
69–70; reelection of, 108; Soviet Union
recognized by, 23; Woody on, 21–22, 53,
55–56, 59, 65, 108, 133–34, 228–29n114
Roosevelt, Theodore, 137
Rotary Club, 25
Russell, Don, 76
Russia, Nazi invasion of, 66, 70, 78
Russo, Mario, 132–33

Sacco, Nicola, 114–17, 157, 225n20
Saidy, Fred: *Finian's Rainbow,* 131
Sanders, Betty, 119, 177
Sands, Carl (*pseud. of* Charles Seeger),
35–39, 213n42
Schaefer, Jacob, 36
School of the Air (CBS), 39
Schwartz, Tony: "The Peekskill Story,"
164–65
Secola, Keith, 203
Seeger, Charles (*pseud.* Carl Sands), 35–39,
213n42
Seeger, Peggy, 189, 195
Seeger, Pete, 1, 39; in Almanac Singers, *68,*
72 (*see also* Almanac Singers); banned
from ABC's *Hootenanny,* 199–200,
239n75; *Broadside,* role in launching,
192; CIO tour by, 73–75; cross-country
travels with Woody, 47; on folk music's
revival through unions, 119–21; on folk
music vs. jazz, 77; at "Grapes of Wrath"
benefit concert, 34–35; at hootenannies,
177; before the HUAC/court battle of,
173–74, *174,* 199; in *The Martins and the
Coys,* 106; McCarthyite blacklist of, xviii;
parodies of, 191, 238n33; at Peekskill,
159–60, 165; People's Songs role of, 121–22,
127, 130, 138, 142; on political analysis,
179; *Rainbow Quest* hosted by, 239n75;
at "Sing for Freedom" workshop, 192; on
Songs for John Doe, 69–70; "This Land Is
Your Land" sung by, 200–201, *201,* 203; in
the Union Boys, 108–9; in the Weavers,
170–71; and Woody, first meeting of, 35,
212n24; on Woody and Lomax, 40; on
Woody's hitchhiking, 28; Woody's legacy
championed by, xviii; Woody's mentoring
of, 47, *48,* 151
—music: "Dear Mr. President," 99, 223n95;
"Deliver the Goods," 106; "Get Thee Behind Me, Satan," 70; *Hard Hitting Songs
for Hard-Hit People,* 44–47, 49, 56, 64–65,

145–46, 163–64; "Talking Union," 70;
"Union Maid," 47–50, 70, 74–75, 90, 91
Seeger, Toshi, 75, 183
segregation in the U.S. Army, 152. *See also*
Jim Crow segregation
selling out. *See* commercial music/success
Seminole Nation, 10, 154
Senate Internal Security Subcommittee, 173
Shafter Farm Workers Community (Cali-
fornia), 57
Share Croppers Union, 49
Shuler, Robert ("Fighting Bob"), 4
Siegmeister, Elie (*pseud.* L. E. Swift), 36, 38
Signer, Ethan, *196*
Silber, Irwin, xviii, 44, 173, 195–96
Simms, Harry, 131
Sinclair, Upton, 4
"Sing for Freedom," 191–92
Sing Out! 121, 192, 195, 197–98
Skid Row areas, 33
skiffle bands, 188–89
Sledge Hammer (Okemah, Okla.), 11–12
Smathers, George, 169
Smith, Fiddlin' Arthur, 106
Smith, Kate, 28
Smith Act (1940), 61, 140–41
Smolens, Marianne ("Jolly"), 171, 234n18
socialism, vii, xvii, 11–13, 46, 104, 153, 167
Socialist Party, 10–12, 14
soil erosion/land reclamation, 58–60
Soroptimists, 25
Southern Tenant Farmers Union, 38, 44
Soviet Union: call for defense of, 99; FDR's
recognition of, 23; Hungarian revolt sup-
pressed by, 181; Poland invaded by, 107;
Red Army's sacrifice/heroism, 100–101;
Robeson's praise of, 159. *See also* Hitler-
Stalin Pact
Springsteen, Bruce, 200–202, *201*
St. Amand, Harry, 185
Stalin, Josef: collectivization policy of,
2; and FDR, 228–29n114; purges by, 2;
Woody's admiration for, xxi, xxv, 54, 129.
See also Hitler-Stalin Pact
Stalingrad, Battle of, 100
Steckert, Ellen, xxii
Steele, Walter S., 135–36
Steinbeck, John, 19–20; *The Grapes of
Wrath,* 7, 12, *24*
Steinbeck Committee to Aid Agricultural
Organization, 19–21, 34
Stern, Arthur, *67, 75, 82, 84*

WILL KAUFMAN is a professor of American literature and culture at the University of Central Lancashire, England. He is the author of three previous books, most recently *American Culture in the 1970s*. Also a professional folksinger and multi-instrumentalist, he has performed hundreds of musical presentations on Woody Guthrie at universities, music festivals, and folk clubs throughout Europe and the United States.

Music in American Life

The University of Illinois Press
is a founding member of the
Association of American University Presses.

———————————————————————

Composed in 10.5/13 Adobe Minion Pro
by Jim Proefrock
at the University of Illinois Press
Manufactured by Thomson-Shore, Inc.
University of Illinois Press
1325 South Oak Street
Champaign, IL 61820-6903
www.press.uillinois.edu